Loren Miller

Race and Culture in the American West

Loren Miller

Civil Rights Attorney and Journalist

Amina Hassan

UNIVERSITY OF OKLAHOMA PRESS : NORMAN

This book is published with the generous assistance of
The McCasland Foundation, Duncan, Oklahoma.

Library of Congress Cataloging-in-Publication Data
Hassan, Amina, 1941–
    Loren Miller, civil rights attorney and journalist / Amina Hassan.
        pages cm. — (Race and culture in the American West ; v. 10)
    Includes bibliographical references and index.
    ISBN 978-0-8061-4916-5 (hardcover : alk. paper)
1. Miller, Loren.   2. Lawyers—United States—Biography.   3. African American
lawyers—United States—Biography.   4. Civil rights workers—United States.—
Biography.   5. Journalists—United States—Biography.   6. NAACP Legal
Defense and Educational Fund.   I. Title.
    KF373.M5315H37 2015
    340.092—dc23
    [B]

                                                                    2015012260

Loren Miller: Civil Rights Attorney and Journalist is Volume 10 in the Race and
Culture in the American West series.

The paper in this book meets the guidelines for permanence and durability of
the Committee on Production Guidelines for Book Longevity of the Council on
Library Resources, Inc. ∞

1 2 3 4 5 6 7 8 9 10

I dedicate this book to my parents,
who wholeheartedly exercised their constitutional rights,
without which, they knew, there is no democracy.
I am indebted to my mother, Mamie Julia Chance,
who provided early-childhood education to African American,
Chinese American, and Mexican American children in the
Los Angeles Unified School District's childcare centers.
I am equally grateful to my father, Alfred Hassan,
an engineer, California state track-and-field champion,
letter carrier, and union man. He taught me that struggles
for justice are interconnected, that the blood of Chinese
laborers lies on our nation's railroad tracks, and that even
though his father, Abdul Hassan (also known as Alfred de
Livera), had emigrated from Sri Lanka, he had been barred
from U.S. citizenship under the Chinese Exclusion Act.

Contents

Illustrations

Acknowledgments

This book on Loren Miller's life has its origins in my growing up in Los Angeles. As a child, I knew Miller's name because he had represented my father, Alfred Hassan, who had been refused service by the Kansas City Steak House. This was in the days that my father worked for the post office, before he became a civil engineer. On the day he entered the restaurant, he was wearing his mail carrier's uniform and was in the company of two white mailmen. Through the lawsuit, Miller succeeded in getting each of the three men the then-standard settlement of one hundred dollars. Although I knew that skeletal story, I only asked my father years later, while in the midst of this biography, just how he had come to know Miller. It was my mother, Mamie, he replied, who was the conduit. An early-childhood educator with the Los Angeles Unified School District, she knew Loren Miller's wife, Juanita, then a child welfare specialist with California's social welfare department. We did not socialize with the Millers, though we shared some similarities. We lived near their Silver Lake neighborhood, away from other black Angelenos; and we were educated, racially mixed, politically progressive, and secular. So it was no accident that Miller's life intrigued me as I took up my research.

Many people have been generous with their encouragement and assistance as this project has unfolded—perhaps more than I can mention here. To my children, Sean Jenkins, Aisha Jenkins, Halima Gilliam, Sumaiya Olatunde, and Fatimah Gilliam, I am grateful for their support, as well as to my artist sister, Johann de Livera Hassan, who supplied me with materials pertaining to Los Angeles's historical black communities. I am especially indebted to Halvor Miller, Jr., Loren Miller's nephew, an invaluable source of family history. Moreover, Halvor granted me the right to use family photographs and to cite from the Loren Miller Papers. I am equally honored to have met and interviewed Edward Miller and Loren Miller, Jr., Loren Miller's two sons, who donated their father's papers to the Huntington Library, as well as Miller's niece, Jane Kerina. I'd like to express special thanks to Quintard Taylor, the Scott and Dorothy Bullitt Professor of American History at the University of Washington and series editor of this book. From the beginning, he encouraged this journey and first suggested that I write a short piece for www.blackpast.org, a web-based African and African American reference center he founded. I am similarly grateful to my publisher, the University of Oklahoma Press, for its insightful assistance from Steven Baker, Kathleen Kelly, Stephanie Evans, Kelly Parker, and Amy Hernandez.

To my dear public radio colleagues, particularly Julia Hutton, who has read several drafts and provided invaluable advice, as well Margaret Summers and Sonya Williams, I am indebted to these extraordinary friends for their editorial comments and advice. I thank Don Foster, who, like me and my four children survived the U.S. invasion of the peaceful island of Grenada, for hunting down several of the unrestricted photographs found in this book. To Harvard University law professor Kenneth Mack, whom I met while researching the Miller papers at the Huntington Library in San Marino, California, and whose *Representing the Race: The Creation of the Civil Rights Lawyer* in 2012 helped restore Miller to the leading ranks of African American attorneys, I thank him for both his encouragement and for taking the time to read an early manuscript. In addition, I thank Martin Schiesl, emeritus history professor at California State University, Los Angeles, whose many intellectual conversations on African Americans in California I cherish.

The clincher for my deciding to launch this project goes to the library staff at the Huntington Library, Art Collections, and Botanical Gardens in San Marino, California, particularly Sara S. "Sue" Hudson, curator of literary manuscripts, and Bill Frank, curator of Hispanic, cartographic, and western historical manuscripts. Before my first visit, I contacted Sue, who informed me that sixteen cartons of Loren Miller's papers had just arrived and that I should contact Bill. When I did, he asked if I would like to go to the basement with him where he was to fill out receivership forms. There I discovered that we were the first to view these documents, which had been preserved but had languished for decades in Loren Miller, Jr.'s, basement. Bill asked if there were things I'd like to see and said he would allow a few hours' access. After three dusty cartons were moved to Sue's office, I hastily examined the contents—barely able to contain my joy. Once cataloging funds were raised, Brooke Black, the Huntington's chief cataloger of manuscripts, cataloged what are now the Loren Miller Papers. Later, Sue invited me to lecture on Miller's life in the Huntington Library's Dreams Fulfilled series. In addition to thanking Sue, Bill, and Brooke, I would like to acknowledge and thank other Huntington staffers: Natalie Russell, assistant curator of literary manuscripts, and Edward "Bert" Rinderle, stacks supervisor. I must say, no library in my experience compares to the generosity of spirit that I experienced at the Huntington.

Many people who contributed to helping move this project along include Susan Anderson, Kim Clark, Lawrence de Graaf, Regina Freer, Sheila Gardette, Angela Holder, Rose Mitchell, Diana Lieb, Clarence Lusane, Ethelbert Miller, Kelly Navies, Arnold Rampersad, and Cindy Stillings, among others.

I'd like to express appreciation to the staff at the following repositories for providing access to their facilities, cited as the source of materials used herein. They are the Bancroft Library, University of California, Berkeley; Beinecke Rare Book and Manuscript Library, Yale University; Billbrew Library, County of Los Angeles Public Library; Center for Oral and Public History, California State University, Fullerton; Central Library, Los Angeles Public Library; Donald C. Davidson Library, Center for the Study of Democratic Institutions, University of California, Santa Barbara; Huntington Library, Art Collections, and Botanical Gardens; Kansas State Archives, Kansas Historical Society; Library of Congress, Washington, D.C.; Moreland Spingarn Library, Howard University; National Archives and Records Administration, College Park, Maryland, and Washington, D.C.; Schomburg Center for Research in Black Culture, New York Public Library; Southern California Library for Social Studies and Research, Los Angeles; Washburn University School of Law; Wilson Library, University of North Carolina, Chapel Hill; Robert W. Woodruff Library, Emory University; Charles E. Young Library, Department of Special Collections, Center for Oral History Research, University of California, Los Angeles. (Note: NAACP staff correspondence and meeting notes cited and attributed to the Loren Miller Papers, the Huntington Library, are equally to be found in the Papers of the NAACP, part 3, series A, B, and C [1913–1951]; and NAACP part 17 [1940–1955] housed at the Library of Congress).

Furthermore, I am particularly thankful to Nancy McWilliams, Ph.D., for permission to quote from the interview with her father-in-law, Carey McWilliams, conducted by UCLA. I'd also like to acknowledge Anthony Nicholas, who graciously granted me permission to publish the interview I conducted with his now-deceased stepfather, attorney Leo Branton. Moreover, I thank the Darhansoff & Verrill agency for use of the Taylor Branch interview of Judge Earl Broady. I was granted interviews by the following people, who knew either Loren Miller, Juanita Miller, or both: June Brown, Janice Carter, Art Drye, Francis Drye, Faye Hopkins Duffy, Thelma Holmes, and Dr. William Hutchinson (for whom Loren Miller was able to get Dr. Hutchinson's eviction ruling by the Santa Anita Municipal Court reversed by the Superior Court). Three others I'm honored to have interviewed who have since died are Attorney Walter Gordon, Jr.; Dr. Marion Maddox, a member of the League of Allied Arts, whose husband Edward C. Maddox was one of Loren Miller's law partners; and Alice McGrath, an activist and supporter of the defendants in the Sleepy Lagoon murder trial. I am grateful to all who helped this biography come to fruition.

Acronyms and Abbreviations

ACLU	American Civil Liberties Union
AFL	American Federation of Labor
ACRR	American Council on Race Relations
AME	African Methodist Episcopal
CAC	California Advisory Committee for California
CIO	Congress of Industrial Organizations
CNA	Crusader News Agency
CP	Communist Party
CRC	Civil Rights Congress
CPSU	Communist Party of the Soviet Union
CPUSA	Communist Party of the United States
ILD	International Labor Defense
JACL	Japanese American Citizens League
JRC	John Reed Club
LAPD	Los Angeles Police Department
LDF	NAACP Legal Defense Fund
NAACP	National Association for the Advancement of Colored People
NBA	National Bar Association

Loren Miller

Introduction

One of the nation's most influential mid-twentieth-century African Americans is little-known today. At his death in 1967, Loren Miller was considered one of the nation's greatest civil rights attorneys, barely second in importance to his friend and colleague and sometime co-counsel Thurgood Marshall. Miller's legal accomplishments as a tireless advocate for full equality were monumental, but his significance was quickly lost to history. As a member of the national legal team of the National Association for the Advancement of Colored People Legal Defense and Education Fund (NAACP LDF), Loren Miller helped change American law and society by writing the majority of the appellate briefs in *Brown v. Board of Education of Topeka*. Yet during many of the fiftieth and sixtieth anniversary celebrations of *Brown*, his role was overlooked, and until recently references to Miller and citations of his work were few.

Miller, along with future Supreme Court justice Thurgood Marshall, effectively abolished racially restrictive real estate housing covenants in two landmark cases before the U.S. Supreme Court; these Fourteenth Amendment victories continue to affect the lives of Americans from every background. Loren Miller's legal argument in *Shelley v. Kramer*, a case that Marshall considered "unquestionably as one of the most important of the whole field of civil rights," is taught in nearly every American law school.[1]

Miller's courtroom victories are only one aspect of what makes him a captivating figure. This biography recounts his forty-year friendship with writer Langston Hughes; Miller's early career as a fiery radical journalist; his move toward the anti-fascist Left and later to left-of-center politics; his ownership of the *California Eagle*, one of the longest-running African American newspapers in the West; and his continued commitment to improving the lives of Americans, particularly the residents of Los Angeles, regardless of color.

A fearless critic of the powerful and an ardent debater who understood that inequality and capitalism go hand and hand, Loren Miller set out for Los Angeles from Kansas in 1929—a freshly minted member of the bar who preferred political activism and writing to practicing the law. By the time he stood before the Supreme Court in 1948, he was a seasoned attorney who had tried more racial covenant cases than had any other lawyer in the nation. All the while, he wrote a regular newspaper column urging readers toward collective action.

His was a career of landmark cases. During World War II, Miller joined the southern California branch council of the American Civil Liberties Union

(ACLU) when it challenged the evacuation and internment of West Coast Japanese citizens and foreign nationals. He also worked to integrate the United States military and the Los Angeles Fire Department. Following his defense of fourteen Black Muslims, who had been arrested in a 1962 street battle in which six unarmed Muslims had been shot down and one killed by the Los Angeles Police Department (LAPD), Miller predicted the Watts rebellion of 1965. His legal skills and civic participation helped establish fair employment practices in the state of California.

This book's eight chapters trace and examine the journey of an American original: a crusader, a dissenter, and a family man, who was also the son of a former slave and was married to a white midwesterner. Miller's personal history offers a lens onto the midcentury race relations and political landscape that shaped him and that he helped shape. His story, moreover, is an American success story, not only because he rose from rural poverty to a position of professional success, civic leadership, and lasting influence, but also because he determined his own path—defying limitations imposed by the larger society and at times bucking convention within the black community. Through Loren Miller's pivotal role in California's civil rights struggles, this volume sheds new light on the lives of African Americans in Los Angeles and, in addition, contributes to the history of the Great Migration to the West Coast.

Miller's early engagement in writing and the arts sparked a friendship with writer Langston Hughes. In 1932, Miller and Hughes traveled to the Soviet Union along with twenty other black Americans to make a big-budget film on "Negro Life."[2] Idealistically enamored of Soviet ideology at the time, Miller wrote sympathetic reports for the Associated Negro Press about Russia's treatment of ethnic minorities as well as on Langston Hughes's impressions of the Soviets. The two men remained friends all their lives. Miller was a dedicated reporter and a prolific writer with an acid wit, quick to burn "holes in the toughest skin and eat right through double-talk, hypocrisy and posturing."[3] His articles were published mostly by black and leftist newspapers during the 1930s and 1960s (*Los Angeles Sentinel, California Eagle, Chicago Defender, Pittsburgh Courier, Atlanta Daily World, Baltimore Afro-American, The Crisis, New Masses, Daily Worker,* and *The Nation,* among others).

Although Miller sought to pursue the writer's life and identified as a fiery, radical writer, the need to put food on the table—especially at the height of the Great Depression—propelled him to practice law. Toward the end of his career, he became a judge, an appointment made all the more remarkable given his early zeal for radical politics, from which he took pains to distance himself over decades, eventually ceasing to represent Communists in court. Yet even though his representation of leftist clients occurred mostly in his early legal career, the "pink" tint remained. Nonetheless, Miller hoped for and in 1964 received an appointment to the Los Angeles Municipal Court from California governor Edmund G. "Pat" Brown, a political ally of many years. At the Los Angeles ceremony, Brown showered Miller with accolades, hailing him as "one of the ablest attorneys I have known. I know he will distinguish himself on the bench as he has in private practice, and as a citizen."[4] Others were less impressed with the appointment, including conservative news commentator George Putnam, who spewed vitriol and scorn on his televised talk show. Within days of the broadcast, the local FBI office received Putnam's transcript and copies of letters sent to the *Los Angeles Times* protesting Miller's appointment.

Over the course of three decades, Loren Miller challenged racial ordinances in California courtrooms and before the United States Supreme Court. Explicit and eloquent in his commitment to making democracy work for every American, he was opposed to discrimination of any kind and held that democracy must work for every American "or in the last analysis we shall not be able to preserve it for any American."[5]

CHAPTER 1

Storming the Barricades

L oren Miller died on Bastille Day, a fitting coincidence for a man dedicated to storming the hush-hush of courtroom injustice. In the coolness of the summer evening, at 9:53 P.M., on July 14, 1967, a Friday, he succumbed to pulmonary emphysema aggravated by pneumonia. Six days earlier, he had entered Los Angeles's Temple Hospital, struggling and barely able to breathe.[1] By noon on July 19, thousands of people overflowed the capacity of the First African Methodist Episcopal (AME) Church at Eighth Street and Towne Avenue. Filling the pews or crowding outdoors was virtually every black lawyer and most of the judges in the city. "A multitude of greats, near greats"—among them dignitaries and just plain Joes—came to pay final respects to the great man. Lena Horne, the show-stopping beauty of film and music, blacklisted in the 1950s for her political views, spoke at the ceremony and later acknowledged hundreds of telegrams, letters, and condolences.[2] Mourners came from far and near to attend the rites of the longtime civil rights leader and prolific writer, lawyer of intimidating rectitude, and key strategist in the legal campaign to overturn racial discrimination, particularly in housing and education—a man, who by sheer force of will and determination, improved the lives of those on the periphery of justice.

The news of Miller's death was a second blow for African Americans in close succession. Two giants of African American culture and longtime friends who even looked alike had died within six weeks of each other. First Langston Hughes, then Loren Miller.[3]

On the West Coast, Reverend Dr. H. Hartford Brookins, the popular pastor of Los Angeles's first church for the "Negro people in the city,"[4] delivered the eulogy. The city's leading black church, housed in an impressive neo-Gothic structure, had been founded and financed in 1872 by Biddy Mason (1818–91), a former slave, midwife, local real estate entrepreneur, and philanthropist, along with Charles Owens, her son-in-law. "Everybody has to say it sooner or later and the time has come for me to say goodbye,"[5] quoted the reverend from one of Miller's speeches. Then he read from Miller's parting article on the sale of the *California Eagle*: "I don't even know whether my writings served a good purpose. . . . But no man can be sure his intentions came to good ends, I'll just have to let the whole thing go with the hope that I did more good than wrong. You can be the judge. . . . We cannot undo our yesterdays. . . . Let us as literal and free men work to overcome the restrictions our yesterdays impose."[6]

The reverend read from the eighth chapter of the book of Jeremiah (verses 20–23), the textual basis for "There is a Balm in Gilead," one of the more important traditional African American spirituals. Miller, he said, often used these passages when addressing the hurt and suffering of society's most vulnerable, asking, "Is there no medicine in Gilead? Is there no physician there? Why then is there no healing for the wounds of my people?"[7] Brookins, profoundly moved, composed a picture of Miller as a doctor treating society's ills, a man who devoted himself to affecting and challenging its social policies. It is interesting that Miller, who believed more in the spirit of justice than in the invisible existence of deities, was known for reciting these Bible verses.

Reverend Lloyd Galloway of Lincoln Memorial United Church of Christ, a leader of civil rights causes in Los Angeles, gave the funeral's opening prayer. Twenty years earlier the Congregational minister had eulogized Miller's brother-in-law, the musician Milton V. Ellsworth.[8] From the hundreds of telegrams and messages received, four were read by Horne: notes from Robert C. Weaver, the first secretary of the U.S. Department of Housing and Urban Development; Ralph Bunche, America's highest official in the United Nations, who received the 1950 Nobel Peace Prize; Roy Wilkins, head of the National Association for the Advancement of Colored People; and the Fair Employment Practices Commission.[9] In a later editorial, the NAACP said that Miller's death "deprives the Negro race and the nation of one of the keenest minds and most persistent workers in the continued struggle to achieve a viable pluralistic society."[10]

At the time of the funeral, Thurgood Marshall, Miller's longtime legal colleague and sometime co-counsel, was sitting through his third day of hearings with the Senate Judiciary Committee on his nomination to the United States Supreme Court.[11] Beforehand, he sent his sincerest condolences to the family. Abraham Lincoln Wirin, "Mr. ACLU," the general counsel for the American Civil Liberties Union of Southern California, was able to attend and speak dearly of his old friend and legal colleague. "Loren Miller did not finish all the work he set out to do when he first began the practice of law forty years ago. Nonetheless, he left a rich legacy for the America he so loved," said Wirin. That work, he continued, included drafting the majority of the briefs in the high court decision of *Brown v. Board of Education of Topeka* (347 U.S. 483), which established that separate was not equal, and that school segregation violated the Constitution. Wirin added, "Not so well known was his close involvement with the American Civil Liberties Union. . . . In 1942, he was one of the two lawyers to join ACLU counsel in the federal courts to challenge the wartime evacuation from California of Americans of Japanese descent," a bold position amid wartime anti-Japanese sentiment.[12]

Dr. H. Claude Hudson, a prominent Los Angeles leader who served with Miller on the national NAACP board, promised to "carry the torch until we have won the victory."[13] Other tributes came from Cecil Poole of the U.S. attorney's office in San Francisco and Edward Rutledge, executive director of the National Committee

Against Discrimination in Housing in New York, one of the many organizations that Miller served on as an executive board member. Nathaniel Colley, director of the national board of the NAACP, described Miller as "Mr. Civil Rights of the Western United States," whose first law office at Vernon and Central Avenue became the battleground of legal work for the fight for justice. He read Miller's obituary aloud just moments before Reverend Brookins began the eulogy. Colley served as Miller's co-counsel in the California state court decree that ended discrimination in the sale of housing "where sales involved the Federal Housing Administration [and] Veterans Administration financing."[14]

As the recessional played, the pallbearers carried the coffin outside to the waiting hearse. James Ronald Derry was one of the pallbearers. A member of the First AME Church, Derry arrived in Los Angeles in 1932 with Langston Hughes, before Miller and Hughes took off for Russia. Another pallbearer was Miller's dear friend and neighbor James H. Garrott, the architect who designed the Miller family home in the Silver Lake district. Norman Hopkins, mortician and owner of Peoples Funeral Home, as well as a neighbor of the Miller family, helped convey the coffin to Rosedale Cemetery, the first cemetery in Los Angeles open to all races and creeds.[15]

Inside the church, a little girl "stepped out of the throng" to present "the widow, Mrs. Juanita Miller, with a lovely long-stemmed rose."[16] Later, Mrs. Miller wrote the *Los Angeles Sentinel* to thank the paper (cofounded by her husband) for its recent issue on him. She wrote, "We found solace and encouragement in your individual and collective tribute and in the words, deeds and prayers of our many beloved friends. . . . That Loren was so valued and respected by so many is a valued inspiration. . . . Thank you so very much."[17]

In truth, the soft-spoken, humble, scholarly looking, mixed-race man had become a municipal court judge at the urging of his wife, Juanita.[18] He accepted the post in 1964, by some accounts to leave a pension behind for his wife and children—for whom he said he was humbly grateful "for their willingness to endure deprivation that I might do my best in the struggle."[19] Though he earned so little during his lifetime of work as a civil rights lawyer and struggling newspaper journalist and publisher, he died free of debt, and the owner of his Silver Lake home, where his wife continued to live until her death three years later. He died confident that the future held great promise.

Loren Miller lived to see Thurgood Marshall on his way to a seat at the U.S. Supreme Court, the first black American appointed to serve there. Together, the two attorneys effectively abolished restrictive racial housing covenants in two landmark cases before the U.S. Supreme Court in 1948 and again in 1953. The impact of those victories and others—founded in Miller's belief that the law "may not eliminate prejudice but it can and does prevent the translation of private prejudice into discriminatory conduct"[20]—propelled him to pave the way for the integration of the U.S. military and the Los Angeles Fire Department, as well as the passage of fair employment practices legislation in California. Brad

Pye, Jr., the sports writer who worked for Miller when he owned the *California Eagle*, wrote how "Cuzz"—as Miller was affectionately known around the newspaper—enriched his life. Using sports metaphors, Pye wrote, "In the civil rights field to me he was the Jim Brown of the legal profession knocking down racial barriers all around him. He dribbled through the courts of the land like Elgin Baylor and scored as many points in the legal field as Wilt Chamberlain does on the basketball courts. As a lawyer, journalist, author, publisher and scholar he was as all-around a man as Willie Mays is on the diamond."[21]

Many of Miller's friends and admirers averred that Miller would have reached federal office had he lived longer. Carey McWilliams, author, editor, and lawyer, wrote that his dear friend Loren Miller, along with William Henry Hastie and Charles Hamilton Huston, were "definite supreme court prospects."[22] Ben Margolis, who, with McWilliams, helped defend the Hollywood Ten, said, "Loren was one of the best lawyers with whom I have ever come in contact." "[He] should have been on the supreme court of the state. He had that kind of capacity, and he had the desire."[23] Judge Earl C. Broady felt similarly: "Loren Miller should have gone to the Supreme Court. But he might not have fit in with his liberal, trade liberal philosophy. But he had the type of mind that belongs there. He not only had knowledge of the laws that existed, but he had ideas about where the law should go."[24] Miller's cousin Leon Washington, cofounder and publisher of the *Los Angeles Sentinel*, wrote, "He should have been on the superior of the district court of appeals or the Supreme Court of the land."[25] A decade later, Judge A. Leon Higginbotham, Jr., justice of U.S. Court of Appeals, Third District, felt the same way, insisting, "In paying tribute to the black lawyers of our country, that one man who 'would have been, should have been' an appellate judge or a member of the U.S. Supreme Court was the late Loren Miller."[26] Others felt that he was barely second in importance to Thurgood Marshall.

Besides racism, what curtailed Miller's prospect for anything higher than an appointment to the municipal court? Certainly his long association with Red Front groups was hardly an aid for advancement, not to mention his defense in court of Communists, his writing for leftist publications, and a stint in 1935 as an editor of the *New Masses*.[27] When Miller was appointed to the municipal court in 1964, conservative Los Angeles broadcaster George Putnam of KTTV became enraged. Spouting vitriol, he told his viewers that Miller voted "Red" and wrote for various Communist newspapers. Putnam's script, "Judge Loren Miller in the *Congressional Record*," found its way into Miller's Federal Bureau of Investigation file.[28]

Up until the year he died, the FBI continued to monitor Miller's activities. In February 1967, the FBI reported that when he spoke at a National Lawyers Guild luncheon in memoriam to Daniel Marshall, who broke the barrier to mixed-race marriages in California in the case *Perez v. Sharp*, "Judge Loren Miller . . . has a hard time breathing and it definitely affects his speaking ability," due to an affliction, "that has been prevalent for some years but has become more pronounced."

Two months before his death, under the pretext of looking for a woman named "Laura Miller," agents called his home. The bureau, before closing out its file on Miller, requested his death certificate from the Los Angeles County Registrar.[29]

Miller took his fundamental creed of equality from Frederick Douglass, whose exploits he discovered as a young Kansas farm boy. He believed that one must do what one thinks is ethical and just. "Of course it isn't always easy to know what is right in a specific situation," wrote Miller to Edward, his youngest son. He continued,

> but the best a person can do is to think through that situation and do what seems to him to be right. . . . Later events may prove that he was mistaken but nobody can foresee everything and if an individual does what seems to be the right thing in light of the information he then has at his command, that is all that can be asked of him. The greatest regrets I have arise out of my failure to use the information at my command as a guide to action.[30]

Underneath, like Marx, thoroughly opposed to the property-owning class, Miller was a good romantic humanist, believing in a just society and the uniqueness of the individual.[31] Though he remained a Marxist, he turned away from Communism in the late 1930s when he "realized there was a great fraud in the communist claims."[32] Nor was he much for conventional religion. From the evidence, he was likely akin to his friend Ralph Bunche, also a Marxist, who said on the prospect of death that he approached the subject "calmly and philosophically,"[33] without fear. A telling comment comes from Miller's son Edward who said the only time he went to church was when his father gave a speech.[34] According to Miller's niece Jane Kerina, neither Miller nor his wife, Juanita, was a churchgoer: "Loren would read the Sunday paper instead."[35]

Three months before he died, Miller was healthy enough to travel in April with Juanita to New York to receive a "special award from the National Committee Against Discrimination in Housing"[36] at the Waldorf Astoria. The surviving record shows Miller in good form mentally, apparently undaunted by the setback of poor health. He had emphysema from years of smoking Lucky Strike cigarettes, and his voice was still strong, though less so than four years earlier when he had spoken on "A Negro Looks at the Fourteenth Amendment" at the Center for the Study of Democratic Institutions in Santa Barbara.[37]

Just before leaving Los Angeles for his final trip to New York, Miller wrote his son Edward, who at the time was serving in the navy aboard the USS *Saint Paul*, off the coast of Vietnam: "No matter how long I've been planning to go some place I am never really ready and the last few days are spent in a tizzy of preparations that should have been long since completed. The situation is worse this time because I haven't been anywhere for a long time. . . . Pete is going to take us to the air port. He will have to come over because somebody has to muscle the bags up and down stairs and I am not up to it."[38] When he arrived in New York, Henry Lee Moon, public relations director of the NAACP, wrote, "Although then suffering from his ailment, he forcefully delivered a memorable address, inoffensive and scholarly. His illness had not dulled his charm and wit and thrust."[39]

While in New York, Miller's old traveling companion Frank Montero and his white wife hosted a party, "which served as a reunion of a group which went to Russia in the Thirties to make a movie."[40] Miller reminisced with the couple in their plush Riverdale home—an evident benefit of marrying an heiress—with Langston Hughes, Ted Poston, married couple Mollie Lewis and Henry Lee Moon, and a few others who had not accompanied them on their Russian travels in 1932. Shortly after the gathering, Langston Hughes, then sixty-five, was admitted to New York's Polyclinic Hospital. Following surgery two weeks later, he died on May 22, at 9:40 P.M.[41]

It is said that most men wish for admiration, long for applause, and seek it. "The wise man," wrote Jean-Jacques Rousseau, "does not run after fortune, but he is not insensitive to glory."[42] Miller, no different, wanted recognition and luckily received it in great quantities. Yet he yearned for more. His friend Carey McWilliams, whom California historian Kevin Starr called California's finest nonfiction writer, recounted, "The black community at [the time of the 1930s to the 1950s] hadn't sufficiently grounded itself so that it could develop elements that would support a man of Loren's caliber. This was a great disappointment to him and to everybody else. And this was unfortunate because he had an extraordinary background and experience."[43]

Although Miller's fearlessness was matched in his other spheres of life, his particular tendency toward razor-sharp outspokenness stood in the way of many serious career aspirations and advancements. He was in some respects like Dwight Macdonald, the mid-twentieth-century journalist who was said to write with "a lot of salt and pepper" and whose work showed similar curiosity and skepticism.[44] Miller did not hesitate—in life or in his newspaper writing—to point out shortcomings of others, even those of his friends. For example, in 1931 he did not pull any punches when reviewing *God Sends Sunday*, a novel by former Angeleno Arna Bontemps. Of Bontemps, Miller wrote: "It seems to be quite the fashion to lay part of the scene for present-day novels in Los Angeles. . . . Denizens of Watts, now South Los Angeles, will be interested in that part of the story laid there and others who would like to see how many uses the adjective 'nigger' may be put will be quite intrigued."[45] It might be that Miller enjoyed provoking others since he had a tremendous appetite for humor; certainly, he did not suffer fools gladly. When reviewing *Recessional*, a play written by William Hurlbut, who later wrote the screenplay for Fannie Hurst's novel *Imitation of Life*, Miller said, "The worst has been preserved for the last. It is *Recessional*, a play by William Hurlbut. The only things that qualify Mr. Hurlbut to write a book about Negroes are that he probably owns a typewriter and is totally ignorant of psychology."[46]

Miller's intellect, admired by virtually everyone he met, might have endeared him more to others if his acid wit had not been quick to burn "holes in the toughest skin and eat right through double-talk, hypocrisy and posturing,"[47] wrote his longtime friend, Lester B. Granger, executive secretary of the National Urban League. Whatever Miller ever hoped to become, he was explicit and eloquent in his commitment to making democracy work for every American:

> It goes without saying that I am opposed to any discrimination of any kind on racial and religious grounds, or on any other grounds. I think that we must do that, not only in simple justice to minority groups of any kind, but out of a realization that the majority has as big a stake in it—if not bigger—than the minorities. We can't stand still. Either we shall have to make democracy work for every American or in the last analysis we shall not be able to preserve it for any American.[48]

CHAPTER 2

The Making of a Dissenter

Loren Miller came into the world on the western edge of the Omaha Indian reservation in Pender, Nebraska, on January 20, 1903. He was born during the American coal famine of 1902–1903, when fierce industrial warfare erupted in the coalfields of Pennsylvania and caused a fuel shortage with a broad ripple effect. In Nebraska, people turned from burning coal to burning corn to heat their homes and cookstoves. In neighboring Council Bluffs, Iowa, fuel-starved factories threatened to shut down. Public schools in many states were closed as coal supplies dwindled. In Indianapolis, along the railroad yards, poor people scavenged lumps of coal and hauled them away in wheelbarrows and sacks in broad daylight in full view of guards with rifles. Eventually, the federal government intervened, turning from strikebreaker to peacemaker for the first time in U.S. history.[1] Perhaps the atmosphere of social and political unrest surrounding Miller's arrival presaged what lay ahead for him: a life on the frontline of justice where he would shine a light into the dark shadows of racism and inequality.

Loren Miller was the second of seven children born to John Bird Miller, a former slave, and Nora Magdalena Herbaugh, a white midwesterner. Miller's father was born on May 4, 1861, three weeks after Jefferson Davis, president of the Confederate States of America, ordered the bombardment of Fort Sumter. John's birth took place somewhere near the Kansas-Missouri border town of Saint Joseph, Missouri, a town whose claim to fame is the 1860 inaugural run of the Pony Express and the site where Robert Ford, "that dirty little coward," shot the outlaw Jesse James in the back in 1882.[2]

What is known of John Miller is that at age fourteen, the ever-stubborn and independent John ran off to Leavenworth, Kansas, where he found work laying the right-of-way for the Union Pacific Railroad. He laid pavement in Omaha, worked the wheat fields of North Dakota, and got an entry-level post as a porter in a saloon before moving up to bartending.[3] Though he supported himself through tough, physical jobs, John was immensely proud that he could read and write. According to family lore, he had been educated by his cousin Nancy Bruce (née Gee), who was also the sister-in-law of Blanche Kelso Bruce, the second African American to serve in the United States Senate.[4]

Loren Miller's mother, Nora Herbaugh, was born on February 16, 1877, in Stoutland, Missouri, eighty miles from Saint Joseph. She was a fair, blue-eyed redhead of German and Irish stock. Nora's parents were Martha Caroline Burke, a homemaker born in 1853 in Tennessee, and Henry Wilford Herbaugh, a Baptist minister, farmer, and railroad man. Born in 1853 in Indiana, Henry was the son of Isaac Herbaugh and Anna Weaver.[5] Nora, the oldest of eight, traveled from Missouri to Colorado as a young child in a canvas-topped, mule-drawn wagon train with her parents and three younger siblings.[6] By 1900, the Herbaughs were living in Beaver, Nebraska. Settled nearby was Henry's brother, John W. Herbaugh, a Civil War veteran of the Eighty-First Regiment of the Indiana Infantry.[7]

Sometime around 1899, the nearly six-foot-tall John Miller, then a hotel porter, met the rosy-cheeked, auburn-haired Nora Herbaugh in what is today Ravenna, Nebraska, a railroad stop at the time that served travelers in the era before "passenger trains had dining or sleeping cars."[8] Plagued with eye problems for most of her life, Nora had already given up earning a living as a teacher. At the time the twenty-two-year-old met John Miller, she was making beds in a hotel, keeping the fireplaces lit, and ensuring that the guests had plenty of hot water.[9]

Nora made no diary entry as to whether the mixed-race couple's courtship caused a stir in the boardinghouse shared with thirty other lodgers, mostly northern Europeans who had emigrated from Germany and Sweden to work as cooks and porters in the local hotels.[10] On August 28, 1900, the couple married in Council Bluffs, Iowa, 245 miles away from Ravenna, because "white and colored couldn't marry in Nebraska."[11] Nora's diary, a record of her hardscrabble life, makes no mention as to why she took a leap of faith and crossed the color line to marry a former slave. Perhaps, blinded by love or simply naïve, she foresaw little of the social isolation and limited work opportunities that lay ahead. Or rather, perhaps because of an ever-advancing eye disease, she needed the protection of John's self-assuredness. In time, she would tire of a husband whose staunch pride kept them in a state of unrelenting poverty.

In the beginning, Nora's family was bitterly opposed to her choice of a former slave as a life partner, not because John was black or sixteen years older, but, as strict Baptists, they disapproved of John's divorce. They believed that sacramental marriages are permanent.[12] Attitudes softened as the babies kept being born. Although Nora stayed in contact with her siblings, two sisters and one brother in particular, there is reason to believe that when they did meet, hovering overhead was the cloud of racism.

The couple, who had moved to Omaha, welcomed their first son Cloyd on November 19, 1901; Loren followed thirteen months later.[13] Contrary to what the Millers originally hoped for, Omaha was unwelcoming to their mixed-race family. Fortunately, they relocated well before the Ku Klux Klan (KKK) established a stranglehold on the city. By the time Loren was born in 1903, the family was living in the village of Pender, on the outskirts of the Omaha Indian reservation, where, as the only black family, they posed no threat to the white population.[14]

The genealogical history of slaves in America is often unverifiable and in some instances little more than a tangled web of oral histories. Most of what is known about the Miller family comes from Loren Miller and his younger brother Halvor, who took the time to write down family stories. We are told that their paternal great-grandmother, Daphne, was born into bondage sometime around 1795 in Tennessee, where Henry, her husband, also was born. However, the census enumerator for Doniphan County, Kansas, where the family eventually settled, wrote on June 15, 1880, that Daphne's older sister Patsey and their parents were born instead in Virginia.[15] According to Miller family lore, Daphne's father may have come directly from Africa, as Virginia in the 1700s had the largest slave disembarkation ports on the Lower and Upper James River basin of the Chesapeake Bay region,[16] which was a gateway for "the first blacks brought from Africa to the colonies."[17]

We learn from Loren that Thomas Miller, his paternal grandfather, born in Tennessee in 1828, was given as a wedding gift—along with his mother Daphne, brothers Henry and Joseph, and an older sister—to Leander Miller, the son of a wealthy Kentucky tobacco farmer, who took all of them by covered wagon to Missouri.[18] After they cleared the Missouri timberland for farming, Daphne, Joseph, and a sister who was "never heard from again" were sold at auction in front of the Saint Joseph, Missouri, courthouse.[19] In time, Thomas married Jane Gee, born in 1832 in Missouri, one of Leander Miller's slaves. The couple later fled from Missouri to Kansas—possibly after 1861 when Kansas was admitted to the Union as a free state—and eventually reunited with Jane's parents, Elijah and Ritter Gee, and her eight siblings.[20]

At some point Daphne escaped to Kansas with the help of Thomas,[21] who assisted his wife's sister, Martha Fouts Hubbard (née Gee), flee slavery with six of her seven children.[22] There is reason to believe that Thomas returned to Missouri, where he successfully retrieved Martha's seventh child.[23] After the Civil War, Loren's granduncle Joseph rejoined the Miller family in Kansas, as did Henry, who had been living in Lexington, Missouri.[24]

It is unclear why three of Loren Miller's maternal granduncles decided so late in the Civil War to march to the beat of the Seventy-Ninth United States Colored Infantry (New), but they did.[25] Fortunately, Loren's grandmother Jane Gee, the second daughter and the third child of nine, lived long enough to see brothers Greenbury, Smith, and Bird leave Kansas for the Civil War.[26] When twenty-seven-year-old Smith Gee mustered in on March 10, 1865, he stood in for Wesley Wood, a slave owner, even though the U.S. Congress had repealed the practice of substitute war draftees in 1863. His twenty-four-year-old brother Bird Gee mustered into the same infantry on the same day. Greenbury, the eldest, managed to muster in ahead of his two younger brothers by eighteen days.[27] Sadly, he did not survive the war, having been "attacked by a chill & fever" in Arkansas; he died aboard ship on a steamer headed for Leavenworth, Kansas.[28]

As for Bird Gee, his war record proved remarkable, not for its battlefield exploits but as one of the few examples of an African American Civil War veteran taking legal action in an effort to secure pension benefits. After war's end, Bird and Smith Gee returned to Kansas weakened and unhealthy. For the most part, black males prior to entering the Union Army were as healthy as white recruits; in some cases, they were actually healthier, their diets fortified by such "throwaway foods" as turnips, beets, and greens from the plantation house.[29] However, by the time escaping slaves reached unsanitary camp conditions, they were "often nearly naked . . . with swellings, open sores, and eaten up with vermin." The Civil War, according to Jim Downs, "produced the largest biological crisis of the nineteenth century claiming more soldiers' lives and resulting in more casualties than battle or warfare and wreaking havoc on . . . the newly freed."[30]

While in the army, Smith contracted measles, which permanently damaged his eyesight. Bird, who weighed one hundred and sixty-five pounds and stood five foot seven and three-quarters, suffered the effects of pleurisy, inflammation of the lung membranes, just five days after he joined up. In 1896, he swore in a series of Civil War pension claims, beginning in 1890, that when "changing heavy clothes at the time of enlistment to light uniform,"[31] he contracted pleurisy. He was hospitalized first in the Leavenworth Hospital and later transferred to the Saint Louis Hospital, where in all probability Bird fell under the care of negligent white doctors who viewed his condition through the lens of racism.[32] His attempt at meaningful citizenship and equality through military service were dashed by illness.

Bird was treated repeatedly in Highland, Kansas, and later in Oklahoma by Dr. C. B. Bradley, who removed Bird's inflamed uvula and swore in his 1901 physician's affidavit that Bird was "disabled from following his occupation farming 1/2 for the reason that the slightest exposure aggravates the condition."[33] Bird fought hard for his pension. He hired legal counsel, arranged for his brother Smith and others to testify on his behalf, and tolerated two medical examinations; however, although the Bureau of Pensions acknowledged that his claim had merit, the administration stated, without explanation, that it wanted "another medical examination." Prior to 1907, Bird ran up against restrictions based on age and length of service. In 1909, when he last applied, at age sixty-three, he was eligible. Although, he provided "copious documentation" and engaged in "never-ending correspondence with pension personnel,"[34] Bird, like many black Civil War veterans, never received his pension, but the records show that it was not for a lack of trying. The good part of Bird's story is that his dogged determination inspired Loren Miller to pursue a lifetime of social justice advocacy.

By late 1904, Lorin Raymond Miller (who later replaced the *i* in "Lorin" with an *e*) was christened, and the household welcomed its third child, Cecil. In quick succession, Ruby arrived, followed by, Halvor, Helen, and Roland.[35] Overwhelmed with the drudgery of so many small children, Nora devised a plan, in opposition to her husband's demand that she braid Loren and Cloyd's hair daily. Instead, she decided to cut their brown curls "a little at a time" "so their father did not miss (their long hair) for a long time and [by] then it was too late."[36] Later, the ordeal of a haircut and John's handheld clippers with two missing metal blades, was, according to Halvor, "just about as much pain as going to the electric chair."[37]

In fall 1908, Loren's older brother set off for his first day of school. Dressed in his best clothes, he waited for John to hitch the buggy to old Kate, the horse. Little Loren began to cry when the horse and buggy pulled away. "'Hush,' said his mother, recalls Miller, 'You can go to school someday.'"[38] But he would not hush. As the year wore on, Cloyd's excitement dimmed as Loren eagerly waited to flip through the popular *McGuffey's First Eclectic Reader*—sprinkled with Christian anti-Semitic themes such as holding Jews responsible for the death of Christ or "Shylock and the Jews' attacking Jesus and Paul."[39] Hardly discouraged by Cloyd's lack of interest, Loren coaxed and pled tearfully for his brother to decipher the "queer little signs."[40] When he refused, Loren cried even more. Nora quickly saw how exceptionally bright her second child was. As he grew, she read to him from *Robinson Crusoe* and a *Barnes History of the United States*, adult books borrowed from the newly formed local library.[41] She described his zest for learning and his remarkable memory as a miracle of the Lord—a reflection of someone having come from a deeply religious family, a family who "thinks it is wrong to ride on the train or street car on Sunday."[42] Amazed by her son's early ability to decipher *ing* and other phonetic symbols—approving his evident thirst for knowledge— she had him exhibit his small share of budding literacy for his father.[43] In a short time, he could read, even better than his school-age brother could. Later in his life, others recognized Miller as a keen intellect and a sharp wit. As he grew older, he stayed indoors, lying on his stomach reading the *Omaha Bee*, his father's newspaper, while the other children played outside. More likely, besides enjoying the solitude that comes with reading, he read *Frank on a Gun-boat* (1864) and *Frank on the Lower Mississippi* (1867), the most popular adventure stories for boys at the time.[44] Reading offered entry to a world beyond the limited circumstances surrounding him. However, the reality of his poverty would steer his future course to change the human condition more deeply than what he would ever find in a book of fiction.

His siblings, perhaps jealous, said he was "spoiled by his father who spent most of his own leisure time reading." Loren's "always sour" and serious personality earned him the family sobriquet "Lemon."[45] In school, Mrs. Farnham Baker, his schoolteacher, "very impressed by his eagerness to learn,"[46] encouraged him to excel, which he did. It was around this time that the townspeople of Pender began saying that ten-year-old Loren was "the brightest child in school."[47]

From time to time, John Miller took his son along with him to the Thurston County Courthouse, an impressive, Victorian-style brick building on Fifth Street, where he worked as a janitor. There, Loren developed an interest in the law. "He had been going around with my father at the courthouse and used to go to the courthouse alone as a child and sit in the courtroom and listen when trials were being held," wrote Halvor Miller. Judge Frank Flynn of Thurston County, a stout, blue-eyed farmer and father of three, took notice of the handsome brown boy who sat in the courtroom's wooden chairs watching the trials.[48] Much like Clarence Darrow, who wrote how as a child he had enjoyed "the way the pettifoggers abused each other,"[49] in court a young Loren Miller savored the atmosphere and the spectacle. Whenever people asked what he was going "'to do when he got big,'" his answer remained always the same: "'I'm going to be a lawyer.'"[50] His father hoped to live long enough to see him do so. Early on, Judge Flynn recognized what a remarkable memory Loren had; he took a special interest in the boy, which continued after the family moved to Kansas.[51]

Miller came of age in the Jim Crow era. Yet, it was a time, according to W. E. B. Du Bois, that "the backbone of segregation" was beginning to crack.[52] New legal precedents were being set just as Miller was poised to enter the profession. Fixed on becoming an attorney, and encouraged to do so by his family, he discovered later what his real ambition was: to be a writer. Ultimately, he would sacrifice that dream for the stability of planting his feet in the courtroom and hurling brickbats at the legal underpinnings of institutional racism. His career path reflected his father's dreams, but it was likely rooted in a more extensive family legacy, especially the example of his granduncle Bird Gee, a contentious persistent contrarian "as far as his rights were concerned."[53] It might be said that Bird's influence, a man Loren never met, propelled him to finish what his granduncle was unable to do—win. Well before Bird unsuccessfully fought the pension bureau for his war pension, he sought justice under the Civil Rights Act of 1875.

On October 10, 1875, Bird Gee was up early.[54] Dressed in his Sunday best, he headed west for the City Hotel in Hiawatha, Kansas, sixteen miles from his hometown of Highland. When Bird reached the hotel steps, he hesitated for a moment. Fresh in everyone's mind was the reign of terror of the Ku Klux Klan, which in Highland had burned down Reverend Dana Fox's barn.[55] Nine people out of ten would have turned back, but not Bird, "a natural born troublemaker and agitator,"[56] according to Miller's history of the Supreme Court of the United States and African Americans. He headed straight to the dining hall, drew a chair close to the supper table, and sat down. Allen McCowan, a commodities speculator from Indiana, complained to the waiters.[57] "Mr. Stanley's waiters" told Bird "in no uncertain terms that Mr. Stanley did not serve Negroes,"[58] according to Miller. Thereupon, Murray Stanley, the hotel owner's twenty-six-year-old son, "appeared in the dining-room and ejected the colored man."[59] Soon after, Bird made a beeline to the township of White Cloud to complain to the United States commissioner Casper W. Shreve. Shreve, a civil engineer, who sat on the local school board for twenty-five years, "devoted his energies to the drug business"[60] and politics.

Afterward, Bird Gee headed south to Topeka, eighty-five miles from Highland, to pour "out his grievance"[61] to George Record Peck, the United States district attorney for Kansas (1874–79). Peck listened sympathetically to Miller's granduncle. Perhaps not surprisingly, Peck agreed to help Bird because he was an easterner from upstate New York whose liberal ancestors had helped found New Haven, Connecticut, or perhaps because, like Bird, he was a Civil War veteran—a captain in the Thirty-first Wisconsin Volunteer Infantry who had marched with Sherman to the sea.[62] Although it is unknown what words passed between the two, Bird was adamant that he had been kept from eating a meal at the hotel for no other reason than that he was a Negro.[63]

On April 10, 1876, Peck convinced a federal grand jury to indict and arrest Murray Stanley; two months later a federal marshal did. Allen McCowan, the white customer who had complained when Bird Gee sat next to him, put up Stanley's $500 bond.[64] On October 10, Stanley appeared in the circuit court of Leavenworth, where his attorneys Clemens and Rossington asked the court to dismiss the indictment. They argued that "Congress had no authority under either the Thirteenth or the Fourteenth Amendments to enact a public accommodations law,"[65] or to have passed the Civil Rights Act of March 1, 1875, which addressed public accommodations for former slaves.[66] In Miller's account of the case, he wrote that Peck "decried the constitutional heresy that Congress lacked authority to protect the rights of the new freedmen and insisted with equal vigor that Mr. Stanley must be punished for his wrongdoing."[67]

Unable to make up their minds, circuit Judges Dillon and Foster certified the case to the United States Supreme Court,[68] where it languished for seven years until the solicitor general submitted the case for review. On October 15, 1883, with neither appearances nor briefs filed by the defendants, the Supreme Court rendered its decision.[69] In an eight-to-one vote, the court decided that Congress had "no authority to enact public accommodations statutes."[70] The court stated that the Civil Rights Act of 1875, passed to prohibit racial discrimination by states, was unconstitutional. This ruling was a slap in the face to the Civil Rights Act of 1866, which accorded equal rights to blacks before the law, and to the Fourteenth Amendment. The Supreme Court's decision on Bird Gee's petition ushered in the end of the era of Reconstruction. With hotel owner Stanley's appeal upheld, he was free to serve whichever customers he chose. "Civil rights in public accommodations was a practical failure,"[71] according to civil rights historian Valerie W. Weaver.

What the Supreme Court had done, well before the *Plessy v. Ferguson* (1896) ruling of "separate but equal,"[72] was to take away Congress's authority in the first and second sections of the 1875 Civil Rights Act to protect all citizens' civil and legal rights. Naturally, across the nation, African Americans denounced the court's decision as an act of betrayal.[73]

Though Miller's granduncle lost in the courtroom, he had "fired the first gun in what would be a long constitutional war and end in a momentous Supreme Court decision"[74] many decades later. Though Bird would not live long enough to savor any future victory, he told relatives "that he was going to spend the rest of his life among the 'heathens' where there was no racial discrimination."[75] In

1889, he left Beeler, Kansas, and headed for Indian Territory at the time of the Oklahoma land rush.[76] Forty years later, Bird Gee's determination, tenacity, and unmet demand for basic rights compelled Miller to set aside his own aspirations of becoming a creative writer and to choose instead to practice law for the greater good.

During Loren Miller's boyhood, the population of the quiet village of Pender in Thurston County, Nebraska, numbered below one thousand people. Recalling life there later, he wrote, "When I lived there it had a substantial number of first generation German and Swedish families, at least one Irish family and an Italian couple (called Wops behind their backs), who had nine children, but the majority of its inhabitants were Americans whose European ancestry was so remote it didn't count."[77]

For the only "Negro" family in the county, race issues were insignificant compared to the anxiety Loren felt moving a half dozen times within two or three years, always just one step ahead of the landlord. He would often hear the rent man at the door, banging "angrily that he had to have his rent or the whole kit and caboodle of them would have to clear out."[78] The family was what some might call off and on squatters, living in weather-beaten, dilapidated frame houses.

Among the places they moved to in Pender was a "house out east of town." In reality, it was a three-room shack built of rough clapboards. Miller wrote, "Mama looked at the holes in the floor and remarked that the place was alive with rats. Papa made his usual answer about poor people not being able to have everything they wanted." On their first night, Roland, who never forgot the experience, said he "was awakened in the middle night by the sound of something scurrying across the floor and cried out." The next night, Nora set out a trap "at the rat hole in one corner of the room. Then she blew out the kerosene lamp. In a few minutes, there was a sudden clamping of the trap and the squeal of a rat. They caught fourteen in a few hours and all through that summer the trap was set every night, with each night yielding a catch. Despite that fact, the rats continued to race up and down the house every night during that summer."[79]

Little by little, the immutable, unbearable poverty began taking its toll on Miller's mother. She nearly had enough the winter John suggested banking the house with manure to keep the cold winds and frost from coming in under the rotten floorboards. Nora knew the house would stink in the spring.[80] It was during times like these that she leaned heavily on her Bible to keep cheerful despite the hardships. At other times, she used a steady gaze to restrain her husband from following through when he came up with such schemes.[81]

By the time they moved to a larger place in Pender, which they called "Fisher's place," Miller's parents began quarreling bitterly and often, which made the children fearful, wondering when the bickering would end or the next fight start up. In constant debt—still owing the doctor for helping deliver the last baby—John began staying out until late to avoid his wife's griping that they lived like pigs. At

Fisher's place, Miller "learned there were other children in the world besides his own family."[82] At first, he was shy and afraid because he had never ventured far from home; the only children he had played with were his siblings. "He never knew how it came to him but it was there that he learned that children were divided into groups." From Freddy, who was white, Miller learned that he was black; Freddy also played with Earl, whom he termed "an injun." Freddy's playground wisdom included the belief that Injuns always had lice—black people did too. This prejudice extended to Fritz, a boy with a Dutch accent. When the trio saw Fritz coming in their direction, Earl said, "Come on let's run him on home.' 'Sure,' said Freddy, 'He's a Dutchman; they eat kraut.'"[83] Miller was bewildered.

On Miller's first day of school, he met other children. When his teacher spoke to him, he kept silent, refused to go out for recess, and "cried more than ever when he wet his pants." Small, soft-spoken, and easily terrified (he liked playing with dolls but understood that it was not manly), he played just enough in the schoolyard to keep from being called a sissy and a crybaby. Three weeks into the school year, and urged by his teacher, Miller began to speak up in class. He surprised everybody by announcing, untainted by pride, "'I know everything in this book.'"[84]

When the handsome brown boy (whom scholar Arnold Rampersad has described as having "straight, shiny black hair, vaguely Indian in his features")[85] went out for recess, "Freddy turned away and didn't say much. So did Fritz and even Earl acted funny. They began to titter among each other. Suddenly one of them called: 'Cinnamon bear, cinnamon bear,' then they all began to shout it.'" When his teacher ran over to him, he did not "know why he was crying but he knew that they were making fun of him,"[86] Miller wrote.

The next day at recess he played pom-pom-pullaway, a popular game of the early 1900s where competing lines of children clasp hands, chanting "If you don't come, we'll fetch you away," with a new boy. The following day, the new boy told him, "My papa said not for me to play with niggers anymore." "Who called you a nigger," his father stormed when told what had happened. "The next time anybody calls you a nigger, you slap him in the mouth, do you hear. Slap him down. He kept on talking in that vein until [Miller] began to cry. Then he became tender again. 'What is a nigger, papa'?" The question took his father aback, and he told him that meant black people. "Colored people are brown like we, like you, like I am—But they're just as good as other people."[87] It occurred to Loren later that Freddy and Fritz looked different. All of the children looked different from him. "They were white! And he was brown. That is, all of them were white except Earl and he was an Injun."[88]

Returning the following day, Miller says he "took savage delight in holding up his hand to answer every question that the rest of them could not answer." After school let out, one of them shouted: "Teacher's pet." The chanting turned to "Nigger, nigger, nigger, nigger" as they followed him home. Later, he told his father that he could not fight them all. When he started to cry, his father took him in his arms. "Never mind, you'll be a great man some day and they will all remember what they did."[89]

In looking back at his childhood, Miller recalled, "Our gangs were organized on a territorial basis with no regard to race and we had lots of fun learning to count, and use dirty words, in German, Swedish, and in the Omaha and Winnebago Indian dialects. The Italian kids were no help: their parents didn't permit them to speak their native language."[90] He also recalled "feelings against Indians: they were dirty, they were lazy, they were shiftless. At least that's what the grown-ups said but we children gave the matter little thought." In time, a friendship developed between Miller and "a little half Indian boy, Herschel Essex," Pearl Essex's son. The friendship was a "fifty-fifty affair," with Miller slipping his pal notes in class and whispering the answers to him. Herschel set things right outside on the playground. Herschel's athletic prowess made him "generally one of the most sought after" to play on the ball team. He had one invariable rule for picking sides: if you wanted him, you had to take Loren too, and "no amount of pleading could move him."[91]

In time, the word "nigger" nearly disappeared from the playground. In his second year, Loren Miller wrote the best story about why one should use Colgate toothpaste after a man came to the school and talked about "Colgate's new Ribbon Dental crème." Handed a half-dollar and a package of toothpaste when told to come forward to get his prize, "'You can give the paste to somebody else, we don't use it at our house,' he said, frankly." Although Miller expected approval, "instead, a ripple of giggles started across the room and broke into a wave when the speaker joined in with a hearty guffaw."[92] Miller would be a senior in high school before he owned a toothbrush.

Such public embarrassment prompted an already-shy boy to feel mortified when Emma Bohling sent him a valentine and told the other children that he was her fellow. Emma gave him the valentine the day before Valentine's Day, and the next day Linabelle Ammons gave him another; he heard the boys whispering that he had two girls. Feeling bashful around girls, he wrote later that he was "sex-shy," a trait that stayed with him throughout his life.[93]

Springtime in Nebraska brings more than fresh garden foods and newly emerging corn; it brings fast-moving storms with hail the size of golf balls and wind blowing clouds of dust far off in the distance after the tornado passes. In April 1908, the Miller family took shelter in their storm cellar to ride out one of the worst tornadoes in U.S. history at the time; it swept through the outskirts of Pender, killing three white residents and causing serious damage on the Winnebago Indian reservation.

More pressing than seasoning storms was Millers' chronic poverty. There were many Saturday mornings when the family had no breakfast until the boys brought home milk from a neighbor and Nora made some corn mealmush.[94] She wrote in her diary proudly that Cloyd and Loren "were always ready to do anything they could"[95] to earn a little money doing chores for neighbors. When Loren was eight, he began selling *Grit*, a weekly newspaper that carried the subtitle *America's Greatest Family Newspaper*, which Miller described later as "a strange re-hash of the week's news."[96] The job netted ten or fifteen cents a week, which he took home and gave to his mother.

One of Miller's happier memories was

> pop toting me off to the [baseball] diamond in the one horse town where I was born. It seems, to let him tell it, that he had been a pretty hot shot in his own day as a player. And that story of his about slamming out a homer in the last inning with the score tied and two men down never got old to me. My mother always insisted that the only time she ever saw him play he did nothing except drop two fly balls in succession but her cynicism may have been due to the fact that she was always tired, caring for seven children all day long.

When Miller was about ten, "Pop" saved up a few dollars and bought him a catcher's mitt that

> made me the envy of my side of town and cinched my place as catcher with the Ivan Street Blues. That might have been the beginning of a beautiful career except for two things. The first thing was my inability to throw to second base. I have been known to cut off a man stealing second by throwing to: (a) the center fielder (b) pitcher (c) left fielder but no living person ever remembers my rifling one to the second baseman who, after all, was supposed to be involved. . . . The second fly in my ointment as a major leaguer was the fact that I grew up and learned that organized baseball was lily white. I upbraided my father about not telling me that but he turned it off by mumbling something about times changing, what he looked for in the future and that anyhow it was a swell game. I think now that he suffered more about it than I did.[97]

In the summer of 1909, Miller's mother stayed in the bed quite often.[98] Ordinarily, she baked bread twice a week and "did all of our laundering, did all of her cooking on a wood burning stove, canned enough foods, including jelly, etc, dried sweet corn . . . raised enough chickens so we had plenty of eggs the year around." From the garden, she harvested "plenty of cabbage, turnips, onions and potatoes in the storm cellar to last until the next year's crop was ready,"[99] wrote Miller. But, after the death of her mother a few months earlier and following the birth of Helen on July 5, 1909, Nora stayed sick a great deal. After fixing John's breakfast, she would ask the children not to bother her. Like most children, they welcomed any lack of supervision. But there was nothing to eat in the house. Sometimes their neighbor Pearl Essex, Herschel's mother, would come to the house and cook up a nice pot of vegetables. She always helped when "each of us 6 children were born in Pender,"[100] recalled Halvor Miller. Pearl, part Omaha Indian, was married to Fred Essex, a white salesman.[101]

Three years later when Loren was nine, Nora was hospitalized for three weeks. It was her eyes. She had given up teaching because of them. Now she barely could see one foot in front of her face and could not see well enough to thread a needle. Although she lacked the money to see a specialist, she decided to write the local newspaper.[102]

Dear Editor:

I am a woman with seven little children. For the past four years my eyes have been getting worse. In a little while I will be blind unless some kind friend will give me money to go to Omaha where a specialist can treat me. I am asking this in the name of my little children and I am praying that God will answer my prayers. Please write to the editor who will explain who I am.[103]

John "stormed and raged for an hour" when he discovered that she had written the editor exposing their plight to the public. Late in the night he returned home with two strange men. "'Drunk,' mama muttered as she opened the door."[104] Later, two German women came to the house and left "mama some money" because they had seen her letter in the newspaper, wrote Miller. Others brought money, too.

The next week, Nora packed her bags and caught the train to Omaha, where she saw Dr. Harold Gifford, a well-known ophthalmologist.[105] Diagnosed with blepharitis, chronic inflammation of the eyelid, more commonly known as granulated eyelids, the doctor clipped away the granulations. Afterward, she wore heavy dark glasses. Once home, "papa burned [the granulations] out," wrote Miller, "with blue vitriol every night. Mama would sit down in a chair and roll her eyelids back with a match. Then papa would take the blue stone that was attached to a holder and run the stone over her eyelids. Each time he did, she would flinch and her eyes would water. But she bore the pain uncomplainingly."[106] Two months later, Nora returned to Omaha for more treatments, and every month thereafter for a while.[107] Though her condition improved, it was not until 1927, fitted with glasses, that Nora was able to properly read again. It was Miller who helped make that happen, and her deferred request suggests that, like her husband, she was largely resistant to turning to others for help. On the advice of a friend, she wrote Loren for help. "He immediately sent me the money to purchase glasses." After twenty years of severely limited vision, she finally was "able to read perfectly."[108]

In June 1913, the family moved to Highland, Kansas, when Loren was a fifth grader. "John took a notion to go back to Kansas, to his old home town where he grew to manhood,"[109] wrote Nora. By the time they moved, after ten years as the only black family in Pender, other black families had moved into other parts of Thurston County, ten miles away, to the nearby village of Bancroft in Cuming County.[110] But the Miller's had never met any of them, and John wanted to be near his relatives despite the relative calm of Pender and the absence of any overt racism. At least that is one story explaining the move; there is another.

In Pender, the family experienced little or no racial segregation or "visible signs of racist attitudes towards blacks . . . [although] it did seem there was some toward the Indians,"[111] according to Halvor Miller. Loren Miller felt otherwise. He had not forgotten that the schoolchildren had called him "cinnamon bear" and "nigger." There was the time his father was placed on probation for throwing a beer bottle at one of Jim Mallory's white saloon customers. The man "tried to force John to talk and called him a nigger when he wouldn't."[112] In some respects, John's personality was like Earl Little, Malcolm X's father, who lived part of his adult years in Nebraska, frequently getting "into heated arguments with whites who resented his air of independence."[113]

Overall, the townspeople took no particular interest in the Millers until John's drinking became too noticeable to be ignored. In Nora's diary, she makes no mention of her husband's drinking while Loren Miller writes that he overheard "the boys whispering at school and learned that one of the reasons they were poor was because papa spent his money on drinking."[114] In Miller's description of his father's evening routine, he wrote that when John came home from work, he had the habit of sitting by the fire and flicking at the calluses on his left hand with his right thumb—as if making a mental calculation, summing up his whole life— then taking "a long drag at the whiskey bottle."[115] While racism is no excuse for drinking, it does supply an adequate explanation for the Millers' penury despite John's working one and two jobs simultaneously for low wages all his life. Despite being literate, he had limited opportunities in the farm towns of the Midwest at the turn of the twentieth century to rise above his low status.

At the time that John's behavior came under scrutiny, the powerful Anti-Saloon League was actively lobbying for Prohibition, and Prohibition groups had successfully kept parts of the state dry, including Pender. Whether John Miller drank to excess is debatable. Family alcoholism is a slippery topic, and there are no accounts of John missing work, being out all night, or having whisky-fueled rages. He may have been a typical drinking man of his time—not a wastrel, but enough of a drinker (and enough of an outsider in all-white Pender) to draw the ire of the local Prohibitionists. If he was an alcoholic, the direct expense and the broad impact on his work life would have added to and perhaps account for the family's continual poverty.

Perhaps it is of little consequence whether they were pressured to move or whether Miller's father truly wanted to be near relatives. Drinking was important enough of a memory that Miller wrote on it extensively. The story goes that a delegation headed by John's saloon boss, Jim Mallory, came to the house to speak with Nora. "He's been drinking too much . . . and the best thing you folks can do is to move."[116] When the family reached Omaha, the first leg of their journey to Kansas, Halvor Miller, who was five years younger than Loren, wrote that they boarded a horsecar and headed to the home of relatives. "My father met one of his old friends, Hugh Eubanks, and Eubanks' cousin, Albert Ewing. It had been several years since they had been together and though my father drank *very moderately* I presume that (they) had quite a celebration because when we got back it was too late to catch our scheduled train."[117]

Miller's version of what happened, though similar to his brother's, differs on the state of their father's sobriety during the journey.

> It was almost midnight when they got to Omaha and as soon as they got seats in the Webster Street station papa went out and said that he was going to call up Jim Ewing so they could go out and see the people before it was time to leave again. Mama tried to dissuade him: "you've been drinking enough already," she said but papa didn't pay any attention to her. He was gone about an hour when he returned with another man.[118]

Afterward, "the whole family got on a [horse-drawn] street car and went out to Aunt Nan's." By the time they boarded the train for Saint Joseph, Missouri, "papa was staggering a little and mama said something very sharply about how glad she would be when they got to Kansas where they didn't sell the dirty stuff." She was particularly happy about leaving because "it would give her an opportunity to rear her boys where they couldn't get any more liquor."[119] However, many years later, Miller would admit that he "violated the 18th Amendment intermittently ever since its inception."[120]

As the train pulled into the small station in Saint Joseph, Missouri, the Millers were nearing the end of their three-hundred-mile trip. For more than an hour, huddled together on the wooden benches, they waited for "Aunt Mary," Nora's sister to arrive. Over the years, Mary Jones had kept in contact. Worried, she would write when she had not heard from Nora.[121] On the station platform, the travel-weary Millers asked to stay the night at Mary's house before making the final leg of their train trip. But Mary refused to have a black man in her home, saying, "'You know how Missouri is.'"[122] Now angry, "Papa turned away and went out the door." The two sisters sat down and talked until the train for Kansas arrived.

What Miller took away from the journey was not so much his father's drinking, for that was nothing new, but rather his aunt's distain for John. And that for the first time he "saw to his surprise that papa was the same color [as his friend] and had the same kind of hair; he had never noticed that before." He had discovered that his father's friend "was black and crinkly haired." He had also discovered that his aunt was a racist.[123] It was after 10:00 P.M. when they arrived at the Highland, Kansas, station. Nobody was there to meet them. They learned later that the church where Nora sent her letter announcing their coming no longer had a regular pastor to check on the mail.[124] They walked until they found Uncle Joe Miller's house, three blocks away and up a hill. "Papa had to hammer at the door for a long time. Finally, an old man came to the door. He was brown too and his hair was white but crinkly too." "Know me, Uncle Joe, I'm John? 'Reckon you are at that,' grunted the old man. 'Joe, Joe,' came a quivering voice from the side room, 'who's that. I'm sick and ain't fit to be bothered at this time of night.' 'It's John, Tom's boy,' said Joe."[125]

When the door opened, the family of nine trooped into a small room, where the stale smell of tobacco smoke still lingered. "'That your wife?' There was a finite touch of contempt in his [Joe Miller's] voice. 'All them your kids?'" asked Uncle Joe. From the other room, Joe's wife, Martha, whined again. "Never expected to lay eyes on one of Tom's boys again in life. . . . That your wife, John? You look like Tom did. You just like him though; all of them Gees [who were mulattos] was crazy about being white. I ain't surprised you marryin' a white woman."[126]

The veiled insults went back and forth, coupled with a touch of curiosity. After kneeling and praying, Aunt Martha Miller sniveled that the children who stood while the two couples prayed were "like heathens, ain't they never heard nobody pray. Don't they know no manners?"[127] After Joe wheeled his wife back into her room, he laid pallets down the length and width of the floor for the family to sleep on.

The very sight of the old couple and the little house made Nora "very unhappy." "And the next day I could not keep from crying,"[128] she wrote. All through breakfast, Joe's wife complained about the "children's enormous appetites"[129] and how she and her husband could not afford to take them in. After breakfast, "papa said he would take them to see Aunt Martha Hubbard (née Gee), whom Miller's grandfather Thomas had helped flee from slavery. In Highland, she was living down a dusty hill at the end of a long lane. "The house," in Miller's description, "leaned heavily to one side as an old man does when he rests on his cane." In the yard, he spotted an old, white-haired woman seated in a wheelchair. Unlike Martha Miller, Uncle Joe's wife, she had a kindly face. She told them, "'I have been praying for one of you to come here and he has answered my prayers.' Then she turned toward mama. 'You are John's wife. I am so glad to see you. And these are your children. I am glad to see them before I died.'"[130] She died not long after their arrival.

Miller's first black community experience continued the next day when they visited Betty Williams, "an old dried up black woman," who spoke in the "queerest way. Lawsy, me, Lawysy. Lawsy."[131] Nora liked Betty and saw the old washerwoman as friendly, cheerful, and "full of fun." Betty lived with her granddaughter, Hazel Craig, "a skinny legged black girl who had the shortest, funniest looking hair, all gathered into tiny little braids all over her head. The funniest thing was that her hair wasn't really braided. Each of the little tufts was wound tightly with white twine," recalled Miller, whose wavy hair, typical of many racially mixed people, was neither kinky nor straight. The other children giggled instinctively as they "trooped off with the strange creature, who took them a 'piece up the road'" to play with two other little girls and Grundy Hammond, their brother, whom later they would see in school. Hazel reckoned, "'Y'all don't know much about playin. Done been raised with white folks.'"[132] This rub he would hear repeated.

The Millers stayed with Betty and her granddaughter for eleven days until their furnishings came in on the train. By then John had found work "on a farm at $2.00 a day and his dinner." At age fifty-two, the mile-and-a-half walk to work was "very hard for him but he continued to work through the summer but when fall came and his service wasn't so much needed," wrote Nora, "his wages were reduced to $1.00."[133]

Once settled, the Miller family began to farm as they had done in Pender, scratching out a living as best they could in a town that, Miller noted, "had no foreign-born residents but there were a dozen or so Negro families, all related to us in some degree, and I became conscious of some group feeling but it was never quite clear to me whether it was based on common color or common ancestry. At any rate there was no organized discrimination and life went on much as before."[134]

Slowly the new pattern of life unfolded. There were about twenty "colored" families in town; unlike life in Pender, "the colored people and the white folks didn't mingle much. . . . The little white children who lived in the neighborhood stayed to themselves and the colored children stayed to themselves."[135] Unhappy with his new life, Miller wasted little time writing "a long and almost a tearful letter to Herschel [Essex] in which he said that he sure wished that he were back in good old Nebraska," and fishing at the back of the house in Rattlesnake Creek.[136]

On June 27, 1913, his grandaunt Martha Gee Hubbard died. The funeral at Saint Martha's African Methodist Episcopal Church, founded in 1882 and named in her honor, was packed with black folks as well as white people. They listened to the pastor retrace her life as a slave, sold three times over, each time, "suffering starvations, beatings, and at one time she was seriously burned because a severe beating at the hands of the wife of one of her masters caused her to fall into a faint into the fire-place; the scars of the burns which extended to her face where outward manifestation of an inward hurt she carried to her grave."[137] A respected cook who had forgiven her trespassers, Martha had years before successfully sold baked goods to raise money to buy her first husband's freedom. Out of her endeavors she saw the fulfillment of one of her many dreams in the establishment of the little church in Highland, which stood on the southwest corner of Main and Canada Streets.

The elderly preacher droned on about how Martha had gone home "to live forever with her wings around a golden throne. All at once a transformation came over him and he threw his head back. . . . It reminded [Miller] of how the storm came up over the Nebraska prairies. The sky actually seemed to get dark." His delight in the hand clapping and the foot stamping and the singsong of the preacher and the people rocking back and forth gave way to fear when suddenly Betty Williams "leaped from her seat and began flailing her arms wildly. She danced up the church aisle."[138]

After the funeral, Nora came to regret having moved in with Martha Hubbard's daughter, Emma Fouts. Her old rickety house, which was near John Miller's job, was no better than the places they had rented or squatted back in Pender. This time they lived in three rooms while their cousin Emma kept the other room. "It was impossible to get along with her"[139] because she fussed about everything. Emma "was a queer witch-like old woman," wrote Miller, "who went around forever mumbling to herself always bundled up in a half dozen dresses and skirts no matter how hot the weather was."[140] No matter how eccentric, Emma represents another relative on Loren's Gee family side who could read.

Each night, Emma came home after work about 8:30. When Loren Miller heard her bustling about her room, "arranging and re-arranging furniture," his curiosity grabbed hold of him. What could she be doing? Miller, writing years later of the experience, said he enlisted the help of his brothers Cloyd and Cecil to pry open Emma's window and sneak in. Disappointed with what he saw—a room crowded with old furniture, chairs piled on top of each other—he quickly jumped back out of the window, but not before pocketing a dime he spotted on the floor. "'What was in there?' his brothers demanded. 'Nothing,' he said." When Miller "refused to be a party to further exploration,"[141] his brothers, he said, threatened to tell their papa. Miller shrugged them off, focusing instead on how to slip away and get to town to buy an ice cream.

On the way there, Miller ran into Willie Starr, his second cousin, Aunt Martha Hubbard's great-grandson.[142] When he tried to walk past the burly older boy with "enormous lips and tightly curled little knots of hair,"[143] Willie blocked his path, he wrote. "'Oh, no you don't, you little white folks' nigger. All of you-all think you are better than other colored people. Might as well get it in your head you ain't nothing but a nigger yourself even if your mammy is white.'" Frightened, Miller began to cry. "He screamed, let me alone." Amazingly, Willie grumbled, "Aw go on kid, ain't nobody goin' to bother you."[144]

Miller trudged on up the dusty main street, where another lesson in racial status soon unfolded. When he entered the drugstore, he saw two white children sitting at the counter sipping ice-cream sodas. Hesitant to ask for a cone, he sidled over to the counter and climbed on the stool. "'Well, what do you want, boy?' asked the clerk. . . . 'Give me a ice cream soda,' he said." The clerk responded, "Don't you know you can't drink at this fountain. You will have to buy something you can take out." Not understanding, Miller asked again. "He wants to drink it here," guffawed the clerk. "Hear that. Oh, ho, ho, he wants to drink it here. Now listen sonny. . . . You might as well learn now as later. No colored people get served here. Get that. Maybe you don't know it but you're colored and colored people don't drink here. See." Humiliated, Miller burst into tears. Then he shouted, "I'm going to tell papa on you." The clerk, even more irritated, ejected him from the store. "Now you get out of here and stay until you learn how to act when you're in the presence of white folks."[145]

As he walked home, tears continued to rush to his eyes. Then "an overwhelming feeling of humility enveloped him,"[146] more so because there was no one to tell. How would he explain where he got the dime? For a while, he lived in terror: Emma would miss her dime and "papa would find out about it and tan his hide but nothing came of the episode and he finally gave the dime to mama one day when she wanted to buy a quart of milk for the baby."[147] He resolved one day to buy his own drugstore and "let everybody come in who wanted. Yes, he would even let Willie Starr come in, ugly as Willie was,"[148] wrote Miller.

Still, there were advantages in having moved to Highland, set at the northeast edge of Doniphan County, "where the corkscrew Missouri makes a sharp turn to the west, and is hurled back upon itself by a huge wooded bluff."[149] He adored the "wonderful woods all around the town to which [he] could walk in a few minutes." There, he fished in swamps and watched "squirrels leaping from tree to tree and rabbits that would run from almost any brush pile if you jumped up and down on it."[150] It was comforting, the beauty of the rounded hills and broad valleys, blooming black-eyed Susans, enormous oak and hickory trees, tall prairie grasses, and whitetail deer. In time, these would become familiar places to roam.

It was too late their first summer to plant a garden, but they "raised chickens and the next summer [they] had a garden." They ate wild berries, mostly gooseberries, and lived off fish that Miller and his brothers caught. In exchange for a quart of milk a day, the three boys cleaned their neighbor's chicken house. In the fall, they gathered and stored black walnuts for the winter.[151]

"Cloyd and Loren," wrote Nora, "earned a little money pumping water for the cattle and Loren and Cecil trapped ground squirrels."[152] With the money, she sent off to Kansas City for suits for Cloyd and Loren. "Roland," she wrote, "came down through the cornfield to meet me and asked what I had. I told him I had some new suits. He asked 'for me'? I said no, for Cloyd and Loren. The poor little fellow cried like his heart would break." Cloyd, his mother said, longed for a gun, but his father felt that they could not spare the money. Eventually, after a bit of scolding Cloyd got the gun, which he put "to good use killing rabbits," for the family table. Unlike his brothers "Loren, cared very little for the guns."[153]

By summer's end, Miller had adjusted to his new life, although he never got used to the fact that the black people moved "in a circle to themselves. Somehow he never quite fitted into that circle."[154] While his siblings seemed to have "made themselves at home, in it he never did." As Miller's awareness of racism grew, he had to have realized that he was cast onto the periphery of separate worlds, one black and one white.

Disturbed apparently when overhearing his parents talk about a black school, Miller wrote, "Papa raved and stormed and said he wouldn't have his children attending any Jim Crow School. . . . Besides he said it was against the law for them to have Jim Crow schools in Kansas." News of his father's attitude got out. A delegation of "colored citizens" came to the house, warning John not to kick up "a rumpus about the school." In the end, John agreed to send his children to Saint Martha's African Methodist Episcopal Church, which had served as the black children's schoolhouse since 1908. The white clapboard building, which survives today, featured a short steeple, gable roof, and Gothic Revival windows filled with wire-mesh glass.

There, Miller found Miss Eva Johnson of Wathena, Kansas, his new teacher, to be a great disappointment.[155] "A thin dark girl, she was amazingly ignorant. . . . She couldn't even talk good English. . . . It was hard to distinguish her dialect from that of the children," he wrote. Johnson taught all the grade levels. The shared room was noisy. While one class was reciting, the others would try to study. Miller soon discovered that he knew much more than the other fifth graders. When he asked to be moved into the sixth grade, his plea fell on deaf ears. Johnson explained, "There wasn't any sixth grade and that she wasn't going to make any because she had enough work to do as it was."[156]

Miller vented his anger on the playground. Warned repeatedly to stop fighting, he brooded, knowing that when school ended he would have to stay behind. One day, when he got home he "lay down on the floor behind the stove and slept uneasily" until his father awakened him and asked, "What is the matter with you, groaning and crying in your sleep?" When "quick sympathy" flitted over his parents' faces, Miller made a plan. "I'm sick," he whimpered, "Oh, I'm sick."[157] He meant to feign sickness just until everything blew over. A week went by. It lengthened into two and then stretched into the entire winter.

In those months, religious revivalism reached Saint Martha's Church. "Up to this time," wrote Nora, "John had not been to church since we were married. But he wanted to go to this revival. So I went with him through cold and mud and snow. To make a long story short he was converted to my great joy."[158] That winter had many privations, perhaps the worst they had ever experienced. John came home with a "crick in his back" and was unable to return to work. Their credit ran out at the grocery store. There were nights that "the family crept to bed without food save for a few pieces of bread and sugar."[159] Days went by like that: getting up mornings with nothing to eat. Miller cleaned up Lizzie Doakes's barn "for a half gallon of thin colorless milk," which his mother believed Doakes watered down. When the ground thawed a bit, they dug in their cousin's garden for frost bitten potatoes, which, when cooked, had a vague, watery sweet taste. When the potatoes ran out, they gathered walnuts and "made a meal of walnut kernels." It was not enough to squelch the hunger pains. Over John's objections, his wife put on her best clothes and went to town. She spoke with the justice of the peace. "Sure enough," wrote Miller, "late that afternoon a basket of groceries arrived and thereafter for a week they got a few things to eat."[160]

By spring, John's back improved, and he returned to work. As for eleven-year-old Miller, he knew he could not drag out staying home forever. He dreaded having to apologize. "It was a bitter dose for him to swallow and he mumbled an apology to Miss Johnson and was restored to his class."[161]

Even though he was called, like before, a "sissy and a 'fraidy cat,"[162] Miller did not yield easily. His anger over his new school unchanged, he wrote Mrs. Farnham

Baker, his former schoolteacher back in Pender. On July 14, 1914, she replied: "Don't you get discouraged about your school work. . . . If you do your best you will surely become far greater than the teacher who won't give you credit for what you do. . . . Maybe [you] will be our president some day." If not president, she wrote, "You will surely fill some other good place if you do your best, always."[163] Though these sentiments could be said to verge on platitudes, she acknowledged the vexations he described and, affirming how remarkable he was, encouraged him to take the long view—without limiting his potential because of race, which is notable for a white teacher of that time and place. Baker's letter shows a serious regard for Miller and tacitly suggests that the atmosphere of her classroom was far superior to his "colored" school without mentioning race at all. Determined to succeed more than ever, Miller returned to his studies. When his cousin Emma J. Starr, the next year, replaced the incompetent Eva Johnson, he improved significantly.[164] By 1915, all of the Miller children except for Roland, who was barely four, were in school.

In a home with few books, Miller tired of reading the Bible, which at first he found interesting, even though he "couldn't make much sense of Revelations."[165] One dull winter day, he remembered cousin Emma's book-crammed room. The first one he sneaked out, after climbing through the window, was the *Narrative of the Life of Frederick Douglass, an American Slave*. Reading Frederick Douglass was a turning point for Miller. It helped him understand the family's poverty and his father's anger. Like Douglass, Miller's "cowardice departed and bold defiance took its place."[166] This first glimpse "of the drama behind the story of the Negro people in America and . . . the entrancing story of the great Negro abolitionist" later left him "starry eyed." Miller continued, "He could see it all clearly now. He would be a great man." Miller fantasized that one day he would walk into the town's white-owned drug store and demand service. Influenced by Douglass, who had changed his name, Miller, by 1926, changed his first name by replacing the *i* in "Lorin" with an *e*. Eventually, he dropped "Raymond," his middle name, entirely.[167]

When Cousin Emma realized that her book was missing, she told John that his family had to move out. She would not have a "bunch of thieves living in her house."[168] Reprimanded for his actions, but apparently aware how hard it was not to have anything to read, the next day his father gave him "15 cents and told him to order the *Kansas City Star* and the *Times*, but that he must never, never steal, no matter how poor they were."[169] At the end of the summer, they moved. "We got a place on a farm just a little ways from John's place of employment. I can't describe how glad we all were to move. It was a very old house but we had plenty of room," wrote Nora. Living with Emma had proved so disagreeable that Nora "kept out of her sight in order to have peace."[170]

On September 6, 1916, Miller entered Highland High School, which shared the building with Highland College, the same institution that had accepted George

Washington Carver's mail-in application but had turned him away once the school realized he "was a Negro."[171] By the time Loren Miller entered high school, a little more than a mile away, his former segregated grade school had closed. At Highland High School, he found it "only mildly hostile because another Negro family living in the district had preceded them there."[172] It had "a library no matter how incomplete it was," where he read and reread *The Last Days of Pompeii* by Edward Bulwer-Lytton, Richard Henry Dana's *Two Years before the Mast* and "an assortment of books by Shakespeare."[173]

His older brother Cloyd had doubts about whether he would pass the county examination for high school, "but Loren was confident," wrote his mother. "However, both passed and Cloyd did not go to high school long but Loren continued and finished."[174] Like their father, Cloyd began working on Mr. Smith's farm, where "he received very small wages," which he gave to his mother. "He worked hard and never complained. He put a few dollars in the bank each month. I encourage him to do this because I was afraid he would get discouraged and unhappy."[175] As for Ruby, Miller's sister, she worked in town "for her board and went to school from home."[176] The remaining children, Halvor, Helen, and Roland, walked a mile and half to the elementary school, even in the winter snow and spring mud. The two youngest would become the most religious of the seven children, with Roland eventually becoming a minister.

On May 14, 1920, Miller graduated with honors from high school, the only boy and the only African American in a class with thirteen white girls. He intended to give the valedictory address, but he took sick, his mother said, "with the flu and couldn't attend the graduation exercise."[177] Unable to attend the ceremonies, Judge Frank Flynn of Thurston County wrote to say:

> My Dear Lorin, rec'd invitation to attending Annual Commencement. Am sorry it is so far would sure attend. Lorin you do not know how much pleasure it is to myself and family to hear that you have done so well. Keep up with your good work and always try to do better. Give our regards to all your family. Let's hear from you and how they are getting along. Your friend Frank Flynn and family.[178]

After graduation, Miller worked through most of the summer. "Well we all struggled on working together each one helping all he or she could but John's health began to fail,"[179] wrote Nora. John had managed to work through the spring, but on August 18 Nora noted that her husband had stopped working entirely, too sick to keep at it anymore. In spite of the difficulties, she noted, "we arranged for Loren to attend the state University at Lawrence, Kansas." As John's health continued to decline, Cecil quit school and got a job making one dollar a day including board. "Cecil said it is better for Loren to go to college than for me to go to High School," wrote his mother. "He was such a sweet boy. Only fifteen years old yet he took the place of a man and brought his check home and gave it to me most of the time. Cloyd too was a wonder. He shucked corn and when he finished one place he went to another and then another."[180]

With no resources beyond themselves, Cecil's decision to drop out—and Nora's okay—indicates how far the family would sacrifice to invest in Loren's future. Cecil's reported comment may reflect simple pragmatism or a desire to put a good face on things. There are few clues whether Cecil disliked school as much as Cloyd, but leaving school undoubtedly shaped Cecil's life course. He became a chauffeur.[181]

On August 28, just before Loren left for the University of Kansas (KU), Nora prepared a big celebration dinner. She recorded, "Although our wedding anniversary was not mentioned, I could not help but think of it. John was sitting around in the yard in the shade. He finally went to bed and slept a great deal."[182] By the time John woke up, his son was on his way to Lawrence, Kansas, one hundred miles away.

Soon after Miller reached KU, midwestern lynch mobs and the terror they brought against blacks created a pervasive climate of racial intimidation. In Omaha, a crazed mob of thousands took Will Brown, a black packinghouse worker charged with assaulting a white woman, from the courthouse. The crowd tore off Brown's clothes, beat him unconscious, and hung him by a rope from a nearby lamppost. Whites riddled his body with bullets, tied Brown behind a car, and towed the corpse "to the intersection of 17th and Dodge. There the body was burned."[183] Film actor Henry Fonda, Nebraska-born and fourteen years old at the time, witnessed the lynching from "the second floor window of his father's shop" across the street from the courthouse. "It was the most horrendous sight I'd ever seen. . . . We locked the plant, went downstairs, and drove home in silence. My hands were wet and there were tears in my eyes. All I could think of was the young black man dangling at the end of a rope."[184] C. Eric Lincoln wrote that the first year after World War I, "seventy Negroes were lynched, many of them still in uniform. Fourteen Negroes were burned publicly by white citizens; eleven of these martyrs were burned alive."[185] In Duluth, Minnesota, for example, three black circus workers were lynched by a mob.[186] The year before, during the "Red Summer" of 1919, no less than twenty-six race riots occurred across the nation in cities such as Elaine, Arkansas, Charleston, and Chicago, among others.

Once settled in at college, Miller fell into the impractical habit of sending his laundry to his mother through parcel post, and she would return it. Nora wrote frequently with updates on his father's health. She recorded, "But one day he decided to come home and see for himself. So here he came bounding into the house surprising us completely." "He was seventeen," and so short, she wrote, that he was called "The baby of K.U."[187] However, according to a physical examination he took in 1941, Miller was five feet ten inches; apparently, he continued to grow after college.[188] Soon after visiting his family, the news reached him that his father had died on Thursday morning November 18, 1920, three months from the day he took sick.[189] He was fifty-nine.

After signing his father's death certificate and attending the funeral, Miller returned to college, where, on February 9, 1921, he joined Kappa Alpha Psi, the second-oldest black collegiate Greek-letter fraternity. There he burrowed into his studies, hoping to escape the "dozen little discriminations" he had known all of his life. He discovered campus life proved little different.[190] He tried being like the other black students, affecting cigarettes, liquor, and wild parties and even feigning athletic ability, none of which was in his nature. Of course, he knew that even if he had had real athletic ability, he could never play on KU's all-white football team in its newly constructed Memorial Stadium, dedicated to students who died in World War I.[191] Still, he pushed to belong to what he knew best, "literary societies or pep organizations or any other extra curricula activities." Disappointed, he wrote:

> A year or two passes thus. . . . You have not found what you sought at college despite
> your mad efforts. That vague something which you called Ideals still eludes you. . . .
> Your own groups [i.e., black] are far from satisfactory. For the most part they are
> engaged in a mad effort to conform. . . . Underneath this outward show you find
> them cynical enough. . . . They are in the grip of a terrible inferiority complex and
> hope for a chance to be allowed to achieve a small success. That's all they ask.[192]

On May 31, 1921, as Miller's first spring semester drew to a close, possibly one of the worst race riots in American history unfolded two hundred miles away in Tulsa, Oklahoma. Trouble had been brewing there for several years. The *Chicago Defender* reported that "an orgy of rioting and bloodshed such as America has never known except in the Indian massacres was precipitated in this city when an army of whites [enabled by the Tulsa police chief who deputized hundreds of white men] sought to storm the jail intent on lynching a prisoner there."[193] It would be decades before the state of Oklahoma acknowledged that "up to 300 people were killed and more than 8,000 left homeless," and that aerial bombings destroyed forty blocks and nearly 1,300 homes.[194] How the Tulsa riot affected Miller is not recorded; however, given his sensitivity and growing political acumen, surely his outrage equaled what other African Americans felt.

Plagued by a lack of funds and an uncertain future, Miller left his studies in Lawrence and returned home to Highland, where he and his brother Halvor found work chopping down trees and cutting them up for fuel. After a year of odd jobs, which included working on the railroad, Miller raised enough money to return to KU in September 1922. He faced constant financial difficulties working his way through school, and when he could not make ends meet, he would write his mother for help, as cash-strapped as she was. She wrote, "I knew if he had to give up school it would break his heart. I had moved to town and had brought several dozen chickens with me, so I sold a few chickens now and then and sent him the money. This small amount of money was just better than nothing as his needs were many."[195]

Intellectually, it had been hard for Miller to leave school. Like John Adams, Miller was "fired by an inexhaustible love of books."[196] In high school, he had read Cicero in Latin and reveled in Shakespeare. In college, he dug deep into the writings of W. E. B. Du Bois, Henry James, Sinclair Lewis, and Bertrand Russell, among others. He read the brilliant protest poems of Claude McKay, whom he admired; and he was given a complete set of Shakespeare's works by a friendly teacher, an unmarried white woman forced to resign when it became known she was having an affair with a married man.[197]

Although Miller later realized that "there is more Jim Crow per square inch in Kansas than any place north of the Mason-Dixon line,"[198] it was in college where he came face-to-face with barefaced segregation:

> Negro students couldn't play on the athletic team; they couldn't swim in the pool; they couldn't attend class parties. Negro students had their own fraternities, their own parties, their own separate way of life. I tried to buy a sandwich and learned that a Negro couldn't eat in Lawrence restaurants—Negroes served only in sacks, the sign said. I went to a movie and was told to sit in the gallery. Fellow students from Wichita, Kansas City and St. Louis, amused at my naiveté, finally taught me that there were Negro sections of the city, of all cities, where Negroes had their own restaurants, their own shows, even their own schools. What, they demanded of me, could an educated Negro do if he didn't have his own institutions to work in. I didn't believe them. I turned to my teachers and they confirmed what I had heard. I dug into my text books and written between the lesson that the Negro had a place, a subordinate place, in America. I was, in turn, hurt, then stunned, then angry, then driven to sullen acceptance.[199]

Miller persevered and completed his sophomore year at the University of Kansas in the spring of 1923. The following summer, he raised enough money working long hours as "a dining car waiter"[200] for the Pullman Company to enter Washburn College in Topeka, Kansas. There, he studied alongside his cousin Leon H. Washington, Jr.; met Ivan J. Johnson III, his future law partner and the godfather to his oldest son; and bonded with Floyd C. Covington, who would come to serve as executive director of the Los Angeles Urban League.[201]

For the next three years, Miller attended Washburn until 1926.[202] Ever restless, he left Washburn that fall and headed to the nation's capital on a personal quest of discovery, which was also, in part, an effort to find the camaraderie of black students. On September 28, 1926, he entered Howard University, in its fifty-ninth term.[203] Before the Thanksgiving break, Miller achieved a small measure of success, reported in the *Washington Post*: "Loren Miller, Howard University student, was announced winner of the Amy Spingarn prize for art and literature for 1926. He offered an essay entitled 'College.'"[204]

Miller, at age twenty-three, penned "College," a brilliant, heart-rending tale that described his struggle of whether to pursue his love of writing or practice law:

Oh, yes, your career; you must have a career. . . . You will be a lawyer after all; a lawyer to confound these fools with their own laws giving life, liberty and the pursuit of happiness. . . . You will show them just how far you will rise in spite of them. You will be ruthless and make them give you a place. You plunge into law. You secretly loathe it. You still find yourself writing bitter little sketches, tragic bits of verse but you repress them; then you find your superlative emotions slowly receding.[205]

On October 25, the *Crisis* magazine awarded prizes totaling $600, donated by Amy Spingarn, at the International House in New York.[206] Arna Bontemps, an up-and-coming poet and future Langston Hughes collaborator, read his prize-winning poem "A Nocturne at Bethesda." John Frederick Matheus, grandson of slaves, read his short story "Swamp Moccasin." It is not certain whether Miller knew that the prestigious panel that selected his winning essay comprised W. E. B. Du Bois, scholar and editor of *The Crisis*; Mary White Ovington, journalist and suffragist; and Joel Elias Spingarn, literary critic and civil rights activist. Whatever Miller knew of the committee, surely he was pleased to accept the $75 cash award that came with such a distinguished literary prize.[207]

Like most educated African Americans of his era, Miller felt obliged to become a "race man" committed to "uplifting the race" rather than to pursue the life he wanted, unencumbered by race-related discrimination or responsibility. In an interview conducted by Paul Weeks of the *Los Angeles Times*, Miller said, "I was dragged kicking and screaming into the practice of law because, you know, in those days a Negro could be a doctor, lawyer or schoolteacher—and that's about all."[208] No black American writer before him had made a living simply from writing. Even for Langston Hughes, it would take years before he pulled off supporting himself as an artist, and still he went through periods of being broke.

Not a man given to brooding or self-pity, Miller accepted the career path he chose, yet his decision to become a lawyer did chafe for the remainder of his life. Like James Baldwin, who did "not allow himself the freedom of pure creation,"[209] because he took on the burden of race, Miller never entirely relinquished his dream of a literary life. But, as journalist R. J. Smith wrote, "It was his legal work that put food on the table."[210] Though Miller ultimately yielded to the demands of practicality and compromise when he took up the practice of law, his short poem "To My Father," written in 1926, reveals a deep bitterness:

> I sat and listened while you
> told tales of the dreams you dreamed
> and how time and fate effaced them.
> Why do you weep now?
> I took a page from you and murdered
> Dreams before my Dream had become
> executioner.[211]

Although Miller yearned for artistic expanses beyond the segregated world into which he was born, where he could breathe freely, he found in journalism, at least temporarily, a rational outlet. And, in it he found enough excitement that did not force him to sell little pieces of himself to the drudgery of boredom in order to buy them back in leisure each night and weekend.[212] Unlike Jean Toomer, the mixed-race fiction writer,[213] who admitted publicly for the last time in 1922 that he had Negro blood in his veins, thereby making his ethnicity ambiguous, Miller, instead, claimed his ethnicity through journalism. In that way, he used his talents to bang away at racial injustice in black newspapers—and quietly compose the occasional poem on the side and safely put it away, unpublished, in his desk drawer.

Miller remained at Howard University—the "capstone of Negro education"—through the fall of 1926, studying English, economics and political science.[214] In all probability, when Miller applied for admission, he included the requisite photograph. "The common legend," writes Audrey Kerr, "was that a prospective student's skin tone was 'evaluated' and was a key factor in whether or not one would be accepted. The admission picture custom was often used to poke fun at dark-complexioned Howard students."[215] The light-skinned Miller easily passed the "brown bag test," meaning he was no darker than a grocery bag, for entry into Howard parties or campus organizations. In the spring of 1927, he became a member of the Stylus Club, a campus organization devoted to producing race literature.[216] Subsequently, he joined the Howard chapter of Kappa Alpha Psi, which at the time had the reputation of preferring lighter-skinned students. Miller would emulate W. E. B. Du Bois in becoming "an acid-tongued Negro graduate of Harvard and of German universities."[217] Both Du Bois and Miller were unaccustomed to mixing with large numbers of blacks. When Du Bois left New England to attend Fisk University in Nashville, Tennessee, he developed "a belligerent attitude to the color bar."[218] At college, the two were thrilled to be among so many black students for the first time; however, Miller tired of Howard University's obsession with color gradation. He left Howard primarily, according to his grandnephew Halvor Miller, Jr., because he "couldn't stand segregated Washington[,] D.C."[219]

Langston Hughes, who in a few years would become Miller's lifelong friend, sketched a portrait of the color-conscious hierarchy of Washington's middle- and upper-class blacks. In 1927, in "Our Wonderful Society," Hughes wrote that the students at Howard University were the "most Nordic and un-Negro" and not above "passing a dark classmate or acquaintance with only the coolest of nods, and sometimes not even that. Washington's black socialites, for Hughes, were "ostentatiously proud"[220] snobs. Miller, who shared Hughes's critique, in 1931 dubbed them, D.C.'s "synthetic black bourgeoisie."[221]

Like most African Americans of his generation, Miller was aware that certain social and economic "advantages went to mulattoes and other fair-skinned blacks.[222] To a certain extent Miller was privileged with greater opportunities because of his skin tone. The historical trajectory of lighter-skinned African Americans having greater wealth and privilege than those who are more recognizably African in appearance is well documented.[223] According to sociologists Verna M. Keith and Cedric Herring, "Fair-skinned blacks had higher levels of attainment than darker blacks on virtually every dimension of stratification," and "higher-status blacks tended to have lighter skin tones than lower-status blacks and that light skin tone was an important criterion for attaining prestige within the black community,"[224] and often was the basis for marriage selection.

In 1933, Miller followed what might be called the traditional trajectory of color when he married a woman as light-hued as himself. According to the American sociologist E. Franklin Frazier, "The majority of prominent Negroes, who were themselves mulattoes, married mulattoes."[225] Unlike her husband, Juanita Ellsworth was not the child of a biracial marriage. However, in the 1920 U.S. census for Los Angeles, she and her seven-member family were light-skinned enough that the enumerator wrote in his binder that the Ellsworths were mulattoes.[226]

In Miller's lifetime—and still today—the most educated and wealthiest group of African Americans were light-skinned. Although he avidly sought intellectual camaraderie, his field of prospects was determined and limited to some extent by a color-ranking system. No available evidence bears out whether Miller preferred to interact with light-skinned African Americans or whether he felt less comfortable with darker blacks. Nonetheless, many of his lifelong friends, such as Langston Hughes, Ralph Bunche, and the architect James Garrott, were fairer skinned. Colleagues like Arna Bontemps and Chester Himes and Washburn classmate Floyd Covington were medium brown rather than light-hued. After he moved to Los Angeles, Miller became close friends with the dark-skinned Lloyd Griffith, the son of a prominent Los Angeles Baptist minister.

Before Miller returned to Washburn College, he had another "run on the railroad as the phrase goes . . . which meant I lived in Chicago . . . and I had lived in Kansas City in that same sense."[227] After a short visit to Wyoming, Miller reentered Washburn to complete his study of law. His travels, his varied encounters with black and white communities, and his contrasting campus experiences helped develop a broader view of the world—or to foresee—his place in it. Echoing Du Bois, who wrote, "Into this world I leapt with enthusiasm. A new loyalty and allegiance replaced my Americanism: henceforward I was a Negro,"[228] Miller declared, "I went to college an American. I emerged a Negro. In the process I swapped pride of country for pride of race, traded the dream of becoming president for the hope of becoming a Negro leader."[229]

On June 5, 1928, he graduated from Washburn with a bachelor of laws degree. "Not one of us there to witness the occasion," Nora noted in her diary. "But we were very glad for him that he was through school at last. It had been a hard pull for him, much harder than any of us realized."[230] Afterward, Miller set up a private law practice in Topeka, but dramatic events in California made that situation short-lived.

CHAPTER 3

Moving to Los Angeles

Dear Mama,

You must know how shocked I was to be called out of bed and get your message. I can't believe it, even yet. Yet it must be true. You haven't told me the details. I can't imagine what must have happened. I am more than ever sorry because I can't get there soon enough. I will leave Topeka either Saturday night or Sunday night.

   Love,
   Loren[1]

Ruby Lillie Holmes, Loren Miller's sister, died unexpectedly on Tuesday, September 10, 1929. That morning, Halvor Miller agreed to fill in for their brother Cecil, who wanted to take off early from his chauffeur's job. After Halvor finished his shift as assistant chef for Pacific Mutual Life Insurance in downtown Los Angeles, "I went to work at Cecil's job,"[2] he later wrote. As he descended the steps to the street, "I dropped my keys and immediately remembered my father's superstition about dropping keys on steps . . . a sign of death of someone close." Nora had called Halvor earlier to say that because Ruby "wasn't feeling well," she "would not be able to work that day" in the cafeteria with him. That morning when Ruby got up, she did some housework, fed and dressed her young children, and, after dressing for work, suddenly took ill. A neighborhood physician, Dr. Porter, prescribed medication but did not indicate that her condition was serious.

   "When I got home about 6 P.M.," after Ruby had suffered all day, "we took her to Los Angeles General Hospital, but too late," wrote Halvor. "At 10 P.M. that night she died and perhaps that was the saddest day of my life. Ruby and me have always been very close."[3] The cause of death was "due to a hemorrhage resulting from a rupture from a tubal pregnancy," according to the autopsy performed by the Los Angeles County coroner's office. Feeling guilty, Halvor believed that if he had not gone to Cecil's job, he would have been home and taken her to the hospital sooner. He fell "all to pieces." He said the night before Ruby died he grabbed her and "ran down the stairs," which he believed "might have jolted her in some way to cause the hemorrhage."[4]

   Two days before Ruby died she had attended evangelist Aimee Semple McPherson's Angelus Temple in Echo Park, along with her mother and a few others. On their way back home, according to Nora, they talked about the return of the Lord. Someone in the group voiced doubts that He would ever come. "Whether He comes or not," Ruby responded, "death is coming and it pays to be ready.

We don't know when we may be snatched away from here."[5] The morning after Ruby's death, Nora wrote that she went into her grandchildren's bedroom. "The baby was standing up in his bed. He was so happy to see me. Helen, the oldest said, 'Is Ruby still sick?'" Just twenty-three years old, Ruby left behind a husband, Fred Holmes, two small girls, Helen and Irma, and a nine-month-old baby boy.[6]

At the time of his sister's death, Loren Miller was the sole family member remaining in Kansas.[7] "I had planned," he wrote in a letter to his mother,

> to keep it a secret from you that I was to stay [in Los Angeles]. I wanted to surprise you, and tell you when I got there that I was to stay. Now—this. I regret more keenly than my words will ever tell you this terrible mishap. . . . Now I envy you your faith, your religion. I, too, would like to have your unshakeable faith. I would like to have your . . . calm knowledge that God must know better than his frightened children what is for their best. . . . Don't sorrow too much, mama, don't cry too much, don't lose hope or faith. I shall see you in a day or two.[8]

When Miller left Topeka, he collected money owed to him, paid some debts, and then boarded the train west to Los Angeles. Many years later, he told historian Lawrence de Graaf that "the California myth was sweeping across the nation and people had begun to say and believe that California was a land of opportunity and the Negroes had, I guess, made the same decision because it was such common talk and it was if you look back at it historically one of those periods in which a migration was mounting to California and Negroes simply came along with the migration." Once Miller reached Los Angeles, he never returned to the Midwest. "I lived here ever since," he said.[9]

The family's migration to California began with a letter from Elizabeth, John Miller's sister, who by then was calling herself Bessie Seals. For several months, Nora kept the letter, which she received sometime in 1922 or 1923, to herself. "She wanted some of the children to go and live with her as she was sick," wrote Nora. "She must have known something of us or she would not have known there were any children or even known of John's marriage. But when she needed help it was easy to find us."[10] Since John's death, Nora and the younger children lived in even more severe circumstances than they had before. Bessie's request for help essentially brought new opportunities and better housing for her brother's widow. At first glance, Nora saw it as self-serving; Bessie had waited until she needed help before reaching out. Possessive and worried, Nora feared that once her children learned of their aunt, whom no one had heard from in decades, they would leave Kansas, one by one, never to return. She confided her concerns with Loren, who, at the time, was away at college. She explained, "He said he thought it would be just the thing and that we would all plan to go in the near future and then we would be together."[11] Cloyd, the eldest, headed for Los Angeles to care for his aunt, who suffered from diabetes; shortly afterward Cecil followed. "Cloyd," wrote Nora, "did not remain there but a few months but while he was there he and Cecil sent money home, a few dollars at a time, until Cloyd returned to Kansas."[12] When Bessie died in late 1924, the family speculated that she might have worked as a madam.[13] By spring 1926, Halvor was living in Los Angeles. When Cecil became sick, he sent word to his mother to come at once. On June 8, 1927, Nora arrived from Kansas. By 1928, Helen, Ruby, Roland, and Cloyd, who by then was married, were all living in Los Angeles.[14]

In mid-September 1929, twenty-six-year-old Miller arrived in Los Angeles; the Southland was in the grip of a heat wave.[15] When he moved into the three-bedroom bungalow to join his mother, Halvor, Helen, and Roland,[16] Wall Street was on the verge of financial collapse.[17] Despite the eventual wipeout, the largest financial crisis of the twentieth century, the Millers considered themselves lucky because their unit came with a nickel-plated ring shower.[18] By 1930, Miller and his family had moved a short distance down the block on East Twenty-Second Street. Not too far away lived Cloyd and Cecil on Twenty-Seventh Street. When Halvor married Ida Jackson on October 30, 1930, he moved out.

George S. Schuyler, sensitive to the crisis at hand in his position as editorial writer for the *Pittsburgh Courier*—a leading black newspaper—predicted that thousands of American households would experience a gloomy Christmas. The crash, he wrote, "parallels the case of the American Negro. He is receiving many bad breaks. Sometimes it seems as if he is facing a sort of perpetual crisis and often one begins to question whether he is going forward or standing still. . . . Unlike American business, the Negro cannot afford to go 'back to normalcy.'" The collapse, he added, would affect "our best white friends," too, who had given investment advice and urged wholehearted support for the market. To this end, Schuyler, who eventually shifted to the extreme political right, called on intellectuals within black America to come up with programs to restore confidence and continue "our achievements, our contributions and our potentialities as an integral part of the American people." He attacked the millions of dollars spent by organizations "every summer staging fruitless fraternal conventions," when there were already at hand trained, experienced and "nationally respected propagandists already at work. We only need to drop our petty, asinine and enervating prejudices and put our shoulders (or pocketbooks) to the wheel."[19]

Langston Hughes, typically at odds with conventional thought, saw the "chaos, confusion and agony" of the socio-economic crisis differently than Schuyler. In keeping with his Marxist point of view, an exultant Hughes told a Los Angeles audience in 1932, "No group of workers the world over has more to gain from the demise of Capitalism than the Negro. Unfortunately, too few Negroes appreciate this truism." He continued,

> As a Negro it is a source of constant pain to me to note the absence of clarity of
> voice and vision among those leaders who have influenced the thought streams and
> actions of the race since the passing of chattel slavery. While the masses yearn for
> a realistic program and leadership that would point the way out of the economic,
> social, political and spiritual pit, these leaders (bleeders) seek to silence the masses

with puerile prattle. . . . This leadership can describe with infinite accuracy the unknowable topography of heaven while it remains woefully ignorant of the plight of the masses here in this living hell of capitalist. The few among the recognized leaders of today know what it is all about dare not speak out having long ago been chloroformed into a state of silence by the deadening hand of philanthropy.[20]

Miller felt similarly about capitalism and the idle babble of black leaders, topics which he and Hughes—soon to become lifelong friends—would write profusely, causing more than their share of agita.

Still averse to lawyering and several years away from proving himself an attorney of eminent fortitude, Miller found work as a reporter at the *California News*. He explained, "I had had a little newspaper experience because I had worked on college papers . . . so I fancied that I knew something about newspapers."[21] It was not much of a newspaper, "even as Negro newspapers of that time go. It had nothing but local coverage and such national news or statewide news as we might secure by clipping things from other newspapers." The paper's editor and publisher wrote poorly, opening the way for Miller to become "responsible for the rewrites, for generally determining what went into the paper by way of news and I wrote editorials of course under his supervision."[22] At that time, Los Angeles had several black newspapers, including the *California Eagle*, one of the longest running African American newspapers in the West (originally established as the *Owl* by John Neimore in 1879) and the *New Age Dispatch*, founded in 1912.

After a year or so, Miller wrote his cousin Leon H. Washington, Jr., "salesman par excellence," and suggested he leave Kansas City and come to Los Angeles. "I thought with my ability to write and his ability to sell that we would make a good team as far as the newspaper is concerned."[23] When "Wash"—as everyone called him—reached California, he joined Miller at the *California News*. The paper kept getting into financial difficulties, and eventually the printer came to the two of them with the proposition that they take over the newspaper. The printer said he could secure the paper "because Taylor [the editor-publisher] was so heavily in debt to him. So we agreed to that and then of course Taylor found out about it and we got fired. That's the reason we left the *California News* and went to the *California Eagle*."[24]

Once at the *Eagle*, from 1931 to 1933, Miller wrote political savvy articles with a touch of humor. On February 13, 1931, reporting on the local scene, he wrote:

I have yet to see a business street in any so-called black belt of the country that presents a more bedraggled appearance than Central Avenue. The avenue is cluttered up with smelly chicken ranches parading as markets, and down at the heels speakeasies from one end to the other. I might add that I have no objection to either of these legitimate businesses, providing the chicken markets stay in their proper districts and the speakeasies maintain the proper fronts. But where they are permitted to flourish indiscriminately in any state that drives away other business that might be induced to invade the district and help bolster up that mystical prosperity the *L.A. Times* says we enjoy down here.[25]

In time, Miller became the *Eagle's* city editor, appointed by "J.B." Joseph Blackburn Bass, the editor, and his publisher wife, Charlotta Amanda Bass (née Spear). When John Neimore died in 1912, Mrs. Bass inherited the *Eagle*. When Charlotta Bass hired J.B. sometime in 1912–13, he was a "fifty-year-old veteran journalist who had edited the *Topeka Plaindealer* and had founded the *Montana Plaindealer*."[26] She married him in 1914. "From the beginning of their association with the paper," writes Regina Freer, Charlotta Bass's biographer, "this husband-wife team used the *California Eagle* as a vehicle for advancing a range of social justice causes."[27] To an even greater degree than her husband, Charlotta Bass was "a committed activist, organizer, and bridge builder," who moved "between liberal and radical political circles whose activities sometimes intersected, but whose relationships were often fraught with tension and suspicion."[28]

The *Eagle*, like other black newspapers of its era, filled a void left by the mainstream press, who concentrated on crime, white sports teams, and sensational news.[29] In the crusading tradition of African American journalism, the *Eagle* supported the "hiring of Negroes as a matter of right. The abolition of enforced segregation and the patronizing of Negroes by Negroes,"[30] among other principles. In serving "the special needs of a militantly struggling people,"[31] the *Eagle*, inspired by the activist example of the *Pittsburg Courier*, waged the Don't Spend Your Money Where You Can't Work campaign.[32] When the *Eagle*, in concert with the NAACP, pushed to block the film production of D. W. Griffith's racist depiction of blacks in *Birth of a Nation*, the paper lost. Afterward, Mrs. Bass warned her readers, "As long as the Afro-Americans of this country sit supinely by and raise no voice against the injustice heaped upon them, conditions for them in this country will grow worse."[33]

When Miller first joined the *Eagle*, J.B. handled the business end of the newspaper; his wife ran everything else. J.B. leaned more toward the philosophy of Du Bois, but for political purposes he publicly "subscribed to the Booker T. Washington philosophy," said Miller. "Mr. Bass," Miller recalled more than three decades later, "was a cagey politician who came up during the terribly difficult period that stretched from 1900 or maybe from 1890 on up into the middle Twenties and Thirties, that period in which it seemed that segregation was going to triumph all over the United States." J.B. believed that "Negroes would get first class citizenship . . . but in the meanwhile they must do the best they could with the situation that then confronted them. He was a very adaptable and, in my opinion, a very clever man."[34]

Far less complimentary of J.B.'s wife, Miller felt that Mrs. Bass "lacked the profound integrity that Mr. Bass had. . . . Essentially, he had a line beyond which he wasn't going to retreat. Mrs. Bass was far more adaptable, far more prone to accommodating herself to passing whims. . . . But of the two I would have said that Mr. Bass was the human being with the most integrity basically with the most courage."[35] Apparently, once Miller left the *Eagle*, the gloves were off between the two; by 1947, their antagonism played itself out publicly and continued well after

Miller purchased the *Eagle* in 1951. Eventually she sued him, charging that he failed to pay "the installment of the purchase price due" adding that she was due an annual percentage of the papers net profits.[36] He denied everything.

Like Woody Guthrie, the American folk singer and activist for left-wing causes, Miller was bound for radicalism. Perhaps it was the extreme poverty and hunger of his childhood or the example of his cantankerous granduncle Bird Gee's lawsuit or the brilliant mind—which everyone who met him acknowledged—that led him onto the path for societal change. As a newspaperman who agitated for reform in his weekly column "On Second Thought," he kept a watchful eye on race and class issues. He mused, "The devious ways of organized charity leaves me puzzled. For instance, I am told by social service workers that needy members of one race group (Negroes by the way) get less county aid per person than members of other groups. Again, I am told, there are instances in which electric light bills will not be paid for applicants under the theory that they could and should use kerosene lamps."[37] Most likely, Juanita Ellsworth, his future wife and local county social worker, provided such information.

As a spokesperson for the local International Labor Defense (ILD), the legal arm of the Communist Party of the United States (CPUSA), Miller used his trademark dry wit both publically and privately. The "loose talk floating around Topeka and Lawrence that I am either brilliant or radical," he wrote Langston Hughes and Louise Thompson, "is just the usual old home baloney. . . . As for the radical part, I earned that title by asserting back in 1926 and 1927 . . . that capitalism was bound to end in a crisis, a theory that I copied badly from the Communist International of 1926."[38]

Miller, an admitted admirer of John Reed, who wrote *Ten Days That Shook the World* and who was considered America's first literary Bolshevik, joined the local John Reed Club (JRC). "The John Reed idea," he told Hughes and Thompson, "is quite a thing for this neck of the woods and is popular, too popular for any good but as soon as the cops raid the joint and clean up a little, the hangers on will be eliminated."[39] Miller's association with the Hollywood chapter of the JRC continued at least until the club dissolved in 1936.[40]

The ILD, founded in 1925 by the Central Committee of the CPUSA, was primarily concerned with defending workers and opposing racism, positions supported easily by Miller. "The ILD," writes cultural historian Michael Denning, "was a radical legal-action group built by the Communist Party to defend jailed unionists, immigrants facing deportation and African Americans facing southern terror."[41] It led the failed campaign to free Sacco and Vanzetti, two immigrants convicted of murder in 1921 and executed in 1927; it also represented the Scottsboro Boys, nine black teenagers accused in 1931 of raping two white women in Alabama. Two African American attorneys, William L. Patterson, who served as executive secretary of the ILD (eventual leader of the Civil Rights Congress [CRC] and husband to Louise Thompson), and Ben J. Davis, Jr., led the behind-the-scenes efforts that brought about the release of four of the nine Scottsboro defendants.[42] In 1935, when Miller moved to New York, he and Davis would work for the Crusader News Agency (CNA).

In 1931, the Scottsboro case was a cause célèbre. The nine young black men charged with assault had been riding on a crowded train from Tennessee to Alabama, as were a half dozen white young men and two white women, Victoria Pace and Ruby Bates, poor women who were likely casual prostitutes. It was said that the black teenagers chased some of the whites off the train, who later "told law enforcement officers that the Negroes had attacked them and the white women."[43] Early on, Miller took up the Scottsboro cause, which became the focus of the Left for the next several years. In his articles, Miller addressed the struggle between the ILD and the NAACP. At hand was which of the two organizations "shall represent the eight Alabama boys who are threatened with legal lynching." The controversy, Miller pointed out, was "more than a mere word battle; it has widespread significance to the Negro and on its outcome may depend the trend of Negro thought for the next few years. . . . No doubt both organizations want to save the boys but each wants the credit because of its propaganda value. Each wants to appear before the Negro public and say, 'See we saved these boys join us.'"[44]

As the case loomed large he found the time to write Hughes to ask how he managed "to stay in the good graces of the NAACPers. . . . Away out here, I reflected with some animus on their Scottsboro case and brought down on my head the combined wrath of White Collar Walter White and Funnyman Pickens."[45] For Miller, above all else, his commitment was to his readers, whom he felt deserve to know the tactics and philosophies behind each organization. In his article of May 15, 1931, he offered a straightforward analysis: "Frankly, the ILD is a Communist organization. . . . The cornerstone of Communist teaching is the solidarity of the working class. . . . If the Negro is to raise [his] status, say the Reds, he must join hands with the white workers and destroy the 'system' which, they say, makes men poor." As for the NAACP, everyone knew, he wrote, that "it proposes to aid the Negro by first winning . . . his civil and political rights . . . once he can take an active part in national life he can win his economic battlers. In short the NAACP wants to make this fight a racial fight and the ILD wants to make it a working class fight."[46]

When the NAACP attacked the ILD for how it handled the case, Miller, clearly biased, wrote,

> The efforts of the national office of the NAACP to excuse its monumental blundering in the Scottsboro case are growing pathetic. It has so far lost its balance that it continues to heap abuse on the Labor Defense offers of aid and comfort to the would-be lynchers of Alabama. . . . But why go on insisting that the ILD is going to have the boys lynched? . . . Giving aid and comfort to the common enemy is a poor way to fight one's own battles even if one doesn't agree with one's fellow soldiers in the matter of tactics.[47]

He continued that on any given day, "he could reach for the morning mail and be certain" that either the ILD or the NAACP "will have sent me a long epistle either condemning the other or assuring me that it will not cooperate with its 'rival' in the fight. This bickering is reaching the point where the boys themselves are almost overlooked."[48]

On other matters, Miller kept his readers up to date on the harassment of local Communists by the Los Angeles Police Department. On March 6, 1931, he wrote that he witnessed "some of the [police] heroes in action at a Red parade" attack "women and children of their own race with a relish that I had been taught to believe died with slavery. They literally smashed a Red restaurant out in Boyle Heights because they knew they could hide behind the fact that they were preventing a radical meeting."[49] Later, the *Los Angeles Times* reported that the police, in a similar incident, used "tear gas and night sticks" when they dispersed "1,500 communists and their sympathizers"[50] at a meeting at the Philharmonic Auditorium. "'Rabid Red' Paul Walton," reported the *Chicago Defender*, "fled the scene by climbing a tree to evade the police."[51]

In January, a few months later, acting as the morals squad, the LAPD raided the Carthay Circle Theater and shut down *Lysistrata*, the ancient Greek comedy by Aristophanes, which had been performed there since Christmas.[52] Gilbert Seldes's risqué translation of the Greek classic had been a hit in Philadelphia, but when it opened beneath the Carthay Circle Theater's "iconic octagonal tower" on swanky San Vicente Boulevard, the bawdier elements attracted the attention of the police. Mockingly, Miller wrote Langston Hughes: "One of the coppers—in that ritzy joint-says to another, sez he, 'Let's arrest the guy who wrote this thing. Where is this guy, Aristophanes?'"[53] The trial of the fifty-two cast members, arrested for performing an "indecent show," would go on for months.

Not long after the Carthay Circle incident, the Red Squad, Los Angeles's police intelligence unit, pounced on the John Reed Club, blocking the production of Langston Hughes's new play, the *Scottsboro Limited*. Miller explained later to Hughes that when he reached the play's performance where he was slated to speak on the program, "Up steps the Red Squad. . . . Me, I was standing on the street corner trying to look like any other up and coming Babbitt in burnt cork when one of the Protectors of Womanhood steps up to me and tells me to beat it."

After dodging the police for half an hour, Miller said while he slipped away the police grabbed one of the scheduled speakers, a Communist who started the rumor that Miller had been arrested. "Imagine my disgust. Just after I had conjured pictures of the workers of the world demonstrating in Moscow . . . Topeka, New York and Birmingham parading with demands that Loren Miller be released . . . and me a guy who would give anything for a little publicity."[54] That jest contained an element of prophecy. Within a few months, Miller met Hughes face to face for the first time; soon after the two set off for Moscow on one of the biggest adventures of their lives.

CHAPTER 4

Sunday, We Leave for Russia

S outhern Californians must have been chanting "water" more often than the Mojave spirit god on the morning that four travelers climbed into Langston Hughes's little Ford in 1932 and started their cross-country drive.[1] Perhaps the rain was a good omen since the dry streets of Los Angeles rarely sparkle in June.[2] In any event, the men were off to make the "first great Negro-white film ever made in the world."[3] Sympathetic toward the Soviet Union's commitment to people over commerce, "Russia," as far as Loren Miller was concerned, "is the only place on the face of the globe where a serious picture of Negro life can be made."[4] Hughes knew if ever he was to "work in motion pictures or learn about them, it would have to be abroad."[5] Before pulling out of town, Miller assured his *California Eagle* readers on June 3, 1932, that if they missed his weekly column, it was not because the cops had "raided one of my favorite speakeasies and cast me into the outer darkness of the Lincoln Heights jail. . . . The simple truth is that I shall be out of the village" for the next few months. "I leave only because of a valid curiosity to see what the other ends of the world are like and because I think that I detect a chance to perform some valuable service during my absence."[6] To Miller and his friends, the adventure held the promise of unbounded freedom, a jumping off into the void.

"It was for the most of them a glorious opportunity to travel and see the world . . . the land of the Bolshevik,"[7] wrote Louise Thompson, Hughes's New York friend (and occasional stenographer), whom he met during one of his early readings when she was teaching at the Hampton Institute.[8] For years, Miller had been trying to get to Russia.[9] His admiration for the Jamaican writer and poet Claude McKay, who enthusiastically described his own experiences in the Soviet Union, was a powerful catalyst for taking the trip.

Opportunity arrived with an invitation from the Meschrabpom Film Company, through James W. Ford, to come to its Moscow studios and make a movie about American blacks—undoubtedly a Communist propaganda film, but one with the potential for high production values, artistic integrity, realistic screen portrayals of African Americans, and freedom from demeaning stereotypes. Ford, one of the leading black Communists in the nation—who rose rapidly within the ranks of the Communist Party after joining in 1925—secured the group's invitation during his winter visit to Moscow. Ford was charged with the task of forming an interracial organizing committee "for the purpose of securing a cast of from twelve to twenty to participate in the production of a film in

Soviet Russia depicting the life of Race folk in America."[10] At the time, Ford was running on the CPUSA ticket for vice president, alongside William Z. Foster, candidate for president.

Miller and Hughes's initial friendship developed through letters. It is unclear, however, as to who initiated the first contact. Suitably impressed, Hughes acknowledged Miller's "sympathetic line or so . . . in the [Kappa Alpha Psi] Journal," when some critic was giving him the blues. In the interim, somehow Hughes lost contact with Miller until in 1930 Louise Thompson, "said you'd turned up in California."[11]

After Miller received a copy of Hughes's first book of prose, *Not without Laughter*, he duly thanked him for "the courtesy you have shown me in sending me an autographed copy." "Louise has told me," wrote Miller, "that you once sent me a copy of your collection by the four Lincoln poets. I regret that I never received it and for that reason never acknowledged the favor." After making a favorable comment on Hughes's novel, Miller closed by saying, "Now that a contact (how I hate that word) has been established I shall look forward to boring you at greater length with some of my pet theories and I hope that you will some time find occasion to write me a line or two."[12] On August 21, 1930, Hughes replied, "I thought you'd at least understand it," unlike the "Strivers" who struggle so hard to forget their hue. After expressing his wish for the still-distant literary freedom to present black characters as individuals, rather than "representative of the whole race," Hughes signed off: "Glad to meet you Loren."[13]

Throughout 1930 and 1931, their correspondence continued—well before they met face to face in 1932—sharing philosophies, commenting on the works of others, and critiquing each other's writing. Miller's correspondence, notably self-deprecating and frank, declared:

> Let me rise to say that I have long entertained more than a sneaking suspicion that what you have set yourself to doing is what the country has been needing for these many years. Anybody looking critically at the output of the NEW NEGRO ARTISTS must have been struck with the thought that the stuff has been written too much with a main eye on the good White Folks. . . . Having said that permit me to suggest that it seems to me that you are still a little too afraid of propaganda. . . . Art can't do anything but mirror life and to set a mirror to catch the reflection of the life of the Negro masses will be propaganda because the upward struggle of the masses is a ceaseless propaganda against the upper classes. I use "we" only as a compliment to myself since I write nothing but you (if you have blushes, prepare to shed them) are the only valid artist of that Harlem group of a few years ago. Your stature grows as your consecutive books testify. At grips with reality, you can are destined to outstrip not only the colored artists but the white ones—the latter are even more in the grip of the bourgeois ideology than the blacks.[14]

By March 1931, Miller, now Hughes's West Coast literary agent, began promoting his friend's first visit to Los Angeles: "Langston Hughes, poet who so far outranks others that comparison is odious, will soon be in our fair village. I have laid plans for a number of public appearances for Mr. Hughes but there are dates open (adv.) Organizations that would like to hear this poet can hunt me down and I will be glad to let them know what dates are available."[15] After Hughes's successful appearance, Miller praised the integrated Los Angeles Civic League— which, though a member of, he criticized from time to time—for "beginning to take a more active part in community affairs. It was this organization," he wrote, "that sponsored Langston Hughes's"[16] presentation at the Second Baptist Church.

Before the fun of movie making could begin, the drudgery of raising funds for the ocean voyage fell to Louise Thompson. Already she had recruited W. A. Domingo to chair the Co-operating Committee for the Production of a Soviet Film on Negro Life, which saw the making of such a film, devoid of black buffoonery and banality, as both bold and unprecedented. Domingo, according to historian Faith Berry, "spared no words in making public statements about the relevance"[17] of the film. Such a film, he wrote, "produced under the best technical and artistic experience of Russia, will be welcomed by discriminating patrons of the cinema and those people sincerely interested in the Negro."[18] Though James Ford headed the committee as executive secretary, Thompson's shrewdness as corresponding secretary brought the enterprise together. She possessed the skills and social connections to reach out to a broad section of supporters as the cofounder of the Harlem branch of the Friendship Society with the Soviet Union and as secretary of the Committee for the Defense of Political Prisoners. During the last days of the Harlem Renaissance, her spacious apartment on Convent Avenue with Sue Elvie Bailey,[19] who later married theologian Dr. Howard Thurman, was a well-known center of cultural and political activity.

At the outset, Thompson recruited film participants from those within her social and political circles who "were willing to pay their own fare,"[20] which was no easy task with a country on its knees financially. She assured others, like Miller, unable to pay the full fare, that accommodations and food rations would be paid for when they reached Moscow; once there, they would receive "between 400 and 600 rubles per month ($200–$300)."[21] Miller quipped to Thompson and Hughes, "I have no money with which to go to the U.S.S.R. but would be more than glad to go if I did have it. Do you suppose I could be the villain in the play? I wear a mustache, which is an invaluable part of every rascal's equipment and I can utter blood curdling oaths when the lines require."[22]

Because America remained the only Great Power that refused to recognize the Soviet Union in 1932, Meschrabpom was unable to exchange its rubles for American dollars. The task fell to Louise to figure out how to purchase the $110 one-way fare from New York to Leningrad on the SS *Europa*.[23] Once Communist affiliation was no longer required, her situation brightened. Now she was free to paint the trip as "a glorified tour and vacation"[24] to students whom she hoped had the dollars to take part in the film. The reality, wrote Hughes, was that "very few professional theater people were willing to pay their own fare to travel all the way to Russia to sign contracts they had never seen."[25] Despite warnings that the Soviets "only want to make Communists out of you all,"[26] as Hughes put it, Thompson recruited a group of ambitious, "adventurous young students, teachers, writers and would-be actors . . . looking forward to the fun and wonder of a foreign land as much as to film-making." There was not a "single worker—in the laboring sense"[27] among them.

Nowhere in Thompson's early correspondence with Hughes had she indicated that she, too, wanted to make the trip. After securing a loan from a friend and the assurance of a one-month paid vacation, she dashed off a note to Hughes confessing excitedly—and in capital letters—that she was joining the tour.[28] She was "tickled pink" when earlier Miller confirmed that he would come along, too. Apparently, the 10 percent cut he received for organizing Hughes's series of Pacific coast lectures did the trick.[29] "Plans seem to be working out so perfectly," Thompson wrote, "that it seems almost (not quite) too good to be true. . . . I shall breathe a mighty sigh of relief when we board the *Europa* on June 14," and, "if we starve we will all starve together."[30]

On May 29, Hughes wrote Miller, "Trust you have your [passport] by now but if not speed it up (and send it on registered to Louise for visas)."[31] By June 20, the group was to arrive in the port of Bremerhaven, Germany, and proceed via boat train to Berlin, where they were to stay for two days. By July 1, they were expected in Moscow to begin filming.[32]

For Miller, Hughes, and Thompson, the trip came at the best time, politically. Organized labor in the United States—which in this period included the Industrial Workers of the World, the International Molders' Union of San Francisco, the Seattle Central Labor Council and the Share-Croppers' Union in Alabama, among other groups—was at the helm of social unrest, leading a wave of union members staging strikes and condemning the false imprisonment of Tom Mooney and the Scottsboro Boys, international causes célèbres.[33] African American artists and intellectuals such as Miller and Hughes, who drew on Claude McKay's affectionate extolling of the virtues of his days in Russia as "the most memorable of my life," came to know that Lenin "grappled with the question of the American Negroes and spoke on the subject before the Second Congress of the Third International."[34] American Studies scholar Kate Baldwin asserts that writers like McKay and Hughes were interested in the "boundary-challenging formations put forth by the promise of Soviet internationalism—as by definition a multilingual and hybrid project—led these men to the Soviet Union in the first place and to contemplate U.S. race relations from a new perspective."[35]

As soon-to-be filmmakers Miller, Hughes, and their Berkeley chiropractor friend Matt Crawford barreled down U.S. Route 80 at breakneck speed on a concrete and asphalt-paved road, heading toward New York City—occasionally slowing down to avoid "speed cops" and already having dropped George Lee, the fourth member of the group, in Monrovia—they drove past desert stretches of

mesquite, sage, flowering yuccas, and the threadlike, orange nets of the chap-
arral dodder plant. Toward evening, they crossed over the Colorado River on
the Ocean Highway Bridge.[36] Darkness had fallen when they noted on the bluff
above them the old Arizona Territorial Prison Cemetery, a burial ground filled
mostly with Mexicans.

Close to 10:00 P.M. they reached Yuma,[37] where they spotted a Greek café. Given
the poverty of the locale where the café was located, Miller naïvely thought its
owner might be pleased to turn an honest penny. They found a table and watched
the waiters fly "back and forth" refusing to even look their way.[38] Finally, Miller
placed his order, while the "darker member of [their] party went to park the
car." Just as Crawford reentered the restaurant—delayed because he had lost his
way—the waiter snatched Miller's steak back and shouted, "You ought to know
better."[39] "Not a restaurant on the main street," wrote Hughes in his "Here to Yonder" column in the *Chicago Defender*, "would serve us a sandwich."[40] Their road
experience was no different than the blatant racism many other African Americans of the era experienced. As the stressor of racism requires all manner of cop-
ing strategies, Miller turned the pain of humiliation into a droll guessing game.
In his unpublished essay "Look Down, Look Down," he wrote, "It is in its way,
quite a sport and I have won, and lost sizeable sums laying bets as to whether we
could, or could not eat in a given place. In case the reader wants to try the sport
with Negro friends I can give the rule that works best. It is the same one used by
experienced crapshooters: always bet that the dice won't hit."[41]

Despite the Jim Crow encounters and the ninety-degree heat, nothing damp-
ened their spirits. Before bedding down for the night, Hughes wired Thompson,
"You hold that boat . . . 'cause it's an ark to me."[42] When they reached Texas,
Miller wrote his mother that his first trip across the South "turned out fine. Of
course, we could not eat in the restaurants but there was nothing else in the way
of color discrimination. The men at the gas stations treated us fine. They acted as
if they were very glad to get our money and thanked us cordially as well as calling
us 'Mr.'" He assured her that he was "feeling fine, in fact better than I have felt for
a long time. I guess that is because I do not have to go to work."[43] However, he
carefully shaped his letter most likely as to avoid upsetting her; privately Miller
revealed that he had been "insulted and Jim Crowed on every hand" from Los
Angeles to New York.[44] As for Hughes, he estimated that "AT LEAST a hundred
times" he had been refused service "in public restaurants in strange cities."[45]

On June 8, the Russian-bound trio reached McAlester, Oklahoma, where they
ran into a "first class thunder and rain storm" which reminded Miller of Kansas.[46] As the storm receded, the sun's rays the next day poured down like molten
lead. With marked earnestness, Miller wrote Nora that seeing men and women
plowing and hoeing the fields and gardens made him feel like he had returned
home. "But, in spite of all that, I do not believe that I would ever like to live in this
heat again after having been in California where it is cool at night."[47]

Forced to stop for piston and bearing repairs, the travelers left before the heat turned the little Ford into a cauldron.[48] Hoping that the vehicle would no longer bob, pitch, or sway, Miller slipped the clutch into gear; they were back on the road again. Writing later that day, he reminded his mother to ask his cousin Leon Washington to send him the *California Eagle* every week while he was in Russia. "Tell Wash that we are not going to Kansas City. . . . We may go to St. Louis but we will not have time to stop."[49] When they reached Ohio, Miller quipped sardonically that they had arrived "just in time to pass within a hundred miles of a city where a Negro was being lynched."[50] In Cleveland, Hughes "hardly had time to tell his mother goodbye."[51] He left her "several hundred dollars,"[52] as he often did, to help with expenses. Then the three rolled on toward New York.

By the time they reached Pier 4 in Brooklyn, at the foot of 58th Street,[53] they barely had time to board the SS *Europa*. Running late, "accompanied to the wharf by [Hughes's] 'Aunt' Toy Harper,"[54] they had missed the rousing sendoff and the many friends who had come to wish them farewell.[55] They missed the group's historic photograph and, perhaps more importantly, the opportunity to stand alongside the film's committee chair, Jamaican-born W. A. Domingo.[56] A former Marcus Garvey supporter, Domingo had cofounded, along with Cyril Briggs and Richard B. Moore, the quasi-secret African Blood Brotherhood.[57] In 1935, Miller would come to know these men when he worked in New York at the American Communist Party–subsidized Crusader News Agency and the *Negro Liberator*.[58] The three West Coast travelers arrived far too late to enjoy the many parties thrown in the film group's honor, including the bon voyage cabaret "for a dozen of the 25 colored players"[59] who were leaving for Russia. The *Baltimore Afro-American* reported that such prominent guests as Nancy Cunard, heir to the Cunard shipping line, political activist, and titled Englishwoman, attended the gala sendoff party at the Unique Colony Circle on West 135th Street. Bronx resident Thelma Clement gave a party for Dorothy West and Mollie Lewis—members of the James Weldon Johnson Literary Guild; likewise, intimate friends of news reporter Ted Poston threw the journalist a sendoff party.[60]

Hughes, the last member of the twenty-two would-be "thespians" to board, scrambled up the gangplank, "loaded down with bags, baggage, books, a typewriter, a Victrola, and a big box of Louis Armstrong, Bessie Smith, Duke Ellington and Ethel Waters records."[61] Years later, Thompson averred that legendary popular music producer John Hammond provided the records and the Victrola.[62] Finally, by midnight, on June 14, the *Europa* pulled out of port with 1,950 passengers—as well as $8 million in gold—and headed into the open Atlantic. The world's fastest steamer, the *Europa* was Norddeutscher Lloyd's newest and largest passenger ship and would take the adventurers to Bremerhaven, Germany. It felt as if nothing could bother them now, not even New York's inclement weather. They were off on a sea of adventures.[63]

By the time the trio reached the high seas, introductions were complete. Thompson knew most of the participants, at least by name. Hughes and Henry Lee Moon knew each other from having attended high school in Cleveland, Ohio, at the same time. Moon knew Mollie Lewis, now a graduate of Meharry's School of Pharmacy, "when he had been a playground instructor at Mollie's school when she was a girl."[64] Though Moon persuaded Dorothy West, the up-and-coming writer from Boston, to make the trip, he "admonished her not to encourage Mollie," whom he considered a bit wild. Hughes knew West from when he lodged one summer with the writer Wallace Thurman, who had been briefly married to Louise Thompson.[65] As for Miller, the only participants he knew were Thompson and Hughes. He barely knew Matt Crawford prior to driving to New York together. Poston, a reporter and assistant editor with the *New York Amsterdam News*, though newly acquainted with Thompson, knew many of the other passengers.[66] The band of twenty-two travelers was well educated, young, and in many instances quite attractive. All were eager for a summer's adventure.

By any standard, they were a motley crew of young intellectuals who, for the most part, lacked any actual stage or film experience. There were a few exceptions—for example, the singer and actor Sylvia Garner, who appeared in a minor role with Ethel Barrymore in *Scarlet Sister Mary*, based on Julia Mood Peterkin's Pulitzer Prize–winning novel. "Sylvia was a large woman who had gone into the theater in the days of the shimmy-sha-wobble,"[67] wrote Hughes. Also on board was Wayland Rudd, a cast member in Eugene O'Neill's *Emperor Jones*, who had performed in *Othello* and *Porgy and Bess*. Hughes called Rudd "The only really seasoned actor accompanying us."[68] A few dabbled in the theater; Thurston McNairy Lewis, a social worker from Mississippi, who "once had been a member of the Communist Party of the United States,"[69] had acted with the Stuart Walker Players. Juanita Lewis, a dramatic reader, had sung with the Hall Johnson Negro Choir. The petite light-skinned Harlem Renaissance novelist Dorothy West, who came from a somewhat sheltered background, had very little theatrical experience other than once performing alongside Rudd in *Porgy*. Of the trip, she later said there was "not a live actor in the group."[70]

Poston saw the proposed film production as a "chance to get a free trip with all expenses" paid, to see for himself the much-publicized Soviet Union.[71] He was aboard ship thanks to the generosity of his coworkers, who threw a "Send Poston to Russia" fund-raising party.[72] The "bespectacled, dignified, and friendly Henry Lee Moon,"[73] Ted Poston's polar opposite at the *Amsterdam News*, was the more conservative of the pair; Poston was bold and flamboyant, with a tendency to embellish. The two—called "Mutt and Jeff" by some—became best pals for life, with Poston naming Moon as the executor of his estate. They lived with Thurston McNairy Lewis after Poston moved out of his brother Ulysses's basement apartment. When they reached Moscow, the threesome bunked together.[74] Lewis would align himself, at least for a time, with the radicals in the group—Crawford, Hughes, Miller, and Thompson.[75]

The group's job skills had little bearing on making movies. Thompson earned her living as a research assistant, working on labor issues. Leonard Hill and Katherine Jenkins were social workers. George Sample, a law student at Fordham University, tagged along as Katherine's fiancé. Frank C. Montero, whose parents paid his boat fare, was "a smart-aleck radical from New York"[76] who had heard about the movie from faculty at Howard University. Other students were Constance White and Mildred Jones, "a very pretty divorcee who traveled on alimony,"[77] according to Hughes. Jamaican agriculturalist Laurence O. Alberga and Lloyd Patterson, a paperhanger and Hampton Institute graduate, rounded out the group of intrepid "thespians." The only confirmed member of the Communist Party of the United States among them was Alan McKenzie, who worked as a salesperson.[78] McKenzie "astounded" his fellow travelers by bringing along a white woman, according to biographer Arnold Rampersad.[79] Homer Smith, a former Minneapolis postal clerk with a degree in journalism from the University of Minnesota, cherished hopes that once the film was over, he remain in the Soviet Union.[80] For the next fifteen years, he wrote "A Column from Moscow" under the pen name "Chatsworth Hall" for the *Chicago Defender*.[81]

Few in the group knew that the film's title was *Black and White* (*Blek end Uait*) or what it was about. Neither Miller nor Hughes knew the title came from Vladimir Mayakovsky, an iconic Russian poet, who in 1925 traveled to Mexico, Cuba, and the United States.[82] Few, if any, had ever heard of Mayakovsky, who was so taken aback by American racism in the mid-1920s that he wrote that Americans were a people who refuse to "shake hands with a Negro."[83] By the time Miller reached Europe, he wrote his mother, "We hear that it is to be called 'Black and White'. . . . All everybody knows is that we expect to work by July 1."[84] Hughes had the daunting task of translating the script.[85] Once the initial excitement of boarding faded, the group splintered into political cliques. Discord surfaced during discussions of whether or not to send a petition in support of the Scottsboro Boys. Thompson's request to hold a nonpolitical "informative meeting relative to the Scottsboro case" was voted down "on account of the captain's disapproval."[86] Urged to drop the matter, she circulated a petition to the other passengers. "In fact," as Miller explained to Juanita Ellsworth, his fiancée, nicknamed Elly, "we have been clearly divided since the start into the 'left' and 'right' factions."[87] The friction, according to Miller, was opposition to "the Communist movement since they are petty bourgeois and simply hope to utilize the trip for their own benefit." It did not take long for the others to dub Langston Hughes, Loren Miller, and Louise Thompson the "L-raising Trio."[88]

On board were two former students of Howard University philosophy professor Alain Locke, on his way to the world's leading medical spa in Bad Nauheim, Germany.[89] When Locke learned that Langston Hughes would be on board, too, he was distraught. Possibly in deference to Locke's age and position, his informants agreed to keep him posted on the activities of their fellow travelers, particularly Hughes's movements.[90]

Locke had a well-known and contentious history with both Hughes and Thompson, whom he called his "friendly enemies."[91] Locke's strained relationship with Hughes began with Hughes's unsuccessful attempt to enter Howard University. "Hughes wanted to get into Howard; Locke wanted to get Hughes in bed,"[92] writes historian Arnold Rampersad. There were plans to live together once Hughes gained admission. However, once that possibility no longer was on the table, the relationship stalled, with the fastidious petulant Locke repeatedly professing his love and Hughes stringing him along.[93]

Despite Locke's earlier attempts "frantically to change his own travel arrangements"[94] to avoid encountering Hughes and Thompson, his curiosity got the better of him. Perhaps his adoration of the babbling gossip in the air got the better of him.[95] Whatever it was, Locke wanted to know what the "Russian Negro Party"[96] was up to; his informants assured him that they would continue to stay in touch after he disembarked at Cherbourg, France.[97] Unable to shake off his obsession with Hughes, Locke mailed photographs of the group to Mrs. Mason, his benefactor, pointing out that Miller and Hughes were in the last row. "Loren Miller," he added, "is another young poet gone Communist. He really never was a poet, was one because that was then the latest wrinkle—and is now Communist for the same reason."[98]

As the SS *Europa* made its way across the Atlantic, Miller met Ralph Bunche, who was on his way to Africa courtesy of the Rosenwald Fund. Miller would later write disparagingly of Julius Rosenwald, who made his fortune from the mail-order house of Sears, Roebuck and Company, saying that his vast paternalism, built on the principle of racial separation, was "capable of exerting a tremendous influence over Negro life."[99] He singled out Booker T. Washington's Tuskegee Institute and the NAACP, who in their search for aid complied "with the wishes of the Fund directors."[100]

In Miller's youthful eyes, Bunche compromised his ethics when he accepted a $2,000 Rosenwald field fellowship to conduct a comparative study of French colonialism in Dahomey and Togoland rather than his intended study of Brazil.[101] Before Miller wrote "Mail Order Dictatorship" for the *New Masses*, he complained to Joe North, its editor. Bunche is "an opportunist of the rankest kind" for switching his intentions to study interracial issues in Brazil to the problems of colonial Africa because the proposed study was considered "too dangerous." He "has ambitions of his own that far outweigh all else for him."[102]

In fundamental ways, Miller changed his preconceptions. Ostensibly, he decided that Bunche's Marxist ideals and support for the working class above "all else" were the same as his own, or perhaps Juanita Ellsworth played a role in softening Miller's earlier harshness. She and Bunche, former high school sweethearts, remained friends long after their graduation in 1922 from Los Angeles's Jefferson High School.[103] More than likely it was Miller, the black intellectual, who changed over time when he went from the far left to the political mainstream—although his "radical and activist engagement" did periodically resurface. By the time Miller bought the *California Eagle* in 1951, the two men were old friends.[104]

At mid-voyage, Thompson was busy dealing with two irritants, Ted Poston and Thurston Lewis. Though they agreed to "represent the race creditably,"[105] she felt that they made fools of themselves by chasing after white women on board. However, Dorothy West, although sympathetic toward Thompson, felt that she was "out of tune" with the others.[106] Even Miller, who was sympathetic politically, felt that "Louise is very stubborn and had rather make a point than be right at times" and "has a genius for getting herself disliked by those who might elevate her to higher positions."[107] Thompson, whom the *Crisis* called the "leading colored woman in the Communist movement,"[108] would remain in leftist politics all her life, becoming particularly active with the National Negro Congress in the mid-1930s as would Miller for a time. At some point, the two grew apart as the country became more anti-Communist.[109]

Once temperaments settled down, the travelers spent the remainder of their time at sea playing cards, drinking, and genuinely have a good time. "The traditional last night-before-landing parties," wrote Thompson, "found some of our group down to their last dollar after imbibing much champagne."[110]

After six days, the *Europa* anchored at the port of Bremen. Then the passengers were loaded straightaway onto a boat train toward Berlin for the next seven hours. "Third class trains," wrote Miller as they passed breathtaking landscapes, "are a marked departure from American trains . . . about one half to two thirds the size of an American car."[111] When they arrived in Berlin, what got their immediate attention was the number of Hitler's Brownshirts, Sturmabteilung (SA), roaming the streets. Luckily, they arrived months before the SA shadowed foreign visitors or banned "race music."[112]

"Germans seem to expect something to happen soon. Maybe a Fascist ascension to power," predicted Miller, who wrote how he was confronted by beggars "on every hand" and was "accosted by at least a dozen prostitutes who ask only a mark or sometimes a half mark [twenty-four cents]."[113] Thompson, apparently more incensed by the number of prostitutes who "try to take [the men] away from any young women in our party with whom they were walking,"[114] ignored the realities of Germany's war-torn economy. Hughes found "the pathos and poverty of Berlin's low-priced market in bodies"[115] depressing. In contrast, the much younger Dorothy West wrote, "Dearest Mummy . . . I loved Berlin. . . . It's a thrilling and beautiful city. Marvelous buildings, night life, everything enchanting."[116] Despite feeling racial freedom for the first time—eating in any restaurant he could afford—Miller found Berlin depressingly wretched.[117]

When they reached Berlin on June 22, the group members expected to travel onto Moscow immediately.[118] To their amazement, the Russian consulate was completely unaware that they were coming—their first encounter with "the famous Russian red tape."[119] As they waited for their visas, they toured and enjoyed Berlin's nightlife. Unimpressed, Miller found its nightclubs

> no different in size and language from the American gyp joints which flourish after
> 12. The only different one we saw was the famous El Dorado. It is a homosexual
> place in which the "women" are all men dressed in the clothes of women. Some of
> them were so feminine as to delude one and some of them were very obviously men
> with large hands and voices. It is their boast that the place is the only one of its kind
> in the world.[120]

Finally, after two days, their visas arrived.[121] Miller wrote,

> The priceless part of Berlin was our leaving. We were slated to leave at 11:30. Part of
> the crew got on the train and was waiting when word arrived that there had been a
> hitch in our passports and that we were not to leave until 4:30. After much scram-
> bling to get off word got around that we were to be stranded there and the looks of
> dismay must have caused the whole city to tremble. You can't appreciate it without
> knowing these European trains and the manner in which everybody hands the bag-
> gage in and out the window.[122]

The next stop: Stettin, Germany.[123]

From there, the group boarded the spotlessly white "good ship Ariadne" which after the *Europa*, Miller wrote his fiancée, "looks like a canoe." "On this boat there is little difference except in the time we eat. We use the same dining room but the first class eats first, gets better food and so forth. Contrary to the case on the *Europa*, we may use the entire ship. Incidentally, it is a Finnish ship with the crew speaking that language. And just when I had worked up a passable com-mand of German."[124] The two-day boat trip across "the Baltic to Helsinki" for Hughes "was most like a fairy-tale journey."[125] The travelers were spellbound by the celestial ballet of what an earlier American sojourner, Benjamin Franklin, had called the "mystery of the northern lights."[126] Despite some travel weariness and the bone-chilling winds of the Baltic Sea, Thompson recalled the strange experience of reading by natural light on deck at midnight as magical.

On the 24th of June, they reached Helsinki, where they found the Finns friendly though unaccustomed to seeing "so many colored folks." By evening, after send-ing Juanita a postcard—"Country boy who made good in Finland"[127]—Hughes and the others left for Leningrad and "the land of John Reed's Ten Days That Shook the World, the land where race prejudice was reported taboo, the land of the Soviets."[128] Such was Hughes's enthusiasm.

In Miller's eagerness to sample everything, he fell ill, possibly with a bout of food poisoning with underlying pangs of homesickness. To boost his spirits, he wrote Juanita, something he did throughout his travels: "I should like to see you (why do people say things like that when they are so remote?). What I mean to say is that I am missing you and that I am not yet used to the fact that you are so far away. It had got to the place where it seemed to me that you should always be close somewhere and now to find that you are eight thousand miles from here!!"[129]

When they reached the border, a banner reading "WORKERS OF THE WORLD UNITE" waved above the railroad tracks; what immediately caught their eye was Soviet soldiers wearing red-starred caps. Impulsively, some in the group left the train "to touch their hands to Soviet soil, lift the new earth in their palms, and kiss it."[130] At Leningrad, formerly Saint Petersburg, they were "met by a brass band," which blared "L'Internationale," the Communist anthem. On the platform waiting with the Meschrabpom officials to greet the newcomers was Lovette Fort-Whiteman, a prominent black Communist from Chicago, who in 1925 had helped establish the American Negro Labor Congress. Afterward, a fleet of cars threaded its way to the October Hotel, where they stayed the night.[131] While the "celebrity" guests were being dazzled by a banquet, which Hughes described as "all the way from soup on through roast chicken and vegetables right down to ice cream and black coffee,"[132] unknown to Miller and his companions, ordinary Russians paid exorbitant prices for inferior bread and parts of the USSR suffered intermittent famine.

In anticipation of the Americans' morning arrival on June 26, ordinary Muscovites crowded the city's Nikolayevsky Railway Station.[133] Amid the cheering throng of citizens, government officials, writers, and actors stood Emma Harris, affectionately known as the "Mammy of Moscow." "Bless God! Lord! I'm sure glad to see some Negroes! Welcome! Welcome! Welcome!"[134] Whisked away in long, shiny Buicks and Lincolns, careening past Lenin's mausoleum near the Kremlin wall, the travelers reached the Grand Hotel, in the heart of the capital.[135] Emma Harris, in Russia since the turn of the twentieth century, showed the would-be thespians "what the guides did not: where to find a place to drink, no matter the hour, where vodka and brandy were served."[136] The former actor, who preferred the tsarist system to the Soviets, "added a big dash of color all her own to the grayness of Moscow,"[137] wrote Hughes.

Once settled in at the hotel, Miller and his two roommates, Hughes and Crawford, ragged on about what Miller called that "Bitter Amerika Fakeration."[138] It was a reference to the Better America Federation, a superpatriotic California-based organization that crusaded against what it considered un-American activities, including people such as Miller and Hughes who adhered to Marxist philosophy. Openly committed to similar political sympathies and perspectives, the trip to Russia for the two writers would solidify and deepen their friendship and commitment to the "Negro masses" and what they saw as the divide between the black and white working class.

Though considered Communists by the others in the group, the men's main link to the Communist Party was through the John Reed Club, the League of Struggle for Negro Rights, and now Moscow's apparent interest in American Negroes.[139] Working as a foreign correspondent for the Associated Negro Press,

Miller reported that Langston Hughes was convinced that "Communism is the only force that is fighting actively for the alleviation and ultimate abolition of the poverty and misery which he found so widespread among Negroes." "The hysterical fear of Communism," declared Hughes, "displayed by whites is born of the fact that they fear it will awaken the Negro and lead him to take active steps to better his condition and thus disturb the present economic regime with its riches on one hand and poverty on the other."[140]

After all the hurrying and scurrying to get to Moscow, Louise Thompson, believing that the bump in Berlin was an anomaly, nonetheless, was surprised to find that their Russian co-creators "were not ready to start the picture, had not even decided upon a location for shooting."[141] After ten days in Moscow with no tangible work on the film to show, they consoled themselves that as *Negrochanski tovarish* (Negro comrades) they were honored and welcomed almost everywhere they went; weeks went by before Hughes laid his eyes on a translated version of the script, recalling "At first I was astonished at what I read. . . . I could not keep from laughing out loud to the astonishment of my two roommates," Miller and Crawford.[142]

The screenplay for *Black and White* was improbable. According to Miller, it was "full of Europeanisms transported to the American scene."[143] A white Southerner is depicted waltzing with a black housemaid, and northern whites rush to Alabama to defend black steelworkers. Hughes, cautious not to offend or blame the screenwriter Georgi Grebner, who knew neither English nor anything about America, promptly returned the unworkable script with his "red penciled" marks and his apologies to the Meschrabpom officials and to the members of the Communist Party in Russia, the Comintern.[144] Thompson later postulated that problems might have been avoided if the film company had waited to complete the "necessary preparations for the production of the picture" before sending for the group members.[145]

On July 7, Loren wrote Elly: "Thus far we have done little towards starting the film. To be exact, barely anything."[146] Reported earlier by Thelma Harden of the *Chicago Defender*, both Hughes and Miller would rewrite the film script.[147] Miller told his fiancée that the screenplay "is being re-written by Langston chiefly, assisted by some of the rest of us. It will not be finished for a few days. Then the fun begins." At least he hoped so. The script was such a mess that all Hughes could do was to "start over and get a new one, based on reality, not imagination."[148] Hughes went through "the scenario with the studio heads page by page, scene by scene, pointing out the minor nuances that were off tangent here, the major errors of factual possibility there. . . . I made it clear that one could hardly blame the scenarist who had, evidently, very meager facts available with which to work."[149] To begin with, the screenplay—"a hodgepodge of good intentions"— had been written by a committee of three people, consisting of a Russian and a German film director, both completely ignorant of the ways of Negro folk, and the "colored Comrade" Lovett Fort-Whiteman.[150] At the time, Lovett was a teacher at the Anglo-American school in Moscow. He and Harry Haywood had arrived in Moscow in 1924 "as scholarship students at the Comintern's Communist University of the Toilers of the East."[151] Homer Smith, who later denied having visited the Soviet Union alongside Miller, Hughes, and the others, wrote that Forte-Whiteman was so "steeped in party dogma that he had completely lost touch with America."[152] Equally agitated, Miller wrote, "It is true that Whiteman had read the work but evidently he had done nothing to correct the false impressions that the authors had of America and the American Negro."[153] Fascinated by the "excessive flamboyance of the man,"[154] Haywood was equally repelled. Fort-Whiteman, whom *Time* called the "Reddest of the Blacks" in 1925, died tragically in 1939 in a prison labor camp hospital in northeastern Siberia from starvation, a broken man whose teeth had been knocked out.[155]

Throughout his stay, Miller felt "doomed to disappointment" due to the slowness of the mail. This led to conjuring up a series of fantasies and rash proposals for Juanita. "I wish that I could think of some way to speed up the [mail] service or hasten the letter that I feel sure you must have written. Unless I get some mail soon I may have to leave the whole film in the lurch and go home to see you. Imagine that, if you can."[156] No matter how the novelty of the Russian scene absorbed him—sightseeing in the day and partying at night—the distractions were of little comfort to the idleness and loneliness he felt. He wrote, "I can not remember when I have wanted to hear from anybody so badly. What makes it worse is the fact that I cannot tell whether or not you are getting the letters that I am writing you. . . . I am afraid to start out telling you how badly I would like to see you for fear that I will induce a mood of melancholy that will get the best of me entirely."[157]

Atop feeling frustrated by the film production, or lack thereof, Miller and the other travelers developed a skin condition, which they blamed on the daily consumption of meat and potatoes, heavy bread, and cold caviar and sturgeon for breakfast. It was "some kind of rash which breaks out all over the body and which the doctors say comes from eating too much protein food," Miller wrote. "However, I have recovered completely both from the sickness and from the rash, by the simple process of buying strawberries, tomatoes and other fresh fruits on the streets."[158] Meanwhile, Robert Robinson, a midwestern African American inventor and toolmaker, who stopped by their hotel weekly to offer assistance and tips on how to navigate the city, invited Hughes to a lavish performance at the Bolshoi Opera House—an accomplishment in itself for Robinson, since tickets were hard to come by.[159] Impressed with Robinson, Miller wrote a laudatory article in the *Izvestia*, the most widely circulated newspaper in Russia. Miller mused, "It is an interesting commentary on the complete absence of color labels and standards that newspapers carrying Robinson's picture and the story of his work do not see fit to mention the fact that he is a Negro. He is referred to simply as an American specialist."[160] Having been branded a "dupe of the Soviets" by *Time*,[161] Robinson knew that he would be unable to return to his job in Detroit. After falling into disfavor, a fate similar to Fort-Whiteman's—though not as drastic—Robinson came to regret becoming a Soviet citizen. He remained in Russia for the next forty years, until 1974, when he was allowed to leave.[162]

What Miller found wearisome was his inability to communicate with Russians. On July 7, he wrote Juanita, "A great deal of unnecessary confusion and mis-understanding occurred because the group was not provided with a competent English interpreter. Repeated requests were made that such a person be provided and many promises were made that this would be done."[163] Even the pleasures of outings to movie theaters were diminished. The familiarity with the language "might have made some difference had I been able to translate."[164] However, the Soviets did provide a language tutor. Miller was joined in the effort to study Russian by Poston, Moon, and Thurston Lewis.[165] Even with tutoring, Miller never acquired a real command of Russian; he continued to find the intricacies of political speech and film dialog difficult to follow. The truth was that he and his companions had grown tired of waiting for something to happen. Though Miller knew that Meschrabpom had to go over the script to see if it conformed to the correct political line, he told Juanita that he foresaw "that it will be some six or eight months before the thing is finished. However the coming of winter makes it more or less necessary that the work be speeded up."[166]

For the moment, the novelty of the Russian scene kept boredom away. When there was nothing else to do because public places closed early, the lively Har-lemites played jokes on the hotel staff.[167] "Their ignorance of English is only matched by our profound lack of Russian," wrote Miller. "So we call them and ask for bacon and eggs, for example. After a parley of a few minutes or hours they disappear. Then you wait and hope. They may return with door knobs or electric irons or anything else but bacon and eggs. Anyhow it is great fun."[168]

Unable to avoid being polite, Miller reluctantly accepted an invitation to attend a gala park celebration in honor of the Russian Constitution. "There will be the usual speeches and music," he told Juanita. "But I don't like music,"[169] which he had confessed to his *Eagle* readers.[170] Still, he wrote, "the spectacle of these crowds and their devotion to the ideals of the new Russia have not yet grown old to me. It is so different to the lethargy with which we greet these things in America that I am still intrigued by it."[171]

Unsurprisingly, romances blossomed in Moscow. "One of the boys," wrote Hughes, "took up with a female truck driver, very buxom, hale, hearty and wholesome. But the others kidded him so about going with a truck driver that he ceased being seen with her near the Grand Hotel."[172] Reminiscing later, Ted Poston said Russian women "flung themselves at him and the other males in the group." He believed that the Soviet authorities used the women as enticements to convert the Americans to Communism.[173] Others in the group thought that Mollie Lewis and Thurston Lewis were sweethearts until Mollie "told people that we were brother and sister since we had the same last name."[174] As for any roman-tic possibilities between Dorothy West and the ever-quiet and reserved Henry

Moon, she turned down his proposal—telling him she was already "going with a handsome man."[175] That was not entirely the truth; she was having a fling with the beautiful, giddy, tempestuous, "bob-haired, peach colored Mildred Jones."[176]

Years later, Poston told Lucile McAlister Scott, the first wife of William A. Scott—the publisher of the *Atlanta Daily World*, the nation's first black daily newspaper—that when men such as the debonair Constantine Aleksandrovich Oumansky, chief of the Press Division of the Foreign Affairs Commissariat (later the Soviet's ambassador to the United States, from 1938 to 1941), showed an interest in Mildred Jones, her response was, "Sorry, I'm looking for the same thing you are."[177]

The Moscow love affairs hit a serious note when Sylvia Garner attempted to take her own life by swallowing potassium formaldehyde. Without mentioning who it was, years later Dorothy West said she had received a friend's call threatening suicide. "Perhaps if we had been hard at work making a film," wrote Hughes, "the near tragedy of the suicide attempt might not have occurred."[178] When the poison burned Garner's stomach, "she screamed, not once but half a dozen times . . . so loud that everybody in the hotel came running to see what the matter was. She was taken to the hospital and saved." According to several writers, Constance White, who Miller wrote was a lesbian, had tossed Sylvia Garner aside for the "Russian woman who served as their translator." It simply was too much for the jilted lover. Once the suicide attempt brought the situation to light, "the secret police (NKVD) confiscated their love letters and quickly exiled the translator and her family to Siberia."[179]

A few days later, Sylvia was back to "rehearsing spirituals with us," wrote Hughes. "But the other girls declared that she, a Negro, had 'disgraced the race,' creating all that excitement in the Grand Hotel."[180] Miller wrote Juanita, "Constance White: Homo-sexual YWCA [Young Women's Christian Association] worker who admires beautiful women and speaks Russian well. Ugly and bulky, she likes to be mistaken for a man and jots down notes to take up time."[181] His letter to Juanita, reflecting the era's homophobia, appears inconsistent with his seemingly neutral impressions of Berlin's gay nightlife; nonetheless, like the others, he was equally embarrassed by the incident.

From the available evidence, Miller avoided frivolous flirtations and sexual escapades while in Europe and Russia; perhaps his impending marriage kept him focused. In the interim, he wrote a running account of his travels, jotting down descriptions of official galas and ordinary street scenes while he waited for word from Juanita. Beyond his cryptic comments on July 17 to Elly that "Los Angeles had not disappeared from the face of the earth despite my own leaving," he replied to her news on the latest efforts of the LAPD to rid the city of Communists: "I have long contended that Los Angeles is in for a bloody massacre unless something is done to relieve the pressure of the Red Squad against radical and liberal meetings. . . . Something should be done to get these people together to protest and curb the police. . . . It seems to me that people like you with left sympathies and others who are not even as sympathetic could find some common ground for protest."[182]

Since 1930, Juanita Ellsworth, a graduate from the University of Southern California's School of Social Work, had been working as a social case worker at Los Angeles's bureau of welfare.[183] Aware that she had a keen interest in Russia's social welfare programs, Loren offered, before leaving Los Angeles, to respond to any questions she might have. Although he regretted his inability to read Russian newspapers, what he conveyed to her reveals a certain naïve enthusiasm about all things Soviet—unsurprising for a young idealist. After visits to several social agencies, he wrote, "Social service is not the same thing that it is in the states. There is, so far as I can gather, no class of professional social service workers such as you know."[184] He noted that a children's nursery he visited was located conveniently next door to a factory: "When the child reaches age of two months it is taken to the day nursery where a staff of trained nurses take it in charge. The women workers get one hour off each three hours to nurse the children as long as that is necessary."[185]

He told Juanita, who wanted to know about Russian prostitution, that he "heard that there are less than 500 prostitutes in the city," a metropolis with a population of three million. "Like you, I can do little but accept that figure."[186] What he did know was that he could walk "for ages in the city without being accosted by one (prostitute)." Unlike his stay in Berlin, "I have never been accosted myself nor do I know of any member of the group who has. That in itself is remarkable."[187] He was told that in the days of the czar "when Jews were forbidden to enter the city of Moscow that many Jewish women asked for and obtained registration slips as prostitutes, since prostitutes of any race were free to live there."[188] Despite being hailed by the press in front-page photographs and stories, the novelty of the visit was wearing thin. With ironic detachment, Miller, now fully aware of Meschrabpom's striking incompetence or what he called the company's tremendous ability to "dilly-dally around,"[189] he wrote, "We have not taken a single scene. We have made no screen tests. We have done nothing. This is July 17 so you can gage our progress."[190] With few new film details to report, Miller let Juanita know that he was receiving the monthly 400 rubles, which was "more than one can spend easily, it must be spent because one can not take it out of the country."[191]

With so much free time on their hands, Thompson and Hughes organized a concert at the Moscow International Library, where, as reported in the *Pittsburgh Courier*, "Langston read his poems. Loren Miller also talked on Negro literature."[192] Other members of the cinema group sang. The resulting screeching startled the audience and made a wreck out of Karl Junghans, the film's director. "The discordant sounds that arose from that first rehearsal in Moscow failed to fool even a European. These Negroes simply could not sing spirituals–or anything else,"[193] wrote Hughes. Sylvia Garner was a shining exception, though she became upset when the others joined in. The evening's "laurels unquestionably" went to the professional singers "Wayland Rudd and Sylvia Garner, who also sang trios with Juanita Lewis and the fearless Louise Thompson,"[194] who marched up and down and singing slogans such as "black and white, unite and fight."[195]

The cast of inexperienced, college-educated city dwellers, who barely knew any of the old Negro spirituals other than "All God's Chillun Got Shoes," was not what the Soviets expected. On the other hand, once the Russians heard Sylvia Garner perform, she became "an American folk-song star on the Moscow radio—except that in doing spirituals they wouldn't let her sing 'God,' 'Lord,' or 'Jesus 'on the air,"[196] wrote Hughes. Sylvia Garner responded, "Them Russians don't understand English and I'm tired of faking. I'm gonna get God into my program." And she did: "Rise and shine, And give Dog the glory! Glory! Rise and shine! Give Dog the glory!"[197]

"We are slated to go to Odessa August 15. . . . Perhaps we will get off by the first of Sept,"[198] wrote Miller to Juanita. Instead, they departed Moscow twelve days ahead of schedule.[199] However, due to illness, Henry Moon and Leonard Hill stayed behind.[200] "As to whether the script would be entirely rewritten, or not," wrote Hughes, "no official would commit himself."[201] Truth be told, no one other than the Meschrabpom executives, director Karl Junghans, Hughes, and possibly the Comintern had seen the screenplay.

The group headed south toward the Black Sea, all the while asking questions about race. Were there any black Russians? Did they have problems? When their train reached Kiev, nearly five hundred miles from Moscow, their handlers located a young black man, possibly a descendent of former Turkish slaves. "I have never seen a more astonished human being, for this Negro in Kiev had probably never seen a black face before other than his own in the mirror,"[202] remarked Hughes. Although they lacked any true understanding of Russian race relations, the travelers were overwhelmed by the many monuments, statues, and streets they encountered named in honor of Alexander Pushkin, the father of Russian literature, a descendant of African and Russian-Slavonic ancestors.[203]

What they did learn more of was the ferociousness of anti-Semitism under the tsarist system. "Jews," wrote Miller, "were barred from government jobs, forced to live in jim-crow districts and refused work in the industrial works."[204] Whenever the tsarist regime perceived a threat, it let "loose a race riot . . . in a manner that would have made the hearts of our southern gentlemanly defenders of white womanhood turn green with envy. . . . (Does any of this sound familiar and Negroid?—I fear so)."[205] Old Russia had its "lynching bees" like America; ethnic minorities were exploited in every possible manner and kept illiterate. Miller passed along what he heard with little skepticism: "Problems once thought as insoluble as America's Negro problem have disappeared in the short space of 15 years."[206]

On August 7, the group arrived in Odessa—"quite a swanky" seaside city with a climate similar to that of Los Angeles, noted Miller.[207] Prior to the revolution, Odessa was a famous resort town. Vestiges of its opulent past remained. Unlike the "mad bedlam" of Moscow, Miller found it engaging, modern, European, with excellent food and a peaceful atmosphere. Once settled into the luxurious seaside Hotel Londres, Miller mentioned that Pushkin once lived a few doors away.[208] "One of his dwelling places," in recognition of the writer's exile from Petersburg (1823–24) for attempting to curb the power of the Tsar, "is kept as a memorial at Odessa."[209] "You probably do not realize how famous Pushkin is in Russia," he told Juanita. "He is the Shakespeare of the nation and whenever a discussion arises about literature, the Russians rush to Pushkin to back their claims for great poets. The fact that he was part Negro is well known also and that is a point of pride with them."[210] Miller reported to the readers of the *Atlanta Daily World*: "One of the many stories current about Pushkin is that of his meeting with Edgar Allen Poe, an American Poet." Unaware that Pushkin was black until meeting him, Poe allegedly "turned his back and refused to shake hands because of his color prejudice."[211] The story is apocryphal. Poe never traveled abroad, let alone to Russia. Miller was clearly off the mark.

As Miller walked to the nearby harbor, he realized that he neglected to fill Juanita in on the latest fracas among his companions who remained divided into left and right factions since their first days aboard the *Europa*. "At heart," he wrote that the opposing coterie

are antagonistic to the Communist movement since they are petty bourgeois and simply hope to utilize the trip for their own benefit. Members of this group are in the majority. They spend their time exploiting the fact that they are colored and hence in demand in Russia were color prejudice is unknown. They are always asking us to make impossible demands on Meschrabpom in the way of food, pay and similar things. To complicate matters the "left" faction is torn by dissention. That faction includes Lang, Mat, Louise and few others including myself. One of the others is a member of the CP [Communist Party] by the name of McKenzie.[212]

Regarded by the others as a Communist sympathizer, Miller wrote, "Truth to tell, I have heard it whispered around that I am an intellectual and 'dicty.' Nothing is better calculated to keep people at arm's length than the reputation of being an intellectual. . . . It is an incipient comedy of the first order." He would be more explicit later as to "the humorous situations developed by taking 22 Negroes to a foreign country."[213]

Throughout his trip, Miller maintained a steady stream of correspondence with his mother. She kept him up to date on his siblings' weddings, new babies, and the family's general welfare. He replied that he would be happy to hear from his brother Halvor and his cousin Wash: "[A]sk Wash to look in the colored papers and see if any of the stuff that I write to them is being printed. Tell him to save all of the clippings that he can find with anything in it and that I want it when I return."[214] He made sure to tell Nora that the Russians "are very much interested in Negroes over here and whatever one wants to write is accepted. I could get a job on the English newspaper if I wanted to do so."[215] Although he mentioned that Langston Hughes's poems would be included in a Russian anthology "of poetry by colored American poets,"[216] he failed to tell her that he would write the preface. That fall, the state publishing house planned to publish those poems, which were intended as a teaching tool for Russian poets on how to write topical poetry.[217]

When the travelers reached Odessa, Ted Poston and Thurston Lewis repeated their skinny-dipping, as they had done in Moscow, with Poston leading "his faction to prance nude on the white sands of Odessa,"[218] according to Faith Berry. All play and no work—as the film kept being postponed—led to embarrassing incidents for Thompson, particularly when earlier Poston and Lewis cavorted "nude among the nude Russians . . . in the Moscow River near the Park of Culture and Rest."[219] Horrified, she wrote to her mother that Lewis's pranks were "disgraceful"[220] and that Poston was a "malicious trouble maker . . . thoroughly irresponsible."[221] In their defense, Moon explained that nude bathing was something blacks knew nothing about. "Our people went in with their shorts on. The Russians asked 'Why they covered up?'"[222] So the "always forthright" Poston "didn't cover anything."[223]

No matter how much they splashed in the Black Sea or enjoyed the warmth of a Mediterranean sun, "One faction," wrote Hughes, "had begun to feel that the Soviets were deliberately giving them the run-around. An indication of the widening split. So why go out of their way to please the Russians anyhow? As to bathing nude in Odessa, why not? . . . The result of this reasoning was that, in spite of the pleas of our group leader," astonished citizens from all over the Soviet Union "would suddenly see streaking down the Odessa sands a dark amazon pursued by two or three of the darkest tallest and most giraffe-like males they had ever seen—all as naked as birds and as frolicsome as Virginia hounds, diving like porpoises into the surf, or playing leapfrog nude all over the place."[224] No matter how common nude swimming might be in the Moscow River, it was not the custom in Odessa. Louise Thompson and Alan McKenzie, the group's nominal leaders, believed that "the boys" did it out of spite. By then, Thompson's influence over the others was at its lowest ebb. By Miller's account, "part of the 'left' splits its strength often enough to permit the 'right' to carry things its own way many times. As for me I am not involved in these factional disputes."[225]

While others frolicked on the beach, Miller worked on his novel, a fictional vehicle to portray the rise and decline of the "Negro petty middle class."[226] He wrote "prefaces for two forthcoming books of Negro poems and work songs . . . brought to Russia by Langston Hughes."[227] Before his overseas journey, Miller had registered with Claude Barnett's Associated Negro Press, which subsequently distributed his articles with the *Atlanta Daily World* and the *Pittsburgh Courier*, among other papers. As he had throughout his travels, he wrote of Hughes's Russian adventures; from time to time he wrote of others in the film group such as Homer Smith, a former Minneapolis postal clerk, who became a consultant to the central post office in Moscow. When the Theatrical Trade Union extended an invitation to cruise the Black Sea aboard the *Abkhazia*, hostilities were tempo-rarily set aside. Although many in the group, according to historian Faith Berry, saw the offer as a diversionary ruse,[228] Miller saw it simply as an opportunity for the travelers to enjoy themselves. He had, by this stage in the journey, developed a love for water travel. He hoped one day that he and Juanita would take a boat trip: "However the state of my finances will probably preclude such a thing for years as I shall be plunged into the midst of dire poverty when I return."[229]

On August 10, the tourists reached Sevastopol and the next day Tuapse, for-merly part of the Ottoman Empire; then the group traveled on to Sukhumi and the Georgian port of Batumi, near Turkey. His postcard to Juanita read "East meets West," which he explained was "the clash of old customs and habits lends an aura of enchantment to what might be a very ordinary sea port."[230] There they strolled alongside dark-skinned Tatars, Khirghiz (Mongols), and blue-eyed, blond-haired Turks in native costume. Miller saw Muslim women wearing the veil, which they "half-shame-facedly draw over half their faces when a stranger appears." He was told that before the revolution, women "were forbidden to remove their veils in the sight of men other than their husbands on the penalty of death."[231]

On his return to Odessa, he read with particular interest Juanita's report that A. Philip Randolph, the president and general organizer of the Brotherhood of Sleeping Car Porters, had visited Los Angeles. Randolph was in Southern Cali-fornia as part of a campaign to renew and encourage loyalty in the West "on the part of the porters to the union."[232] Miller responded to her account: "There are many of us who are prone to accuse Randolph of being a has-been in the radical movement. We construe many of his latter day activities as being altogether lack-ing in class-conscious content. But he is, I know, a relief from most of the fakirs who parade as statesmen and leaders."[233]

On August 15, the very day that shooting on the film was scheduled to begin, Henry Moon dropped a bombshell: "Comrades, we've been screwed!"[234] In the *Paris Herald-Tribune*, the headline read, "Soviet Calls Off Film On U.S. Negroes: Fear of American Reaction Cause."[235] "The story had been given to the news-papers," as Hughes put it, "before any of the cast learned about it."[236] Though reported by Eugene Lyons of the United Press, the story ran without his byline. What began so optimistically now started disintegrating into acrimony, accusa-tions, and ideological hysterics. According to Hughes, all "hell broke loose."[237] Some believed that they were pawns in some international scheme. Others cried that their budding film careers were over before beginning. Everyone had an opinion. For several months afterward, black newspapers would carry long accounts of the controversy.

Boris Babitsky, a Meschrabpom official, arrived the next day to assure them, according to Arnold Rampersad, "that, no, the film was not cancelled, only post-poned, and only because of the quality of the script."[238] He told them "that the film is artistically too weak as the scenario now stands and that it must be thoroughly revised, a work that it is said will take several months."[239] There was nothing else for them to do but to return to Moscow.

On August 20, when the travelers returned to Moscow, they found it overrun with American and British tourists. Unable to secure their old rooms at the luxurious Grand Hotel, Meschrabpom placed them in a small, third-rate hostel, the Minskyaya, which Homer Smith called a "flophouse."[240] For Hughes, he preferred its location "between the Moscow River and Lenin's Tomb, and right across the street from the big gate through which the sleek cars of Voroshilov and Stalin sped past the Kremlin walls." He found it more fascinating and more "an integral part of Russia" than the Grand Hotel.[241]

Naturally, the film's apparent cancellation disappointed all the Americans, who mostly now were united under the leadership of the "L-Raisers"—Miller, Hughes, and Thompson—plus Alan McKenzie, the only confirmed Communist among them.[242] For those who did not believe that it was merely postponed "on account of scenario difficulties,"[243] a major uproar rose within the opposing faction: Ted Poston, Henry Lee Moon, Laurence Alberga, and Thurston Lewis. Matt Crawford laughingly dubbed them the "Black White Guard," who denounced Meschrabpom for betraying "Negro workers of America and the International Proletariat."[244] They accused "Stalin himself for selling out the black race."[245] In a clear break from the others, they declared: "WE BELIEVE that the production of the film, 'Black and White' has been cancelled primarily because of political reasons."[246] Heated tense debates continued "all day and every day for over a week . . . about the reasons for the cancellation of the film,"[247] noted Thompson. Speculation ran wild: some members "are said to be unfitted for the picture"; other black Soviets are "not now available"; or the film company lacked the "technical facilities."[248]

Poston's faction charged that government complicity led to the film's demise, while the majority, the "L-Raisers," accepted the official nonpolitical explanation. Ultimately, they became Soviet apologists. Poston called Hughes an opportunistic son of a bitch and a "Communist Uncle Tom."[249] Along with Henry Moon and Leonard Hill, Poston *rightly* alleged that Colonel Hugh Cooper, the American builder of the immense Dnieprostroi Dam, and Ivy Lee, a public-relations man who represented Rockefeller business interests, used their influence with Stalin to stop the film "because it might retard American recognition of the Soviet government."[250]

The group's fury continued. With marked earnestness, Miller prepared a formal statement that read in part: "We, the (fifteen) undersigned members of the Negro group," deny "all slanderous charges and rumors concerning the postponement of the film."[251] In effect, the leading faction denounced Poston and the other dissenters as counterrevolutionaries, enemies of the state, and opportunistic propagandists. The formal statement ended with a deeply apologetic tone, extending regret for "malicious and unfounded attacks" made upon their

Russian hosts. The opposing group remained adamant. Dissatisfied with the abandonment of the film, they "appealed . . . to Stalin repeating their charges against Meschrabpom."[252] They had been had. Later, Thompson wrote how ironic and unfortunate it was that the dissenting minority, which had enjoyed complete racial equality for the first time in Russia, "should walk into the trap of becoming the weapon against the Soviet Union of those capitalist forces that oppress them in America."[253]

On August 22, a delegation representing both factions stood before "several old Bolsheviks sitting at a long table in a gloomy room."[254] Miller led the discussion while Hughes demanded "the immediate production, distribution and exhibition of the film."[255] Otherwise, they predicted that counterrevolutionaries would use the film's abandonment as propaganda to "confuse Negroes" and turn them against Communism and smear the Soviet Union's reputation.[256] Though the Comintern agreed to censure Meschrabpom for "gross administrative inefficiency," the Americans' plea to immediately resume film production was put off until spring as winter was approaching.[257] The film was done. Subsequently, the majority in the group accepted the official position that the cause of the postponement was the script and technical difficulties.

In measured tones, Miller expressed his disappointment to Juanita: "It would be un-social if I were to say what were my feelings when I learned that the picture could not be made this year. You have not spoken your own thoughts on that subject but I think that I can guess just what you felt. At any rate, the journey is over."[258] Gladdened by the prospect of returning to his fiancée, but dissatisfied with the film's outcome, he appreciated having had a firsthand view of revolutionary Russia.

By then, the folks back home had either seen the headlines—"Negroes Adrift in 'Uncle Tom's' Russian Cabin"—or read articles about how the Americans were stuck penniless in the USSR.[259] Miller consoled his mother and countered the newspaper reports of abandonment: "We are no such thing. . . . We have plenty of everything to eat and a good place to stay. . . . Those who say that we are stranded do so merely because they hope that we are and not because they think that we are."[260] On September 22, reporting for the *Atlanta Daily World*, Miller wrote, "Nothing could be further from the truth than these rumors, obviously inspired by hostile newspaper men."[261] He chastised Floyd Calvin's *Pittsburgh Courier* article as "a strange concoction of lies, half-truths and abysmal ignorance. . . . The picture has NOT been cancelled. . . . The group is NOT stranded."[262] He closed by adding, "I am not a member of the Communist party and have no desire to debate political questions with you, but I do want you to know that members of this group strongly resent your falsification of the facts. Will you be fair enough to retract?" Despite his public display of bravado, Miller imagined that back in Los Angeles some were rejoicing "that something untoward has happened to me with the hope that it will reduce what must seem to them an insufferable ego."[263]

Though the black press in the northern U.S. continued to carry conflicting stories about the reasons behind the film's cancellation, members of the white press mainly ignored the issue. When they did write about it, their coverage was slanted. The Crusader News Agency, the *Atlanta Daily World*, and the *New Masses* scoffed at the suggestion that politics had put an end to the film. That November, the New York branch of the Workers Film and Photo League, a branch of Meschrabpom, published a press release in the *New Masses* that questioned the credibility of Ted Poston and Henry Moon.[264] What evidence, it asked, did the two *New York Amsterdam News* reporters have to declare that Colonel Hugh Cooper had returned "to Moscow for a conference with Stalin"?[265]

In truth, that is exactly what Cooper had done. Poston and Moon were correct in stating that Cooper had the support of Rockefeller counselor Ivy Lee. Though Stalin was absent, Cooper met with Vyacheslav Molotov, chair of the Council of People's Commissars, who promptly shut down the film production. That such high-powered players determined the fate of this seemingly small film suggests how important this Afro-centric project—and race relations in America—was to global politics of the time. From widely different vantage points, the Meschrabpom Film Company, American black progressives, and leading U.S. industrialists all recognized the movie's potential power. "One would have been naïve indeed to expect Stalin to risk his promising chances of obtaining diplomatic recognition from Washington for the short-range propaganda success of mounting a film exposing America's racial problem,"[266] wrote Homer Smith, whose views "moved from outright enthusiasm to pessimism to a kind of ambivalence over his fourteen-year tenure in the country."[267]

Soviet historian Woodford McClellan, citing archival evidence released by the Russian Federation after the disintegration of the Soviet Union, writes that the Comintern chief Manuilsky knew that Cooper "threatened to delay completion [of the Dnieprostroi Dam] if plans for 'Black and White' went forward."[268] The dam was a major investment for the Soviets, who spent $420,000,000 building it, and for Cooper, who drafted the original plans.[269] A key component and symbol of Soviet modernization, the dam would contain the world's largest hydroelectric power plant, with a generating capacity of 800,000 horsepower, until surpassed in 1936 by the construction of the Hoover Dam on the Colorado River.[270]

Apparently confident in his strategic position and his contacts with Stalin and Molotov, Cooper was not about to let a potential flap over a small film about African Americans interfere with his company's ability to continue to make enormous profits on future engineering projects.[271] As early as 1926, he had spoken publicly in favor of reopening diplomatic relations between the Soviets and the Americans. He felt that once the Americans got over their antagonism toward Russia, the pendulum would swing back to open trade relations.[272] Even after he met with Molotov, Cooper remained agitated over the kindly treatment the African American group was receiving from the Russians. On his way back to New York,

Cooper stopped by the American consulate in Berlin. There, on August 29, he spoke with Raymond H. Geist, longtime Berlin consul, and told him that the Russians, who were considering another enormous engineering project, had sought his advice. The next day, the American consul general, George S. Messersmith, cabled the U.S. secretary of state in Washington, D.C., informing him that Molotov had met with Cooper and had listened to his objections to the making of *Black and White*. An immediate investigation took place that "resulted in the scheme being entirely forbidden."[273] According to historian Glenda Gilmore, as revealed in Stalin's private papers, "Colonel Cooper did indeed meet with Molotov."[274]

The chaos over the film's ending evoked a sense of melancholy in Hughes. Though he regretted the project's cancellation, he agreed that, since the script was "so mistakenly conceived,"[275] ending the production was a wise decision. Frank Montero declared many years later that as far as he knew, the film "was never made because it was such a goddamn lousy movie."[276] Although the whole affair was over and done with, the bickering continued. After Meschrabpom refunded the group's passage to the Soviet Union, a heated argument broke out between Sylvia Garner and Thurston Lewis, "whose ticket to Russia," according to Rampersad, "ironically had been subsidized . . . by Hughes and Sylvia Garner." The situation grew particularly nasty when Lewis "almost slipped away with their refund." The dispute ended when "Garner whipped out a knife on the stunned Soviet paymaster, who at once saw the wisdom of her position."[277] In the aftermath, Poston and the rest of the dissenting faction spurned the Soviet Trade Union's invitation to tour, deeming it an attempt to pacify the group.[278] The majority of the American crew, exhilarated by the invitation, celebrated triumphantly in Thompson's room.

Setting out in eager haste to explore Uzbekistan, Turkmenistan, the Caucasus, Armenia, and beyond, the group, now whittled down to twelve members, left Moscow.[279] Before they caught the five-day Moscow-Tashkent express train, Hughes sent Miller's fiancée a postcard: "Russia is too tight. We're off for Middle Asia today. Loren says he'll have you on his mind even in Samarkan!"[280] Homer Smith, Wayland Rudd, Sylvia Garner, and Lloyd Patterson chose to remain in Moscow, determined to continue their Russian employment.[281]

Homer Smith, using the pseudonym Chatsworth Hall for the *Chicago Defender*, reported that on September 17, the first to head back to the United States were Frank Montero, Henry Moon, Leonard Hill, Ted Poston, and Thurston Lewis.[282] Poston and Moon lingered a bit longer in Berlin, where they met with a German director, who "expressed belief that the picture could be made for $50,000"[283] in the United States. On October 3, the two left Boulogne-sur-Mer, France, aboard the SS *Saint Louis* for New York.[284]

Meanwhile, Miller's faction, before heading for Uzbekistan, loaded up on "cheeses, sausages, teapots and enormous loaves of black bread."[285] According to Miller's account, they passed the endless expanse of the Aral Sea: "Thus far, we have plunged far across the Kazakhstan steppes, passed the tip of the Aral Sea and are still going south to the border of Afghanistan. Riding in a fine train and with excellent care, it has been an interesting journey for us." He recounted, "One of the porters on the train came to us with the news that the train crew desired a meeting with us to discuss the international situation. Can you imagine that? Mere porters, brakemen and conductors wanting to discuss the international situation?"[286]

On September 27, the tourists reached the capital of Uzbekistan, Tashkent, where, according to Hughes, they saw "exotically clothed Uzbek, Turkomens and Tartars" and smelled "a kind of mixture of musk, melons and dust that seemed everywhere a part of the East."[287] There they met a group of African American agronomists from Tuskegee, who were "helping to modernize the Soviet cotton industry."[288] The "Negro specialists" from Alabama, wrote Miller, "are experimenting with crossing Native and American cotton and in trying to adapt Egyptian cotton" to Uzbek's "short (planting) season here." That experiment "rest[s] primarily in the hands of three men: Oliver Golden, John Sutton and James Sloane."[289]

The travelers left Tashkent for Samarkand. From there they traveled to Bokhara, by then travel weary.[290] Although Louise Thompson, in a good mood, enjoyed smoking her Russian cigarettes, Mildred Jones and some of the others could barely endure one more "triple translated" speech.[291] Though Miller continued to marvel at the modern-day nurseries and the state farms, what truly disturbed him, after four months of travel, was how Thompson and the other women "have no conception of being involved in an equal experiment with men and make demands simply based on sex," he wrote Juanita. "They cannot eat this, they do not like this dirt, this place is impossible and similar things flow from them. Such mannerisms suit them well enough in countries where one may find middle class comforts but they are irritating and galling where there is not much to be had at the best. Perhaps you understand the situation. Since I am not gifted with patience, I find it very difficult."[292]

Not just the women, however, had had enough of dirty bazaars, blazing sun, and Soviet lectures, which made "even the radicals drowsy."[293] Hughes, too, had enough of touring medical schools and visiting universities, "of dust and sun, statistics and speeches."[294] His plan was to leave the group when they reached Ashkhabad, but "exhausted and running behind schedule,"[295] the others voted not to stop. Angered, Hughes jumped "off the train without handshakes or farewells."[296] He would remain in Russia, travel from Moscow to the Soviet Far East, to Japan, and to China before journeying back to the States in 1933.[297] As for the two friends, Miller and Hughes, the cross-country road trip and months together in Russia solidified a friendship that continued for the remainder of their lives. With Langston Hughes gone, Miller and the others set out by car over the Georgian Military Highway to Tiflis (now Tbilisi), Georgia, famous for its bubbling hot sulfur springs. There he profiled a young Russian of African descent named Bashir Shambi, who had been purchased in Persia, sixteen years earlier, by two officers of the old Russian tsarist army and brought to Georgia. Writing for the *Atlanta Daily World*, Miller reported that, since the revolution, Shambi had become "one of the police chiefs"[298] of Tiflis. Next, the group members headed for the Dnieprostroi Dam, which had apparently doomed their film project. Miller, who felt the dam itself worthy of a great novel, compared the different influences of socialism and capitalism on the Dnieprostroi Dam and the Boulder Dam—which, along with Langston Hughes and the Oregon poet Norman Macleod, he had visited that spring.[299]

On the last lap of Miller's seven-thousand-mile "momentous trip," unrestrained, he wrote Juanita, "I learned much not the least of which are the facts that I was, and am, woefully ignorant of both history and geography." What he was not ignorant of was how weary he had become of the incessant harping and grumbling of his companions. He had had about as much as he could stand: "I am ashamed to sit down to the table with them because I know that their demands must begin at once."[300] In an effort either to amuse Juanita or to pass the time, he described the personal piques of his fellow travelers and the general souring of relationships of people cooped up together for too long. "Perhaps a few one-sentence characterizations of the members of the group will let you see what difficulties we bear," he wrote. Was he going out on a limb—jeopardizing his coming marriage—by revealing how critically harsh he could be? Would he, once married, turn that searing gaze in his wife's direction one day?

He described Alan McKenzie, the lone Communist among them, as having "only a cursory and scattered knowledge of Marxism and Leninism. His enthusiasm supplies the deficiency in . . . his lack of political knowledge."[301] Louise Thompson, who continued for the remainder of her life as an important player in American Communist circles, he characterized as someone who "thinks the world owes her as much spoiling as her mother gave as an only child."[302] Of the youthful Dorothy West, he wrote lightheartedly, "One of New York's new Negroes who is painfully scatterbrained, she "regrets that Russia has changed because the new order cannot produce any Dostoevskys."[303] His remarks precede what West wrote later, that at fourteen she discovered Dostoevsky and other Russian writers who for her became "gods of good writing."[304] In 1934, when West founded the short-lived literary journal *Challenge*, she wrote affectionately of Russia as her "lost youth and all things lovely."[305] When the *Challenge* reemerged in 1937 as the *New Challenge*, Miller helped it stay afloat (though briefly) by reaching out to young writers willing to contribute to her magazine.[306]

Sparing not even himself, Miller wrote a brief, facetious self-appraisal: "Loren Miller: Aloof and cold, his intellect breeds fear in his fellows rather than any genuine liking. Too precocious during the age of Menckenian cynicism, he has difficulty shedding that attitude for enthusiasm for socialism (a thing which he feels)."[307] Perhaps what prodded such acidity was the reaction he had received from writing a scathing article earlier on black professionals and how they exploit the black worker: "My article has got me in bad with certain friends. I have learned that I am: dumb, an upstart, ignorant, a Red, a reactionary, a smart aleck and other things, too harsh to mention."[308]

Nonetheless, he reserved his harshest assessment for Mollie Lewis, whom he considered, the "modern interpretation of a gold digger: one of the few women in the world who has been able to trade her slight interest in Socialism for concrete returns."[309] In 1938, Mollie and Henry Moon flabbergasted everyone by getting married; he had once thought her too wild to associate with the less worldly Dorothy West. Still, Miller, more tolerant once he was back home and happily married, stayed on good terms with Henry and Mollie.[310] In the fall of 1934, the two men traveled to North Carolina as delegates to the first southern interracial conference, held at Shaw University in Raleigh.

Over the years, as Miller made frequent trips to New York, he and Henry Moon socialized, more so after Moon became director of public relations for the NAACP. Most letters between them were polite and courteous, a simple thank you to their New York hosts followed by an offer of the same. "If you come to Los Angeles, we will be happy to entertain you with a fried chicken dinner,"[311] wrote Miller. Decades later, Moon told Ted Poston's biographer, Kathleen Hauke, "A few years after we returned [from Russia], Loren Miller said he had made an error in taking so strong a position on the side of the Communists."[312]

Interestingly, when Henry's first cousin, novelist Chester Himes, moved to Los Angeles during the war, he and Miller became friends.[313] Who is to know if Miller resisted a chuckle or two when Himes, in *Pinktoes*, depicted Mollie Moon (fictionalized as Mamie Mason) as a pretentious "social celebrity in Negro circles."[314] In Himes's harsh novel, "Really, all Mamie Mason ever wanted was just to be 'Hostess with the Mostess.' . . . just to serve the Negro Problem up to white people and be loved by white people for this service."[315]

In Miller's pithy commentary on his Russian travel companions, he reserved his kindest words for his pals, Hughes and Crawford. Matt Crawford, he wrote, was the "most genuine of us" and never complained. "One of the finest chaps on the trip has been Matt. . . . He has intelligence and discernment as well as personal generosity and engaging mannerisms."[316] Their friendship survived the trip, and by 1934 all three men were serving together on the national council of the League of Struggle for Negro Rights, for which "Hughes willingly became a figurehead for the general secretary, Harry Haywood, a communist."[317] In Miller's dispatch to Juanita, he described Hughes as sincere and sensitive, shrewd and resourceful. He further mused that Hughes belonged to the future as one of the great artists of his time.

In fundamental ways, the trip proved as beneficial to Miller's personal life as it did to him professionally. He accomplished some measure of success as a writer by publishing a great many articles, thus influencing a wider audience of black readers than ever before. At twenty-nine, this former farm boy from Kansas crossed the Atlantic Ocean, traveled the Baltic and the Black Seas, witnessed life in much-celebrated Mother Russia, and visited the building of the world's largest dam, the Dnieprostroi. He thrived abroad. His friendship with Langston Hughes deepened as did his devotion to his future wife through their exchange of letters. His travel experiences smoothed the uneven edges shaped by a rough childhood. Mostly, Miller simply felt better than ever before and understood that traversing foreign lands and cultures had given him a new sense of self, steadfastness, and commitment.

Nothing he had ever done before this trip had brought him such pleasure. "It has been a grand vacation for me,"[318] he wrote his mother. "It seems almost like a dream." It was the first time he had escaped "the burden of color as it exists in the United States. No Negro in the United States knows what it really means to really be free until he has left that country. Certainly, I do not think that I shall ever feel satisfied with it again." In his naïve enthusiasm, he told her "there is no such thing in Russia as color prejudice and one may do whatever one has the ability to do. The contrast to America is so great that I feel that I have never been 'free' except in the few short weeks that I have spent in the Soviet Union."[319] He felt like Paul Robeson did on entering Moscow a few years later: "Here I am not a Negro but a human being for the first time in my life."[320] In heading for home, he wrote Juanita that "two events mark milestones in my learning: my going to college and my making this trip. Both of these things must be division points to direct me in new channels."[321]

Loren Miller. Reproduced by permission of
The Huntington Library, San Marino, California.

Edward and Juanita Miller descend church stairs after Loren Miller's funeral.
Reproduced by permission of The Huntington Library, San Marino, California.

John Miller, father of Loren Miller. Courtesy of
Edward Miller and Halvor Thomas Miller, Jr.

The Miller siblings: (*back row, left to right*) Loren, Cloyd, Cecil; (*front row, left to right*) Halvor, Helen, Ruby. Courtesy of Edward Miller and Halvor Thomas Miller, Jr.

Martha Gee Hubbard, Loren Miller's grandaunt, a former slave.
Courtesy of Edward Miller and Halvor Thomas Miller, Jr.

Frederick Douglass, ca. 1850–1860. Courtesy of the Library of
Congress Prints and Photographs Division, LC-USZ62-15887.

Holbrook Law Building, Washburn College, 1922–1939.
Courtesy of Washburn University School of Law, Topeka Kansas.

Jane Miller Kerina, Loren Miller's niece, and Leon Washington,
Loren Miller's cousin and publisher of the *Los Angeles Sentinel*. Reproduced
by permission of The Huntington Library, San Marino, California.

Group heading for Moscow aboard the *Europa* (June 17, 1932): (*front row, left to right*)
Mildred Jones, Louise Thompson, Constance White, Katherine Jenkins,
Sylvia Garner, Dorothy West, and Mollie Lewis. (*Middle row, left to right*)
Wayland Rudd, Frank Montero, Matt Crawford, George Sample, Laurence Alberga,
Langston Hughes, Juanita Lewis, and Alan McKenzie. (*Back row, left to right*)
Ted Poston, Henry Lee Moon, Thurston Lewis, Lloyd Patterson, and Loren Miller.
Reproduced by permission of The Huntington Library, San Marino, California.

Film group touring Central Asia: (*back row, left to right*) Loren Miller,
Matt Crawford, Langston Hughes. Reproduced by permission
of The Huntington Library, San Marino, California.

Loren Miller, ca. 1933. Reproduced by permission of
The Huntington Library, San Marino, California.

Juanita Ellsworth Miller, ca. 1933. Reproduced by permission
of The Huntington Library, San Marino, California.

Ruby Terry, Juanita Miller, and Loren Miller. Reproduced by permission of The Huntington Library, San Marino, California.

Lena Horne, singer and actress, and Juanita Miller. Reproduced by
permission of The Huntington Library, San Marino, California.

Supreme Court justice Thurgood Marshall. Courtesy of the Library of Congress Prints and Photographs Division, LC-USZ62-60139.

Loren Miller, holding a copy of the *California Eagle*, 1951. Reproduced by permission of The Huntington Library, San Marino, California.

Nobel Peace Prize winner Ralph J. Bunche and Juanita Miller, ca. 1950s.
Courtesy of Edward Miller and Halvor Thomas Miller, Jr. Reproduced
by permission of The Huntington Library, San Marino, California.

Halvor Miller, Sr., Helen Miller Addison, Nora Herbaugh Miller, Roland Miller, and Loren Miller. Reproduced by permission of The Huntington Library, San Marino, California.

Join The
COMMITTEE
TO DRAFT
Loren Miller
FOR CONGRESS

1. IN 1962, CALIFORNIANS ARE GOING TO ELECT THEIR FIRST NEGRO CONGRESSMAN. WE NEED YOUR HELP NOW TO SHAPE THIS HISTORIC MOMENT TO OUR NEEDS

2. WE MUST CHOOSE THE MOST ABLE MAN IN OUR COMMUNITY TO BE OUR FIRST REPRESENTATIVE IN THE U. S. CONGRESS FOR ACTUALLY THIS MAN WILL BE THE VOICE OF 1 MILLION CALIFORNIA NEGROES.

3. THAT MAN IS ATTORNEY LOREN MILLER – MR. CIVIL RIGHTS IN CALIFORNIA,

"Mr. Civil Rights"

Loren Miller

1962 congressional election campaign flier from
Miller's FBI file, U.S. Department of Justice.

Edward Miller, Loren Miller, and Loren Miller, Jr.,
Los Angeles Municipal Court, August 21, 1964. Reproduced by
permission of The Huntington Library, San Marino, California.

Loren Miller, Jr., and Halvor Miller, Jr., Los Angeles Superior Court, 1977.
Reproduced by permission of The Huntington Library, San Marino, California.

Returning to America

Miller wrote Hughes in fall 1932, "The Yard Apes, got back to New York and are raising hell as you will see from the papers I sent you if you ever get them. They sent out a story from Berlin saying that the Soviets had betrayed us for big money."[1] Most likely Miller eventually accepted the reality that Russia canceled the film because it wanted official recognition from the Unites States. When that reality set in is unclear. From Moscow, he boasted to Langston Hughes that he shared a "swell" two-room apartment with Matt Crawford and Alan McKenzie where a neighbor woman "cooks our breakfast and you should see us eating ham and eggs and kasha and everything else dictated by our jaded appetites." He added that he had signed a contract to write a pamphlet for the "International Publishers and the Cooperative Publishers. But the damned thing will not get going and it may be that I will not write until I get to America. Either through laziness or through something-or-the-other I can't make the pamphlet click."[2]

That "something-or-the-other" that kept Miller from working on the pamphlet was perhaps a touch of wedding nerves over his pending marriage to Elly. "I am inclined to the opinion," once married, "that the best thing to do is to rent one of these god-[undecipherable] furnished apartments. They look like hell, cost little and call for no external campaign whereas the project of unfurnished and buy-on-the-installment-so-you-can-furnish-it places look like hell, cost more and call for a long period of time of figuring and re-figuring."[3]

Before Miller left Moscow on November 9, he stayed long enough to witness parading soldiers, sailors, workers, and peasants celebrating the fifteenth anniversary of the Bolshevik Revolution.[4] When he reached Berlin, he wrote his mother to say that he was sorry to hear of his brother Cloyd's serious illness, whom he had written a few days earlier: "One never leaves home without something very untoward happening. . . . Also sorry to hear of Aunt Flora's husband's death."[5] He assumed that his mother could borrow the train fare to attend the funeral from Mrs. Bass at the *California Eagle*. But, as he assured his mother not to worry since he had plenty of money, the matter of the ticket would require her "personal attention." When he returned, he would "be able to help again. . . . Also you will have a coat. I would like to buy you one here but I doubt that I could get out of Europe with it. . . . At any rate I will see that you get the kind of a coat that you want when I get to America."[6] He thanked Juanita, who offered earlier to help finance his return trip, "but as it happens [because of the ticket refund from Meschrabpom] I shall not need any money at least until I get as far as San Bernardino, I think."[7]

During his return visit to Germany, Miller interviewed George Padmore, the "tall, dark, well groomed and well informed" West Indian radical and intellectual, at the time the editor of Hamburg-based the *Negro Worker*, an organ of the International Trade Union of Negro Workers. Typically, Padmore spoke on the international solidarity of all workers, white or black, and of the oppressions suffered by Africans "under English rule surpass[ing] those of the American southern states."[8] More newsworthy at the time was Padmore's bitter opposition to reducing "Liberia to a vassal of the League of Nations or to put it under an American dictator." Two years later, by then expelled by the Communist Party, he raised the party's ire when he questioned why it "never conducted a campaign in defense of Liberia's independence."[9]

Before Miller left Paris on 22 November, he dashed off a postcard to his flamboyant cousin Leon Washington: "The prodigal son sails tomorrow from Cherbourg. See you and Hoover lost at the polls."[10] When he reached New York six days later, adamant not to remain on the East Coast too long, he sent his future mother-in-law, Mrs. Francis Ellsworth, a postcard: "You can always tell country people. They send cards from every stopping point."[11] By then, Miller recalled Hughes's earlier advice and encouragement before he left the United States to "gather up your novel" and to not "stop work just because you're going to Russia."[12] Restless, he wrote Hughes: "Only a week or so and then to Los Angeles and to my novel. The damned thing is just about all in my mind and if the words look as good as the idea (which they won't) I will like it despite the fact that I will probably be the only one in the world who will."[13]

Wryly self-deprecating like many writers, Miller struggled with self-doubt about his writing ability. "I have no very grandiose plans," he told Juanita, "for myself except that I plan to work on my forthcoming novel and that seriously. I have my private doubts that I shall write a successful one right off the bat but I want to finish one draft of it this winter. With the spring I hope to be able to re-write it and then do whatever one does with such things." He asked if she would aid him "in picking out, and writing, what are the most typical and at the same time the most human incidents." However, he needed more, "much more to make it really go. Your pay? ****????"[14] which Juanita supplied until he returned to the practice of law.

Within weeks of Miller's return, Norman Macleod, then editor of *Contact* (a short-lived proletarian literary quarterly in New York), asked him whether he had any "unpublished revolutionary poetry or prose"[15] from his Russian experience. First, Miller apologized for the long delay in answering, then added,

> The reasons are the same ones that prevented me seeing you when I was in New York: the radicals. You can imagine that I have been in their hands ever since my return from the Soviet Union. However, I am taking a sort of leave of absence in

order to catch up on my work and hope to write a number of things that I have
promised. Having nothing on hand at the present moment but if I do something
that I think suitable I will submit it to you.[16]

He closed by saying that he had seen Macleod's Boulder Dam poem in the *New Masses* and noted, "Lang and I had the best intentions of writing something when we went to Moscow but time simply slipped by us."[17]

What did not slip away in Russia from Hughes was "Cora Unashamed," a story he published in 1934 recounting the tragic story told to him by Miller of a grief-stricken black servant who finds the courage to speak "her piece concerning love and morals at the funeral"[18] of a white girl who had been forced to have an abortion. Later, in the shadow of the Cold War, Hughes published his second memoir, *I Wonder as I Wander*, in 1956, which literary critic J. Saunders Redding called "Hughes lite." Although the book included an account of the trip to Russia, Hughes assured Miller that for obvious reasons, "Nobody's named" in the account "due to the aura of the era"[19] of the 1950s. However, that was not entirely true.[20] Hughes credits Miller by name as the person who gave him the material for "Cora Unashamed," his first short story since 1927. "None of the situations in my story were as in the real one, but its inspiration came from Loren Miller's tale."[21] As much as Hughes might have wished to protect those who traveled to Russia with him, on December 1, 1953, all the names of the *Black and White* film group came out during the testimony of former communist African American Louis Rosser, in which he named names before the House Un-American Activities Committee investigation of Communist activities in California.[22]

Sweet though it was for Miller to be home again among friends and family, he was elated by a bit of minor celebrity, particularly when he was "feted by newspaper men of Southern California with a cabaret party at the Club Alabam"[23] on Central Avenue, which was attended by Lawrence La Mar, Harry Levette, Cullen Fentress, Max Williams, and Miller's cousin Leon Washington.[24] For Miller, 1932 ended well. However, bittersweet tones lay ahead.

NEWLY WEDS WILL THROW BIG BRAWL
Brazenly admitting that his stock in trade of groceries consisted of one can of
tomatoes, three half spoiled turnips and a half loaf of last week's bread, Loren Miller,
today wheedled his bride of a month into aiding him entertain newspaper friends
at a party which will pay off his own obligations and which he is advertising as a
party.[25]

In the *Ellsworth-Miller Weakly Blather*, a humorous broadsheet meant for friends, Miller merrily added, "MILLER BAMBOOZLES BRIDE INTO ENTERTAINING TO PAY OFF OWN DEBTS. . . . 'I do not know what the guest will eat,' sobbingly admitted Miller, long suspected of being a Red, 'but that will be no novelty for them,' . . . and, the first hoodlum who masquerades as a journalist at the party scheduled for nine o'clock March 29 who throws [cigarette] ashes on the floor will be summarily ejected by the threat of Juanita Ellsworth, bread winner for the household at 207 East 45th street." Jokingly, he warned reporter friends Max Williams and J. Cullen Fentress that Juanita would not take it kindly if they "squirt tobacco juice at the nearest receptacle."

How long Loren Miller and Juanita Ellsworth courted is unclear. During the time Miller was in Russia and later in New York, no mention of it is found. However, as early as March 1930, the *Chicago Defender* reported that the two attended a dance party hosted by the Upsilon chapter of Kappa Alpha Psi, Miller's fraternity.[26] Like many light-skinned African Americans, the couple fell into the color hierarchy of marrying within their color complexion, hair texture, and aquiline facial range. As for Juanita, many said that with her full face and sleek, soft brown hair she was more beautiful than Kathryn Dickerson, the wife of the Chicago attorney Earl Dickerson and an acknowledged beauty (as well as the first woman honored with the Man of the Year Award by the Chicago Urban League).[27]

Throughout their thirty-four-year marriage, the Millers appear equally resolute in candor and affection in their love for one another. Her reserve, grace, "poise and intelligence"[28] balanced his wit, a certain ebullience, and down-to-earthiness. Still, they were a bookish couple, with Juanita a bit more educated in having attained both a bachelor's degree in social work at the University of Southern California in 1927 and a teacher's credential at the University of California, Los Angeles, the following year.[29] Together, they championed housing issues, she more officially as the relocation supervisor for the Los Angeles City Housing Authority from 1942 to 1944.[30]

Juanita married well, knowing that a man who treated his mother right would treat his wife right. On Friday, March 17, 1933, just before midnight, according to accounts reported by the *Chicago Defender*, "a huge heart, which decorated one side of the [Elks banquet] wall was opened and showed an announcement of the marriage of Miss Juanita Ellsworth and Loren Miller on Tuesday, Feb. 21."[31] Among prominent educator Mrs. Cornelia Bradford's many guests were Dorothy Johnson and Irma Hopkins, Juanita's Delta Sigma Theta sorority sisters, the newlyweds' brothers Halvor Miller and Milton V. Ellsworth, and Jimmy Garrott, Lloyd Griffith, and Thomas Griffith. Earlier, at the home of Mrs. Ursula Pruitt Adams, a member of the Los Angeles Civic League, the couple, who lived at 207 E. 45th Street, directly across the street from Juanita's parents, Mr. and Mrs. Edward T. Ellsworth, were presented with a wedding gift.[32]

After Miller married, he received a letter from Langston Hughes, who was still in Moscow:

Dear Loren,

I'll keep all my news till next time. Yours is the best. . . . You lucky guy—marrying a grand girl like Juanita. (I sent you-all a cable last night). I'm glad as hell about it. And I'm sure you two will be happy together. I think she's a swell person—as I've told you before—and this is one time that fate (or whatever you'd call it in your Marxian vocabulary) has been kind to you, even if you have got a lot of kicks coming on other scores. . . . Jesus, I'm glad. . . . Getting married to someone you love ought to be a much better thing than writing novels or seeing the world or making revolutions as you'll now admit. . . . You're a damned lucky guy. And I'm glad you can't yowl about life this time. . . . Tell Juanita I like lemon pie with lots of meringue—if you ever invite me to dinner.[33]

Overshadowing the couple's new happiness was the March 10 death of Cloyd, Miller's older brother. Although Cloyd had been ill for six months, his death from a pulmonary disease—the exact diagnosis unknown/unrecorded—shattered Nora. First, Ruby in 1929, and now, less than four years later, her oldest child lay dead at thirty-one. On his brother's death, Miller wrote:

To My Brother Dying in a Hospital
While Death sits there at your side
Plucking with eager fingers at your bed
To feed the crimson pool by your bed
I will frequent my usual haunts . . .
But my mind is not there with you nor yet here
on these familiar things.
It has fled back eagerly to recall those
Hours your numbed brain has forever forgot:
When the first bird called the spring . . .
Or the smell of the sweat of horses
When we raced to unharness them at noon time; . . .

These things are interwoven in my memory
Like a crimson thread—they are woven
Into the very pattern of the poverty
By which our lives were cut . . .

For I shall grieve secretly a while
And suffer the white hot touch of sorrow in my heart,
Then I shall remember again.
And your memory will be the strong scent of courage in my nostrils.
And sinews of steel for my arm
And a cloak of mail; and a sword for my hand.
Together we shall renew our war with Poverty . . .[34]

Funeral services, arranged by Angelus Funeral Home, were held the following Monday at Bethel Church of Christ Holiness. Interned at Evergreen Cemetery, where Ruby Holmes and aunt Bessie Seals lay buried, Cloyd left behind a wife and two children from his first marriage.[35]

The day Cloyd Miller died, a 6.4-magnitude earthquake struck southern California at 5:54 P.M., along the southern segment of the Newport-Inglewood Fault Zone. Long Beach, Compton, and Huntington Park were hit the hardest. Hughes, unaware that Loren's brother was dead, wrote playfully, "Say, where were you when the earthquake came? I bet you thought it was the Red Squad arriving."[36] Compelled by the magnitude of the Long Beach earthquake, President Roosevelt immediately asked Congress for $5 million to aid California's earthquake zone. The earthquake (which generated the first record of a local earthquake by newly designed motion instruments) caused substantially more damage than originally thought; repairs ran between $40 million and $50 million (in 1933 dollars).

Los Angeles County launched an inquest into any possible criminal negligence on the part of builders, particularly at school sites, where most of the damage occurred. According to Archie Clifton, superintendent for the Los Angeles County Schools, "The original arts building of the Whittier Union High must be torn down and rebuilt,"[37] in addition to buildings at six other schools that were seriously damaged. Jefferson High School, where Juanita Miller graduated in 1922, followed in 1926 by her sister Calme H. Ellsworth, was one of two last schools to reopen.[38]

After Miller married, he left the *California Eagle*, where, following his return from Russia, he resumed his duties as city editor. Although he left the *Eagle* on reasonably friendly terms, the same was not true of his cousin Leon Washington's experience, who sold advertising, in addition to writing an entertainment column. Wash left mostly because "he and Mrs. Bass didn't' hit it off,"[39] according to Libby Clark, food editor at the *Los Angeles Sentinel*.

After leaving the *Eagle*, Wash, with the aid of Miller, started *Town Talk*, a free, small tabloid, the precursor to the *Los Angeles Sentinel*. "I said that is no name for a paper *Town Talk*, it sounded like a gossip sheet. We ought to have a new name," said Miller to Lawrence de Graaf. "So we had a contest to find a name for the paper and a Presbyterian minister whose name I can't recall now suggested the name Sentinel and we had promised a prize of five dollars to the winning name and I recall we had to dodge him for about two months because we didn't have the five dollars."[40]

By Miller's account, he was "affiliated" with the founding of the *Los Angeles Sentinel*, though his cofounder contribution usually goes unaccredited. Through his guidance in the 1930s and 1940s, the *Sentinel*, which continues today, became one of the primary newspapers read by black Angelenos.[41] Essentially, Miller's role at the *Sentinel* was what his nephew, Halvor Miller, Jr., called a "shadow relationship." In the early years, he wrote a great many of the articles as well as the editorials without a byline. Once he began working full-time as an attorney, he pulled back.[42] During the 1940s, every Sunday morning at 10 A.M., Southern Californians could tune into KFOX for an hour to hear "Leon H. Washington, publisher of the Sentinel, and Loren Miller, prominent attorney" discuss "what 15 million Negroes are saying, doing and thinking."[43] However, after a severe stroke in 1948 paralyzed Wash's entire right side and clouded his mind, Miller, the newspaper's legal counsel, became its executive editor, writing the occasional editorial.[44] Wash wrote, "Our close relationship," which deepened during college, "continued when we came West to seek our fortunes. . . . Not only did he send me the money to come to Los Angeles but I lived with his family during those first lean days. . . . And, since even relatives do not often have as close a relationship as we enjoyed, I shall always think of him as a dear friend, with James Boswell's description in mind: 'A companion loves some agreeable qualities which a man may possess, but a friend loves the man himself.'"[45] It was an enduring friendship bound by love and the added joy of poking fun at one another.

Wash's tenure as the editor and publisher of the *Los Angeles Sentinel* would have major, long-term significance for Los Angeles, and in particular for black Angelenos. Before the start of World War II, in 1940, California governor Culbert L. Olson, urged by state assemblyman Augustus F. Hawkins, appointed Wash to the State Immigration and Housing Commission, headed by Miller's good friend and legal colleague, Carey McWilliams. Like other black newspaper publishers, Wash launched the "Don't Spend Your Money Where You Can't Work" campaign and gained distinction later as one of the leaders in the "Double V" wartime campaign and other urban reform initiatives. It was around this time, according to Halvor Miller, Jr., that Wash took to calling himself "Colonel Washington," although there is no evidence that he ever served in the military. He worked on campaigns, no matter how small, such as the time he made sure that "two Negro janitors" got hired by Paramount Studios in an era when those positions were reserved primarily for Japanese workers.[46]

The *Sentinel* was a liberal newspaper until Washington's stroke. "Following his illness its entire editorial policy," according to Miller, "was overhauled, and it has become a mouthpiece of reaction."[47] In 1953, disturbed by the anti-labor and "dictatorial, reactionary policies" of Dora Moore, then manager of the *Sentinel*, Wash picketed his own newspaper.[48] That unprecedented action prompted Wendell Green, columnist for the *California Eagle*, to write: "You've got to give him credit for the great fighting heart he has always had. With his whole right side paralyzed from the stroke he suffered he got a sign and marched up and down in front of the newspaper."[49] In time, he recovered to the extent that, through the 1960s, he served as the *Sentinel*'s acting publisher.

After Loren Miller quit the *Eagle*, he spent his time at the *Sentinel*, where he barely earned anything resembling an income. Urged by his wife, Miller decided to sit for the California state bar exam. On June 7, 1934, Miller, along with ninety-five others, was granted the right to practice law.[50] By July, Miller, accompanied by Lloyd C. Griffith and Thomas L. Griffith, Jr., sons of the pastor of the oldest African American Baptist church in Los Angeles, the Second Baptist Church, sued the Rollerdome Ice Skating Rink for $25,000.[51] Earlier, on March 9, George Prioleau, a student at Polytechnic High School, and a number of other African American students were denied admittance to the rink while their white classmates were admitted. After a protest waged by the League of Struggle for Negro Rights, of which Miller was a member, George's mother turned to the local NAACP legal committee. The three attorneys alleged that an "act of discrimination occurred last March 9 when young Prioleau," accompanied by his "classmates to the rink to take part in class day exercises," were "refused on the ground that the rink did not cater to Negroes."[52] Before Miller gained national recognition as a brilliant civil rights litigator who shined light into the shadows of racism, he handled ordinary divorce and probate cases. Other than the occasional estate matter, his income depended on the "high volume of small-fee . . . practical day to day disputes in his community,"[53] which ranged from two to twenty-five dollars. Through "constant hustling" for new clients and honing his courtroom skill defending victims of Los Angeles's racist public accommodation policies and of the city's brutal police force—including those falsely arrested— his name recognition grew.[54] For example, he received favorable newspaper coverage defending Rachel Gibbs and Miss Emma Tanksley. When the two women entered Gunther Drug Store in Beverly Hills and ordered two milk shakes, the soda jerk told them "they had no dining room for Negroes."[55] Subsequently, the women received a favorable ruling from Judge Kurtz Kaufman, who ordered the owner to pay $200 for refusing to serve them.

There were other thankful clients. On February 11, 1937, the *Los Angeles Sentinel* published a thank-you card from a grateful Baron J. Lawson, executive secretary of the United American Democratic Club. "I wish to thank my many friends of all walks of life and two clever attorneys, Loren Miller and Curtis Taylor . . . in their undaunted belief as to my innocence regarding my trial . . . in which I, Baron J. Lawson was acquitted of narcotic charges placed against me by the Policeman Stovall."[56] In 1939, following his well-publicized success in saving George Farley from the gas chamber, Miller took up the cause of Los Angeles's black garbage workers, who opposed plans by city's Bureau of Engineering to inaugurate a "one man truck" collection policy. "We view the move," asserted Miller, "as one that involves grave and fundamental questions of public health, public safety and as calculated to result in drastic restrictions in personnel."[57] Subsequently, he called for an impartial public hearing with the Municipal Refuse Collectors Relief Association. What he did then—shine light on inequality—he would do for the remainder of his legal career.

As for married life, Juanita Miller continued her role as "a society maven," attending soirées and raising funds for indigent children. As president of the Los Angeles City League, she planned and organized meetings and hosted bridge luncheons, and, as treasurer of De Amicus Puellas, she attended meetings as far away as Atlantic City.[58]

Through his wife's connections, Miller moved within the social cocoon of Los Angeles's black elite, where his appearances at banquets, dances, cotillions, and other charitable and social events were duly and often noted by the *Chicago Defender*, the *Los Angeles Sentinel*, and the *Pittsburgh Courier*. On March 2, 1935, the *Courier* commented that Loren Miller arrived "early with his lovely wife who is a prominent soror of the Delta Sigma Theta Sorority"[59] for the swanky dance party hosted by Dorothy Johnson and her attorney husband Ivan Johnson, III. By fall 1936, Johnson and Miller, who had become chums at Washburn College, formed a law partnership, which lasted throughout World War II. During this period, Juanita and Dorothy Vena Johnson, the first African American female principal to run a secondary school in Los Angeles, established a venue for artists and musicians, the League of Allied Arts, which brought plays by Langston Hughes and others to Los Angeles.[60]

As a prominent sorority member and as "one of the foremost social workers in the city,"[61] Juanita maneuvered unhindered by marriage to a fiery proletarian rhetorician, whose leftist rhetoric, writes Scott Kurashige, "belied the fact that [Miller] was himself a member of the city's Black elite."[62] Seemingly, Miller's professional status and his marriage to a well-known and well-liked socialite softened his radical persona to the degree that it "led him to work with the city's most prominent African American leaders to combat discrimination." He had attained a truly Herculean accomplishment, climbing out of the depths of staggering poverty; his life was a far cry from ramshackle homes and rats skittering around at night.[63]

Juanita's status as a social worker put her in contact with various organizational venues such as the local American Red Cross, the League of Women Voters, the Wives of the Bench and Bar Club of Los Angeles, and her beloved Delta Sigma Theta sorority. Through these like-minded organizations, she gained considerable public-speaking experience.[64] On May 1, 1938, Juanita Miller, reported Gladyce Clark, society columnist for the *Chicago Defender*, served as mistress of ceremonies for Mary McLeod Bethune, "one of the best loved women in the country and one of the greatest women of our times," founder of the Bethune-Cookman College,[65] in town for the annual Delta May week conference. By 1945, Juanita had become president of Nu Sigma graduate chapter, where, speaking at that year's Delta May week—built on the theme of peace—she told her sisters, "It is most important that our women gear their activities and interest on demands of the post-war era . . . and the rehabilitation of our returning servicemen. Our job has just begun."[66]

During Loren Miller's early Los Angeles legal career, he continued, though mostly unpaid, as the *Sentinel*'s city editor, all the while writing articles for the Association of Negro Publishers. His writing leaned toward analysis rather than simple coverage, or the old journalism credo of "show, don't tell." Before resuming his lawyering career full-time, Miller continued to write a regular column called Screenings for the *Liberator* (a.k.a. the *Harlem Liberator* and later the *Negro Liberator*), the official organ of the League of Struggle for Negro Rights, founded by the Communist Party in 1930. Subsequently, Ben Davis, its editor, let Miller know that his column clearly had become the most popular feature of the semimonthly communist publication, saying that it "is winning a great deal of favor in the Negro press and we have every desire for you to continue it regularly."[67] As a member of the league, the successor of the American Negro

Labor Congress and earlier the International Labor Defense, both organized by the Communist Party, Miller found an easy outlet for his political musings. "Dear Comrade Miller," wrote Davis on October 8, 1934, "Your column is swell. Keep up the good work. Now about a few matters. . . . First of all, will you consent to become one of the editors of the CNA, the other being myself? That is, to have your name appear on the letterhead with mine? Also we'd like to syndicate your column through the CNA. Many of the Negro papers would be glad to reprint it. Is this OK with you?"[68]

A few weeks later Miller received more praise from Davis: "First, I want to tell you that your column is excellent. The style is simple and clear and the subject matter is always timely. One of the catchy things about your style is that it conveys the impression of complete and 'holy' impartiality that is the writer has no particular fanatical love for the movement but must through the sheer correctness of its program find himself in accord with the revolutionary way out. Such a style is most convincing. Keep up the good work." More exultations, this time from the *Liberator*'s managing editor, Maude White, wrote that his articles were "just the thing our paper has been in need of for a long time."[69]

Elizabeth Lawson, a member of the *Liberator* staff, wrote Miller on November 27, "We've changed the name of the column to The Way Out (which the printer changed to This Way Out but we caught it in time.) The Way Out is Ben's suggestion based on your suggestion: The Way it is."[70] Lawson's letters duly and promptly kept coming. In December, she pressed Miller to use his influence with Langston Hughes. "Boy, if you can get Hughes to write poetry for the Lib. . . . What do you think about the idea?"[71]

It is unclear whether Miller ever contacted Hughes on Lawson's behalf. What is clear is that when she reproached Miller on what others were aware of—his tendency to procrastinate—she did it lightheartedly. "Thanks for the [photo] mats. I was getting impatient and was going to pick up the ugliest man I could find and have his picture taken and label it Loren Miller. So you see from what a fate you've saved yourself."[72] Six weeks later, a humorless Ben Davis wrote, "Almost a week ago we sent you a wire asking you to rush the final installments on the relief exposure series in the LIBERATOR. Thus far we have not heard from you. Please get busy and send these installments at once."[73] After another week and still no word, he wrote again:

> Dear Loren, Say what on earth is the matter? Are you sick dead or what? Here is what you must do at once: 1st, send at least 2 "way out's" at once, by air mail special delivery; 2nd, send at least a wind up installment to the Jim-crow FERA series. First you sent us four, but there is a note at the end of the fourth one calling for a fifth. Send this fifth post haste. . . . Evidently you do not understand what a big part of our paper and CNA your material is. . . . You can't let us down."[74]

Four more times Davis pleaded. Finally, Miller responded: "I am ready to eat worms and die. I have no excuse for my dilatory conduct in getting columns to you beyond the fact that I have been busy as hell. I shall do better in the future."[75] But he did not; he continued to drag his feet.

In between writing for the *Sentinel*, the *Liberator*, and the Association of Negro Publishers, in 1934 Miller became manager of Augustus F. Hawkins's campaign—a bitter battle won by 1,500 votes.[76] The twenty-six-year-old Hawkins, a graduate of Jefferson High School, the University of California, Los Angeles, and the University of Southern California, defeated Republican Frederick Roberts, the sixteen-year African American incumbent of California's Sixty-Second State Assembly district. With Hawkins's victory, the two radicals [members of the League of Struggle for Negro Rights] shifted the "political balance of power as Black [Los Angeles] voters switched en masse to the Democratic Party."[77] Hawkins would serve in the state assembly from 1935 to 1963; he would become California's first black elected to the U.S. House of Representatives (1963–91).

Although Hawkins, the youngest state legislator in 1934, was a supporter of Upton Sinclair's End Poverty in California (EPIC) campaign, Miller was not entirely enamored with the darling of the Left, the muckraking novelist of *The Jungle* and *Oil!* Miller had written critically during Sinclair's unsuccessful bid for the California governorship in 1934. "Sinclair has made few direct promises to Negroes," wrote Miller. His record,

> as far as Negroes are concerned shows that he has had little to say about their status in America, almost as little as his opponent. . . . Yet not one of his books has ever concerned itself with the so-called Negro problem. . . . I asked him whether or not he would lend his influence to abolishing California's anti inter-marriage law and residential restriction covenants. His public meeting answer was a "no" based on his claim that he would have to stick to his Epic plan.[78]

Following Upton Sinclair's bruising defeat, the Reverend W. A. Johnson, pastor of Los Angeles's Trinity Baptist Church, brought a one-million-dollar libel suit against the former candidate. The pastor had taken offense at an article in the *Nation* in which Sinclair stated, "The Sunday before election day every Negro preacher in Los Angeles received $50 to preach a sermon against me." Sinclair's statement and earlier charges during his campaign that certain prominent preachers "were in the pay of the Republicans" reflected "a subtle anti-Negro prejudice of which Sinclair has never been able to rid himself despite his 'socialist' beliefs," wrote Miller for the *Pittsburg Courier*.[79] Subsequently, the reverend and Sinclair met. Afterward, Sinclair retracted his post-election statement: "I have made an investigation of this matter I find that this statement was ill-advised and I desire to withdraw it. . . . I have had the pleasure of meeting Reverend William A. Johnson . . . and I have found him to be a man who does not indulge in politics in his church."[80]

Praise for Miller's writing—however welcome—came without any sort of regular paycheck. With sporadic lawyering fees, he continued to depend on his wife's employment with the Los Angeles County Bureau of Public Assistance. From 1930 to 1939, Juanita Miller, working first as a field caseworker, alongside her Delta sorority sisters Irma Hopkins and Alma Thomas, advanced within the county charities division from case supervisor to special case auditor and eventually to supervisor for twelve southern California counties for the state.[81]

Unquestionably, Juanita's steady employment provided Miller with the means to pursue what is today considered advocacy or citizen journalism. Without his wife's moral and financial support—something she provided before they married, during his Soviet travels—Miller would have been unable to accept not just one but two virtually unpaid editorial positions on the East Coast. Obviously, his decision to relocate to New York was easier to make while the couple had no children. Essentially, the couple was of one mind when it came to political and racial affairs and his career. Still, Miller risked uncertainty by deciding to go to New York.

By May 1935, Miller's plans were set to join the editorial staff of the *New Masses* magazine in New York, where he anticipated meeting the influential Marxist literary critic Granville Hicks. In addition to the *New Masses*, Miller planned to work as assistant editor of the Crusader News Agency, the nation's first Negro national news service. There, he would work alongside Harlem's most prominent black Communists, Cyril Briggs and Benjamin Davis, editor in chief and assistant editor, respectively.[82] By the time Miller actually joined the news agency, established by Briggs in 1919 to fight Marcus Garvey's Back to Africa and pro-capitalist policies, the CNA reached "some 200 Negro papers throughout the country, and in the West Indies and Africa. Since we made no charge for the [weekly] service, it found immediate acceptance, particularly among the smaller Negro papers."[83] "The CNA," argues Gerald Horne, "helped to shape the leftist tilt of the Black press and at the same time reflected the fact that Jim Crow had in effect pushed Blacks to the Left."[84] Miller was part of that tilt.

On May 27, 1935, before Miller shook the dust of California off his heels, he wrote Juanita from Missouri that, while visiting friends and relatives in Kansas and Saint Louis, he had "a great old heart-to-heart talk in that 'do you remember when' and 'I knew you would make good' vein."[85] Perhaps in an attempt to lessen any anxiety Juanita might have regarding money matters, he wrote, "Thus far I see no need to put you to stealing. I still have a little cash and when I think of the many times I've left various places with so much less I really feel quite the capitalist." Two weeks later he wrote complaining that the weather in New York

> was hot as blazes until quite late. . . . Little clouds begin to come up in the sky and you look up hopefully. A few more clouds and you say to yourself that surely it will rain. Then the sun seems to be winning the battle. Finally, it rains. The first onrushing drops clear the air. It feels fresh again and then gradually it becomes cooler again. You know that it will but make it hotter for tomorrow but one day's respite is something.[86]

Although there is no clear indication that Juanita joined her husband in New York, Fay M. Jackson, political editor for the *California Eagle*, reported that her fellow cofounder of the Upsilon chapter of Delta Sigma Theta sorority, Juanita, "may join him in the fall."[87] After the two graduated from college, Juanita served "for a time as a member of the staff for Flash,"[88] Jackson's short-lived black intellectual newsweekly. By 1937, as the first African American woman foreign correspondent for the Association of Negro Publishers, Jackson covered the coronation of King George VI in London.

After a few months in Harlem, Miller realized that he was living in the center of a cultural mecca, where a young Billie Holiday performed before tough audiences at the famous Apollo Theater.[89] He arrived as Harlem was recovering from its first major race riot. The March 19, 1935, uprising claimed three lives, wounded hundreds, and left just about every plate-glass store window from 116th to 145th Street smashed. According to Nannie Helen Burroughs, the pioneering educator and Washington, D.C.–based religious leader, it was a "human revolt," not communistic propaganda as alleged: "A colored boy, a nickel pen-knife and a screaming woman were no more the cause of the Harlem uprising in 1935, than was a shipload of tea in the Boston harbor, in 1773, the cause of the Revolutionary War. The tea party was only the manifestation" of discontent and abuses buried beneath a mountain of injustices. Burroughs continued, "An unknown boy was simply the match—a frightened woman's screams lighted it and threw it into the magazine of powder and Harlem blew up."[90]

"That is Harlem," wrote Miller. "Not a giant but a long-suffering strong youth who awoke from passivity March 19 and turned on his tormentors in bitter wrath armed with the memory of a thousand wrongs. . . . When angry Negroes surged through the streets, defied police and smashed windows in the 125th street region. . . . Violent conflicts involving Negroes are no novelty to Manhattan Island. As long ago as 1712 a group of Negro slaves revolted and marched on the scattered settlements."[91] It was apparent to Miller that the violence was rooted in unemployment. When the Great Depression struck the nation, Harlem was hit particularly hard. "Jobs vanished overnight. Professional men found that their clients had no money for fees. Discrimination is the norm in American life and it was altogether natural that when relief agencies were established they should discriminate against Harlem folk in a thousand and one subtle and not so subtle ways."[92] Such conditions, he wrote, breed unrest.

Once the powder keg blew, a mayor's commission formed, and committees, such as the Joint Conference Against Discriminatory Action, met, followed by rallies. The United Societies League for Negro People, an ad hoc committee, planned a mass trial of city officials and employees. Loren Miller, Edward Kuntz, attorney for the Communist Party, and Ben Davis agreed to "assume the role of lawyers for the prosecution."[93] Rev, Adam Clayton Powell, Jr., pastor at the Abyssinian Church, and William Lloyd Imes of Saint James Presbyterian Church, served as jurors, along with other community leaders.

Miller found it "rather odd to be living in a community like this one where . . . preachers speak on the same platform with [James W.] Ford and other Communists and permit the use of their churches and it seems quite the thing." Here in New York, he told Juanita, "the Communists are almost respectable. No group or groups planning to make a fight on civic abuses, for example, would think of setting about the task without the support and to some extent the sanction of the Reds."[94]

True to form, Miller criticized the esteemed sociologist E. Franklin Frazier, who later wrote the seminal book *Black Bourgeoisie* (1957). Miller called Frazier, the head of the mayor's commission, a conservative who "will do little more than hatch an elaborate report detailing conditions that everybody knows exist."[95] "Harlem folk," he continued, "have a certain advantage over the [mayor's] commission; they know beforehand just what will be found out and they need not wait for publication of the report." Privately, to Juanita, he revealed more:

> Franklin Frazier is here as the man to make the survey for the highly touted mayor's committee which is looking into the Harlem riots. I saw him the other day when I attended the hearings. It is plain that nothing will come out of the hearings. They are merely circuses when you sift it all down. A great show of democracy is kept up with persons in the audience having the right to question those who testify. That leads to trouble, although undeniably it is much better than the old kind of hearings where self confessed experts do all of the talking and the master-minding. . . . All in all, the troubles that led to the first riot have not been curbed and it is only a question of time until the Harlem people, encouraged by their first taste of power, will flare into violence again.[96]

Nonetheless, the investigation did conclude that the primary causes for the riot were the result of overcrowding, high rents, employment discrimination, unequal treatment by relief agencies, and an overly aggressive police force that curbed discontent with billy clubs.[97]

In the midst of political turmoil, Eugene Gordon, Miller's *New Masses* colleague prepared to leave for a position with the *Moscow Daily News*.[98] Like Miller, he, too, was a member of the League of Struggle for Negro Rights. Gordon assured Miller, before departing, that his scathing *New Masses* article "Mail-Order Dictatorship," which indicted the philanthropic Rosenwald Fund for making gifts in the fund's name that "went to support and encourage racial institutions built on the principle of racial separatism," "contains such excellent material that we feel it should be published, with very slight changes."[99]

While at the *New Masses*, Miller wrote of Paul Robeson's "self-imposed exile in England . . . because he could no longer bear the humiliations and discriminations heaped upon him" and of the "limitations that hedged him [Robeson] in as an actor."[100] In "Last in Peace, Last in War," an overview of the wartime efforts in the Great War to quell black discontent at home, Miller wrote of "Marauding bands set upon Negro soldiers in southern states," lynching and mob violence in

Brownsville, and riots in Omaha, Nebraska. He reminded readers of the Camp Logan mutiny of 1917, in which thirteen black soldiers were hanged in Houston, Texas, within hours of their guilty verdict. He disparagingly criticized W. E. B. Du Bois, who at the outset of World War I, wrote Miller "vacillated, writing stinging editorials sneering at American and Allied hypocrisy—and then capitulated"[101] by later issuing a stunning editorial appeal in support of the war. Miller told Juanita of an article that ran without his byline: "Just between you and me and the guidepost that article on Why Japan Risks War was mine."[102] He was busy.

At first Miller had few assignments. Then that changed: "I wanted to write you sooner," he told Juanita,

> but I have been busy as hell what with a half dozen different irons in the fire and having to keep office hours again. Nothing is worse than the latter fate especially after you have had a measure of freedom for the moment. I'm almost sorry I was so anxious to go to work. The job I am doing for New Masses is not exactly in my line. . . . I am now at work on an article on the threatened split in the Socialist Party. That's rather out of my line but I rather welcomed the job because I want to do something other than things about Negroes to take away the idea that I am just a Race Man holding a job as a figure head as do the Zigs in the U.S. government for example.[103]

As soon as Miller learned that the *American Spectator* had accepted his article on the "administration and the Negro," he shared the good news with his wife: "What I really want now is to publish an article in New Republic or Nation. When, as and if I do I will try out one of the monthlies, perhaps Harpers. Survey Graphic ought to be a cinch for something in the social workers' field if we ever get around to it. That kind of thing, writing I mean, accelerates with each published piece. Once you break in on one rag the others take you out of fear that their competitors may if they don't, if your stuff has merit at all."[104]

Although he never quite succeeded shaking off the "race man" mantle, Miller eventually did find an outlet for his essays in "white" publications, but only years later when he had achieved considerable recognition for his courtroom success. During Miller's six-month tenure in New York, in addition to writing for the *New Masses*, the *Liberator*, and the Crusader News Agency, he helped launch *RACE*, a short-lived, 1930s literary quarterly dedicated to the struggle for complete equality.[105] Edited by Genevieve Schneider, *RACE* carried articles by Miller; the *New York Times*'s first black reporter, George Streator; Howard University's E. Franklin Frazer; and Alexander Lesser, Columbia University anthropologist.[106]

On the assassination of Huey Long, Louisiana's populist governor, Miller wrote disapprovingly of President Roosevelt: "Was F.D. talking through his hat when he lamented Long's death?" Astounded by Roosevelt's statement "that the 'spirit of violence is un-American and has no place in a consideration of public affairs,'" Miller added, "Although I am opposed to assassination as a means of settling political disputes, I am sure that Mr. Roosevelt is dead wrong. The truth is that violence has long occupied a very prominent place in American public affairs. . . .

In fact, it's so easy to think of examples of the use of violence in American public affairs that it isn't even a good game." As an example, Miller made reference to the victims of thirteen lynchings that year. He concluded, "However, the killing of one office-holder always strikes other office-holders as a terrible matter. That's the time when those who have winked and connived at all sorts of violence get excited. But as I was saying, I am opposed to assassination too."[107]

Mostly as a demonstration of collegiality, Miller wrote the vacation column of "the old pigs' knuckle detective," Roi Ottley, columnist for the black-owned *New York Amsterdam News*. He wrote, "NOW WHY would Roi Ottley ask me to write this column for him? It's practically impossible for me to satisfy his clientele because I don't know Harlem well enough. I can't fall back on snappy little items to the effect that Miss Jones, who was out with Miss Smith's boy friend looked charming at Miss Williams' party." However, he did try: "The more I think of it the more convinced I am that what Harlem needs is a Society for the Demolition of Stuffed Shirts. While the gossip boys waste their time on non-essentials the town is being inundated by a wave of solemn nonsense that passes for wisdom. Something ought to be done and, unless there are signs of action in the mighty near future, I'm going to . . . undertake the job myself."[108]

The longer Miller stayed in Harlem, the more he realized it was not as unified as he had once thought, and not everybody saw things eye to eye. He remarked in the *New Masses*, "There are deep and thoroughgoing divisions of opinion reflecting economic groupings . . . bulwarked behind such organizations as the YMCA [Young Men's Christian Association], the Urban League and National Association for the Advancement of Colored People, these middle-class folk preach a doctrine of gradual reforms and protest of invasions of civil liberties." He singled out James Hubert, secretary for the Urban League, as "a man who has a pathetic faith in a return to the farm as a cure for the ills from which the urban Negro suffers."[109]

In late June, Ben Davis waited anxiously in Harlem for a "real juicy, original story"[110] from Miller, who was in Saint Louis covering the twenty-sixth annual conference of the NAACP. Miller came down hard on Roy Wilkins, editor of the *Crisis* magazine at the time. The July 27 edition of the *Baltimore Afro-American* carried the headline: "Wilkins Is All Wet on His Inferiority Theory—Miller."[111] What angered Miller was Wilkins's extolling the virtues of such star athletes as Jesse Owens and Joe Louis and saying that they were "ambassadors of good will who had done more for the race than a box-car of Du Boises." Miller argued that Wilkins's focus on individual merit rather than economics in effect supported a concept that underlay the abuse of black Americans—a belief in their intrinsic inferiority. The *Crisis* editor, Miller asserted, put "the cart before the horse. As slavery became more and more profitable in the South and subject to more bit-ter attacks from the North, the theory [of inferiority] was born to justify it." In Miller's mind, black athletes suffered no differently than the rest of the black population when it came to discrimination. "Eddie Tolan was Michigan's ace sprinter; Michigan," Miller opined, "turned right around and barred Willis Ward from the Basketball team. Michigan is going to keep on doing such things until the colored man helps destroy the foundation of the system which holds him down. . . . It isn't hard to see that if you destroy the economic reasons for keeping the race down, you strike a body blow at the whole superstructure of inferiority theories."[112]

A few weeks earlier, in "How 'Left' Is the NAACP?" Miller questioned the organizational structures and policies of the organization, which for years "had been agitating members." He referenced a bitter fight launched by delegates in 1933 against a "'self-perpetuating oligarchy' charged with ruling the Association." The desire for a policy change, he insisted, "has been growing steadily out of the realization that despite twenty-five years of struggle, discrimination against and segregation of Negroes have been on the increase." Delegates charged that a decline in influence followed the victory in the Scottsboro case by the International Labor Defense and a move by the masses to the left. After the delegates heard reports on the membership and claims that the organization opened twenty-three new branches, Miller wrote that the delegates overwhelmingly "adopted a program pledging the Association to 'foster the building of a labor movement which will unite all labor, white and black' and calling for the laying of 'the intellectual basis for united action between white and black worker.' Minor democratic reforms were also adopted."[113]

As the conference wore on, "it became increasingly evident," continued Miller, "that the Association leaders weren't nearly as militant as the program indicated." In Miller's mind, the conference had failed miserably. The leaders "were long on words but very short on concrete proposals for action." In his analysis, the NAACP program was "almost criminally inadequate" and was based on an "old dream of a petty bourgeois utopia in which an assured clientele would be guaranteed to the professional and business man." W. E. B. Du Bois, who guided the association under the old plan, reported that Miller now proposed "that the organization give up its old constitutional fight and advise Negroes to take 'advantage of segregation.' Du Bois quit when his program was rejected." That departure opened the door for Walter White to become the organization's guiding spirit, whose "real function," in Miller's opinion, "is to please the Board on one hand and make the Negro membership like it on the other."[114]

During the conference, Martha Gruening, a former member of the *Crisis* staff, along with Helen Boardman, circulated a pamphlet titled "Who Is the NAACP?" Earlier, in 1917, Gruening had covered the Camp Logan mutiny in Houston in which thirteen soldiers of the all-black Third Battalion of the Twenty-fourth United States Infantry had been executed.[115] The two women, who had done investigative work on what many considered one of the most remarkable trials of the South, and its defending attorney Charles H. Houston "pushed the issue believing justice had not been served."[116] The NAACP contended they had not sold out the defendant, George Crawford. "In the final analysis," as Genna Rae McNeil put it, "Houston had acted in accordance with his client's wishes."[117]

Finally, when Miller returned to New York, he wrote at length to Juanita, telling her that the Saint Louis conference "muddled along with a great many left promises and really nothing to indicate that the NAACP intends to do more than make a few gestures." Impatient toward the end of the conference, he told her, "I refused to be polite any longer and broke out with some acute and acid observations." Then he told her, "I wrote an article [on the NAACP] and sent it ahead but I hope that I can get to revise it. So if you read it and don't like it just remember that I didn't either." He closed describing his rail trip back to New York: "You know how terribly dirty it is through the coal mining regions. Honestly, coal dust was a quarter of an inch thick on the window sills."[118]

From the beginning of his New York stint, Miller often leaned on Juanita for small infusions of cash: "Received the ten and thanks a million, or better say ten million. You probably rescued me from having to resort to a tin cup or to be more optimistic at least to the Home Relief Bureau, the chief dispenser of alms to the poor in these parts."[119] Despite Miller's attempt to make light of his situation, he was embarrassed—guilty even—about always being on the receiving end of Juanita's generosity. It was her sacrifice that bothered him most:

> There is no use of your telling me that you aren't depriving yourself of something that you need. Twenty dollar bills do not grow on trees and you need it. I swear at myself every time you send me something. But, you are thinking to yourself that is all he does. He keeps on taking it. Which is true and I wouldn't if I could make it otherwise. So—but the argument is fruitless. The one with myself, I mean. Some time I hope I'm going to do something as nice as you.[120]

A bit later he felt buoyed up by the prospect of getting paid for his *American Spectator* article, though the timeframe was uncertain: "I don't know when I will get paid because, as I observed once before, those damned magazines pay on publication and it is a monthly. . . . Still it will be cash when I get it and will put me in a new field"[121] as a writer. He mused, "I hope that . . . I get paid before the Second Coming."[122]

In order to avoid spending unnecessarily, Miller tended to scale back on social and cultural functions. However, Lester Granger, his dear friend and roommate, would have none of it; he insisted that Loren attend the "various phases of social programs as they affect Negroes"[123] in New York. When Granger wanted him to attend the second annual New York State Conference on Social Work on June 8, at first Miller declined.[124] Later, he explained to Juanita, "Granger insisted on taking me, although I did not want to go because I felt that I could not spend the money. . . . He wanted to take me to see *Waiting for Lefty* but I felt that was too much so I did not go."[125] Instead, the two went over to Small's Paradise nightclub on 135th Street and Seventh Avenue. "Despite their many advertisements,

Harlem night clubs are just night clubs," he wrote her. "The show is a little better than the one we saw at the Club Araby [in Los Angeles] but it wasn't worth spending much money on at that. One of the mysteries of my life is why people can get such a kick out of going to a night club. But there is no accounting for taste."[126]

Miller eventually did see Clifford Odets's play *Waiting for Lefty* at Harlem's Rockland Palace. Afterward, an "evening of fun, theatre and festival" followed the performance. The floor cleared, wrote Marvel Cooke, columnist for the *New York Amsterdam News*, for "the dancers to do a little light trucking or lindy hopping or bumping or just plain fox-trotting to inimitable tunes furnish[ed] by Teddy Hill's Roseland Orchestra."[127] Cooke reported fleeting glimpses of Loren Miller, Lester Granger, Roy Wilkins, Mollie Lewis, Bessye Bearden, her son, the artist Romare Bearden, Miller's painter friend Aaron Douglas, and his wife Alta.

An event at the Rockland Palace was more business than pleasure: "By the way, I am going to my first party since here. . . . Maybe it isn't a party at that. The darned thing is a pay-affair given by a group of goils in New Jersey who call themselves the Girl Friends. They, apparently, might as easily be called the Granger Friends as he seems to be one of their prime heroes. Anyhow, Granger and I are going to drive over and pay $1.25 for the two of us to see what happens at a barn dance in the effete east."[128] Afterward, Miller assured Juanita, "Fortunately for me, there were no old ladies there with designs on me. The sad part of it is that there were no young ones with those thoughts, which must be by way of proof that my charm is declining severely or that I have forgotten the fine art of intriguing young gals."[129]

Miller had planned to travel in late September to Atlanta with Lester Granger to form some sort of "valid judgment" of the south.[130] He changed his mind. The next month before Granger left, this time for the American Federation of Labor Convention in Atlantic City, "He says to tell you to come to New York and accompany me to the west," wrote Miller to his wife. "He certainly is a swell guy; there are people whom you like as long distance friends and all of that but he is as nice when you happen to room with him. As you observed once, we have a good time with our own wit. We seldom have company because we refuse to answer the bell. If we didn't the place would be full of argufiers all the time."[131] After Lester Granger arranged for them to speak in New Jersey to "a bunch of high school students," Miller discovered that the invitation had come from Mrs. Tate, a secretary at the YWCA. Mrs. Tate, an old Topekan, he recalled, was "a star-spangled pain in the neck (only it wasn't the neck)."[132] "I was quite the hero and it all contrasted strangely to the days when I was Topeka's bad boy and a rather sad example of how a young man should *not* waste his talents. I'm important now only because I represent *New Masses*—'I knew him when,' I don't exactly appreciate such an attitude but I took a kind of malicious pleasure in my position." He admitted to Juanita that he eventually warmed a bit to the high schoolers, concluding, "They weren't bad." He continued, "Speaking of speeches, I am sure that you have seen announcement of the damned Nov. 11 meeting at which I am to be chairman,"[133] where Earl Browder, general secretary of the CPUSA, and Heywood Broun, president of the American Newspaper Guild, where scheduled to speak. "I hate the job like poison. . . . I guess that I will have to stop. I have a million things to do. Please pray for me while I'm over in New Jersey making those damned speeches and listening to these silly people."[134]

Pleased, and even proud, that back in Los Angeles Juanita had found a new site for the Civic League meetings, Miller mused, "I hope that the meetings flourish and prosper so that your pal, Baxter, can feel duly taken aback for his part in ridding the YMCA of us."[135] He wrote again two weeks later, this time aware that Juanita needed encouragement

in preparing to fight for your right to take your civil service place on the list of appointments. I feel that Gus [Hawkins] will do his very best by way of exertion of political pressure. I am not at all convinced that such a fight will win but it is worthwhile. . . . I do not agree with you in thinking that you ought not to appeal to the politicians except in a certain sense. . . . Certainly, they ought not to be asked to gumshoe for you but my own idea is that they must be put on the spot when and if the time comes for mass pressure. After all, they pretend to be serving the masses. Let them. They should be asked, indeed it should be demanded, to join in with a public pressure campaign for your appointment. After all, your case is not that of a person seeking a job that rightfully belongs to him. It is that of a *Negro* and that demands that every person who stands for Negro rights do something. The larger perspective is that such organizations as the Inter-professional Association, your social workers group, the NAACP, etc., ought to be made to pitch in. When and if it gets that far, the American Civil Liberties Union ought to be asked to do something too because after all the matter is one of the denial of fundamental civil rights. The first thing for you to do is to go back again, if that is possible, and make copies of the one list and then the Jim Crow list.[136]

From the outset, when Juanita's letters took too long to reach him, he stewed and fretted like he had done in Russia. Such was his loneliness. He wrote her,

Seeing as how this is Tuesday night and I haven't heard from you yet this week I thought that I would write to you. . . . Well, it may be that the Amsterdam News strike is upon us. In fact, I announced it in *New Masses* this week only to take it back at the last minute. The publishers went on a spree Sunday and announced that seven of the Guild members would be fired only to take it back when they heard rumblings of a strike. . . . The Guild feels that perhaps it would be better to go ahead and strike fearing that the whole thing is only a trick on part of the rag to gain some time. We ought to know pretty definitely tonight. In fact, I am on my way to a meeting right this very minute where the whole matter will be settled, once and for all I hope.[137]

On October 19, 1935, the *Chicago Defender* reported that the publishers and owners of the *New York Amsterdam News*, William H. Davis and his wife, Sadie Warren Davis, locked out seventeen members of its staff: "It was charged that the staff was summarily discharged and locked out . . . because of activities in the American Newspaper Guild in which they sought better working conditions, and security from being fired." The owners claimed that the lockout was based on the economy. Aiken Pope, attorney for the owners, had stated earlier in the summer after meeting with the staff, "The Amsterdam News will never recognize a union among its editorial employees."[138] Other efforts failed despite the enlistment of the Harlem Citizen's Committee, whose members included Justice James C. Watson of the municipal court, noted historian and writer Arthur Schomburg, and Elmer A. Carter, editor of the *Opportunity* magazine.

The Newspaper Guild took up the fight on behalf of the fifteen locked-out newspaper workers, members of the local guild. Among those dismissed and on strike were the paper's city editor, Ted Poston, and Henry L. Moon, Miller's former Russian film nemeses. In response to the owner's charge that the guild was out to "destroy Negro business," Poston declared, "We don't want to destroy the *Amsterdam News*, we simply want our jobs back and acceptable union conditions."[139] When Juanita queried her husband about Poston's social philosophy, he replied, "The curious part of it is that he is the most aware of all of them of the class struggle. In fact, he calls himself a revolutionist and his disagreement is with the Communist Party rather than Marxism. The real trouble is that he is gifted or afflicted with a supreme cynicism that is an effective bar to any real participation in any organized movement."[140]

By mid-October, picketers carrying "Boycott the Amsterdam News" banners formed lines in front of the newspaper's headquarters. Miller was there along with other union supporters. As the lockout dragged on, he wrote Juanita that "the paper has lost money and advertisement in a disastrous manner and were Mrs. Davis gifted with any horse-sense at all she would settle it post-haste but the whole affair to her is based on emotional and not business prejudices and so she holds out. It must terminate in one way or another: either the paper will be ruined or she will give in."[141] He compared Mrs. Davis to Charlotta Bass, owner of the *California Eagle*. Mrs. Davis, he wrote, "is some such kind of a person as Mrs. Bass. Were we dealing with rational people we would have won before this time." But, he explained, Mrs. Davis "apparently doesn't intend to give in until she is beaten right down."[142]

"Blame it on the strike," his groveling apology to Juanita began. "I have been on the go ever since the darned thing started and what with walking my shoes out on the picket line and making speeches here, there and everywhere I haven't taken time to write you."[143] On October 30, after reading a copy of the *California Eagle*, he wrote again: "With what appeared to me almost a jubilant announcement of my arrest. . . . I am not as hopeful that the announcement of the dismissal of the complaint will merit as much publicity. But there is at least one piece of consolation; as *Time* is so fond of observing names make news. And when your name makes news the inference is that you are important."[144]

The eleven-week strike ended in December. The locked-out employees returned to work when Drs. C. B. Powell and P. M. H. Savory bought the *Amsterdam News*. Conditions of the agreement, reported the *Chicago Defender*, called for the "reinstatement of the striking employees . . . a 10 per cent wage increase; the establishment of a Guild shop; a five-day 40-hour week,"[145] and an annual two-week vacation. The employees won!

During the strike, Miller alerted Juanita that Langston Hughes might "be back in Los Angeles in the near future" because he "had received an offer from Hollywood but he doesn't know exactly what there is to it but it seems that movie makers are thinking of doing some Negro pictures and there is the possibility that he will get some good offers out of it. I hope so. He sends his best regards. etc., etc." Toggling between sentences, Miller mentioned that Hughes's play *Mulatto*, which examines miscegenation, "is a very melodramatic thing that has little proletarian content. But it was written several years ago and it has a very great racial content. Certainly it is not 'counter-revolutionary,' whatever that happens to be."[146]

True to form, Miller did not let friendship interfere with his principles. Miller's review of *Mulatto* in the *New Masses* was unsympathetic:

> Langston Hughes breaks with this tradition in his play, *Mulatto* . . . only to escape the pitfalls of melodrama by the narrowest of margins. He drops all attempts to make his drama colorful and strives for a realistic description of the relations between an illegitimate mulatto son and his white planter-father. . . . It is evident that Hughes hoped to depict the manner in which the racial set-up in the South damns both white and Negroes. Unfortunately, *Mulatto* was written several years ago when his grasp of the situation was not as complete as it is now and the play does not offer a well-rounded picture of that phase of southern life with which it deals. But primary weakness of the drama is in its internal construction.

The failing, he wrote, was not in the acting of Rose McClendon, who kept the play from "slipping over into blood-and-thunder melodrama." According to Miller, Hughes relied too heavily "on the device of having the characters explain what is happening." All and all, *Mulatto* for all its faults, he wrote, is "at least a realistic attempt to grapple with a problem that is begging for honest dramatic treatment."[147]

From the moment Miller arrived in New York in late May, he had fallen easily into the "political cockfights between the Stalinists and the Trotskyists."[148] Although *New Masses* had long separated itself from its Trotskyite beginnings, the paper's sectarianism, ill-humored Communists, and ideological rigidity, which had driven away Richard Wright, eventually led Miller to leave for the same reasons. After six months, he quit. Four months before Miller died, he told Lawrence de Graaf, "I don't know that there was ever a time that it was said you can't write this or you can't say this or you can't say that. But as a newspaper man by that time you know the boss doesn't have to tell any newspaperman what he wants in his newspaper." He continued, insisting that any staff reporter "knows what the boss wants and he does what the boss wants or else he quits."[149] Miller quit.

Although Miller left the magazine on good terms, he confided in Hughes that its rigidity encouraged a "stifling of many things that are too valuable to lose."[150] Yet privately the thirty-two-year-old Miller revealed something quite different to his wife: "Working on *New Masses* has been a swell thing for me. I have liked it and I have learned more than you imagine about writing since I have been here. Things that I hope to put to good use."[151] And he did, particularly the publishing and pamphleteering experience he acquired.

Like Thomas Paine, the inveterate propagandist and radical pamphleteer, Miller aimed his *New Masses* rhetoric at the "uninitiated general public"—those ignored by the mainstream press. He set out to persuade readers in a way the Communists had been unable to do. Whether Miller knew that "a substantial portion of the total communist propaganda effort"[152] lay in pamphleteering, during his tenure at the magazine, he put great effort into attracting new members—essentially luring them away from their Popular Front competitors.

From the beginning of Miller's eastern sojourn, he and Juanita puzzled over what to do about his cousin Leon Washington, who along with his wife was staying with Juanita during Miller's absence: "I have an idea that this business of Mr. and Mrs. Washington is going to get funny before it is over. If I know anything about Wash I guess that he did not tell his bride that he and she would have to vacate the house in such a short time. . . . And this whole business will probably leave them in a first class hole. Where in the hell will they go? The prospect of a rooming house won't be so hot after having stayed with us."[153] He advised Juanita to "please start moving my cousin out of your house so I can see you there pretty soon without interruption."[154]

Seven days later, apparently feeling some regret about suggesting she kick out the couple, Miller wrote again:

> I see no need for your remorse over what you wrote me in connection with Leon. If I have failed to say the same things on occasions it has only been because I never got around to it and not because I did not think that it should be said. He's the kind of a guy, nice fellow that he is, that drives one to saying things that one didn't know were in one's vocabulary. I still cling to the hope, rather to the demand, that you get them out of the house. I have no hard and fast rule denying my hospitality to those who talk baby-talk. That isn't exactly the idea. But I just don't want to be favored with a lot of company right off. Of course, if you can't get them out by gentle persuasion don't call the eviction squad. I leave it to you and your superb sense of management. I'm always leaving something to you aren't I?[155]

Resigned to the whole affair with his cousin, he became wildly exuberant when word reached him that the situation had changed: "So—my cousin will move upstairs? . . . The mere fact that he is actually planning on moving is an item that cheers me to say nothing of my happiness on learning that he has given you $20.00. What hath god wrought?"[156]

After another night of speech making that fall, Miller could barely wait to get back to New York to write his wife. He wrote, "You will probably be both surprised and pained to get this letter in long hand. I am using it because it is late—about 1 A.M. Monday—and I remember how terrible a typewriter sounds late at night. You remember, of course, the guy who typed over us."[157] He suggested that she should "go ahead and make plans for Friday, November 22." Earlier he had warned,

> If I hear of you telling anybody that I will get there before Friday night I will take wings and fly back to New York. . . . What I am trying to dodge is any possibility that there will be anybody at the station to meet me but you. I feel that it is necessary to give you these sad-faced warnings because I remember that you fetched several to meet me when I got back from Russia. Of course, you didn't have a car then but you have now and so you need bring nobody. To repeat: don't tell anybody, not even my family, that I will get into town on the morning train. Be pleasantly vague about the matter. . . . Then we can drive out and see my mother and drop in—later that night—on those people whom it is necessary for me to see the day of arrival.[158]

The next few weeks, he later wrote, "will be a very long time in passing, so afraid that I try to keep from even thinking about it. I'm intrigued by your plans and your fear that you may lack restraint which you [can] count upon me to supply. Should I pray for the Lord to grant me that strength?"[159]

When Miller's train reached North Platte, Nebraska, on November 20, he stepped off briefly, long enough to send a postcard to Langston Hughes: "Thanks for books was glad to get them. Am on my way home. Will write you later."[160]

After the dealer shuffled and dealt, "The pinochle game is where all the politics came out,"[161] said Miller's niece, Jane Kerina (née Miller). After Miller returned from New York, his Wednesday night card game, sometimes with two card tables and sometimes six, started up and continued all through World War II and a bit afterward. At the card table, everybody's opinion counted. According to Jane, "They could say anything." No subject was off limits. At age ten, "Daddy let me pour beer." If no bubbles stuck to the side of the glass, Jane got a tip; so adept at keeping the frothy foam no more than an inch thick, she became the games' designated pourer. She vividly remembers her uncle Loren, whom her father, Halvor, Sr., idolized—a lit Lucky Strikes hanging loosely from his lips and a shout: "Jane, Cliff needs beer." According to Edward Miller, the younger of Miller's two sons, Juanita detested her husband's "filthy habit"[162] of chain smoking.

The card players were a close-knit group made up mostly of old friends and relatives. Cliff White and Lewis Russ, who were Miller's cousins, were among the regulars, as was Jane's godfather and cousin Leon Washington. Cecil Miller dropped in, as did Earl Broady, then a police officer with the LAPD (later an L.A. County Superior Court judge). When Langston Hughes, a chain smoker like Miller, was in town, he came by, too. They were a group to some extent bound tightly by the Long Beach earthquake and the death of Cloyd Miller, Loren's brother. Everyone remembered where he or she was on March 10, 1933. James Ronald Derry, a regular who had come to Los Angeles with Langston Hughes, on that fateful day had scooped up three-year-old Jane and carried her to safety. Ida Jackson Miller, the wife of Halvor, Sr., one of the players, and incidentally Juanita's Jefferson High School classmate, had done the same for little Halvor, her six-month-old son.[163]

Essentially, Miller's time in New York, dissecting racism and capitalism for larger audiences, proved beneficial. His newfound visibility, in turn, brought more clients to his lawyer's door. When Weirick Drug Store on West Pico Boulevard refused service to Allen Woodward and Aaron Johnson, on December 5, 1935, "because of their race," they sought Miller, who filed a suit "for damages asking $2000."[164] Seven months later, he and Thomas L. Griffith, Jr., represented Horace Hampton, who had been beaten by the police. Extricating fact from fiction, the attorneys uncovered that on July 16, Hampton had been picked up at 41st Street and Central Avenue, beaten by six men, three of them police officers, and taken to "Jefferson and Stanford streets, while his captors taunted him with declarations that they were members of the Black Legion. He was released only after he promised to leave the city."[165] The *Los Angeles Sentinel* reported that after the two attorneys outlined the facts of the case, a grand jury ordered a full investigation.

Although Miller continued his legal work throughout 1936, he had not, as yet, abandoned his association with East Coast leftists. Before he left for New York in October to attend "a scintillating theatrical and cultural vivant"[166] sponsored by the Friends of the *New Masses*, Charlotta Bass's *California Eagle* accused him of being a Communist. His peppery defense generated a follow-up by the *Eagle* on October 9:

> Have a letter from our fellow countryman Loren Miller, brilliant young barrister and also a big leaguer in the literary world. Lorren [*sic*] says that we hooked him wrong in stating he was to write publicity for the New Deal. He further slapped us on the wrist for saying he was a Communist. Heard Loren deliver an eloquent speech at second Baptist several months ago in which he beautifully portrayed the glories of Red Russia. Pardon us, we thought you meant it. Have a drink; we'll take a cool one.[167]

Miller's beef with the *Eagle* appears disingenuous. In most circles, he was a known Marxist idealist.[168] Countless times he had written approvingly of the Communists, endorsed them, and published in their newspapers and magazines; he belonged to numerous cultural front organizations. Had he forgotten that he wrote "One Way Out—Communism" which ran in the July 1934 edition of *Opportunity* magazine? In it, Miller celebrated the virtues of socialism; he derided a philosophy that extolled the virtues and righteousness of economic prudence "broadcast to the Negroes of the land" a hundred years after slavery."[169]

The real answer, Miller maintained, requires a "Socialist America and that with that achieved there would be no place for group exploitation as the example of Russia has proved. The common Socialist culture of a Soviet America would operate to facilitate the final merger of Negroes and Americans."[170] Like many black intellectuals during the 1930s, Miller embraced Marxist ideals without the need to join the party. Throughout his life, he always maintained that he never was a member of the Communist Party, a position he reiterated when agents from the Federal Bureau of Investigation visited him on February 20, 1952. Whether he was or not is a matter of whom we believe. According to Miller's FBI file, an "Informant said that LAWRENCE ROSSMORE was identical with LOREN MILLER," who joined the party in 1936. Card No. 75393 was made out to Lawrence Rossmore, a thirty-two-year-old African American who belonged to "Unit 1940, Professional Section, and District 13." In 1951, another informant, a former Communist Party member, said that Miller was seen as a menace because of his ownership of the *California Eagle* and was "not a member of the Communist party."[171] Although the bureau was unable to conclude whether he was or was not, it nonetheless continued to monitor him for the remainder of his life. Miller's niece Jane Kerina believed he belonged to the party.[172]

On March 7, 1937, after four years of marriage, "Attorney and Mrs. Loren Miller of 207 East 45th Street," reported the *Los Angeles Sentinel*, "are receiving congratulations this week upon the birth of a six-pound son who was ushered into the world late Sunday afternoon"[173] at the Methodist Hospital of Southern California on South Hope Street. The announcement continued, "The newcomer is scheduled to be christened Loren Leon Miller as soon as ceremonies are held." The attending physician, Dr. Henry A. McPherson, added, "both mother and baby are getting along nicely."[174]

Dr. McPherson, who was prominent in the National Medical Association as well a bass soloist in the Westminster Presbyterian Church choir, was—like the well-known Chinese actor Philip Ahn and noted Korean physician Dr. A. Kim— being sued for occupying a Los Angeles home legally restricted to Caucasians. McPherson and the Millers were friends. Much later Juanita and her doctor would join forces in the fight against tuberculosis. Still later she would become a member of the Los Angeles chapter of the Links, an elitist black women's organization founded in 1950 by the good doctor's wife, Marjorie McPherson.[175]

At 8 P.M., the same day that the Miller baby—who later acquired the nickname "Pete"—was born, gunfire struck Buron Fitts, the district attorney of Los Angeles County, while stopped at a railroad crossing on his way to the San Gabriel Valley. He recalled, "A shot came from the other machine, and the bullet struck me in the left arm. A second bullet crashed through the windshield." Instrumental in quelling the recent sit-down strike in Santa Monica at the Douglas

Aircraft plant, Fitts said, "It is my best guess that radical labor agitators either associated with the longshoremen or aircraft industries are responsible for this unwarranted attack."[176]

Before Pete's birth, a bomb exploded in Harry Raymond's car, a former police officer and private investigator who was investigating corruption in the administration of Los Angeles's mayor Frank L. Shaw.[177] Seven months after Pete's birth, another bomb, this time filled with chloride of potash, "rocked and partially wrecked" the Los Feliz Boulevard home of Clifford E. Clinton. He was chair of the Citizens' Independent Vice Investigation Committee, vice chair of the grand jury of Los Angeles County, and the owner of Clifton's Brookdale Cafeteria—where the motto was "you may pay what you wish or dine free unless delighted."[178] As questions surfaced as to why a bomb had ripped through the kitchen of Clinton's house, speculation settled on three possibilities: (1) a servant in the Clinton household was the intended target; (2) the attack was an attempt to curb Clinton's crusade to rid city hall of corruption; (3) Clinton staged the bombing himself. Although no assailant surfaced in the bombing, LAPD captain Earl Kynette was indicted and convicted in the earlier bombing of Harry Raymond. Finally, after years of corruption allegations, "Los Angeles voters turned on Shaw and gave him the distinction of being the first U.S. mayor to be thrown out of office by recall."[179]

Though born into a similar political climate of unrest as his father, unlike his father, the newest addition to the Miller clan entered a world with some measure of cultural and intellectual privilege, if richness can be measured as a circle of friendship and lively exchange. The Millers welcomed such friends of such distinction into their comfortable small house on East 45th Street—just a few doors from where Juanita's parents lived—as Arna Bontemps, Aaron Douglas, Walter A. Gordon, Chester Himes, Langston Hughes, Thurgood Marshall, Henry Lee Moon, Carey McWilliams and A. L. Wirin, among others.

Five days after his son's birth, Miller was back in court, along with his law partner Ivan Johnson III. On March 12, the two appeared on behalf of Cecil McIntyre, who testified that Cole's P. E. Café at 118 West Sixth Street served his "two white companions but refused his request"[180] for a glass of beer. Judge Ellis Eagan ordered the café to pay McIntyre "$100 and costs for refusing to serve him." That Easter, Miller, most likely bleary-eyed with a brand-new baby in the house, spoke on world peace at a special vespers service at the new interracial First Church of Humanity, founded by Los Angeles's "homespun philosopher" Eugene Henry Huffman, whose ultramodern church, according to Miller, "dresses religious worship in the garb of art and music."[181]

Interestingly, Miller's enchantment with Communism began to fade around the time he became a father. This was before the Nazi-Soviet Pact of 1939, when many white and black radicals became disillusioned with the CPUSA. He told

Lawrence de Graaf that by 1938, "I was no longer a Marxist."[182] He told Lester Granger, "All such [leftist] activities on my part stopped in 1938.[183] This was not entirely accurate, however.

Ever since Miller and Hughes first became friends, the two traveled on similar trajectories, one never too far behind or ahead of the other, particularly on political and literary matters. Hughes, who had moved toward the "political mainstream after a decade of association with international communism," renewed his "radical and activist engagement"[184] during World War II, according to historian Nikhil Pal Singh. Miller similarly moved away from his early naïve enthusiasm for Communism as a means to combat American racism in the late 1930s. But at the outset of World War II, he took a particularly radical and unpopular stance when he opposed the roundup and internment of Japanese Americans. And though he wrote in the late 1930s of distancing himself from the Communists, in 1942 he filed an amicus brief in *Communist Party v. Peek*, supporting the organization's right to participate in any California primary election.[185]

What changed in Miller's life during this period, according to Harvard law professor Kenneth Mack, was not the "various shifts of CPUSA policy that drove so many into, and out of, radical politics, nor anything significant in national civil rights politics. What had changed was not the world around Miller, but himself. After years of denial, he had begun to ply his trade,"[186] the law. After all "it was his legal work that put food on the table."[187]

Somehow, word got out that on Friday, November 15, 1940, Langston Hughes would "say a few words about his recent bestselling autobiography, *The Big Sea*. While more than six hundred luncheon guests were gathered at Pasadena's swanky Hotel Vista Del Arroyo, waiting for publisher George Palmer Putnam to introduce Hughes, a delegation sent by Sister Aimee Semple McPherson burst into the room waving a copy of "Goodbye Christ," Hughes's 1932 poem: "[It] seems Hughes wrote a poem in which he referred to Sister Aimee and assorted other religious leaders in none too complimentary language." The evangelist, according to the *Chicago Defender*, had warned her followers that the devil "has been appearing in strange guises for untold centuries while telling them of Hughes' scheduled talk."[188]

In the confusion, Hughes made a hasty exit and slipped down a street "packed with pickets, onlookers and police squad cars" to a waiting taxi. He turned up on Sunday morning and read some of his poems at a literary coffee sponsored by Juanita's League of Allied Arts in the home of Pauline Slater. Later, escorted by Miller, Hughes told reporters that "he was unruffled by the experience and absolved the hotel" and his hosts. There would be no legal action of any kind taken. "Looks like one of Aimee's publicity gags,"[189] said Miller. Three months later, the Los Angeles division of the FBI reported: "Subject, a negro poet, announced on circular as speaker at the 'Book and author' luncheon in Pasadena,

California . . . author of poem entitled 'Good-bye, Christ,' which appears to be of a Communistic nature." The FBI report noted that Hughes "did not appear on the announced program."[190]

More serious events were taking place in Los Angeles before Hughes's comedic hasty exit. Between May and August 1940, the Japanese residents of Los Angeles were feeling unimaginably fearful. Looming above their heads was legislation winding its way through Congress, which, when approved, would require the fingerprinting and registration of all aliens living in the United States. On a similar course, the Los Angeles County Board of Supervisors was poised to adopt a local ordinance requiring the compulsory registration and fingerprinting of all aliens in the county.[191] Already, the board had enacted an ordinance prohibiting trespassing around airplane plants "to curb subversive alien activities," reported the *Los Angeles Times*.[192] Unsurprisingly, the civil liberties leader A. L. Wirin opposed any attempt to register noncitizens. As spokesperson for the local ACLU and the Los Angeles chapter of the National Lawyers Guild (and eventually the Japanese American Citizens League), Wirin declared before the L.A. Board of Supervisors that "Such an ordinance has been held by the Supreme Court to be unconstitutional. The Constitution of the United States is for both the rulers and the people of the country alike, applying also to aliens as a recognized class within the country entitled to the protection of the country's law as well as its citizens. The courts have so held."[193]

Amidst the ever-increasing anti-Japanese sentiment, Loren Miller, Leo Gallagher, Charles J. Katz, and several dozen liberal attorneys countersigned Wirin's brief. As usual, they were in the minority. Mainstream sentiments, such as those coming from retired superior court judge John Perry Wood, saw the legal challenge to the ordinance as "subversive opposition."[194] Even before Wirin stood, on June 11, before the board of supervisors, the *Los Angeles Times* endorsed the police commission's suggestion that "the City Council adopt an ordinance requiring immediate registration and fingerprinting of all aliens in Los Angeles." "Congress will move faster," according to the *Times*, "if an example is set by cities and areas throughout the country and it is to be hoped that the Board of Supervisors will promptly consider adoption of the police program for the county as a whole."[195]

On June 29, Congress passed the Alien Registration Act of 1940 (also known as the Smith Act), which required all noncitizens fourteen years old or older to register with the government. The anti-sedition section of the act set criminal penalties for advocating the overthrow of the United States government. In the interim, whether due to naïveté or an attempt at normalcy, representatives from the Japanese American Citizens League (JACL); the city's largest Japanese-English newspaper, *Rafu Shimpo*; and the Japanese-owned Pacific Investment Company appeared before the city council with a request to purchase land "on a hay field near the intersection of Jefferson Boulevard and La Brea Avenue"[196] in the West Jefferson boulevard area, near Leimert Park. Their appeal met with an excoriating, racially charged response, according to the *Los Angeles Sentinel*: "Local American born citizens of Japanese origin bore the brunt of a savage attack [on August 12] when city council chambers resounded to fiery oratory citing the imminence of a frightful 'yellow peril.'"[197] City council objections to the proposed subdivision made reference to what happens when "Negro residents" sought to "make an effort to move elsewhere." Property values, the council thundered, would decrease and the American standard of living would decline.[198]

Miller, incensed by the furor of the city council, declared, "Residents of this community owe it to themselves to urge the City Council to approve the subdivision sought by Japanese residents of the city." The so-called Yellow Peril outcry, which Miller's *Sentinel* editorial called a smokescreen, was yet another veiled attempt to "confine minority groups to undesirable sections of the city."[199] The elected officials' actions led Larry Tajiri, editor of the weekly *Pacific Citizen* and a longtime critic of prejudice and discrimination, to astutely coin the term "Jap Crow."[200]

Undeterred by the objections to Japanese living in Jefferson Park, Miller expressed "solidarity with the Nisei" and their desire to move beyond the boundaries of the Little Tokyo district in downtown Los Angeles. According to historian Scott Kurashige, "Miller assured the Nisei that African American voters would strongly support their efforts to defeat Jefferson Park's political opponents at the polls."[201] His editorials, which tended to shape the *Sentinel*'s policies, zeroed in on the real peril: "The peril to democracy as exemplified by office holders who use their positions of public trust and honor to deny democratic rights and privileges to American citizens whose only fault is an accident of birth. . . . It is safe assumption that an office holder who is willing to deprive any minority group of any of its rights is not a safe person to entrust with the rights of any other minority group."[202]

The Equality Committee of the JACL organized mass rallies to combat the "venomous nature of white hostility" toward Japanese Americans moving into white residential neighborhoods. Japanese developers with white backers filed lawsuits. In the end, the city council approved the subdivision. However, "the controversy had given many Nisei cold feet. As many as half of the lots had been reserved, but an unstoppable stream of withdrawals killed the project. The white residents had lost the legal battle but succeeded in convincing Nisei that Jefferson Park homeowners would have obnoxious racists for neighbors."[203]

On August 28, Toyosaku Komai, publisher of *Rafu Shimpo*, showed up on the first day for registration and fingerprinting at the post office's newly established Alien Registration Center at 660 East 22nd Street.[204] "Several factors," argues Kurashige, "explain why [the Japanese] bent over backward to accommodate government officials. . . . As late as 1940, the *Rafu Shimpo* . . . was still printing news releases from the Japanese government. . . . Second, they received encouragement from prominent officials convincing them they were doing what was right."

The JACL leaders were young, naïve, and confused and, according to Kurashige, "anxious to expunge the legacy of dual nationalism."[205] They pushed the concept of loyalty to America. "We were always told to be as American as possible," said Floyd Mori, national executive director of JACL. There was another reason. Despite present-day Japanese Americans' drive to assimilate, during the war they adhered "strongly to the ancient samurai values of endurance"[206] and duty. That reservoir of stoicism helped them survive internment.

When the news of the Japanese attack on Pearl Harbor reached Miller, he was in his front yard with four-year-old Pete. Following the surprise military attack, President Roosevelt executed Executive Order 9066, authorizing the roundup and internment of approximately 110,000 American citizens of Japanese ancestry and resident aliens from Japan. Not long after, government trucks would arrive, taking Pete's Japanese playmates away.[207]

Within the ACLU, there were conflicting positions on the constitutionality of evacuation and internment. "Leaders of the American Civil Liberties Union bear much of the blame for the outcome of the Japanese American cases,"[208] writes Peter H. Irons, civil rights attorney and legal scholar. West Coast branches of the ACLU were instructed to limit test cases to the unlawful singling out of "Japanese Americans on racial grounds,"[209] not constitutional ones. "My research," writes Irons, "in the files of the ACLU and its West Coast branches disclosed that personal and partisan loyalty to Franklin D. Roosevelt, who signed [Order 9066], led the ACLU's national board to bar"[210] constitutional challenges and subsequent appeals. Interestingly, Harry Bridges, leader of the International Longshore and Warehouse Union, who before the war had been saved from deportation by A. L. Wirin, subsequently accused him of "representing the enemy."[211] Even Carey McWilliams "initially supported what he regarded as the government's surprisingly well-executed and just implementation and administration of internment."[212] Wirin ignored pressure from the national ACLU leadership, and instead as the leader of the southern California branch in 1942 challenged "the wartime evacuation from California of Americans of Japanese descent" in federal court. According to Wirin, Miller was "one of the two lawyers to join ACLU counsel"[213] in this effort.

War years for the Millers were busy. When Miller had the means to build a new home, he chose the hilly part of Los Angeles's bohemian district, four miles north of downtown and four miles south of the Griffith Observatory. The Silver Lake neighborhood is that part of Los Angeles where mid-twentieth-century artists, leftists, and homosexuals chose to live. Historically, it was a small area for early twentieth-century film studios, where Mack Sennett hit comedies and Keystone Cop movies were made.[214] All in all, the Millers did the unconventional when they decided to live across town, in the center of progressive politics and away from the growing number of middle-class African Americans. Perhaps the neighborhood suited Loren Miller's need for greater intellectual stimulation and a safe harbor from churchgoers. In any event, the Miller's increased prosperity allowed the couple to choose an old friend, pioneering architect James "Jimmy" Homer Garrott, an emergent modernist, to design their home.

Garrott designed two parcels of land on Micheltorena Street: one at 647 for the Miller family, the other a Silver Lake lot he designed for himself. Although the parcels were purchased in 1938, it took two years before the Millers moved into the newly built, two-bedroom, split-level house in late 1940. According to Edward Miller, both the land and the house cost $4,800.[215] Jimmy Garrott lived next door with his mother, brother, and Helen Duncan, his wife, in a two-story, three-bedroom, three-bath house.[216]

Garrott, who like Miller had belonged to the League of Struggle for Negro Rights, was a graduate of Los Angeles's Polytechnic High School, had studied architecture at the University of Southern California, and had passed the California architect licensing examination in 1929. Known best for his early important commissions, such as designing the headquarters of the Golden State Mutual Life Insurance Company at 4261 Central Avenue, Garrott designed two hundred homes and twenty-five churches in his lifetime. After the war, he rejoined his architect friend, Gregory Ain, who was awarded a Guggenheim Fellowship in 1940, and the two, in addition to designing attorney Ben Margolis's house, designed and built their modernist, one-story architectural office at 2311 Hyperion Avenue, a ten-minute walk from Micheltorena Street.[217]

The year after the Miller's moved to Micheltorena, Arna Bontemps asked Langston Hughes, "How is Zora [Neal Hurston] doing? I mean is literature her staff?" He also wanted to know just where Miller "built his new house."[218] Hughes replied on October 23, 1941, "Loren's new house is just beyond the West Temple district around Hoover, Virgil."[219]

Coincidentally, the day after writing to Bontemps, Hughes was scheduled to speak in Los Angeles at the League of American Writers dinner meeting on American Negro literature. Three weeks earlier, Hughes had written the league's Maurice Murphy, to say he would be happy to appear as a guest speaker on October 24, if the league would pay his expenses to and from Monterey and hold the dinner in the black part of Los Angeles—possibly the Clark Hotel, his favorite place in Los Angeles. He suggested that the dinner should honor all "Los Angeles Negro writers," particularly Chester Himes, John Kinloch (Charlotta Bass's nephew at the *California Eagle*), Almena Davis, Anita Scott Coleman, and Zora Neal Hurston, "a new resident on the coast," among others "and two or three others whose names Loren Miller can give you." Because Hughes had already agreed to make several public appearances later in the season, he did not want his appearance at the dinner to undercut other "Negro organizations who expect to make some money . . . by attracting their audience."[220]

Hughes wrote Miller too, who had recently joined the League's board: "If they are holding this meeting, then keep that Latin American book and I'll pick it up when I come down." He had lent Miller *Lanterns on the Levee* by William

Alexander Percy. Then Hughes added a bit of gossip: "Six of the Dunham Dancers stayed out here, and Mr. Sullivan had a party for all of them after the recital—which is very good. You ought to see it. It's more entertainment than concert—so you won't get sleepy. Dance patterns based on Wigman, but the hips are colored."[221] Lastly, he told his friend that he received a check for *Jump for Joy*, a sketch entitled "Mad Scene from Woolworth's" he had written for Duke Ellington's all-black musical review. *Jump*—financed in part by the actor John Garfield—starred Dorothy Dandridge and Herb Jeffries at the Mayan Theater in Los Angeles.

Unquestionably, Miller and Hughes were close. Arnold Rampersad writes that Arna Bontemps was Hughes's closest friend; they were like "blood brothers," said Bontemps's wife, Alberta. Miller and Hughes's friendship differed in that they drank, smoked, and played cards together. "Arna hardly touched liquor,"[222] according to Alberta. She said Hughes "could dine with kings and with common people. Arna was not so flexible." Like Hughes, Miller could hang with the high hatter and the plain Joe. Apparently, their friendship of infrequent visits relied on wit and a capacity to turn disdain for the behavior of the petty bourgeois into bawdy humor. Most likely, their unforgiving memories of poverty, a shared appraisal of vicissitudes in life, the adventure to Russia, and an enduring, flat midwestern accent that some call "Kansas twang" helped bind the literary friend to the genius of the courtroom for forty years.

CHAPTER 6

Pursuing Justice

I n 1943, during the battle over who had the right to live in the exclusive West
Adams Heights Sugar Hill neighborhood, it was thought that there was little
possibility that the black movie stars and other prominent black Angelenos
who lived there would be forced to move. The Los Angeles realtor who sold most
of these homes to the stars, assured them that, although the all-white homeowners association had met to raise funds to oust them, it was unlikely they
would succeed.[1] On May 24, 1945, that assurance dissolved when attorneys Loren
Miller and Clarence A. Jones responded to an injunction initiated by Ane Marie
Anderson and her seven co-plaintiffs, all members of the West Adams Improvement Association.[2] Like most whites of the era, they opposed any racial change
to the exclusive character of the neighborhood.[3] The invasion of affluent African Americans, such as Hattie McDaniel—the first black actor to win an Oscar
from the Academy of Motion Picture Arts and Sciences—and other "top flight
Negro movie celebrities"[4] like Ethel Waters and Louise Beavers—whose newly
purchased West Adams home was "once owned by a mayor of Los Angeles"[5]—
fared no better than blacks with lesser means. Celebrity or not, African Americans were purportedly alien interlopers "dragging the Caucasian race down to
[their] level."[6]

Undoubtedly, Miller knew that McDaniel's celebrity "would make this a high
profile case and that her involvement presented a major opportunity to strike a
blow against housing discrimination,"[7] according to Jill Watts, McDaniel's biographer. Walter White realized it too from the moment the black press picked up
the story. After reading of the fate of Ethel Waters, vocalist and actor, and others in Los Angeles embroiled in a legal struggle, White instinctively telegraphed
Thurgood Marshall: "look into the matter while on the [West] Coast."[8] White
advised Marshall to get in touch with Miller (who would become a member of
the national legal committee of the NAACP's Legal Defense Fund).

The West Adams plaintiffs alleged that they were within their legal right, based
on the neighborhood-wide restrictive covenant signed in August 1937, to prohibit
any "person whose blood is not entirely that of the White Race" from living in their
neighborhood, "except in the capacity of a domestic servant of a White person."[9]
They were adamant that Earl Auseth, Sidney Dones, Ethel Waters, Hattie McDaniel, Vada Somerville, and other "Negroes from the area bounded by the Adams,
Washington, Western and La Salle thoroughfares"[10] should be kept out. They used
the standard marketing ruse of falling property values to support their cause.

Despite the plaintiffs' opposition toward blacks moving westward—beyond South Central Avenue—as early as 1938, well-to-do African Americans "willing and able to pay $15,000 and up" for homes on Los Angeles's West Side "had begun moving into the old colonial mansions."[11] Langston Hughes, well accustomed with Los Angeles, wrote that these were "the most beautiful Negro homes I have ever seen. . . . Why should not Negroes have palatial homes if they can afford them. I wish everybody, colored and white, could have a fine home—then maybe some white folks would not be so jealous of Negroes who live well."[12]

In 1941, the same year that silent-film star Harold Lloyd, famous for hanging from the hands of a skyscraper clock tower in *Safety Last!* (1923), led the drive to keep blacks and Jews from moving into nearby Beverly Hills,[13] Hattie's brother Sam McDaniel bought property south of West Adams Heights in the West Jefferson neighborhood of Jefferson Park. At the time, because that upscale neighborhood had already begun to change, racially defined private property restrictions were thought unenforceable. Instead, Sam McDaniel and Mrs. Vetress Howell Walker were ordered to appear in the Los Angeles County Superior Court[14] to answer a law suit brought by a white property owner "bitterly opposed to any letdown in the fight to prevent Negro occupancy"[15] in the 3700 block of South Van Ness Avenue, near the Sugar Hill neighborhood. At trial, Miller argued that "the recent surveys have shown an acute housing shortage for Negroes in the city."[16] Aided by the appearance of the ACLU and the NAACP, Miller's defense revolved around the changing character of the area, which bordered Jefferson and Exposition Boulevards to the south of Cimarron Street and Arlington Avenue to the east.[17] When those housing covenants had been signed in 1925, he argued, few African Americans lived in that section of Los Angeles.[18] He explained, "These recurrent efforts to confine Negroes to restricted areas indicate that the problem is becoming serious and that a renewed fight must be made to break restrictive covenants and secure a larger housing area."[19]

There were other challenges to the status quo besides the two McDaniel suits. Over in Orange County, Judge Albert F. Ross threw out the suit to oust first-generation Mexican American Alex Bernal, his wife, and his two daughters from their Fullerton home. Judge Ross, in wisely dismissing the case, "felt that the restriction is contrary to public policy and more so decidedly unconstitutional."[20] According to Gustavo Arellano of the *Orange County Weekly*, the judge was unconvinced by the testimony of Orange County real estate appraisers, who testified "that having Mexicans live in a neighborhood brought down property values by at least half," and by "anthropologists who claimed Mexicans were not Caucasians."[21] In David C. Marcus's closing defense arguments (he would later argue *Mendez v. Westminster*), he stated that the action of Mr. Bernal's neighbors "was taken from Hitler's 'Mein Kampf.'" Judge Ross, disturbed by the "Hitlerite Attitude" of the plaintiffs, opined, "I would rather have people of the type of the Bernal's living next door to me than Germans of the paranoid type now living in Germany,"[22] an obvious dig at the plaintiffs, some of whom were German

Americans, according to the *Chicago Defender*. Eight miles south of downtown Los Angeles, in the then lily-white city of Maywood (now 97 percent Latino), David Grant and Alice Grommet were summarily arrested for "distributing pamphlets without a license," which blasted, "the Chamber of Commerce plan to re-establish race property restrictions"[23] at a time when almost every liberal organization in Los Angeles had joined the chorus against restrictions. Leo Gallagher, their attorney, succeeded in getting the charges dropped.

When Pauli Murray, one of the founders of the National Organization for Women and the first black woman to become an Episcopal priest, answered the federal government's War Manpower Commission's call for wartime workers in 1944, she and her sister decided to drive cross-country. In her autobiography, she writes that Jim Crow "pursued us relentlessly to the West Coast."[24] Further adversity greeted Murray, a transgender woman defying conventional binaries of gender identity, and her sister Mildred when they arrived in Los Angeles.[25] She recalls, "When I came home one day and found in our mailbox an unsigned typewritten letter with no return address, purporting to be from the South Crocker Street Property Owners' Association and addressed to Mrs. Mildred Fearing and Pauli Murray." The letter read, "We . . . wish to inform you the flat you now occupy . . . is restricted to the white or Caucasian race only . . . therefore we ask that you vacate . . . within seven days or we will turn the matter over to our attorney for action."[26] Unwittingly, they had moved a half block over the "white" line into a dilapidated cold-water railroad flat at 5871 South Crocker Street, "where white people had decided to take their stand to prevent Negro penetration." For Murray, this was not the first time she had run up against such harassment. In 1941, while she was house-sitting in Queens, New York, the landlord chased her out of the building, shouting, "Go back to Harlem where you belong." In New York, she did not feel frightened. But in Los Angeles, because her sister worked the late shift at the veterans hospital on Bonsall Avenue in West Los Angeles, she felt otherwise. Murray turned to Miller, who advised that she seek immediate "police protection." "[S]oon squad cars," she writes, "began to patrol our neighborhood at night and the FBI was asked to investigate the matter. Our greatest protection, however, was public exposure."[27]

That summer Murray wrote about her experiences as a reporter for the *Los Angeles Sentinel*. It was there that she met Miller for the first time: "He and I hit it off beautifully. First of all, we had this common tradition of civil rights and he was really a beautiful human being and so that was a very, very happy relationship and they just turned me loose as a roving reporter and let me go my way.[28] She learned that two hundred people had hurriedly gotten together to form the Southside Property Owners' Protection League and that that the league had decided to enforce restrictions against two families, one of whom was Murray and her sister. She insisted, "[N]o self respecting human being will tolerate this 'white supremacy' twaddle. So long as there's breathe in his body. Isn't that what we're supposed to be fighting for, or am I wrong"?[29] The sisters held their ground. After finishing law school, Murray became the first African American female deputy attorney general of California.[30]

For more than a century, housing and residential issues "were at the heart of the struggle for Black advancement in Los Angeles."[31] According to Gunnar Myrdal, residential segregation based on race "represents a deviation from free competition in the market for apartments and houses and curtails the supply available for Negroes" and "creates an 'artificial scarcity' whenever Negroes need more residences, due to raised economic standards or increased numbers of the Negro population."[32] Residential segregation, as understood by Myrdal in 1944, is determined by factors such as poverty, ethnic attachment, enforced segregation, restrictive covenants, federal housing policies, and the real estate industry. In turn, these factors shape educational options, access to jobs, and quality of life.[33]

"War's end brought no surcease" in housing, wrote Miller in *The Petitioners: The Story of the Supreme Court of the United States and the Negro*. "The migrants kept on coming, the children kept on being born, the population kept on growing."[34] Though the pattern was the same throughout the nation, California experienced the largest population shift with three million new residents between 1940 and 1947.[35] The existence of such exceptional dynamics as population growth and housing shortages brought an increased deployment of restrictive covenants. "Eighty percent of the land occupied by Negroes in Los Angeles," wrote Miller in the *Crisis*, "is covered by racially restrictive covenants."[36]

California's housing history "with its salubrious climate," Miller informed, "has produced racial restrictive covenants far superior, if that is the word, to the ordinary run-of-mine racial restrictive covenant."[37] In the super-paradise of the Pacific, "None could dwell but blond-haired, blue-eyed Aryans, certified 99.44% pure for at least seven generations, all of them five feet 10 ⅞ inches tall, addicts of Little Orphan Annie,"[38] the Sunday comic strip. The herding of nonwhites into racial zones by "hucksters of prejudice"—one of Miller's recurring themes— began not in the South as one might conjecture or even in opposition to African Americans. Its origins are California based, he claimed; its target, the Chinese. "California's 1879 constitution," he continued, "clothed cities and towns with the authority to exclude Chinese or segregated them within city limits."[39] Objections to the newcomers from China had led to California's Anti-Coolie Act of 1862, an attempt to tax Chinese laborers lured earlier to California by the promise of gold. "Throughout the Pacific area and beginning in California, the exclusion movement," wrote Miller's friend Carey McWilliams in 1943, "has followed a definite course: from local agitation against a particular class or race of Asiatics to national movements directed against all Asiatics of every race and class; from economic arguments to cultural and biological arguments for restriction and exclusion."[40]

By 1870, Chinese workers would make up 20 percent of California's labor force, a threat felt most by non-Asian laborers.[41] In an attempt to halt further threats by Chinese workers, reinforced by the depression of 1876, the United States Congress passed the first restriction on immigration, the Chinese Exclusion Act of 1882 (which involved a ten-year period of limitation on Chinese immigrants to 105 per year). The act was not repealed until the passage of the Magnuson Act in 1943. "As a matter of fact the exclusion of the Chinese squared perfectly with the policy of placing Indians on reservations and segregating Negroes by force of law. Modes of aggression which had been tried out against Indians and Negroes were easily transferred to the Chinese,"[42] wrote McWilliams. When the door closed on the Chinese, it cracked open somewhat; Japanese immigrants filled the void. However, according to McWilliams, the Japanese presented a more "potent threat . . . than the Chinese for they demonstrated a remarkable ability to move up into the self-employed and farm-owner category."[43] Anti-Chinese and anti-Japanese agitation became a tool to build a powerful labor movement. For example, the American Federation of Labor, in an effort to preserve the status quo, by 1904 "resolved to exclude Japanese and Korean, as well as Chinese laborers."[44] The subordination and exclusion of Asians, according to scholar Lawrence de Graaf, extended to the 1915 state law barring "non-citizens from public employment."[45] Although restrictive immigration laws affected other Asians, the greatest impact fell earliest on those Chinese who endured months of quarantine in detention barracks on Angel Island, in the San Francisco Bay.[46]

In 1890, in an attempt to control where within the city these Chinese newcomers would live, "San Francisco responded with a segregation ordinance,"[47] the nation's first race-based residential ordinance. A wise Lee Sing "decided to defend [his] rights along strictly legal and constitutional lines."[48] Subsequently, a federal court promptly struck down the ordinance as invalid "on the ground that it denied Chinese the equal protection of the law demanded by the Fourteenth Amendment,"[49] wrote Miller.

Undismayed by the federal court's decision, a group of property owners, wrote Miller, earned the distinction of putting in the "law books the first case involving race restrictive agreements."[50] The agreements read that "the party of the first part shall never . . . rent any of the buildings or grounds . . . to a Chinaman or Chinamen."[51] One of the signers, in opposition to the other property owners, agreed to rent his San Buenaventura (now Ventura County) property to Fong Yet and Sam Choy, two Chinese laundrymen.[52] The other signers "promptly asked the federal district court for an injunction restraining the Chinese from using or occupying the property, on the ground that they were violating a private contract." In 1892, federal district judge Erskine M. Ross ruled in *Gandolfo v. Hartman* that "Such a contract is absolutely void and should not be enforced in any court-certainly in a court of equity of the United States."[53]

Though consistently undemocratic, courts evaded enforcement by continuing to rule that "neighborhood agreements," according to Miller, "were 'private contracts' and hence not violative of the equal protection clause."[54] For the proponents of race-restrictive agreements, Miller wrote, "covenants are merely private contracts with which the state is not concerned."[55] Other courts, despite agreeing that such agreements were discriminatory, held that "the Fourteenth Amendment does not forbid discrimination by individuals but only by states."[56] With the pressure removed, artful covenant agreements and real estate boards, already powerful, grew exponentially. Though residential restrictions were first directed against Chinese immigrants, they were not the only objectionable groups. In time, segregation by contract extended to other ethnicities: African Americans, Armenians, Hindus, Jews, Japanese, Turks, and Mexicans; at times, though of mixed indigenous blood, Mexicans have been classified for purposes of naturalization as "Caucasians" (because of the Treaty of Guadalupe Hidalgo, which ended the Mexican-American War of 1846–48).[57]

By 1915, a wave of appellate court decisions upheld restrictions.[58] Circuitously, the Supreme Court did its part too when in 1917, Moorfield Storey, attorney for the NAACP, argued for the plaintiff in *Buchanan v. Warley*, a Louisville, Kentucky, racial zoning case. In 1914, the city of Louisville designed an ordinance "to prevent conflict and ill-feeling between the white and colored races . . . to preserve the public peace and promote the general welfare by making reasonable provisions requiring . . . the use of separate blocks for residence, places of abode and places of assembly by white and colored people respectively."[59]

The short version of the story is that Robert Buchanan, a white property owner, entered into a sales contract with William Warley, a black man. Warley signed the agreement, which stated that he was not obligated to pay for the purchase unless he had "the right under the laws of the State of Kentucky and the City of Louisville to occupy said property as a residence."[60] Buchanan wanted his money. "Warley, who at once professed legal pain and surprise, said he didn't have to pay," explained Miller, "or accept the deed unless he had a right to build and occupy a residence on the lot." Buchanan took the case to court—a strange spectacle since Buchanan was white—contending that the segregation ordinance was unconstitutional and that Warley was "apparently fighting tooth and nail to uphold racial segregation." The trial judge threw the case out. Buchanan sought relief from the Kentucky Court of Appeals, where "he repeated his argument that the ordinance was unconstitutional." He wanted the court to compel Warley "to accept the deed and pay the purchase price."[61]

Finally, the case made it to the U.S. Supreme Court, and the NAACP, representing Buchanan, convinced the court that the racial zoning ordinance was unconstitutional.[62] "Colored persons," wrote Justice William R. Day, "are citizens of the United States and have the right to purchase property and enjoy the use of the same without laws discriminating against them solely on account of color."[63] As Miller observed, "Everybody but Louisville, other southern cities, and segregationists, North and South, was happy: The NAACP, because it had established the great principle that states and cities could not impose residential segregation by law or ordinance; Buchanan, because he had won, Warley, because he had lost." The rejoicing was short-lived. "[A] cloud no larger than a lawyer's pen rose on the housing horizon. State courts began enforcing racially restrictive covenants,"[64] wrote Miller decades later. In practical terms, white property owners were free to attach private agreements to their deeds, which excluded the sale or rent of "their property to Negroes."[65]

In 1921, John J. Buckley and Mrs. Irene Corrigan, along with a group of twenty-eight like-minded white property owners in the District of Columbia signed an agreement covering "25 parcels" of land that stated no "part of these properties shall ever be used or occupied by, or sold, leased or given to any person of the negro race or blood."[66] The next year, Mrs. Corrigan violated the agreement when she sold her lot to the wife of a prominent black physician, Mrs. Helen Curtis. Buckley, in due course, sued both Corrigan, who refused to nullify the sale, and Curtis. After the case was lost twice by James A. Cobb, attorney of record and Howard University Law School graduate, he "turned for help to the national office of the NAACP."[67] Louis Marshall and Moorfield Storey, two elderly white attorneys and cofounders of the NAACP, responded.

Subsequently, on January 8, 1926, the attorneys argued before the Supreme Court that covenants in themselves were unconstitutional.[68] Five months later, the court decided unanimously that the appeal was "entirely lacking in substance or color or merit." According to Miller, "From a strictly legal and technical point of view, all that the Court had decided was that a racially restrictive covenant was not void in itself, that property owners were entirely free to enter into such agreements abide by them if they chose to so do, and that a court not hold them void on the complaint of a Negro who wanted to buy the land."[69] The court's myopic interpretation skirted the constitutional issues. "The language used by the Supreme Court," wrote Miller, "in the Corrigan case also had the effect of stimulating the growth of a lush legal lore justifying race restrictive covenants and rationalizing their use."[70] Miller further stated, "Segregation imposed by state law was much more rigid and widespread in 1930 than in 1900, and it was growing in scope and intensity."[71]

Miller opined in 1966, "The courts ordered an offending Negro's ouster with no thought and no responsibility for his housing, even where it was apparent that no shelter was available for his use. If he refused to move in response to an injunction, he was in contempt of court and was jailed."[72] Following *Corrigan*, for the next two decades, the Supreme Court, for the most part, refused to review similar covenant cases.

Where Louis Marshall did succeed, according to Clement Vose, was in developing "a line of argument that presaged later efforts to have the judicial enforcement of racial covenants declared to be an unconstitutional expression of state action."[73] "Inevitably, African Americans turned to the Supreme Court, that final expositor of the Constitution," because "there was no hope for legislative relief,"[74] wrote Miller. Since 1875, Congress failed to pass any new civil rights bills. When Marshall and Storey died, according to historians August Meier and Elliott Rudwick, Walter White lamented, "It is going to be almost impossible to replace these two men who were our greatest legal assets as well as immensely helpful through the prestige which each had." However, their deaths led to the development of "a rising feeling among black lawyers that they should undertake the major responsibility in the fight for Negro rights; the appearance of an elite nucleus of black lawyers trained in constitutional law at Harvard and other leading institutions."[75] Even before the deaths of Storey and Marshall, there had been a general unhappiness on the over reliance by the NAACP on white lawyers. It would take people like Charles Hamilton Houston, according to Judge James A. Wynn, Jr., and Eli Paul Mazur, among others, to "lay the groundwork for the test cases that would ultimately come before the United States Supreme Court."[76]

In Los Angeles, it would take a high-profile case such as Hattie McDaniel's trial to begin to turn things around for black Angelenos. Known colloquially first as "Blueberry Hill" at the turn of the twentieth century, West Adams Heights, which later became known "far and wide as the famous Sugar Hill section of Los Angeles" after Harlem's fashionable sector of the same name, was one of Los Angeles's earliest residential areas planned exclusively for the socially elite.[77] In part, it was developed by railroad magnate Henry Edwards Huntington (of the Land and Improvement Company), who "founded the Los Angeles Railway, a massive intercity transit system"[78] and by Hulett Clinton Merritt, the wealthy Pasadena industrialist. For Carey McWilliams, attorney, author, twice awarded Guggenheim fellow and self-proclaimed "rebel-radical," the West Adams Heights district represented "one of the first elite residential areas in Los Angeles" and "one of the few surviving examples of planned urban elegance."[79]

In the 1940s, the neighborhood's stately late nineteenth-century and early twentieth-century Victorian mansions, old carriage houses, and medieval turrets remained resplendent by the time of the influx of African Americans. "Long before the Negro invasion the Heights had experienced a curious inner collapse, a psychological defeat, a social deflation which made the change in occupancy possible."[80] White bankers and industrialists, down on their luck and unable to maintain a lifestyle as they had before the Depression, began selling their West Adams property to well-to-do African Americans, who essentially escaped unscathed by crisis of the 1930s.[81] It was becoming a preferred area for professional black Angelenos and their families, who on any given Sunday afternoon would be seen attending "smartly appointed teas, musicales, and receptions."[82]

Interestingly, during the war, Sugar Hill defendants Mr. and Mrs. Henry T. Elmore, kept four refrigerators well stocked in order to entertain "from three to 40 servicemen in their 17-room home,"[83] providing them full-course dinners, long-distance telephone calls, and comfortable beds. Hattie McDaniel, too, as the chair of the Negro Division of the Victory Committee, filled her home with soldiers.[84] Prominent African Americans such as Sidney P. Dones, realtor, moneylender, and would-be spiritualist; Dr. Vada Watson Somerville, the first African American female graduate of the School of Dentistry at the University of

Southern California (who, along with her Jamaican-born husband, John Alexander Somerville, the first black male graduate of USC's School of Dentistry, built the Hotel Somerville); and musicians Benny Carter and Noble Sissle, "managed to buy homes on unrestricted blocks."[85] For Hattie and Louise Beavers, it was the "preferred neighborhood for actors and other black professionals as the Depression and the expiration of restrictive covenants made housing available."[86]

A decade before Norman Houston, founder of the Golden State Mutual Life Insurance Company, became the first African American to purchase a home in the West Adams Heights Sugar Hill district, property deflations had already begun. Houston, one of L.A.'s leading black elites, a member of the first national black men's fraternity, Sigma Pi Phi, and employer to 135 employees in 1935, "initially rented to a white tenant"[87] rather than submit to racial insult by occupying his property. Eventually, he did move in. His son, Ivan Houston, points out that, although their next door neighbor at 2219 South Hobart Boulevard was Hollywood actor Louise Beavers, "racially restrictive covenants in the city's neighborhoods placed all the black people in close proximity to each other, but this did not bring together black entertainers and their black professional neighbors. They were two entirely different social groups." Though most of Los Angeles's black elite had "no ties to Hollywood," Houston and Miller were the exceptions.[88] The two, along with singer and actress Lena Horne, were board members of the International Film and Radio Guild, a nonprofit corporation whose aim focused on bringing worldwide understanding and "a more realistic presentation on the screen and in radio of various people of the world."[89]

Houston's purchase of the home in 1938, it appears, grew out of a dispute between the previous owner and her unfriendly neighbors. Knowing that the property had never been under any restrictions, the owner decided "to settle scores with her oppressors by selling to a Negro."[90] As the older, more wealthy residents died off or moved away, newcomers realized that the old restrictive covenants were about to expire. This led the newcomers to draft a petition, "asking property owners to consent to the imposition of new restrictions designed to protect the Heights against non-Caucasians until midnight on December 31 in the fantastically remote year of 2035."[91] The older residents refused to sign, which infuriated the newcomers, eight of whom became plaintiffs in what eventually would become the famous Sugar Hill case [*Anderson v. Auseth*]. Before they filed their suit, the Improvement Association's president approached Houston—an amiable man—with an option to purchase his property, but the members could not agree on the amount. The option expired. What followed was twenty-four-hour neighborhood surveillance "to detect the first signs that Mr. Houston intended to occupy the property."[92]

Due to the white owners' inability to reconcile their differences, diehards decided to go to court to uphold their position that the only way a black person could live in West Adams Heights was "in the capacity of a domestic servant of a White person residing on the self-same parcel."[93] The plaintiffs contended that, because the defendants were African Americans, they had violated the terms of the real estate agreements, which restricted occupancy to persons of the Caucasian race and that therefore they should move. The defendants' counterargument contested the validity of such caviled agreements, though upheld as valid and legally binding in countless courtrooms outside of Los Angeles.[94]

Hattie McDaniel faced mounting adversities by the time her case came to court. According to scholar Jill Watts, "She was completely out of work."[95] Although her career had come to a halt, the trial and a pending divorce kept her name in the media. As a child, before she became one of black Hollywood's first celebrity film stars, McDaniel and her brother were vaudeville entertainers; Sam "Deacon" McDaniel did clog dancing, striking rhythms with his heel and toe against the floor.[96] Both were born in Wichita, Kansas, to former slaves. Sam had encouraged his sister "to come westward and give Hollywood a try."[97] According to *Los Angeles Times* columnist Cecilia Rasmussen, McDaniel "hopped a train for Hollywood with $20 and her lucky rabbit's foot in her purse."[98]

Eight years later, amid a "flower-smothered standing ovation,"[99] she strode up to the podium in the 1,000-seat Coconut Grove ballroom of the Ambassador Hotel and accepted an Academy Award for best supporting actress for her role as Mammy in *Gone with the Wind*. The poet Rita Dove writes:

> What can she be
> thinking of, striding into the ballroom
> where no black face has ever showed itself
> except above a serving tray?
>
> No matter, Hattie: It's a long, beautiful walk
> into that flowered-smothered standing ovation,
> so go on
> and make them wait.[100]

The crowd went wild when director Frank Capra and actor Fay Bainter announced that she had won.[101] Earlier, on entering the banquet hall, McDaniel had received a "tribute of applause" before she had been "tendered the palm for the best supporting performance of 1939."[102] Duly impressed, *Los Angeles Times* movie columnist Hedda Hopper wrote, "It was refreshing in this cockeyed world, when we're fighting for freedom of speech . . . freedom of America that in a town at which every poisoned pen in the universe is directing a flow of vitriolic words, that we were actually honoring English, Irish, Jewish and colored. Proving that art is universal."[103]

Award or no, McDaniel came under widespread criticism for perfecting and playing servile roles like fellow actor Stepin Fetchit, who played the consummate Uncle Tom, with giggling and "yas suh boss." "While referring to Uncle Toms," wrote columnist Thelma L. Thomas, "let us not omit Willie Best."[104] The subject of African American actors was a very touchy one for Langston Hughes, since he knew a great many actors, but the time had come to stop degrading the "Negro people on the screen. With defense work running full blast, they can all get jobs elsewhere, if it is still a matter of bread and meat."[105] Hughes seemed to have forgotten how he "paid dearly in a loss of pride," when, in 1939, he was in Hollywood writing *Way Down South*. "In the most humiliating episode, Langston was forced to eat a sandwich under the broiling California sun because a white executive refused to enter any restaurant with him,"[106] wrote Rampersad.

Unlike many other critics of black film actors, Miller faulted "Hollywood's habit of casting the Negro actor as a clown, a fool or an underling." He attacked Louis B. Mayer of Metro-Goldwyn-Mayer and Jack Warner of Warner Brothers: "Certainly, these men are farsighted enough to realize that the movies are valuable aids in preserving the status quo on which their own welfare and profits depend" when they cast the Negro as "the underdog to be laughed at or despised."[107] Reflecting Miller's sentiments that the studios controlled how and when blacks were portrayed on the screen, Robert Jones of the *Negro Digest* wrote, "The solution to protests against stereotyping the Negro has been quite simple for Hollywood; cut them out altogether."[108]

Though the film industry was in the forefront of anti-Negro image making for Miller and Hughes, the blame lay not entirely there. "It would be unfair to tax the movie magnates with inventing their product out of whole cloth," wrote Miller, who partly held the black press responsible for "pumping some Negro bit actor up to the dimensions of a star. One not acquainted with American life and reading only a Negro newspaper theatrical page could believe easily enough that some 45-second Negro bit player, depicting a servant, was the star of the film being reviewed!"[109] He suggested, instead, that black moviegoers should be educated on how to register their resentment of anti-Negro sentiment and how "their feelings can reach the box office. They must let Hollywood know that they object to being shown as buffoons, clowns or butts for jest."[110] Because the "so-called Negro market," wrote Miller, was "far from negligible," with a purchasing power of roughly two billion dollars, he called for organized protest.[111] The fact that Hollywood, according to Hughes, has little regard for the portrayal of blacks on the screen "may be due partially to the fact that in the past the Negro public has paid but little active attention to Hollywood."[112] William T. Smith, author of "The Negro in Hollywood," an undated essay, agreed: "The Negro actor suffers because their own group is lethargic in expressing its approval of them—or their disapproval of the 'Mammy–Uncle Tom' parts they are forced to play."[113] Though Hughes feared black filmgoers would rather "grumble and mutter" about what they do not like on the screen, he offered his readers a list of actions to take, including writing the film studios in protest. And, for those who were unaware, he encouraged them to write and thank film star Bette Davis for helping Eddie Anderson win a part in her film *In This Our Life* (because she had felt that Anderson had the right look and demeanor she encouraged director John Huston to screen test him). Hughes added, "Incidentally, you might also thank her for her influence in the Hollywood Stage Door Canteen," a place for fellow-ship and entertainment, "setup against any segregation of Negro servicemen"[114] before they headed off to war.

On the morning of December 5, 1945, after more than two years, Hattie McDaniel, along with her fellow actors and the wives of fifty plus codefendants and 250 sympathizers, "appeared in all their finery and elegance."[115] Horace Clark, owner of the Clark Hotel, one of the most famous hotels on Central Avenue, musicians Juan Tizol and Russell Smith—the who's who roster of Sugar Hill society aristocrats—the litigants' day finally had come. At the time Miller stepped into superior court department six, scene of the two-day hearing, to argue the case, there were more covenant cases in Los Angeles than in any city.[116] He estimated that "at least twenty cases seeking enforcement of racial restrictions," were pending in the Los Angeles County Superior Court and, "that involved in these twenty cases are more than 150 parcels of property."[117] "Suffice it to say," wrote Cary McWilliams, "that, in 1945, more suits contesting the validity of restrictive covenants were filed by Negroes in Los Angeles than were filed by Negroes in all the rest of the nation."[118] McWilliams predicted that the pattern of segregated housing would be first broken in Los Angeles.[119] That morning, a well-prepared Miller electrified the courtroom. He had worked hard. Speaking extemporaneously as lead attorney, he attacked "the constitutionality of the covenants, insisting they are invalid on numerous technical grounds" in his opening arguments. He alleged that the plaintiffs, in basing their theory on "white blood," were "ethnologically unwise in that most scientists agree it is impossible to tell whether any given person's blood is 'pure' and unmixed in this day and age."[120] He also argued that the defendants had moved in after the subdivision restrictions had expired.[121] He objected to the introduction of any evidence on the grounds that "any decree made by the court would be a nullity because it violates constitutional guarantees"[122] of the Fourteenth Amendment.

The stylish atmosphere in Judge Thurmond Clarke's court "was such," wrote McWilliams, "as to make one wonder if the Judge would pour tea during the afternoon recess."[123] After hearing arguments from both sides, Clarke adjourned the court until the next morning. The *Los Angeles Tribune* reported, "A tour of inspection of the West Adams district was set for that afternoon to enable the court to gather first-hand information on the character of the neighborhood."[124] The two opposing sides accompanied Clarke to the area in order "to determine the present status of the neighborhoods in question," which the defense claimed was now more than "50% Negro," wrote McWilliams.[125]

Thurmond Clarke could easily have bypassed the constitutional issue, like other jurists before him, and rule in the defendants' favor on the basis that the neighborhood's occupancy had changed over time. Instead, perhaps in anticipation of the thinking of the United States Supreme Court, he quoted first from the Fourteenth Amendment that "the rights of citizens shall not be abridged because of race, color, or previous condition of servitude." In tossing out the suit, Clarke remarked, "It is time that members of the Negro race are accorded, without reservations or evasions, the full rights guaranteed them under the 14th Amendment to the Federal Constitution. Judges have been avoiding the real issue too long. Certainly there was no discrimination against the Negro race when it came to calling upon its members to die on the battlefields in defense of this country in the war just ended."[126] After his epochal decision, Clarke told the "TRIBUNE afterwards in his chambers, in order that any higher court of review 'would have to pass on the very constitutionality of all racial restrictive covenants before reversing the ruling.'"[127] His ruling, though not the first to deny enforcement of covenants, became the "first in the U.S. to state clearly why such covenants cannot be recognized as legal."[128] The case had been decided on a point of constitutional law.

Something monumental had occurred; history had shifted. According to emeritus professor of history Carlton Jackson, when Hattie McDaniel stepped out of the superior court, she declared, "That's one fine judge. (I'm) mighty happy I've still got my home."[129] The next day the *Los Angeles Times* headline announced: "Negro owners win contest on occupancy"; the *Los Angeles Tribune* followed with "SUGAR HILL VICTORY SETS U.S. PRECEDENT."[130] The same day the trial ended, Miller wrote Thurgood Marshall:

> The Court sustained our motion and held plainly that enforcement of race restrictions would be unconstitutional and contrary to those guarantees. . . . We are certain that there will be an appeal, and that for the first time our California Supreme Court will be faced with the single question as to the constitutional issue. We are, of course, very anxious to preserve the question and to safeguard it at every step of the proceedings. . . . I think that when the case does get to the California Supreme court, the national office and such other organizations . . . should file proper briefs and perhaps some nationally known lawyers should appear with us as counsel. I am sending a copy of this letter to Bill Hastie, Loring Moore, Charles Houston and Earl B. Dickerson.[131]

At about the same time that Walter White was drafting his "unqualified congratulations," Miller was reading Marshall's thoughtful letter "on the victory so far with the 'Sugar Hill' case"; cc'd at the bottom were secondary recipients' attorneys Earl B. Dickerson, William H. Hastie, Charles H. Houston, and Loring Moore. When the time came for an appeal, Marshall assured Miller that the NAACP would file an amicus brief, along with the National Bar Association and the ACLU. "No doubt that the Lawyers' Guild will also come in so that we should have the fullest cooperation from all interested groups," opined Marshall. He closed asking for a copy of the record "so that we can get together our future action."[132] The next day Miller replied that he was enclosing a clipping from the newspaper with the complete text of the judge's decision. Over the next few months, the two lawyers exchanged several letters. When Miller wrote on

February 16 that the case had been appealed, he enclosed a copy of another brief decided earlier: "It is probable that we will argue the appeals in that case and this one at the same time."[133] Thurgood Marshall responded that his staff was "still anxious to file a brief amicus and to come out personally to the argument if it can be arranged. We would, or course, need the record in the case and your brief and instructions concerning the filing of the brief amicus."[134] Miller's delay, at least this time, might partly have been due to the birth of his second child, Edward Ellsworth Miller (named for Juanita's father), born on January 3, 1946,[135] rather than to his tendency to procrastinate.

Luckily, the same week Eddie was born, Langston Hughes was visiting Los Angeles at the invitation of Juanita's League of Allied Arts.[136] In time to congratulate the new parents and give his lecture, Hughes attended McDaniel's swanky victory gala for friends and movie associates along with Clarence Muse, Louise Beavers, the Reverend Clayton Russell, and others.[137] Afterward, Hughes wrote of Miller's victory, "TRUE TO FORM, prejudiced whites have tried to invoke restrictive covenants and get the Negroes out. But so far, Miller, brilliant West Coast lawyer, has won the Negro case, and it looks as though colored folks are on Blueberry Hill to stay. I hope so."[138]

The victory, by the end of 1946, brought Miller's law practice's coffers to nearly $7,500 "above the national median for solo practitioners,"[139] writes Kenneth W. Mack—as well as a great many congratulatory letters. The unremitting attention, though a bit hard to take in by a man of such reserve and shyness, surely brought certain exhilaration, particularly when congratulations came from A. L. Wirin, one of the first to write:

> I know I needn't tell you how surprised I was to learn that Judge Thurman Clarke of all judges did what the liberal judges of Los Angeles haven't had the courage to do. You are to be doubly congratulated in having made a "liberal" out of Judge Clarke. Years ago I wrestled with his conscience in vain. If there is to be an appeal, please let me help on it. Sincerely yours, Al.[140]

The dean of the School of Law at Lincoln University, Scovel Richardson, wrote, "I was in Louisville last week-end and spent one evening with Charlie Anderson [a Republican, and the first African American elected to the Kentucky legislature]. We both were very elated over the success that you achieved in the 'Sugar Hill' cases." Ohio attorney Jesse Heslip wrote to say, "The few days we spent together with Bill and Tommie were some of the most happy that I have ever enjoyed. I might say this to you, young man, you certainly can bend your elbow [an informal term for alcohol]. I noticed in PM that you won your case for Hattie McDaniel's and others. Congratulations, old Daniel Webster."[141] Heslip suggested that, as an executive officer of the National Bar Association, Miller should organize a West Coast branch.

On December 19, Walter White wrote, "Dear Miller: I send you unqualified congratulations on the magnificent victory you won in the Thurman Clark decision. . . . This is by far the greatest victory of its kind. As you may perhaps have heard, I will be on the Coast in January. I intend to say publicly in Los Angeles what a great contribution you have made."[142] Later, in White's regular *Chicago Defender* column, he declared, "Modesty, concisely, learnedly did Miller relate the facts of the dozen or more cases he was then fighting in Los Angeles to prevent not only movie stars like Hattie McDaniel and Ethel Waters from eviction from the houses they had bought but to smash the iron ring legal chicanery had forged around the Negro on the West Coast and elsewhere in keep [*sic*] him in overcrowded, segregated areas on the other side of the tracks."[143]

Miller's fondness for hyperbole spurred him to write his good friend Lester Granger, executive secretary of the National Urban League (which opposed the Wagner Act in 1935 because it failed to prohibit unions from excluding African Americans[144]):

> As you perhaps know (I assume that you can still read and write) I rushed home to try the "Sugar Hill" restriction case and succeeded in pulling a rabbit out of the hat by inducing a local judge to hold race restriction covenants unenforceable on the grounds that such enforcement would be violative of the 14th Amendment. This was a rather neat trick in view of numerous holdings to the contrary by both state and federal courts . . . of course it is only a lower court pronouncement and we still have the job of making it stick in the state supreme court if we can and of getting to the holy of holies in the United States supreme court.[145]

Though legal hurdles at the State Supreme Court level lay ahead, *Anderson* marked the first favorable constitutional decision of its kind in the nation.

The unanticipated consequences of the Sugar Hill case led the NAACP to set up a Hollywood bureau to monitor the unfavorable images of blacks in the film industry. Although as early as 1942, Walter White is credited with pressuring film executives such as Darryl F. Zanuck of Twentieth Century-Fox and Jack Warner of Warner Brothers Pictures and seventy other important filmmakers,[146] including the Screen Actors Guild (SAG) for "more realistic Negro characters"[147] and a better jobs policy. Leon Washington of the *Los Angeles Sentinel* called White's "allegedly successful Hollywood campaign" a hatchet job during the picket line protest of *Tales of Manhattan*, a film, according to the protesters, fraught with "Uncle Tomism."[148] Fearful that their employment would suffer, several hundred blacks in the film industry agreed to take steps to discourage any future picketing.[149] Resentful that White, an outsider "initiating negotiations that directly affected their livelihood . . . a group of black performers met at the home of Hattie McDaniel to discuss the problem,"[150] according to author Mel Watkins.

Barely two months after Judge Clarke's decision, "a bureau in Hollywood to review the latest films and pass on their contents as regards treatment of racial themes,"[151] was established by the local NAACP. Floyd C. Covington, then executive secretary of the Los Angeles Urban League, beat the NAACP by six years when, in 1940, he formed the National Negro Board of Motion Picture Review.[152]

As early as 1926, Covington, Miller's Washburn College classmate, wrote "The Negro Invades Hollywood," a critique of the film industry's black stereotypes.[153]

All and all, after Walter White met in January 1946 for three hours with a group of "colored film celebrities," which included Lena Horne, Sam McDaniel, Jesse Graves, Anita Brown, Nina Mae McKinley, and Carlton Moss,[154] he hoped that a bureau in Hollywood would encourage filmgoers to "write words of commendation as well as criticism to producers and directors."[155] The *Chicago Defender* called the action meritorious and laudable; however, it also stated, "a clique of Hollywood's Negro actors has gone on the war path" because the self-appointed nonprofessional advisors failed to consult the group of twelve smoldering "members of the Hollywood sepia film colony" displeased with the decision.[156] Clarence Muse, who headed the group, charged that the NAACP was doing "irreparable harm to the Negro's cause and setting back the advancement of Negroes."[157]

Bandleader Ben Carter complained, "You have critized [*sic*] all of us to such an extent that you are about to kill all of us out of pictures. Build on what we already have—don't destroy what we already have."[158] Louise Beaver told the *Pittsburgh Courier* afterward, "This latest NAACP brainchild is a new type of streamlined gangsterism."[159] Three years later, still rankled by White's one-man effort to solve the Negro film problem, she questioned how such a bureau "could be set up without consulting a single member of the local actors.[160] As for Wash, Miller's publisher cousin, he hoped that the bureau's "work will not be hamstrung by picayune jealousness or by the hurt feelings of people who were not consulted."[161] After all, how realistic was it for the actors to meet with their employers with regard to policy?

According to Stephen Vaughn, the SAG, under Ronald Reagan's leadership, "supported black demands for more dignified parts but [he was unwilling] to go as far as White and the NAACP in advocating elimination of roles as butlers and maids."[162] Notwithstanding the NAACP's laudatory objectives, if the association had consulted with the actors first, it might have learned that for the last year and a half many were jobless. Later that September, SAG, in an unprecedented resolution, condemned "the vicious 'silent boycott' against Negro actors and actresses now being adopted by most of the major film studios."[163] The guild accused the studios of either omitting black actors entirely or using white actors in their place. "A committee was appointed and 6 months later," wrote Jones of the *Negro Digest*, "without one meeting, disbanded because its chairman, Gregory Peck, was 'out of town.'"[164] However, by 1947, Louise Beavers "was paid the highest honor that could be given an actress," reported the *Chicago Defender*: "She was urged to accept the appointment to the board of the Screen Actors' Guild negotiating committee for the negotiation of new contracts with producers for fellow actors and actresses."[165]

In the process of handling the Sugar Hill case, Miller, according to Jill Watts, developed a "tremendous respect for Hattie. In 1944, when he ran unsuccessfully for the Fourteenth Congressional District seat on the Democratic Party ticket,

McDaniel turned out to support him."[166] When she died in 1952, Miller wrote sympathetically, "Even the disadvantages inherent in the stereotype roles she took could not conceal Miss McDaniel's real ability."[167] To her credit, McDaniel refused to accept racism outside the studio walls.

During the Sugar Hill case, Miller ran for Congress and participated in the first of three major NAACP strategy conferences on restrictive covenants, all the while assisting in overturning California's Alien Land Law of 1913, which barred Japanese-born aliens from owning land. In 1944, despite the great demand for Miller's legal services, feeling he had something to offer the voters of Los Angeles, he decided to run for the Fourteenth Congressional District seat. "I want to remind our listeners," said Leon Washington, on his regular Sunday morning KFOX broadcast, along with cohost Miller, "that you [Loren] are a candidate for Congress in the 14th district on the Democratic ticket. I urge all of them to remember that when they go to the polls on May 16th. Certainly, the *Sentinel* stands behind you."[168]

Although Miller's political drive was significantly less radical by then—like so many others on the Left who withdrew their allegiance following the Nazi-Soviet Pact of 1939—he had become a liberal Democrat and an upstanding member of the NAACP, the same organization he had so vociferously attacked in the 1930s. By the 1940s, he believed, more or less like Bertrand Russell did, that "None of our beliefs are quite true; all at least have a penumbra of vagueness and error."[169]

That April, Carey McWilliams announced, "I am supporting LOREN MILLER for Congress because of a strong conviction that at this time the nation is in vital need of more Negro representation in Congress." Proud to make the endorsement of the "only Negro" on the Democratic ticket, he declared, "I have known Loren Miller for about 15 years. He is an intelligent, courageous and able individual of unquestioned integrity. He has been a consistent, liberal and progressive with strong pro-labor views during the entire period of our acquaintance."[170]

Miller was beat nonetheless in the primary by Helen Gahagan Douglas, Broadway star and wife of the Oscar-winning actor Melvyn Douglas, despite a bit of controversy because she lived outside of the district.[171] Douglas, a liberal, served three full terms in Congress. Although Miller was on friendly terms with Douglas and had supported her candidacy for Congress in 1944 after she beat him in the primary, and would again in 1946, he warned that it would be the last time he supported a white liberal against a black candidate:

> I am convinced . . . that the time is rapidly approaching in America when liberals must face this issue of color and candidacies. As the matter now stands, it is always the white liberal who presents himself to the Negro voters and says in effect to them that you, as liberals, must support me at the risk of being traitor to the ideals you profess. It is time that these same liberals select Negro candidates and present them to the white voters and with the suggestion that these white voters owe something to their professions of liberalism.[172]

When Douglas ran in 1946, Henry Lee Moon, who had traveled to Russia with Miller, encouraged him to support Douglas again. In reply to Moon, Miller wrote,

> Making a choice between Roberts [a Republican] and Douglas is a difficult matter for me. If Roberts were white, or if both of the candidates were Negroes, there would be no question in my mind, and I would certainly support Mrs. Douglas. However, I cannot overlook the fact that it is very important that Negroes have representation in Congress even if such representation is, in some cases, less competent than the opposition. I am not one of those people who believe that the time has come in America when we can decide on the issue of competency alone. I think the matter of race is a matter of great importance. . . . When I have made up my mind, I will write you again.[173]

He decided in Douglas's favor. However, when she ran again in 1948, true to his convictions, Miller endorsed Colonel Moody Staten, the "only Negro candidate"[174] in the primary filled with twelve white candidates. Douglas won again.

After Miller lost the primary in 1944, he set out for Chicago that summer to join thirty-two others, including Thurgood Marshall, at an NAACP-sponsored conference on restrictive covenants—the first in a series of conferences on methods of attacking restrictive covenants—where after "long hours of discussion emerged a clear-cut blueprint for attacking racial restrictive covenants."[175]

Before Miller arrived, Marshall wrote to say, "It is to be a working conference without any fanfare and we will certainly appreciate your suggestions."[176] "I think," replied Miller, "that the primary job for us is to devise ways and means of securing a United States Supreme Court test and of presenting some of the appeals on the broadest possible social and economic grounds."[177] There, Miller, along with Charles Hamilton Houston, other attorneys, and social justice activists would focus on "the problem of restrictive covenants, in the hope of arriving at a plan as a result of the combined judgment of all members present."[178]

On July 2, the same day Miller replied to Marshall, he sent his apology to Mrs. Wilkie C. Mahoney, wife of the well-known Hollywood screenwriter: "I am extremely sorry that I will not be in the city to participate in the meeting set for July 8th. . . . I am going to Chicago to participate in a national conference of lawyers designed to plan ways and means for an ultimate Supreme Court test of the validity of restrictive covenants." He assured her that on his return, "if there is anything that I can do to assist in the movement [to combat the evils of restrictive covenants], you have undertaken, I shall be glad to do so."[179]

When Miller reached the Chicago office of the American Council on Race Relations—a national research clearinghouse on the underlying problems of race and cultural relations—he, along with the other lawyers and consultants, listened to Robert Clifton Weaver emphasize the economic, social, and psychological "impact of restrictive covenants" and what appropriate steps were needed "to get the issue in front of the court."[180] In explaining that segregated housing caused overcrowding in black neighborhoods, which inevitably leads to increased crime, according to professor of law, Mark V. Tushnet, Weaver urged that statistics and factual data such as the sociological relationship between overcrowding and crime become part of their legal strategy.[181] During the course of the meeting, "Every conceivable opportunity of attack was suggested," with Miller pointing out from his own experiences in Los Angeles that it was "a good thing that a new suit was brought every time a Negro moved in," because the costly burden of constant litigation was borne by those "who desire to enforce"[182] racist agreements. Others noted that it was "no less expensive for Negroes"[183] either. According to Tushnet, Houston "argued that the litigation should be used as a forum for public education."[184] Eventually, assurances would be given by the organization "to individuals that legal support would be provided."[185]

The Chicago conference ended with a blueprint on how best to attack restrictive covenants. Afterward when Marshall announced that the NAACP would undertake a new legal assault on covenants, he promised a publicity campaign and a "full-time staff member on housing."[186] Miller, under instructions from Marshall, "attempted to develop records on which the lawyers' conference had focused."[187] He wasted little time reporting to Marshall on pending cases in California. Approving nearly all that Miller had submitted, Marshall on July 30 added, "There are a number of statements which have been credited to you in other sections of the report, but it is not possible to separate them and submit them to you for editing. Please correct the enclosed draft . . . so that we can go to work on a draft to be submitted to the entire group."[188]

In January 2, 1945, the U.S. Army rescinded its Japanese American internment order, following the U.S. Supreme Court's unanimous decision that American citizens would no longer be detained without cause. Thus began the long journey home of roughly eighty thousand penniless and jobless former internees.[189] What was perhaps the bleakest of hours for the former Japanese residents of Los Angeles—and for others like the former residents of Seattle, who were met with vigilante violence by those intent on keeping them and other returnees out—was the sight of their homes, which in their absence had fallen prey to vandals or had been taken over by strangers, many of them blacks.[190]

Sympathizing with their plight, the *California Eagle*, which earlier had clamored for internment, now "prodded its African American readers to recognize that they stood in a common struggle with Japanese Americans."[191] However, because the city was in the midst of a citywide housing crisis, the two groups were pitted against each other and became competitors. Faced with the monumental task of finding available housing, free of restrictive covenants, many returnees moved into rundown apartments and boarding houses near downtown Los Angeles. The lucky few who had entrusted their deeds with good neighbors such as Miller returned to their homes with few complications.[192]

There were others, like former army sergeant Akira Iwamura. Distraught that the state of California wanted to take away his family farm, he appealed to the *Los Angeles Times*. Awarded combat metals, Akira and Cecil, his brother, believed that they had fought in the war "to keep our family and home safe." Instead, wrote Iwamura,

> I came home and read the alien land law court summons to take away my farm. . . .
> My folks have lived here for 40 years under the present law which bars them from
> citizenship . . . but because my folks happen to come from Japan my farm and home
> are being taken away from me. Why does California with its alien land law keep
> kicking us in the teeth. . . . Why are we hounded like outlaws?[193]

The Japanese American Citizens League; A. L. Wirin; and Hugh Ellwood Mac-Beth, Sr., an African American attorney who earlier had attempted to establish a black agricultural colony in Baja, California, joined forces to challenge the Alien Land Law, which had its roots in the 1882 Chinese Exclusion Act. Passed in 1913 by the California legislature, the law banned "aliens ineligible for citizenship" from owning, leasing, occupying, or transferring agricultural land to their American-born children.[194] Outraged by the state's attempt to confiscate farmland purchased in the 1930s by Japanese-born Kojiro and Kohide Oyama, who had transferred the land to their American-born son, Fred Y. Oyama, the attorneys argued in *People v. Oyama* that the law was unconstitutional. Unsurprisingly, the San Diego County Superior Court upheld the state's position that the Oyama couple had knowingly evaded the law through subterfuge since Fred was sixteen at the time his parents transferred the land into his name.[195]

"Sometime ago," wrote Wirin to Loren Miller, Morris Cohn, Hugh Macbeth, Jr., and Daniel Marshall (president of the Catholic Interracial Council of Los Angeles who had successfully argued against California's anti-miscegenation law), "we talked about taking a California Alien Land Law escheat [confiscation] case to the Supreme Court—first to California and then of the United States . . . in the course of which it was tentatively agreed that amici would send communications to the Supreme Court."[196] After he filed his appeal, convinced more than ever that the law was "conceived in prejudice" and violated the state's constitution, he reached out again to his colleagues: "Let's all have lunch [on October 26] together at Goodfellow's, Friday noon at 11:45 A.M. (so we can get a booth before the hordes descend)." Afterward, according to Wirin, Miller agreed "to get up a statement (an original and eleven copies) for filing with the [State] Supreme Court . . . in behalf of the NAACP."[197] In March 1946, the Court heard the case and by November, it rendered its decision, which, like the lower court, upheld the state's right to seize the Oyama's farmland.

By the time the Oyama case reached the United States Supreme Court, Wirin, joined by law partners Fred Okrand and Saburo Kido, former head of the JACL, argued that the Alien Land Law violated the Fourteenth Amendment rights of American citizens of Japanese ancestry. Short of declaring the law unconstitutional, on January 19, 1948, the Supreme Court justices condemned the law by a vote of six to three. "The States," wrote Chief Justice Frederick M. Vinson, "must accord to all citizens the right to take and hold real estate."[198]

Though the Supreme Court suspended the enforcement of the Alien Land Law in California, it had not entirely overturned it. It would take another case to do that. In 1952, the five American-born Masaoka brothers, represented by Miller, Wirin, and Kido, petitioned the court to determine, under the terms of the law, if the state had the right to confiscate the Pasadena home they planned to give to their widowed Japan-born mother.[199] The last nail in the coffin came on July 9 when the California Supreme Court held that "the Alien Land Law is unconstitutional because it violates the Fourteenth Amendment to the federal constitution."[200]

CHAPTER 7

The Case of the Century

Eye-blurring smog added to the sizzling heat on the Tuesday Loren Miller left for New York on September 2, 1947.[1] He drove southwest from his Silver Lake home.[2] When he reached Sunset Boulevard, he turned right onto the curved road. Luckily, as bad as this particular evening was, the worst of the heat was over, and his steering wheel was no longer a ring of fire. He crossed over Figueroa Boulevard where today Sunset turns into Cesar E. Chavez Avenue (renamed in honor of the late Mexican American union leader).

Years of distinguishing himself in the courtrooms of Los Angeles and on the pages of African American newspapers and left-leaning white journals had brought this man of decidedly slight build to this point in time. He had achieved national prominence as the brilliant attorney who defended both the famous singer Nat King Cole and Hattie McDaniel, the first African American actor to receive an Oscar.[3] Though still a believer in Marxist values, he had left communism to the Communists long ago, just before the Nazi-Soviet Nonaggression Pact of 1939.[4] By 1947, he knew that he had reached one of the turning points in his life. He had much to be grateful for, a supportive wife and two sons. He had enough confidence and social standing to invite 175 guests to his home for afternoon cocktails and expect that they would join him in honoring Sydney Brown, prominent attorney for the Chicago Board of Education, Brown's wife, and "their daughter Donna Brown," a Delta Sigma Theta soror and recent graduate from the University of Southern California.[5]

On March 3, 1947, Philadelphia attorney Theodore Spaulding wrote to Miller: "Congratulations to you on the spread of you in April issue of *Ebony*. The picture is good, the praise is well put and I hope you will continue until you are twice as good. . . . Regards to wife."[6] The *Ebony* article not only characterized Miller as "one of the foremost battlers of restrictive covenants"[7] but later would call the Miller couple one of society's leading figures of the country.

With his public standing greater than ever, Miller would remain in the spotlight as a major player pressing for judiciary justice. Invited by William Hastie to join the national legal team of the NAACP Legal Defense and Educational Fund in 1945, Thurgood Marshall, special counsel of the Legal Defense Fund (LDF), considered him the "best civil rights lawyer on the West Coast,"[8] according to Pulitzer Prize–winning author Richard Kluger. Marshall praised him to C. L. Dellums, president of the Alameda County branch of the NAACP, as having "marvelous success in restrictive covenant cases."[9] Marshall as well assured

Dorothy I. Height, then secretary for Interracial Education for the YWCA that Miller was "tops" in his field in the battle against restrictive covenants and that matter which concerned her most "required [his] expert Judgment."[10]

Ten minutes from the time he left his home on that September day in 1947, Miller reached Union Station, set in the oldest part of downtown Los Angeles, across from historic Olvera Street, transformed in 1930 into a colorful mixture of romance and capitalism for locals and tourist alike.[11] Circumstances could not have been more favorable for Miller then. By the time he finished his oral arguments in Sacramento in the Hattie McDaniel Sugar Hill covenant case, he had amassed the necessary ammunition and perhaps confidence that would help him when, for the first time, he stood before the United States Supreme Court. His caseload of clients was far beyond what might be reasonable for any one attorney or his sometimes two-attorney law firm. His law practice had grown considerably, though earlier the *Atlanta Daily World* had called him a "some-timey lawyer," who "never seemingly [took his] law practice serious"[12] until he focused on race-restrictive housing covenants.

Once in New York, he would map the final strategy "in an all-out war on covenants" with other leading civil rights attorneys, religious leaders, and consultants.[13] After three decades, the NAACP's national litigation equalization campaign was close to achieving its goal of leveling the playing field for African Americans and others, at least in housing.[14] The era where race divided the nation, rife with the legacy of social Darwinism, with its hatred and disdain toward "colored" people, was giving way to a substantial shift of public opinion in matters of race. The time had come for lawyers like Miller to fulfill a purpose greater than their own aspirations. At their own expense, wrote Walter White, "Some thirty attorneys would travel to New York City, to pool their thinking and experience in the several hundred cases now pending in state and federal courts to test the constitutionality of the evil device which is spreading like wildfire all over the country to restrict minorities, particularly the Negro, in ghettoes."[15]

In four days, Miller would join Charles Hamilton Houston, forty-one other attorneys, civil libertarians, and social scientists of note for the last in a series of conferences on the best methods to attack racially restrictive covenants. The plan was to meet in Manhattan at the NAACP's headquarters in the Wendell Willkie Memorial Building, where, beginning at 10:00 A.M., they would plan an all-out legal and political assault on housing covenants. "Mr. ACLU," Miller's friend and ally A. L. Wirin, chief counsel for the ACLU of Southern California, would be there. Other participants included members of the National Bar Association (NBA), the nation's oldest predominately African American lawyers association, in which Miller was vice president; Will Maslow of the American Jewish Committee; Ina Sugihara of the Protestant Council of Churches; Phineas Indritz from the Department of the Interior; and Constance B. Motley, a new law clerk with the LDF. Motley's accomplishments speak for themselves: the first African American woman to argue before the U.S. Supreme Court; the first African

American woman elected to the New York State Senate, and the first African American woman appointed to the federal judiciary.[16]

A measure of Miller's growing stature was his earlier appearance before the federal district court in Los Angeles as amicus curiae, a friend of the court, on behalf of the National Lawyers Guild in *Mendez v. Westminster*. Permitted to participate in the oral arguments as amicus counsel, he condemned the segregation of Mexican American schoolchildren in four southern California school districts on the basis that it violated the equal protection clause of the Fourteenth Amendment. On February 18, 1946, Judge Paul J. McCormick ordered an injunction against the school districts.[17] With the case pending before the Ninth Federal Circuit Court and Thurgood Marshall recuperating from a respiratory infection, Robert L. Carter, then assistant special counsel of the LDF., filed an amicus brief (under the names of Carter, Miller, and Marshall).[18] By the time the *Mendez* appeal reached the Ninth Circuit, A. L. Wirin and his law partner Saburo Kido, president of the Japanese American Citizens League "participated in the oral argument on behalf of the JACL, which was the only group other than the parties to actually present its case before the Court." This was a first for the JACL to intervene in a "civil rights lawsuit involving another group."[19] On April 14, 1947, when the Ninth Circuit struck down racially segregated public schools in California, "Wirin and Kido," according to historians Toni Robinson and Greg Robinson, "accelerated their collaboration with Loren Miller in the fight against racially based restrictive covenants." What *Mendez* did, in addition to being an "initial dry run" for future discrimination cases (i.e., introducing sociological evidence that segregation significantly damages African American children), was to cement the alliance between the JACL and the NAACP. More importantly, it was "the first case to hold that school segregation *itself* is unconstitutional and violates the 14th Amendment," writes Maria Blanco. "Prior to the Mendez decision, some courts, in cases mainly filed by the NAACP, held that segregated schools attended by African American children violated the 14th Amendments Equal Protection Clause because they were inferior in resources and quality, *not* because they were segregated."[20]

Miller remained busy in the ensuing months. Before he set off for New York City, he turned his attention to events beyond California's borders. On August 3, he was in Arizona speaking on "Discrimination in a Democracy" in East Lake Park at a mass meeting sponsored by the Phoenix branch of the NAACP.[21] Uppermost in the minds of the local branch was the "'dual' system of education that existed in Phoenix for Negro children and whites," by which "Negro children are being refused in nearby communities and shipped into" inferior schools. Sadly, shortly after Miller returned to Los Angeles, Juanita Miller's brother Milton V. Ellsworth, the eldest of five—a musician—died on August 16, following an illness of more than two months.[22]

When Miller finally stepped aboard the Santa Fe Super Chief passenger train for New York, his mind wandered away from grief and onto more mundane issues. Did his reservation include a roomette or an upper Pullman sleeper? The Century and Broadway Limited trains—so he was told—were full.[23] Earlier, in *Look Down, Look Down*, his unpublished essay, he wrote, "Whenever I go to buy a Pullman ticket the whole car is sold out except Lower One and Lower Sixteen," which were over the wheels. "I have bought accommodations a month, a fortnight, a week and a day ahead. The story is always the same: 'Sold Out.'"[24] He boasted that he had ridden on the Lower One and Lower Sixteen more "than any white person who has ridden an equal number of miles."[25] Once he boarded the wrong train out of Kansas City on his way to Los Angeles. He woke up the next morning "just as we were crossing the Oklahoma line into Texas. I was sitting in the Pullman smoker trying to figure out what to do when the conductor charged in like a wounded bull. 'Are you colored?' he roared." "Hell, No," Miller roared back.[26] Somehow, the conductor mistook him for Hawaiian. Miller recalled, "The poor fellow outdid himself for the rest of the trip trying to make me comfortable in a manner that would have done credit to a Hollywood version of a humble servant."[27]

Traveling by auto, bus, or railroad, he wrote "is no cinch for the Negro who gives in to the advertisements and starts out to see America first." The Plessy rule of separate but equal was still in full force and effect, but "Negroes must be afforded Pullman accommodations,"[28] wrote Miller. Instinctively bracing for whatever racist slight he might encounter, the three-day journey was a good opportunity for Miller, forty-four, to prepare for what lay ahead in New York before dozing off to the clickety-clack of the wheels on the track.

Miller was not a man prone to self-pity or in need of sympathy, yet at times he felt slighted and anguished that it took others so long to publicly acknowledge his extraordinary brilliance, a situation of which Wendell Green, a former Tuskegee Airman and lawyer, his friend and former managing editor of the *Los Angeles Sentinel* (who along with Miller would purchase the *California Eagle*), was well aware. Miller's pride, sensitivity, and shyness, according to Green, caused him to miss many opportunities for personal gain because of his "deep distaste . . . to engage in the mendacities and banalities that seem necessary for personal achievement."[29] With family and friends, Miller was affable, warm, loyal, and often humorous. But, according to Faye Hopkins Duffy, a close Miller family friend, "Loren was impatient with people who did not grasp ideas, and they resented him for it."[30] He more or less believed that happiness depends on the quality of your thoughts.[31] His nephew, Halvor Miller Jr., said that he simply had to speak the truth. If he had something on his mind, "he'd have to say it, get if off his chest."[32] In fundamental ways, Miller was impatient with complacency, and particularly with people who were inactive in the "Negro cause." His tendency to condemn ethnic boosterism and those who boasted of their achievements and respectability rubbed the upper reaches of black society the wrong way. His acid wit, wrote Lester Granger, could "burn holes in the toughest skin and eat right through double-talk, hypocrisy and posturing."[33]

Whether calculated or not, by the early 1940s Miller was living in the hilly bohemian neighborhood of Silver Lake, across town from Los Angeles's most prominent black families. After all, in Nebraska, he grew up in close proximity to white neighbors. His willingness to raise eyebrows or risk his standing in the black community by physically distancing himself accorded well with his moral principles that a man does what he ought to do in the circumstances confronting him, no matter the consequences.[34] Maxcy D. Filer, president of the Compton branch of the NAACP, later wrote, "It is somewhat ironical, Judge Miller fought to eliminate restrictive covenants in housing" and yet moved to the Silver Lake, "as well he should."[35] Still, Miller was understandably "frustrated," recalled Carey McWilliams, who lived nearby in Echo Park "because of the way in which he was sort of boxed in." He was "one of the brilliant people that I've known . . . a beautiful, beautiful person and an extraordinarily sensitive, perceptive, intelligent man. . . . I loved him." Regrettably, McWilliams recounted, "The black community at that time hadn't sufficiently grounded itself so that it could develop elements that would support a man of Loren's caliber. This was a great disappointment to him and to everybody else. And this was unfortunate because he had an extraordinary background and experience."[36] For all of his frustrations or evident discomfort, Miller set aside bruised feelings for the greater good. Yet none of that would bridge the gap he felt—real or otherwise—between his circumstances and that of his better-situated East Coast colleagues. Not to imply that Miller's eastern colleagues ever snubbed him; the reality was that he was not a graduate of Howard University, Morehouse College, or Lincoln University—the premier, historically black colleges for long-standing black aristocrats—nor was he an Ivy Leaguer. Instead, he was an artist cloaked in lawyer's garb, a farmer's son, distinctly different from his African American colleagues in the East such as William Henry Hastie, Charles Hamilton Houston, and Robert Clifton Weaver. In truth, he had risen from the lowest to the highest social status in one generation. Yet he would never entirely fit in. There would always be a gap between the old guard black elitism and a biracial farm boy from rural Kansas. Still, whether liked or not, Miller by virtue of his education and profession was part of that elite group of African Americans—W. E. B. Du Bois's "talented tenth"—where class and race intertwined. By race, he was no less or more a marginal American than Hastie, Houston, or Weaver, who were born into privilege yet were unprotected from prejudice by their Harvard degrees. As African Americans, they experienced what Du Bois called the personal sensation of "double-consciousness," the "looking at one-self through the eyes of others, of measuring one's soul by the tape of a world that looks on in amused contempt and pity . . . an American, a Negro; two warring souls, two thoughts, two unreconciled strivings; two warring ideals in one dark body, whose dogged strength alone keeps it from being torn asunder."[37]

Undeniably, Miller moved in the same small circle of black professionals as Hastie, the first African American federal judge, who received his law degree from Harvard. Like other educated blacks, the two were members of equally respected black Greek-letter fraternal organizations, established to unify black achievers with the opportunity to support each other and their respective communities. Hastie belonged to the prestigious Omega Psi Phi fraternity, as did James M. Nabrit, Jr., the future president of Howard University, who joined Miller and Hastie in the New York meeting on Saturday September 6. Miller's equally respected Kappa Alpha Psi fraternity was the "smallest of the three old-guard fraternities" and "least identified with a particular stereotype,"[38] and yet he was still somewhat at a disadvantage. His uneven position on the social ladder was the lingering effect of Miller's poverty-stricken, rural midwestern background, as well as his decision not to live in the East but rather to live in Los Angeles, where "some of the old Black [fraternal] organizations were very late arriving in the city."[39]

Miller's upbringing could not have been more different than those of his elite colleagues Hastie and Houston, who were cousins, and Weaver, members of a privileged group of upper-middle-class African Americans.[40] What most set him apart from them were his farm-boy roots, the extreme poverty he suffered throughout childhood, and his experience as the virtual lone African American among predominately-white classmates.[41] In contrast, the three Harvard graduates attended, though at different times, the most prestigious high school in the District of Columbia for African Americans, Paul Laurence Dunbar (earlier known as M Street).[42] Dunbar was a high school described by Dr. Kenneth Clark, the psychologist who played a major role in *Brown v. Board of Education of Topeka* as a "white school in a segregated system"[43] that focused on preparing the district's black middle-class and upwardly mobile students for college. "When it came to elite public schools for black society," wrote black society observer Lawrence Graham, "no school could out-perform Washington, D.C.'s Dunbar High School."[44]

Miller's good fortune was to have had a mother who held a teaching certificate and a father who could read and write, at a time when only one in ten Americans could read and write. However, having a father barely able to scratch out a living married to a white woman brought its own set of complications. In contrast, Hastie, Houston, and Weaver grew up financially secure. Hastie's father, a clerk in the United States Pension Office (now the Veterans Administration), married Roberta Childs, a former Chattanooga schoolteacher, and they provided little William Henry with the cultural values and comforts of the middle class. Charles H. Houston's father, William, was a general practice attorney, and his mother was "a hairdresser whose clientele included senators and cabinet officers."[45] They provided every opportunity they could, including giving Houston professional experience assisting his father's legal firm. Robert C. Weaver, the preeminent authority on housing, had similar advantages. Well before he earned his doctorate in economics from Harvard, his family's accomplishments had placed him (immeasurably) at the top of Washington's black aristocracy.

In marked contrast to Miller's paternal grandfather, who fled slavery and hauled loads as a teamster after the Civil War,[46] Weaver's maternal grandfather, the son of a former slave, became the first professionally trained black dentist in the country when he graduated from Harvard's dental school in 1869, a time when only 1.1 percent of Americans were enrolled in postsecondary education.[47] By virtue of prominent relatives, according to urban historian and legal scholar Wendell E. Pritchett, Weaver was introduced to the theater and cultural life of New York City. Through the agency of family connections, he participated in "what many blacks at the time called the 'wedding of the century,' [as one of ten groomsmen in the 1928] marriage of Yolande Du Bois, only child of W. E. B. DuBois, and poet Countee Cullen, son of one of the nation's most famous black ministers."[48] In time, Weaver would own summer homes on the "Chesapeake Bay and in Connecticut," where he lived a life "much more similar to that of the wealthy whites with whom he interacted."[49] After graduating from Harvard, Hastie, Houston, and Weaver, who became among the most accomplished blacks in the nation, all socialized together, preferring often "to meet in their respective homes [in Washington, D.C.] to drink and play cards."[50] Moreover, during the mid-1930s, Weaver and Hastie easily maintained both friendship and career interests by working for the Interior Department, where the two bonded even further as they met with other black "New Dealers" in the home of Mary McLeod Bethune, at the time the director of the Division of Negro Affairs of the National Youth Administration.

Before Miller's train pulled into New York on September 5, 1947, he believed firmly that "the problem [with overturning covenants] is not so much a matter of law as it is of inducing a favorable public opinion."[51] On that, he was adamant. With various restrictive covenant cases percolating in many parts of the country, Miller wrote three blistering articles that year on the evils of the covenants. He himself served as a member of the Advisory Council for the International Ladies Garment Workers Union, owner of KFMV 94.7 FM in Los Angeles.[52] His purpose was to alter public opinion.[53] Perhaps, thinking more like a seasoned journalist with more than twenty years' experience under his belt and less like an attorney, Miller knew that judges, little different than ordinary people, have a difficult time brushing aside public opinion. Miller, no different from other black journalists, defended the oppressed; he believed that providing readers with accurate and reliable information was important in changing racist behavior. He saw himself as an agent of social change, fully aware of his task. He was a propagandist, a media activist, committed to changing the way the public thinks and understands issues. Repeatedly and consistently, his articles questioned the appropriateness of discrimination based on race and class. Though he wanted recognition as an American writer, not just a black writer, the racial climate of his era stood in the way of that ambition. Even his beloved Langston Hughes was considered a "Negro" writer, never an American writer.

Miller's way of stemming the tide of prejudice and bigotry was to encourage action, which he did as a freelance reporter (citizen journalist), particularly wherever American fascism raised its ugly head.[54] He did it when he critiqued stereotypes in the film industry. He held that if organizations were serious about shifting popular anti-racial sentiment, they should commit time and finances to informing the public. He felt that the public should be bombarded with stories of the various covenant cases winding their way to the Supreme Court, which since 1926 "had circuitously but effectively upheld judicial enforcement of racial covenants."[55] If they were serious, leaders were obligated to reach out to officials in government and private industry, write letters make phone calls, and meet with newspaper editorial staff. Roy Wilkins, at the time the editor of the NAACP's magazine the *Crisis,* on this theme, agreed with Miller. He also felt that the best way to tip the balance of public opinion was to launch a clever campaign bombarding the public, both ordinary and influential people, government and private industry, with the latest legal news.[56] In Chicago, the NAACP branch heeded that call when it took it upon itself to circulate a fundraising flyer in hopes of raising $50,000 for a publicity drive to "BREAK RACE RESTRICTIVE COVENANTS."[57]

Memorable change, Miller believed, comes from an informed and organized citizenry. That belief led him to write Roy Wilkins on July 18, 1947: "The NAACP ought to make every effort to arouse the press of the country" because "I notice that some of the papers buried the news of the granting of [its petition to the U.S. Supreme Court] on inside pages." Success would come "only if we are backed by an aroused public opinion."[58] The next month, Wilkins followed with a memo to Robert Carter. "Loren mentions the possible preparation of 'a series' of articles. I do not know about a 'series,' but perhaps we could prepare at least two articles illustrating the importance of these covenant cases. . . . Perhaps, Mr. Harrington [the satirist and political cartoonist Oliver Harrington] can use it to put together the articles."[59]

Miller spent his life working to shift the tide of opinion in the direction of a free, functioning society. He had an incisive understanding of the media and how it affects the public. A committed writer and speechmaker as well as a radio broadcaster, he seized every opportunity to spur public action. This was well before the American Council on Race Relations (ACRR) undertook a national campaign against racial covenants or Thurgood Marshall's 1945 promise of a publicity campaign at the end of the first strategy conference in Chicago (though reluctant to put too much stress on it).[60] In time, the NAACP, the ACRR, and the ACLU jointly sponsored a pamphlet titled *Race Bias in Housing.* Other groups such as the American Jewish Committee, the *University of Chicago Law Review,* and the *Yale Law Review* published full-length articles on covenants.[61]

Eighteen months before Miller met in New York to strategize with the other experts, he opined to Robert C. Weaver, "It seems to me that we need some 'popular' articles on the matter, say *Survey Graphic, Nation, New Republic* etc. I am not under any illusions as [to] the number of readers of such periodicals but they are important in cases of this kind where we need public opinion in intellectual (?) quarters. I know that you have access to such people. What do you think can be done in reference to publicity of this kind?"[62] Whether Weaver took his advice or not, Weaver did publish "Housing in a Democracy, *Annals of the American Academy of Political and Social Science*."[63]

Despite Miller's desire to attend the second in the series of conferences on restrictive covenants, convened this time at Howard University on January 26–27, 1947, he was not there, most likely because of the birth of his son Edward and the practice of confining new mothers to their hospital beds for two weeks. Willis M. Graves and Francis Dent, with the Detroit branch of the NAACP and the Legal Defense and Education Fund's national team respectively, reported that in *Sipes v. McGhee* the "court of last resort in Michigan had upheld restrictive covenants."[64] Since 1945, the two attorneys had represented Orsel McGhee, a press operator and his wife, Minnie S. McGhee,[65] a postal worker, who had purchased and moved into their Detroit home on Seebaldt Avenue on November 30, 1944, in violation of the local covenant.[66] During and following World War II, the Detroit branch of the NAACP, according to Thomas Sugrue, "alone litigated nine restrictive covenant cases"[67] in their attempt to wipe out ghettoes.

From the start, there was a "clear-cut split" within the Howard conferees on what road to take. Should they emphasize violations of the Fourteenth Amendment, human rights, and fundamental freedoms under the United Nations Charter, or should they stress the sociological effects of overcrowded housing?[68] Marshall held that testimony by economists and sociologists "might persuade the Supreme Court to accept a test case."[69] The plan was to meet once again to continue discussions on *Sipes* and "the California case [with which Miller was familiar] to determine what action" should be taken.[70] Marian Wynn Perry, assistant special counsel, alerted the Howard group that "It was determined that there may be Michigan cases coming up before the court better than the *Sipes* case on which to appeal, and that therefore we would not file a petition for certiorari until the very last moment . . . that in the meantime we watch for further decisions from the Michigan court."[71]

Marshall, however, found himself outmaneuvered by George L. Vaughn, who thwarted Marshall's legal strategy and jumped the gun on April 21 by filing *Shelley v. Kraemer*, the Missouri case, with the U.S. Supreme Court. Marshall was equally provoked because he "did not have a great deal of confidence in Vaughn, and was somewhat annoyed at Vaughn's failure to cooperate with the NAACP."[72] Not to be bested by Vaughn, Marshall filed his petition, too, for a writ of certiorari with the U.S. Supreme Court in *McGhee v. Sipes*. "To Marshall's relief," writes legal scholar William B. Rubenstein, "the court consolidated the cases when it granted certiorari in June 1947."[73] In August, petitions were filed in *Hurd v. Hodge* and *Urciolo v. Hodge*, the two District of Columbia cases.[74] "Thurgood was very reluctant to push the restrictive covenant cases at the Supreme Court level," according to the recollections of Franklin H. Williams, junior staffer with the LDF at the time. "But the lawyers outside the Fund made it clear that they were going to fight these cases all the way, with or without Marshall. . . . If the initiative had not come from outside the Fund office—from Loren Miller in California and the branch people in Detroit and St. Louis—Marshall might have let it go then,"[75] possibly setting the covenant battle back a number of years.

The *Shelley v. Kraemer* case (eventually bundled with *McGhee v. Sipes, Hurd v. Hodge*, and *Urciolo v. Hodge*) originated on September 11, 1945. On that date, J. D. Shelley, who worked at a small-arms bullet plant during World War II, and his wife, Ethel Lee Shelley, an employee at a baby-care products company, moved into their Saint Louis home at 4600 Labadie Avenue with their six children.[76] Within days, Louis Kraemer and his wife, Fern, who had inherited property on Labadie Avenue from her parents, sued the Shelleys for violating the racial covenant, which restricted use and occupancy by "people of the Negro or Mongolian Race." The Shelleys, who had fled Mississippi after a brutal beating of a teenage girl, sought George Vaughn's legal assistance after Ethel contacted her pastor, Robert Bishop, an occasional real estate man, who had arranged the purchase for $5,700 from Geraldine Fitzgerald, a white woman.[77]

Vaughn was prominent in the local NAACP and the Saint Louis's Democratic Party. He ran unsuccessfully for alderman in 1941. Vaughn immediately saw the Shelleys' "case as a good vehicle for the constitutional challenge,"[78] claiming first that the covenants had never been enforceable because "nine of the thirty-nine owners . . . had failed to sign the document."[79] Subsequently, he argued the case before the circuit court of the Saint Louis and the Missouri Supreme Court to halt his client's eviction by introducing "into the record objections on public policy and constitutional grounds."[80]

Assuming that the *Shelley* and the *McGhee* petitions would be granted by the U.S. Supreme Court (as well on the two District of Columbia cases), much had to be done in preparation for the hearings and, more immediately, for the upcoming meeting in New York. Marshall, in letters to Houston and Miller, wrote, "Dear Charlie and Loren, I made the suggestion to Messrs. Dent and Graves, of Detroit, that the two of you should argue the *Sipes* case if it was agreeable with them. I have just received a letter from Graves stating that he and Dent had discussed the matter and that they had reached the conclusion that the 'choice of persons to present argument is excellent.'" He concluded by saying, "All of the lawyers are being requested to do independent research on the sociological arguments, as well as the legal arguments, so that we will be in a good position to discuss the case," at the New York meeting.[81] "Dear Thurgood," replied Miller, "I have your letter of July 10th, and I am very glad to accept the appointment to argue the *Sipes* case. I will be present in New York, Saturday, August 30 [which for various reasons was changed to September 6]." Further, Miller wrote, "It is my opinion that the [illegible] race restrictive covenants should be placed on two planes: First that they be subjected to the due process requirements, and, second to the equal protection requirement. I also believe that extensive 'sociological briefs' should be filed in which the questioner of public policy is implemented."[82] These statements are somewhat at variance with those Miller made back in February, when he was convinced that the cases (particularly the Sugar Hill case, *Anderson vs. Auseth*) pending in the California Supreme Court would "present a better point than the Michigan cases."[83]

Before Charles H. Houston opened the morning session of the New York confab on the 6th of September, where the participants hoped the best plan to overturn the nation's restrictive covenants would be the outcome, the *Chicago Defender* reported that the attorneys meeting the press were Loren Miller of California; Leon Ransom and Spottswood Robinson of Washington, D.C.; Andrew Weinberger and Charles Abrams of New York; George Vaughn of Missouri; and Lucia Thomas of Chicago. In emphasizing the national urgency of the fight against the covenants, Miller pointed out that "pre-war scarcity of homes coupled with tremendous war-time migration has made the question of housing restrictions crucial, as for instance, Los Angeles is 80 per cent covered by covenants." Vaughn stated that 125,000 "Negroes are now occupying the same space as did 43,000 Negroes in 1910."[84]

At 10:00 A.M., Houston opened the meeting "by outlining the fact that we now have five cases pending on restrictive covenants."[85] He asked those actively handling cases for "a brief outline of each case so that the facts could be presented and thus it could be seen where we have common issues involved." By the 12:45 lunch break, they had covered at length the socioeconomic factors. When they resumed, Vaughn, considered an "obstructionist" by some, continued his discussions "on state action and its application to the *Shelley* case."[86] Miller criticized the construction of *Fairchild v. Raines*, a 1944 case he knew well as one of the appellant counsel, along with Willis O. Tyler and George Cryer. He added, "No sharp distinction should be made . . . whether there is only one covenant in a city or a whole series."[87]

As the attorneys chiseled away at the technical points and doctrinal problems of state action, including a legal principle that the Fourteenth Amendment applies only to state and local governments and not private entities, Houston warned an impatient Vaughn, "You will be questioned further than that. We must answer these questions in our own minds." Shad Polier of the American Jewish Committee "cautioned against trying to win too much at one time."[88] Miller, according to the minutes of the meeting, entered into the fray only once. It is doubtful that he was intimidated in the presence of so many knowledgeable attorneys, but why was he so silent? Perhaps it was his natural shyness or the intellectual in him to ponder the comments of others later, or had he felt that his comments on *Fairchild v. Raines* were enough of a contribution?

At 5:45 in the afternoon, the meeting adjourned with no "satisfactory resolution on the doctrinal questions," according to Mark V. Tushnet, "though, the lawyers appeared to believe that the sociological material was important in defining the scope of what they were asking the Court to do."[89] Unresolved was the legal conundrum of finding a sound line of attack that distinguished the differences between state action and the equal protection clause of the Fourteenth Amendment. Houston closed the meeting by requesting the names of organizations intending to file brief amici curiae—which eventually twenty-one organizations did. "Every lawyer here," commented New York attorney Norman Levy (author of the satires *Opera Guyed* and *Theatre Guyed*), "knows what he is talking about and approaches the subject with not only obvious careful study but with profound understanding of the social and economic implications of restrictive covenants. No one wastes any time and nobody is trying to show off."[90]

With the meeting over, Bill Smallwood, a *Los Angeles Sentinel* columnist, reported how pleasantly surprised he was to run "full-tilt into Loren Miller at a recent Sun. nite dancing party in Manhattan. He was east from LA for a restrictive covenant confab."[91] Back in Los Angeles, as Miller read the meeting minutes, did he wonder why of all the participants his was the only name listed without the prefix "Mr."? He was listed as "Loren Miller," whereas each participant's surname was preceded by the honorific "Mr." or "Miss," with no given name. The only other exception was William Hastie, who, appropriately, was listed as "Gov. Hastie." Perhaps a minor oversight?

By the end of October, Thurgood Marshall remained unconvinced that the equal protection argument was the best strategy. Unflaggingly persistent, he wrote Miller to "come up with a better argument on this particular point because we are still not for it."[92] Miller hurriedly replied the following day with three pages: "Summed up, my point is this, legislation setting up a ghetto would deny Equal Protection of the law quite apart from the right of the private property owner to sell his property, and a construction of the common law of a State that sets up a ghetto also denies Equal Protection apart from the right of the private property owner to buy property. Thus, it seems to me that Equal Protection and Due Process are intertwined." A day prior to Marshall's letter, Miller received a draft of the *Hurd v. Hodge* case (companion case to *Shelley v. Kraemer* and *McGhee v. Sipes*), which he told Marshall was "a much better job than the draft in the *Sipes* [Detroit] case. The due process argument is well developed and is entirely convincing. That does not mean," however, "that I am willing to abandon Equal Protection in the *Sipes* case."[93]

Miller shifted the subject to Charles H. Houston, whom Marshall had removed as co-counsel in *McGhee v. Sipes*. He agreed: "Charlie should use all of his time in the *Hurd* case because I think the toughest hurdle we face is a District of Columbia case. . . . Obviously, the person who argues such a case must be well versed in every aspect of the law and Charlie is such a person."[94] Two decades later, in his magnum opus *The Petitioners*, Miller wrote that Houston, as dean of law at Howard University, elevated the law school from what Marshall, his protégée, called a "dummies retreat to a fully accredited school"[95]; produced lawyers who changed society; expanded and improved the NAACP's blueprint for a legal campaign against segregation; and was "a man of vast creative skill and ability."[96]

Unquestionably, Houston was the best attorney to argue *Hurd v. Hodge* and its companion case *Urciolo v. Hodge* in both the district court and in the court of appeals.[97] With Houston removed from the Detroit case, Marshall found himself under considerable pressure to find his replacement. "As I told you," he wrote in his explanation to Miller,

> I am not for having a person simply because he is reputed to be a "big shot." What we need is someone who knows the law on restrictive covenants. If you believe that you will want someone in addition to yourself to handle the *Sipes* case, I hope you will clear the matter with me before you make any decision. There is a tremendous amount of "fast footwork around second base" going on and these cases are too important to tolerate any shenanigans.[98]

Miller left little doubt as to where he stood when he took up his pen to reply:

> As for outside legal help in the arguments, I, like you, and everybody else, am primarily concerned with winning. If we had a Wendell Willkie [the corporate lawyer and liberal Republican nominee for the 1940 presidential election] to assist us I would be all for associating with him. However, I see no sound reason for the association of any person who does not know something of the intricacy of the problem involved. . . . I am entirely willing to shoulder the entire burden of argument in the *Sipes* case or to share the time with some other person as you and the others involved think best. Those of you who are in the east can discuss the matter and I will be guided by your opinion.[99]

Others might have wanted some "big shot," but Marshall's forceful, though charming, verve, what Miller called "bluff," allowed him to get his way.[100] Marshall stuck with Miller, whom he considered "the best civil rights lawyer on the West Coast."[101] He added himself as co-counsel. In a letter to John Doebele, housing director of the Chicago Council Against Racial and Religious Discrimination, Marshall explained why he selected Miller and Houston: "They have argued more appellate cases on restrictive covenants than any other lawyers."[102] As head of the NAACP's Legal Defense Fund, Marshall was "more a coordinator of other lawyers' work than an initial drafter of legal documents like briefs."[103] Aware that Miller's strength lay in his command of the English language, he imported him "to do the bulking of the drafting" for the Detroit case. When the time came for *Brown v. Board of Education*, Marshall turned to Miller again to write the bulk of the briefs, six to be exact.[104]

For two decades, wrote Miller, the Supreme Court, by refusing all requests to review cases, "had circuitously but effectively upheld judicial enforcement of racial covenants."[105] After decades of using the courts as its major weapon in its campaign for equality, the NAACP perceived a shift. Under "heavy attack by liberals and labor leaders,"[106] the court could no longer feasibly cling to its resolve.

Miller calculated that "the Court was on the eve of change in both personnel and attitude on social issues. Negro leaders hoped that during the process of that change they could press their own case and secure some of the changes they desired." "Part of the genius of the "NAACP lawyers," he wrote, "lay in the acute perception of the depth and direction of these changes, and their ability to take them at their flood and translate them into constitutional concepts palatable to Supreme Court justices, who were at once propelled in new directions by social change and architects of that change."[107]

With change on the horizon, particularly in the matter of the *Hurd* case, "a cadre of social scientists and lawyers," according to historian Genna Rae McNeil, "came together to cooperate in the preparation of a 'Brandeis brief' for the Supreme Court. The inclusion of nonlegal material (an approach Louis Brandeis initiated early in the twentieth century defending minimum wage laws for women) necessitated collaboration with economists and sociologists for the development of an appendix of pertinent scholarly articles. Then, with some attention to documentary evidence, Houston, [Phineas] Indritz, and [Spottswood] Robinson refined their legal arguments."[108] Philippa Strum, Brandeis's biographer, credits Houston with writing "the first of the NAACP's Brandeis-style briefs,"[109] a style of brief in which economic and sociological data, historical experience, and expert opinions are marshaled to support the legal propositions.

By November, the consolidated *Hurd* brief was filed with the Supreme Court. Believing that the final showdown on the four combined covenant cases was scheduled for the week of November 17, Miller and his wife Juanita enjoyed a farewell party, held in their honor at the home of Dr. William A. Beck, former professor of clinical medicine at Meharry Medical College, and his wife, new arrivals to Los Angeles from Nashville, Tennessee.[110] Attending were several couples, including Miller's partner Harold Sinclair and his wife. Whether Miller grew annoyed when the Supreme Court rescheduled oral arguments for December 8 is sheer speculation. What we know is, as Miller wrote, "The course of court-made law seldom runs smoothly"[111] from start to finish as planned. He made new plans to leave Los Angeles on November 21, to defend Orsel and Minnie McGhee (whose two sons, twenty-one-year-old Reginald and twenty-year-old Orsel, Jr., were in the army). Despite the threats of abuse, the McGhees continued their refusal to move from 4626 Seebaldt Avenue in Detroit.[112]

While planning for the later trip to Washington, Miller kept busy with a controversy brewing within the Presbyterian Church in Los Angeles and with the three black families that he and his partner Harold Sinclair represented. When Major Frank Louis Drye, a disabled veteran of two world wars moved from Alabama to Los Angeles, he bought his dream house in the upscale Country Club Park neighborhood of Los Angeles at 1032 South Arlington Avenue.[113] Frank and Artokia Drye; prominent business leader Lee V. Steward and his wife, Carney Steward; and Mrs. Blanche Strickland, widow of a well-known Dallas insurance executive, had all moved into the same neighborhood in August 1947.

Reverend W. Clarence Wright, minister of the Wilshire Presbyterian Church, along with eight co-petitioners, filed a temporary injunction to oust these families. The good reverend, who lived directly across from the Drye family, led the charge to prevent the Dryes, the Stewards, and Mrs. Strickland from occupying their homes during the pending action. "A charge," reported the *Los Angeles Sentinel*, "that Negroes who seek to establish their homes outside of the tight, over-crowded ghetto districts in this city are guilty of 'un-Christian' conduct [which] has allegedly been made by a local Presbyterian minister in a restrictive covenant case."[114] When Reverend Hampton Barnett Hawes, the black pastor of Westminster Presbyterian Church (and father of jazz pianist Hampton B. Hawes, Jr.), heard that a minister of his faith was "an active participant in an attempt to enforce segregation," he tried to persuade "the minister to abandon the lawsuit" before the case came to court.[115]

When the case did reach the court, Los Angeles Superior Court justice Stanley Mosk, later appointed to the California Supreme Court, dismissed the suit against the families on grounds that it was inconsistent with the guarantees of the Fourteenth Amendment. It was the second court case of its kind rendered in the Los Angeles Superior Courts, the first having been the well-known Sugar Hill suit argued by Miller. "We read columns in the press each day about un-American activities," read Judge Mosk's memorandum. "This court feels that there is no more reprehensible un-American activity than to attempt to deprive persons of their own homes on a 'Master Race' theory. Our nation has just fought against the Nazi race superiority theory. One of these defendants was in that war and is a Purple Heart veteran."[116] Sixty years later, Richard Mosk, an associate justice of the California Court of Appeals, said of his father's ruling, "It was pretty gutsy for a young Superior Court judge who has to face the electorate."[117] On November 4, following the court's decision, approximately 250 lay and clerical leaders of the Los Angeles Presbytery of the Presbyterian Church held a meeting, where they adopted a "resolution directing ministers to refrain from taking any action to enforce race restrictive covenants and to withdraw from any such action in which they may now be involved."[118]

On the heels of the rousing victory for the Country Club Park families came yet another Supreme Court delay in the *Shelley* case. "Due to the illness of Justice Frank Murphy, the U.S. Supreme Court has postponed until January 5, 1948, its hearing on four cases testing the constitutionality of race restrictive covenants."[119] Finally, on December 29, Marshall telegraphed Miller: "NEW TENTATIVE DATE RESTRICTIVE COVENANT CASES JANUARY FOURTEENTH AND FIFTEENTH. ALTHOUGH DATE NOT CERTAIN LITTLE POSSIBILITY CASES BEING HEARD PRIOR THAT DATE. WILL KEEP YOU ADVISED."[120]

That same day Marshall wrote the Charles Hotel to cancel his reservations "for two rooms beginning the 2nd and also the room for Loren Miller of Los Angeles, to whom I just talked over the telephone. Please make the same reservations for

Rooms 101 and 201 in my name and a room with bath for Loren Miller beginning Saturday January 10th. Please also reserve Room 101 for me beginning the night of Monday, January 5th. I expect to be in Washington through the 8th."[121] After speaking with Marshall, Miller immediately called the Santa Fe Railway office in Washington, whose agent advised that "upon proper application" and return of the two unused tickets he would receive a full refund.[122] The next day, Marian Wynn Perry canceled her Statler Hotel "reservation for a single room with bath beginning January 4, 1948," and instead made "a reservation for January 12, 13, 14, and 15, 1948."[123]

Concerned, even worried, prominent figures such as Walter White, the NAACP's front man, pivotal to eliminating the "menace of covenants," appealed to Tom Campbell Clark, attorney general of the United States appointed by President Truman in 1945. "The Department of Justice owes minorities a deep responsibility to help the court to understand the issues involved," asserted White, "and to arrive at a decision which will not set up in America legalized ghetto life for Negroes, Jews and any other group."[124] He was asking the Justice Department to submit an amicus on behalf of the United States government. According to Richard Kluger, "When [Clark] received Walter White's request that he put the government on the Negro's side in the restrictive covenant cases before the Supreme Court, Tom Clark was on the spot . . . to come to the aid of African Americans."[125] Of the same mind, Rabbi Irvin Miller, chair of the Executive Committee of the American Jewish Congress, pressured the Justice Department to file friend of the court briefs in two pending restrictive covenant cases. In the rabbi's letter to Clark (whose son, Ramsey Clark, would become the sixty-sixth United States attorney general in 1965), he cited President Truman's declaration on civil rights of June 29, 1947, and "called on the Department of Justice to bring its massive influence to bear in the struggle to outlaw racially restrictive covenants."[126] On October 29, the day President Truman published "To Secure These Rights" the government's investigation on the status of civil rights, Solicitor General Philip B. Perlman wrote Rabbi Miller: "The Attorney General has asked me to inform you that he has decided to file a brief amicus curiae in the Restrictive Covenant Cases now pending in the Supreme Court"[127] in support of *Shelley v. Kraemer, McGhee v. Sipes*, and the two *Hurd* cases.

Behind the scenes, Philip Elman, assistant solicitor general (1944–61) and Phineas Indritz, who was employed by the Department of Interior, "cooked up the idea that [Secretary of the Interior Oscar] Chapman "should write to the Attorney General requesting the Department of Justice to file an amicus brief."[128] Then they used their connections with various liberal organizations. Eventually, all the letters came to Elman, who showed them to Philip Perlman. Elman explained, "I then wrote a formal memorandum recommending that the United States file an amicus brief."[129] Elman subsequently assembled a team of government lawyers to write the Justice Department's brief. Though he admitted that the amicus brief "contained a lot of high-blown rhetoric about liberty and equality . . . it was still a solid lawyerlike job."[130] It marked the first time the government went on the record condemning discrimination.

Before the Justice Department submitted its brief on December 5, Louis Lautier of the *New York Amsterdam News* reported that Attorney General Clark received such "prolonged applause" when he made "an impromptu speech to the National Bar Association . . . that he had to take a second bow."[131] During the opening session of the twenty-second annual meeting of the NBA on November 28, Clark declared, "I am for a law that will strengthen the civil rights statues and bring into reality the equal protection under the law that the Constitution of the United States guarantees to every citizen in this country." Clark announced his plans to ask Congress for a full-fledged civil rights division. "Purveyors of hate are striking at the foundations upon which our liberties rest. These termites of democracy," he insisted, "would deny to others the rights that they, themselves enjoy."[132] Over the course of the three-day conference, speakers such as Sadie T. Alexander of Philadelphia (former NBA secretary and one of two African Americans on the fifteen-member President's Committee on Civil Rights) "challenged Washington to correct the undemocratic evils existing here, and urged the support of all the people for the recommendations of the President's report."[133]

Shortly before the twenty-first annual NBA conference the year before, the association had "filed a motion and brief as 'a friend of the court' in the case between the Northwest Civic association of Detroit and a group of colored home buyers and white sellers; and that of other white owners vs. Orsel McGhee, colored, and his wife, Minnie S. McGhee."[134] Association president Earl B. Dickerson declared, "Each of these cases present an issue which affects the civil and political rights of a large body of citizens of the state of Michigan and the United States."[135] During the legal conclave, Miller, voted back into office as second vice president, presided over discussions on restrictive covenants, where he "urged that the United States be directed by the United Nations to establish and guarantee rights of minorities on a sociological basis."[136]

As Miller, Marshall, and the team of lawyers worked diligently on their oral arguments, Miller and Marshall "prepared for their presentation in a moot court held before the students at Howard Law School. Following a tradition of arduous dry runs, originated by Houston, a second-year student reportedly asked 'a long, rambling question,'" which during the arguments Justice Frankfurter addressed. According to legal scholar Mark V. Tushnet, oral advocacy before the court is "a peculiar art. Its point usually is not to persuade undecided justices; rather, it is to inform them about the case."[137] In truth, Marshall was a master trial attorney:

> A great raconteur, Marshall developed the capacity to speak in the different voices of the characters in his anecdotes; and he used that capacity as well as an oral advocate, shifting from a careful legal analysis to sharper tones as the occasion demanded. Having immersed himself in civil rights law and procedure, Marshall was usually in full control of oral arguments, meeting skeptical objections to his positions with a

tenacious insistence that he asked for only what the law required, slipping only when he was forced on to unfamiliar terrain.[138]

When the big "dynamite-laden"[139] day arrived, Miller was understandably nervous; it was his first time arguing a case before the U.S. Supreme Court. By 10:30 A.M. on Thursday, January 15, the first day of debate, twenty-five people lined up outside the door to the main chamber, which seats 268 persons. Mrs. Andrew Ransom, wife of a prominent Washington attorney, had been waiting since 9:00 A.M. and had brought her crocheting. The VIPs were escorted by a clerk dressed in morning coat and striped pants to their plush red-cushioned benches— separated from the other spectators by red velvet-covered ropes. In the audience was Walter White, with "elbows on knees, his chin resting on his hands."[140] At noon, nine justices filed in and took their seats. Each side was given three hours for oral arguments, with the solicitor general granted one hour as amicus curiae.

Before oral arguments began, Justices Wiley Rutledge, Robert H. Jackson, and Stanley F. Reed stood up from their black leather swivel seats and walked out with no reason given for recusing themselves. "The reason commonly repeated was that these three had covenants on properties they own or live in," reported Carl Murphy of the *Baltimore Afro-American*. "It shows how deep the case cuts when one-third of the nation's highest court disqualifies itself," commented Houston.[141] If a fourth justice removed himself, the court could not have heard the case. Ultimately, the remaining Justices, Felix Frankfurter, Harold H. Burton, Frank Murphy, Hugo L. Black, William O. Douglas, and Chief Justice Frederick M. Vinson would decide what had begun three decades earlier.

George Vaughn and Herman Willer argued for the Saint Louis appellants, J. D. and Ethel Lee Shelley; Thurgood Marshall and Loren Miller argued for Orsel and Minnie McGhee of Detroit; Charles Houston and Phineas Indritz challenged the District of Columbia covenants on behalf of James and Mary Hurd and Raphael Urciolo, white attorney and realtor. On the opposing side were three white attorneys: Gerald L. Seegers for Louis and Fern E. Kraemer of Saint Louis and Henry Gilligan and James A. Crooks on behalf of white property owners Benjamin and Anna C. Sipes of Detroit and Frederic E. and Lena A. Hodge of the District of Columbia.

Backed by the Truman administration, the United States solicitor general, Philip B. Perlman, opened the proceedings by declaring that the Justice Department believed covenants were unconstitutional and against public policy: "Racial restrictive covenants on real property should no longer be enforced by any part of the judicial system of our country. They should be relegated to the limbo of other things as dead as slavery. We ask that the decree here involved be reversed." White Americans "are under a heavy debt to colored Americans. We brought them here as slaves. . . . We set them free, promising them . . . equal rights and privileges with all other people. Yet after three-quarters of a century, attempts are made by such devices as restrictive covenants, to hold them in bondage" and to hem them in where "they cannot escape the evil conditions under which so many of them are compelled to live."[142] Aside from the moral issues, overcrowded residential areas pose a public health threat.[143] According to Elman, Perlman, who had clerked for Justice Felix Frankfurter, repeatedly stated, with few questions from the bench, that the judicial branch of government—both state and federal—has no authority to enforce covenants. The central focus was whether the judicial enforcement involved state action. Clearly, Perlman was asking for an end to segregation. Elman, who had written out the solicitor general's oral presentation, said that when Perlman "argued in a courtroom full of blacks," he "was very moved by the experience. It was a transforming experience for Perlman."[144] "The Solicitor General," observed Miller, "spoke out vigorously on their behalf, even quoting the State Department as concerned at the harm judicial enforcement was doing in the area of international relations."[145]

Next up was George L. Vaughn, who, like Miller, was the son of a former slave. He characterized racial covenants as "the Achilles hell" of democracy and repeated the state action theory.[146] If the court did not reverse the Missouri Supreme Court decision, "these covenants would push the Negro back into slavery and involuntary servitude."[147] Vaughn's presentation, according to Elman, was poor and "not particularly distinguished." He argued the Thirteenth Amendment, "which wasn't before the court . . . And the Justices didn't ask many questions." In truth, it was a dull argument until he came to the very end." Elman recalls Vaughn saying something like,

> Now I've finished my legal argument, but I want to say this before I sit down. In this Court, this house of the law, the Negro today stands outside, and he knocks on the door, over and over again, he knocks on the door and cries out, "Let me in, let me in, for I too have helped build this house." All of a sudden there was drama in the courtroom, a sense of what the case was really all about rather than the technical arguments.[148]

Marshall was already concerned with Vaughn's legal abilities, particularly after Vaughn revealed one night to J. D. Shelley, "I ain't never had a case this hard."[149] Disgusted by Vaughn's performance, according to journalist Juan Williams, Marshall reportedly said, "I mean he was a blunderbuss. He stood up in that damned courtroom filled to the gills with people, and said in a loud booming voice that you could hear out in the streets: 'And Moses looked across the River Jordan and looked across the Mississippi River and said, let my people Go-o-o-o-o-o.'" Then Vaughn sat down and "promptly fell to sleep. . . . I got up and said to him, 'Are you goddamned dead?'"[150]

During the proceedings, Herman Willer, Vaughn's white associate, declared, "Racial covenants . . . are morally indefensible, especially in housing where the 'separate but equal' doctrine cannot operate."[151] He pleaded that "the nation's treaties, the United Nations Charter and the Act of Chapultepec, have established a public policy of equal treatment for all and have made the covenants void."[152] If the court upheld covenants, Willer concluded, the international "prestige of the country will be greatly impaired."[153] Gerald L. Seegers, counsel for the Marcus Avenue Improvement Association and nephew to its founder, representing the white respondents, "contended that the Court should disregard the sociological and political aims of his opponents."[154] His position was that problems of race discrimination are not for the courts to solve.

Two hours later, when the time came for Miller to approach the bench—in the only case of the four cases sponsored by the NAACP—the *Baltimore Afro-American* reported that Miller "argued that 'a state cannot support property rights when that right denies another its civil right.'"[155] Miller recommended only one remedy: the right of a citizen to own, use, and occupy residential property. When the state enforces restrictive covenants, he insisted, it constitutes a denial of the equal protection of the laws, a decree that is contrary to the Fourteenth Amendment. Miller argued that "the civil rights cases preclude the states from using any of its powers to impede restrictions."[156] He called for a reversal of the Michigan Supreme Court decision, which he contended was based on an unconstitutional desire to uphold segregation as public policy. Francis Allen, law clerk for Chief Justice Vinson, remembers, "Loren Miller, employed a style that verged on the pedagogic, but which was nevertheless lucid and persuasive."[157]

The *McGhee* brief, written by Miller with input from attorneys Francis Dent and Willis M. Graves, argued that covenants violated treaties between the United States and other members of the United Nations. What we have here, they explained, is either a "united nation or a country divided into areas and ghettoes solely on racial or religious lines,"[158] a position Miller had argued many times before.

As Marshall stood before the mahogany bench, he urged the court, in a delivery typically elegant and articulate, to weigh the impact of racial segregation on "housing problems, crime and disease."[159] Justice Frankfurter, long involved on the side of civil rights, the NAACP, and in particular, sociological jurisprudence, queried Marshall: "What's the relevance of all these [sociological] materials? If you are right about the legal proposition, the sociological material merely shows how it works. If you're wrong, this material doesn't do you any good."[160] Marshall replied that in the Detroit case sociological materials were included to show the "disastrous total effect of covenants on the lives of Negroes. But he quickly added that in a legal point of view, his case would be just as valid if there were only one covenant on one lot in the Nation,"[161] a position Miller advanced in New York, during the third and final strategy meeting in the war on covenants.[162] "If there was only one covenant in the land to base this case on," stated Marshall, "it would be just as unlawful as a great number would be."[163]

Marshall pointed out that the court "is not a mere arbiter in a private contractual dispute but is the arm of the State enforcing a discriminatory restriction in an area from which the State is prohibited by the Fourteenth Amendment."[164] Gilligan, on behalf of his white respondents, "bitterly" assailed the government for intervening and dismissed the sociological data since it was not introduced in the lower court. It has "no place in the Supreme Court debate."[165] His clients, he charged, simply wanted to be "unhampered by the greed of unscrupulous real estate speculators posing as friends of the Negro race while mulcting them of large sums of money."[166] This was an apparent dig at white realtor Raphael G. Urciolo, appellant in the District of Columbia case, who owned four pieces of property on Bryant Street in the matter before the court. Gerald L. Seegers, representing the Saint Louis respondents, argued that the "rule of law" should be upheld or white people will be "vitally affected."[167]

Throughout the proceedings, Crooks, Gilligan, and Seegers held that covenants were thoroughly in line with public opinion and that the Fourteenth Amendment did not apply to individuals. Crooks further contended that the only reason the petitioners were in court was that they were colored and that the "only reason they are deprived of their property is because they bought property with restrictions on it."[168] During the proceedings, Crooks, who followed Gilligan, proclaimed that "Congress has done nothing to alter the public policy and that there is no legislation contradictory to segregation in Washington," a position challenged by Houston.[169] Of all the lawyers arguing, Houston was particularly at ease standing before Associate Justice Felix Frankfurter, his Harvard Law mentor, "a leading advisor of the National Association for the Advancement of Colored People and a mentor for a series of outstanding black Harvard Law School students."[170] One of the advantages that the six petitioning counselors had was the opportunity to argue the four cases in succession, a maneuver used later by the NAACP in *Brown v. Board of Education.*

They had the added advantage as "the country's most distinguished and tested veterans of civil rights litigation," according to Francis Allen. The attorneys for the respondents, on the other hand, were in many instances "engaged in real estate practice . . . practices that likely included few appearances in appellate forums." The oral arguments "may have strengthened the Chief's resolve to reverse the lower court decisions."[171]

In the two District of Columbia cases, Houston and Indritz were on different and perhaps more sharpened legal footing since the Fourteenth Amendment applies only to states, and not to the federal government. Tushnet writes, "To one listener, Houston's argument 'combin[ed] intellectual strength with moral force, and . . . communicat[ed] a sense of personal integrity.'"[172] In closing out the two days of debate, Houston said, "What the courts are doing by supporting these racial zoning efforts is to develop ghettos which are a threat to the national security. . . . We are not trying to change anybody's prejudices . . . but racism must go."[173] After hearing seven hours of argument, the six Supreme Court justices left for a two-week recess.

In the interim, while the high court deliberated whether to abolish restrictive covenants, Miller returned to his law practice, political activism, and commitment to community service.[174] At the annual convention of the Southern California region of the American Jewish Congress, held at the Biltmore Hotel, Miller spoke on a panel on "Law—Potent Weapon Against Discrimination," along with colleagues Daniel G. Marshall, chair of the Catholic Interracial Council, and Charles J. Katz of the National Lawyers Guild.[175] On February 24, Miller, Southern California co-chair of the National Conference of Christians and Jews, along with Lena Horn and Frank Sinatra, welcomed that year's Brotherhood Week principal speaker, former secretary of war Judge Robert P. Patterson.[176]

On March 5, during the West Coast Regional Conference of the NAACP, Miller and Thomas L. Griffith, Jr., president of the Los Angeles branch, led the Friday night discussions on restrictive covenants, police brutality, and public accommodations. Thurgood Marshall came directly from Texas, where he was representing Herman M. Sweatt, who had been refused admission to the School of Law at the University of Texas. He arrived in time to lead the lineup of speakers at Sunday's mass meeting.[177]

While he waited for the high court to reach its decision in the *Shelley* case, Miller was needed in nearby Santa Monica, where approximately two hundred people had turned out on February 27 to picket discriminatory hiring practices at the newly opened Sears, Roebuck and Company store on Colorado Avenue. When Frank Barnes, president of the Santa Monica branch of the NAACP, launched one of the largest pickets against Sears, the Santa Monica City Council, in turn, attempted to rush through "a special anti-picketing ordinance."[178] Though the ordinance was defeated when more than 150 people jammed the council chambers, two months later, Barnes was "suspended from his job [as a letter carrier] under Executive Order 9835 [the president's loyalty order for federal employees] on charges that he was 'affiliated or sympathetic'"[179] with subversive organizations.

In Miller's response to the charges against his client, officially authorized by NAACP executive secretary Walter White to defend Barnes, he wrote, "Our review of the evidence . . . convinces us that the charges are absolutely unfounded. We regret the use of the loyalty order in this connection as an unwarranted intervention of the federal government in a community dispute revolving around the legitimate demand of Negroes for employment on the basis of merit and not of color."[180] Miller and law partner Harold Sinclair "challenged the [postal] board to produce witness to substantiate the charges."[181] The *Los Angeles Sentinel* saw the charges as an obvious ploy to break the antidiscrimination campaign against Sears.[182]

By summertime, Miller and Sinclair jointly appeared before the U.S. Post Office's hearing board, where they "pointed out that such widespread use of the loyalty cloak might induce unscrupulous persons to use it to break the back of Negro leaders seeking their just civil rights." Such widespread use of the loyalty order deprived their client of "his due process of law, equal protection of the law and freedom of speech." By Christmas, Barnes was absolved of all charges and "restored to his former position. Afterward, Miller told members of the press,

"We regard this decision as a significant victory in the fight to prevent subversion of the presidential Loyalty Order to serve private ends." Miller added: "Barnes emphatically denies being a communist or a fellow traveler."[183]

Before Miller departed Los Angeles for Washington, D.C., to attend discussions with the military on integrating the armed forces, he did what he said he would do and switched his pledge of support from Helen Gahagan Douglas, wife of film actor Melvyn Douglas, to Colonel Moody Staten in the race for California's Fourteenth Congressional District, pledging, "I will do whatever I can to help secure [Moody Staten's] nomination . . . a competent and qualified Negro."[184]

The invitation to attend the all-day closed session on race relations in the armed forces had been arranged by Lester Granger, Miller's old friend, now special advisor to James Forrestal, the secretary of defense. S. W. Garlington of the *New York Amsterdam News*, attending the National Defense Conference on Negro Affairs, reported that "16 prominent Negro leaders flatly stated that they would not form a permanent racial relations advisory committee to the armed services as long as segregation continues in the military forces."[185] The most striking element, noted the *Los Angeles Sentinel*, was the participants' unanimous decision "not to participate as individual advisors or as members of an advisory committee to the secretary of the defense unless a program to end segregation was devised and put into effect." "Our attitude," said Miller, "was simply that we would not aid in trying to make the jim-crow system work in our military establishment or be a party to bolstering up a segregatory system. . . . We told Mr. [James] Forrestal that in so many words and requested that we not be called upon again until a non-discriminatory program to integrate Negroes into the armed services had been worked out."[186]

"I do appreciate, kind sir," wrote Granger jokingly to his old friend, "your comment on the report to Forrestal. Your suspicions were well founded; for not only did I have to complete the job alone, but most of the committee, including yourself, kind sir, failed even to acknowledge receipt of the first draft until needled with a telegram announcing imminent draft of the final statement. But that's what a chairman is for, isn't it?"[187]

Over the weekend, most of Washington stayed home as light rains blanketed the area, while the more adventurous assembled at the ballpark to see the Washington-Philly doubleheader until it began raining in the second game. However, on Monday, May 3, 1948, the day the Supreme Court announced its decision, the day began with improved weather conditions.[188] At one o'clock in the afternoon, Gerald L. Seegers received a terse telegram from James A. Crooks, the other white attorney who defended the white property owners: "ALL COVENANT CASES DECIDED ADVERSELY."[189] Any enforcement of restrictive covenants, through the courts, would be unconstitutional and unenforceable under the Fourteenth Amendment.

"The Supreme Court ruled 6–0 today that restrictive real estate agreements which bar Negroes from all-white neighborhoods, cannot be enforced by state or federal courts,"[190] reported the Associated Press. When Mrs. Shelley heard, according to *Time* magazine, that she could keep her house she said, "My little soul is overjoyed. Wait till I get by myself. I'll tell the Lord of my thankfulness."[191] Mr. Paul R. Steward, one of the Washington, D.C., litigants, vented his pent up feelings "on hearing of the decision with a loud, 'Thank God.'" "We figured that we would win out. What's more, we have too much invested in this house to give up."[192]

"Whatever else the framers (the framers of the Constitution) sought to achieve," announced Chief Justice Vinson, "it is clear that the matter of primary concern was established in the enjoyment of basic civil and political rights and preservation of those rights from discriminatory action on the part of the state based on consideration of race or color."[193] In deciding to preserve these rights, the court declared that the Fourteenth Amendment forbade "state action" in matters of racial discrimination. Stripped of the legal verbiage, the decision meant that Americans of every stripe were free to purchase and occupy homes where they wanted. "The short of the matter," Vinson concluded, "is that from the time of the adoption of the Fourteenth Amendment until the present, it has been the consistent ruling of this Court that the action of the States to which the Amendment has reference, includes action of state courts and state judicial officials."[194] The pivotal argument, on which the court cinched its decision, was that "judicial action *is* state action," the very point Miller had hammered away for years in the courts of California.[195]

According to Mark V. Tushnet, Miller rushed a "mash note," to Marian Wynn Perry, "to brag about the fact that in the beginning wasn't nobody but you and me really believed we could restore God to his heaven and sanity to the Constitution—greatest Document ever struck from the minds of men by overthrowing race restrictive covenants—We told 'em so, huh"?[196] On May 6, the *Los Angeles Sentinel* ran extensive coverage of the Supreme Court's decision. "The victory that we won," said Miller, "is a triumph not only for Negroes and members of other minority groups but for all Americans."[197] In thanking colleagues and clients for the aid and encouragement he had received, he said, "Credit for this victory belongs to literally hundreds and thousands of people—in the labor movement, in the churches, in fraternal orders, in civic organizations—who kept up an unending fight against this evil. Briefs on our behalf were filed by the AFL [American Federation of Labor], the CIO [Congress of Industrial Organizations], the Elks Lodge, the American Jewish Committee . . . and the American Indian Congress, to name only a few."[198] Appraising the victory, Thurgood Marshall said, "This blow to racial segregation in the field of housing opens up the pending fight against segregation in education which fight must be carried on with renewed vigor."[199]

In 1951, Marshall wrote that the *Shelley v. Kraemer* decision "is unquestionably one of the most important of the whole field of civil rights. With judicial enforcement of restrictive covenants now held to be a denial of the equal protection of the laws, it becomes possible for colored minorities to break out of crowded ghettoes into unsegregated areas, with consequent opportunity of acceptance as members of an integrated community. Thus increased opportunity is given for eventual solution of racial problems in this country."[200]

Naturally, the court victory, considered a triumphant for democracy, brought jubilant cables, phone calls, and letters of congratulations, including comments from newspapers from across the country. The *Washington Star* said, "The Supreme Court has written new law . . . law which in the long run will serve public policy."[201] George A. Beavers, Jr., of the Golden State Mutual Life Insurance Company, Los Angeles, said it was one of the greatest victories in the history of the NAACP. "Dear George," replied Thurgood Marshall on May 13, "Thanks so much for your letter of congratulations. . . . The victory was made possible only through the cooperation of a whole gang of lawyers, both white and black, including Loren Miller, whose cooperation was better than marvelous."[202] Calling it a triumph for democracy, the *Los Angeles Sentinel*'s editorial blared: "It is no exaggeration to say that [Loren Miller], more than to any other single individual in the nation, belongs credit for arousing opposition to these iniquitous agreements and for perfecting the legal arguments that persuaded the Supreme Court to overthrow them."[203] The president of the *Pittsburgh-Courier*, Ira F. Lewis, rightly cautioned, "Instead of celebrating such victories the fact should be brought home to us that there is much work yet to be done. . . . There can be no turning back. There can be no settlement short of full citizenship rights."[204] Interestingly, the *Wall Street Journal* barely mentioned the victory—it published only a fourteen-line article—whereas it accorded three lengthy articles on the ruling by the high court in a Federal Trade Commission antitrust suit against eight major motion picture distributors.[205]

Los Angeles's black realtors and property owners were "unanimous in expressing to The *Sentinel* . . . their joyous reactions to the hard-won Supreme Court decision." Special commendation was due Miller and the NAACP for the part they played in bringing the case to the Supreme Court and winning it. California State Assembly member Augustus Hawkins (whose first electoral campaign was managed by Miller) said it was "the most important decision affecting the fundamental rights of the Negro since the Dread Scott decision." John W. Bean, Jr., with the Maddox Realty Company, said he was waiting for this decision, so "we could build on our restrictive lot. Thanks to God, Miller, Marshall and the Supreme Court."[206]

There were testimonial dinners in his honor. Attorney Abraham Lincoln Wirin told the "business executives and civic personages" who gathered in the Alexandria Hotel's Continental Room in downtown Los Angeles of Miller's role and the role the ACLU played in the long housing battle. Miller's Kappa Alpha Psi frat brothers presented him with an achievement award for outlawing property covenants. Members of the J.B. Bass Elks Lodge No. 1004, held a mass meeting at the Tabernacle of Faith, on 114th Street and Central Avenue, where they presented him with a plaque recognizing his part in abolishing restrictive covenants. During grand opening ceremonies over the Memorial Day weekend of the Lake Elsinore Community Center, eighty miles south of Los Angeles, he accepted a gold wristwatch for his victory.[207]

In time, he received more praise, more awards, another watch. The *Los Angeles Sentinel* reported that Miller, in recognition of his restrictive covenant achievements, received a wristwatch from the Association for the Abolition of Second Class Citizenship.[208] By Christmas, the Southern California branch of the ACLU honored both Loren Miller and Daniel G. Marshall, at its twenty-fifth anniversary dinner for outstanding work on behalf of civil liberties—Marshall for his civil rights victory that banned "the 76 year-old [California] law prohibiting interracial marriage," and Miller for his "conspicuous service in promoting civil liberties—one of the signal achievements in the cause of democracy in this generation."[209]

CHAPTER 8

Fourth Estate to the Judiciary

I f Gloster B. Current, the national director of branches of the NAACP, chose to ignore Miller's October 16, 1948, plea for change, more than likely the contentious flare-ups between Thomas Lee Griffith, Jr., president of the Los Angeles branch of the NAACP, and members of the executive board would continue. Miller wrote, "I cannot stress too strongly that the (Los Angeles NAACP) branch is virtually stagnant and that it must inevitably recede unless something is done. (Thomas) Griffith's oft expressed attitude that he has "run the branch for fourteen years" and is going to "continue to run it" is the road to ruin."[1] Like Miller, the others had grown weary of what they believed was Griffith's extraordinary incompetence and arrogance, particularly in the lead-up to the 1949 biannual board election. Attempts had failed during the war to oust Griffith and seize control. However, feeling confident, a small clique tried again in 1947. In a surprise move, Miller was nominated for the presidency, but in the final tally he lost by a margin of one hundred votes; Griffith was reelected for his thirteenth term.[2]

By the time the next board election rolled around, opponents to Griffith's long reign was considerably larger. Almena Lomax, editor of the *Los Angeles Tribune*, outraged at the plummeting NAACP membership numbers, which were said to have fallen from somewhere between six thousand and twenty thousand, editorialized: "If we were to fix blame, we'd say the culprit is Tommy, President (for 14 years) Thomas L. Griffith. Tommy did all with his little hatchet." Not satisfied with "his handiwork, he wants to stick around and desecrate the body, which is to say he wants to be president again."[3]

Equally dissatisfied, the *Los Angeles Sentinel* joined the *Los Angeles Tribune* in opposition to Charlotta Bass's *California Eagle*, a powerful supporter of Griffith. To complicate matters, the newly hired executive secretary of the Los Angeles branch complained to Current that Griffith kept her from doing her job; Mary Alton Cutler's complaint initiated a brisk flow of correspondence between the national headquarters and the local branch. As a result, Cutler, along with the *Tribune*, charged—whether accurate or not—that the "so-called Lefts" and "Reds" had infiltrated the branch at the behest of Griffith. Less alarmist, a *Sentinel* editorial asserted that "there aren't a handful of Reds in the branch" to "win a single office if the rank and file members take a hand." In calling for Griffith's removal, the editorial argued, "He is in a rut and he has got the branch in a rut. The branch needs fresh leadership."[4]

Adding fuel to the situation, Miller wrote Current that Griffith, the son of Los Angeles's most prominent black Baptist minister, treated Mary Cutler "as a mere office girl."[5] On October 19, 1948, Current assured Cutler, "[As a former executive secretary] I know exactly what you are going through. . . . My advice to you is to sit tight for a while."[6] He suggested to Miller that "If the Los Angeles branch were to invite me to come in to investigate the situation and offers to pay all or most of my expenses round trip from Dallas, perhaps something could be worked out."[7] Miller agreed.

That same month, as the NAACP controversy continued to percolate, a forty-eight-year-old melancholy Miller turned to poetry:

My Wife at Noontime
Now that spring has gone,
Let us not deny its passing,
And tell the lie so often told:
—that it shall never go.
Know this, My Love
A summer rose is but a brief interlude
Of Beauty—
Between an earth brown seed
——and blowing dust.

Let us savor—this summer:
Breathe its heavy windless air . . .
These palsied summer days are our time, My Love,
To eat our fill of fruit so ripe
It will not last the day,
Our moment—
—and this our only one—
To gather whatever we will
Before it falls victim to the very urge that gave it birth.
The taste of fruit,
The smell of flower,
Strike deeper if the wind is eager, the blood unafraid . . .[8]

By December, Almena Lomax, frustrated at the "weak and futile attempts" to oust Griffith, indirectly accused Miller of cowardice: "There is nobody with nerve enough to run against Tom Griffith who could beat him. The trouble is that there is almost nobody with the nerve; or is there? . . . Last year, a particularly disgraceful situation arose in which a likely candidate stood up, then sat weakly down and mouthed an endorsement of Mr. Griffith at the first sign of disapproval from that worthy."[9]

Apparently, the *Eagle* made similar charges, which led Miller to publicly explain why he declined the offer by the anti-Griffith faction to run for the branch presidency: "I have told all of those who have approached me that I was not a candidate. To put the matter at rest, once and for all, I am not seeking, I do not want and I will not accept the presidency of the branch. My personal commitments and obligations are such that I cannot afford to undertake the responsibilities . . . that office would thrust upon me."[10]

In the interim, on December 27, two days after the executive board fired Mary Cutler, Gloster Current wrote Noah Griffin, the regional secretary of the West Coast NAACP: "We believe it is time for the National Office to step in a quiet way to direct the strategy behind the scene. You can understand the need for diplomacy and tact because we are dealing with an explosive matter and can be charged with "outside interference." You must be discreet and firm and success-ful in either ousting Griffith with the aid of [Norman O.] Houston and others or electing a completely non-Communist executive committee."[11]

On January 9, 1949, Griffith beat Harold M. Kingsley, director of the interracial social center Pilgrim House, by a margin of 135 votes. The next month, acknowl-edging defeat, Miller wrote Thurgood Marshall, "A new election would do little good."[12] Miller's concession, according to historian Kevin Allen Leonard, offered "the national office a way to avoid further embarrassment by simply ignoring the serious divisions within the branch and suggesting that its only concern with branch affairs was keeping Communists from dominating the branch. Miller dwelled on the fact that 'no Communists or fellow travelers were nominated' for office by the nominating committee."[13] The brouhaha ended nine months later, when—after fifteen consecutive terms as branch president—Griffith wisely announced that he would not run in the next election.[14] Apparently, he realized that it was time to walk away. Not long after his loss, Griffith and Miller went head on, arguing in court the legitimacy of four newly elected officials to the Broadway Federal Savings and Loan Association board of directors.[15] Although H. A. Howard, founder and director of the association, was under indictment for fraud, embezzlement, and false entry, the judge, who ruled in favor of Griffith's clients, ordered a new election. Howard was later found guilty on two counts of falsifying records.[16]

Whether it was Miller's sense of humor, the money, or the publicity, he repre-sented Martha Green of 117th and South Avalon Boulevard. The case, according to the *Los Angeles Sentinel*, "caused consternation in the entire city." Green swore that when she came home from the feed store with a headless chicken, it "jumped up on the sink and started to crow," sending her screaming from the house. Sub-sequently, the L.A. Department of Animal Regulation gave her twelve hours to put the bird to death or face animal cruelty charges. By then she had grown "quite fond of her rather notorious chicken" and was undecided what to do with the offers from a circus. "What offer she will take or what she will do depends on her attorney, Loren Miller. . . . Mr. Miller was equally vague when called by the *Sentinel* but managed the 'guess' that his client would take 'the best offer.'"[17]

More seriously, the trouble between Loren Miller and Thomas Griffith, Jr.— who was elevated to the Los Angeles Municipal Court by Governor Earl Warren in 1953 and later became the first black judge "elected to the Superior Court by county voters"[18]—apparently started long before the NAACP election controversy. What particular event initiated the discord or when it began is unclear. Walter L. Gordon, Jr., who occasionally co-counseled with Miller, said, "They didn't ride in the same wagon."[19] Although Miller was professionally friendly with Tom, tensions between the two, at least where Miller was concerned, had developed by the early 1930s. Most likely it began when they worked on discrimination cases as members of the legal staff of the local NAACP, along with Thomas's brother Lloyd.[20] What is certain is that as early as 1935, Miller confessed to Juanita, he clearly disliked Griffith:

> How in the devil did Tom ever manage to get so far from Papa? All the same if ever there was an ass, Tom is it. I actually and actively dislike him for his grade of Uncle Tommery. Lloyd is a curious case with me. I like him despite his bluff and his real mental laziness. At least one has the sense that Lloyd is a friend while Tom goes in my classification of snakes-in-the-grass. There may be some biological contradiction in the spectacle of a man being at once a snake and a jack-ass but I insist that Tom is both, which must be some sort of a record for Darwin and his followers to ponder.[21]

Miller's formal shift into fair employment issues led to a new range of personal attacks, which surfaced following the 1946 defeat of Proposition 11, the Fair Employment Practices Act. Miller, and others closely involved in the campaign, were assailed as undemocratic, unchristian, and pets of the Communists and the CIO.[22] Intensified and perhaps strengthened by those attacks, Miller agreed to serve on the Los Angeles Committee for Equal Employment Opportunity and later on the California Committee for Fair Employment Practices, for which in 1953, among hundreds, Miller marched on Sacramento to help turn the tide against employment discrimination. In the forefront of that tide was Augustus Hawkins, state assembly member, who in 1945, 1949, 1951, and again in 1953 pressed for passage of the Fair Employment Practices Act, along with support from C. L. Dellums, Berkeley's NAACP branch officer. The act was signed into law on April 16, 1959, by Governor Pat Brown. Later, as a member of the Legal Committee of the Los Angeles County Conference on Community Relations, Miller challenged a proposed state assembly bill to establish a Department of Human Relations. In his six-page recommendation, he pointed out that the bill suffered from a lack of specificity.[23]

Besides Thomas Griffith, Jr., there were others within Los Angeles's black leadership community with whom Miller crossed swords. For some time, he had disliked his former employer, *California Eagle* publisher Charlotta Bass. It could safely be said that the two more or less assessed their relationship as equally acrimonious, more so after Miller and his cousin Leon Washington left the *Eagle*, where not long after they established the *Los Angeles Sentinel*. If Miller ever said anything good about Bass—other than keeping up a public relations front during his tenure at the *Eagle* in the early 1930s—there is little evidence on record.

Near the end of his life, Miller told Lawrence de Graaf that Mrs. Bass leaned whichever way the wind blew and that she was a chameleon, a person of accommodation more prone to whim, a behavioral trait he disliked. He accused her of going from the Republican Party in the 1920s—swallowing "the Republican Party whole no matter what it did or what it didn't do as far as Negroes were concerned"—to running unsuccessfully in 1944 on the Progressive Party ticket as a candidate for the U.S. Congress. Later, in 1952—by then "widely identified with Communism"—Bass ran for vice president (the first African American woman to do so), along with her presidential running mate, San Francisco attorney Vincent Hallinan.[24]

Bass's leftist leanings, according to Miller, came more from her devotion to her nephew John Kinloch, attracted as a youth to the Communist doctrine, than from her own political acumen. Kinloch, a Harlem transplant, began working for his aunt at sixteen. According to journalist R. J. Smith, "He edited, wrote reviews and editorials, and ghostwrote Bass's column; on the small staff he was the consummate polish man, the stylist who would take the raw copy from others and give it a snap that could be heard round the corner."[25] When, on April 4, 1945, Kinloch died from German artillery shells, his aunt was devastated. Afterward, with the backing of the Communist Party, the John Kinloch Club was formed for Los Angeles's youth activists.[26]

Regina Freer, professor of politics at Occidental College, contends that Charlotta Bass's move from the "Republican Party to the Progressive Party reflected a political evolution that also characterized her evolving role as a political activist." One of her main rivals was Almena Lomax of the *Los Angeles Tribune*, who, along with the California State Un-American Activities Committee, labeled Bass a Communist. "Whether she actually joined the CP," writes Freer, "her active participation in groups with large numbers of CP members and leaders, such as the Civil Rights Congress, indicated her comfort in working with CP members and CP-influenced groups and her defiance of an increasingly virulent anti-Communism."[27]

Miller's opinion of Bass's husband, Joseph Bass, was diametrically opposite to what he thought of her. "Mr. Bass," said Miller, "was the human being with the most integrity, basically with the most courage."[28] If Charlotta lacked courage, as Miller implied, it certainly did not appear so when, in 1936 her newspaper called Miller a Communist.[29] Perhaps it was a generational divide, Miller's harsh and unsympathetic opinion of someone born in 1874. Charlotta Bass's forty years of activism, expressed mostly on the pages of the *Eagle*, were huge accomplishments, not so easily dismissed, despite Miller's opinion regarding her character. After all, Bass was a major force behind the Don't Buy Where You Can't Work and the Los Angeles Negro Victory campaigns, which brought together labor, Communists, radicals, and conservatives alike;[30] her newspaper pressed hard to end racially restrictive housing covenants; and she was elected president of the Home Owners Protective Association in 1945—all issues supported by Miller.

At first glance, generational, cultural and political differences separated the two rivals. While she belonged to the same Victorian generation as Charles H. Houston and Raymond P. Alexander, Miller belonged to that generation of "younger black professionals and intellectuals," who, according to Harvard University law professor Kenneth Mack, "were in active revolt against their predecessors' Victorian ideas, which had celebrated hard work, thrift, savings, and success in the market economy as the route to responsible manhood."[31] Men like Charles Houston saw the "law as an opportunity to gain some upward mobility." Although, in 1935 Miller openly chastised Houston for being too lax during the George Crawford murder trial, he eventually softened, even to the point of congratulating Houston on his victory against the University of Maryland Law School's discriminatory racial admissions policy.[32]

Miller did not extend such conciliatory sentiments to Charlotta Bass. Apparently, he never relinquished what he felt toward her, which appears more a situation of two clashing personalities, beyond the confines of generational differences. The bad blood between them would play itself out long after 1951, when Bass sold Miller the *California Eagle*. Miller might have been less provocative if he knew what lay ahead.

On Thursday, May 3, 1951, the caption under the photograph of Loren Miller and Dr. Ralph J. Bunche standing together read: "Dr. Ralph J. Bunche, Nobel Peace Prize winner, took time out from his crowded schedule to wish Loren Miller success in his new venture as publisher of the California Eagle."[33] The front-page photograph shows the two "viewing first proofs of the current issue of the paper." Wendell Green, the *Eagle*'s new editor, who in a few years would became one of its owners, along with Violet Brown, wrote, "The change will result in a sharp break with the Eagle's immediate past and a repudiation of its stands on many issues. . . . We shall oppose Communism, and oppose it vigorously and with every means in our power."[34]

Miller failed to convince everyone he had changed political horses. Thomas H. Werdel (1949–53), the U.S. representative from California, apparently "riled because of the high praise heaped upon" Miller, issued a vicious attack. He charged him with having "connections with Communist support" and insisted that "any statement bearing out a change of policy may be deceptive."[35] To make his point, Werdel, a Republican, read into the *Congressional Record* a litany of Miller's Communist affiliations.

In an effort to quell critics who questioned his sincerity, Miller professed that he had learned about new beginnings and hope in the class of Mrs. Baker, his white Nebraska schoolteacher. Miller explained, "It's a heartening thing to remember that 'Yesterday now is a part of forever.' It tends to loosen the cords that bound men to that yesterday's tight little patterns of thought.'" He continued,

> A newspaper, any newspaper, can do a lot in fitting men's thoughts into new molds.
> A Negro newspaper is to the average daily paper as the pioneer to the established
> citizen of present day America. It can have a mighty big part in setting new patterns
> of thought for a whole people. . . . Yesterday is done with. Today is in the making.
> Tomorrow the pattern will begin dissolving into the texture of yesterday and the
> Negro newspaper is in on the whole picture. . . . Everybody is invited to get on the
> bandwagon. TODAY IS OURS AND TODAY ALONE. Let's go![36]

During the *Eagle*'s first year, Wendell Green introduced more in-depth coverage. He exposed the shameful white-only burial policies at Forest Lawn Cemetery, unlike managers of Evergreen and Rosedale Cemeteries, who in the late
nineteenth century "approached Negro residents and sold them plots without
regard to color and creed."[37] The *Eagle* assured its readers that the newspaper
would "re-establish" its proud reputation as well clarified any doubts that Bass
remained behind the scenes.[38] After the sale, Charlotta Bass left for New York
City, where she stayed for some time before returning to Los Angeles in spring
1953.[39]

When Miller and Clyde B. Denslow purchased the newspaper for forty thousand dollars, it was financially, according to Miller, "at very low ebb."[40] As early
as 1937, rumor had it that the *Eagle* was in trouble even though Bass dispelled the
report as "preposterous" and that her newspaper, "was to pass from her control"[41]
into the hands of Lucius Lomax, the future publisher of the *Los Angeles Tribune*.
At the time that Miller purchased the *Eagle*, it had become "an extreme left-
wing newspaper," having "lost ground."[42] According to historian Josh Sides, the
California Eagle editorial of May 1, 1952, "took a swipe at the CRC [Civil Rights
Congress], drawing a clear link between the Communist Party and the CRC."
The change in *Eagle* ownership, according to historian Scott Kurashige, was perhaps "the most historic Cold War shift in Black community leadership" in Los
Angeles. When Bass wrote her last Sidewalk column, she claimed that American
fascists and her own people had run her out of business, "a thinly veiled refer-
ence to Miller."[43]

Running a law firm, mostly singlehandedly, while simultaneously managing a
weekly newspaper, tested Miller's abilities. Feeling overwhelmed and disheart-
ened, he did what he did when troubled; he took up his pen to dissuade his
spirits and wrote a poem:

> **Prelude for Suicide**
> Waste no time on the spring that has gone:
> For it will come again
> Save some tears for the spring-sown seed
> that lies rotten in the ground
> and for the husbandman who laid it there.
> Rotted seed and blasted hopes
> have become part of the everything that is everything
> identical with the everything that is nothing.

Being nothing they will remain everything,
And being everything they will always be—nothing . . .[44]

Between the spring and autumn of 1951, Miller handled more discrimination cases than were manageable. During the inaugural period of running the *Eagle*, Miller, along with A. L. Wirin and Stewart Udall, the future United States secretary of the Interior, filed a lawsuit in the U.S. District Court, on behalf of the Maricopa County, Arizona, chapter of the NAACP against the board of education in Phoenix for refusing "to admit Negro" high school students to the area's high schools other than those "set apart for Negro pupils."[45] On the Millers' home front, Loren, Jr., graduated from Virgil Junior High School—where actors Carole Lombard and Marilyn Monroe had attended—with a C+ average.[46] If it were not for that D in handicrafts, he instead would have graduated with a solid B. His middling average academic performance raises an issue. Did his parents spend too much time on their careers, advancing their social statuses?

Despite a slow start, after graduating from Belmont High School, and attending Los Angeles City College, Loren, Jr., graduated from the University of Oregon with a bachelor's in history; in 1962, he earned a JD from Loyola Law School. While waiting for his bar exam results, Pete worked "as a student deputy in the office of Atty. Gen. Stanley Mosk (purely on his merits, you will understand),"[47] wrote his father to Henry Lee Moon. That July, Franklin H. Williams, then with the Peace Corps (which he had assisted Sargent Shriver in organizing), wrote Miller: "I don't know what you did to deserve it, but let me congratulate you on Loren Jr.'s success. I must confess. . . . I found myself reacting to the news story as if he were my son. I know that you and Juanita are justifiably proud."[48] He suggested that Junior consider working in Washington at the attorney general's office. Before Loren, Jr., entered private practice, he litigated as a deputy attorney general for the Fair Employment Practice Commission. Appointed to Los Angeles Superior Court in 1975, Loren Miller, Jr., served until 1997. His friend and colleague Judge Arthur Gilbert wrote on his death in 2011,

> A firm commitment to justice is firmly ingrained in the DNA of the Miller family. Loren was a judge of unscrupulous fairness. He applied the law and imposed tough sentences when required, but at the same time had a heart. He was compassionate and kind. Even the most hardened felons who received tough sentences at his hand revered him. Loren's daughter Superior Court Judge Robin Miller Sloan and his son Michael, a public defender, and daughter Nina, a school teacher, carry on the tradition of their father and grandfather.[49]

Interestingly, in 2003 Sloan became the "first linear third-generation judge in the history of the California court system."[50]

By October 1952, Miller returned to his mainstay, restrictive covenant cases. This time, assisted by Franklin H. Williams, then director of the NAACP's western region, Miller submitted *Barrows v. Jackson* to the United States Supreme Court, a case equally as important as *Shelley v. Kraemer*.[51] Did a covenant owner have the right to sell her property to an African American? At issue was whether the plaintiffs, Olive B. Barrows, Richard Pikaar, and M. M. O'Gara—three white residents of Los Angeles—had the right to sue Leona Jackson because she sold her property to a black couple, Parenell and Florine Smally, on the theory that she violated, as a co-covenantor, their restrictive residential agreement.[52] "Desperately embattled Negrophobic real estate interests," explained Lester Granger, executive secretary of the National Urban League, "have brought in a new device, trying to get the courts to uphold the covenants on the ground that to break them is a violation of a legal contract rendering the violator liable for civil damages."[53] Arguments were set for the 28th and 29th of April, 1953.

Two months before Miller stood in the courtroom of the U.S. Supreme Court for the second time, surrounded by friezes of ivory vein marble from Spain, portraying allegorical representations of law and historical lawgivers,[54] he and Juanita set off for New York City. When the "personable and popular West Coast couple," arrived on the afternoon of Sunday, March 8, 1953, they barely had time to "catch their breath and rush through a change from traveling to cocktail attire in time for the smart and intimate cocktail party and supper given in their honor by Mrs. Aaron Douglas,"[55] wife of the famous Harlem Renaissance painter. Attending were Robert C. Weaver, Henry Lee Moon, and many other prominent figures in law and the arts.

Miller wrote Franklin H. Williams afterward that, while in New York, he discussed the *Barrows* case with Thurgood Marshall, who believed that "it would be better if the entire argument is handled by one lawyer . . . that I handle the argument for the obvious reason that I know the case and am familiar with the law involved. That strikes me as a valid view of the matter and under present plans I will make the appearance, although he will be present." Miller let Williams know how anxious he was about the outcome of the case and that he wanted as much local "credit as possible in the matter" because it will affect "our membership campaigns and for the purpose of furthering our plans for our Legal Committee."[56]

On April 28, Miller argued before the Supreme Court that allowing "damages for breach of the agreement would result in residential segregation."[57] The attorneys for the plaintiffs, according to the *Chicago Defender*, came under a barrage of questions from Chief Justice Frederick M. Vinson and Justices Hugo Black and Felix Frankfurter. How could Mrs. Jackson keep African Americans from occupying property she sold in 1950? How legally feasible is it to award a suit for damages when under *Shelley v. Kraemer* covenants were no longer enforceable?

On Monday, June 15, the court, in upholding *Shelley v. Kraemer*, agreed with Miller; the *Barrows* plaintiffs had no grounds to sue for damages.[58] Their constitutional rights had not been violated. There was no breach of contract, no forthcoming payout of damages. What Miller had done, wrote his friend Lester Granger, was to "put the last nails in what should be the coffin of legally-backed race restrictions in home-buying."[59]

Soon after, Miller was back in full force publishing the *California Eagle*, and attacking the Broadway Department Store with the *Eagle*'s Don't Buy Where You Can't Work campaign. Then the *Eagle* turned its focus on the Jim Crow policies of Los Angeles fire chief John H. Alderson, whose commissioners subscribed "to the old folk tale that a little Jim Crow, like a little pregnancy, doesn't count."[60] In "Memo to the Mayor," the *Eagle* editorial charged, "Neither Chief Alderson nor the weak-kneed Commissioners deny the existence of such [segregation] practices. They advance the mealy-mouthed and stultifying argument that there isn't 'complete racial segregation' because four Negroes work in the fire preven- tion bureau and another in the bureau of supply and maintenance. They oper- ate on the theory that a little Jim Crow isn't bad."[61] Dr. H. Claude Hudson, vice president of the local NAACP, along with attorneys Edward C. Maddox (Miller's future law partner), Elbert Hudson, Thomas Neusom, and Herbert Simmons, Jr., charged the fire department with spending "public funds unlawfully to maintain racial segregation."[62] Of the city's eighty-seven fire stations, only Stations 14 and 30 served African Americans. The Board of Fire Commissioners ordered Alder- son to integrate, though "'gradually,' but integrate it nonetheless.'"[63] Alderson countered with a five-year estimate to integrate, which was rejected by churches, civic groups, and labor unions, who, hastened by the NAACP's petition, moved to oust Alderson: "We, therefore, call upon the Mayor, the City council, the Fire commission and the Civil Service commission to take immediate action to remove Alderson as chief engineer of the Fire department for insubordination and failure to act in good faith in integrating firemen in the department."[64] Sub- sequently, the U.S. attorney notified Miller, who headed the petition delegation, insisting that "the petition alone was unacceptable" because it lacked "documen- tary evidence."[65]

Depositions and countersuits followed; however, after attempting for two years to bypass integration, Alderson announced his intention to resign no "later than Jan. 1, 1956." "Thus, it would seem, the harassed chief bowed out," heralded the *Sentinel*'s editorial titled "Dear Chief: Bye Bye!" The chief "ran his integration program—in a pack of lies. . . . Thus, the tough, whip-cracking Mr. Big whim- pered" away after two years of community pressure, the editorial continued. "The merit of the segregation issue, as time went on, became the least important factor as the problem unfolded. Finally, one question emerged above all others: Was Alderson's will superior to that of constitutional government? Alderson's resignation gives the final answer."[66]

There were unintended consequences to Miller's ousting the fire chief, winning the *Barrows* case, and drafting the majority of the *Brown v. Board of Education* briefs; it caused the *California Eagle* to stumble. Who is to say whether Miller miscalculated the impact on his newspaper, or in spite of the consequences decided, for the greater good, to devote his time to writing *Brown I* (1954) briefs Nos. 2 and 4 (*Briggs v. Elliot and Davis v. County School Board of Prince Edward County, Virginia*, along with William R. Ming, Jr., Constance Baker Motley, and

Oliver W. Hill, among others) and *Brown II* (1955) briefs Nos. 1, 2, 3, and 5 (*Brown v. Board of Education*; *Briggs v. Elliot*; *Davis v. County School Board of Education of Prince Edward County, Virginia*; and *Gebhart v. Belton*)? In spite of the court's vague 1955 directive in *Brown II* to implement desegregation "with all deliberate speed," Miller, with the aid of various colleagues, changed American law and history forever.[67]

Interestingly, the *Briggs* appeal, to which Miller devoted such large swatches of time honing the facts relevant to the brief, was particularly pivotal in the victory over racial discrimination in public education and its role in dismantling Jim Crow. Many legal scholars, including professors Carol B. and Robert E. Botsch, consider *Briggs* the most important of the five cases from Delaware, Kansas, South Carolina, Virginia, and Washington, D.C. They argue that "Although history books record that the case which ultimately ended school segregation was *Brown v. Board of Education*, one could justifiably argue that the decision really began in South Carolina with *Briggs v. Elliot*," the first of the school segregation cases, which began with "a simple request to provide bus transportation"[68] and ultimately targeted teacher salaries, buildings, and educational material.

Change, however, moves at its own pace. Although a few months after *Brown*, one of the first minor after effects—more symbolic than substantive—was the appointment of fifteen-year-old Charles V. Bush, the first African American to serve as a U.S. Supreme Court page.[69] More substantial and severe was the manner in which the NAACP came under attack "in almost all the eleven former Confederate states," according to Robert L. Carter, at the time general counsel to the NAACP and later a United States district judge in the southern district of New York. "Typically, for example, NAACP lawyers at the national level would announce that the organization was now prepared to sponsor litigation outlawing segregation in state colleges." Virginia followed by amending its statues "to make this methodology illegal."[70] In Alabama, the attorney general demanded the NAACP membership list. If the association defied the court order, it risked a $100,000 fine. Carter surmises, "It would be finished in Alabama. All the black people would be afraid to join for fear their names would be given to the local officials."[71]

Ever the contrarian, Miller urged defiance, recalls Judge Carter: "Thurgood [Marshall] gave up the fight and said it was up to Roy [Wilkins] to decide. His abdication was interesting because all three of us knew Roy would do whatever Thurgood told him to do." The non-lawyer board members voted to defy the court, whereas "almost all the [NAACP] lawyers voted to obey the court's order."[72] However, according to Carter, Miller "broke the pattern and said risk the fine. When the board's votes were counted, I was able to relax because a majority had voted for defiance."[73] When the case *NAACP v. Alabama* reached the U.S. Supreme Court, the high court sent it back to the Alabama Supreme Court. "The Supreme Court . . . would not tolerate deprivation of constitutional rights through evasive application of obscure procedural rules,"[74] writes Miller in *The Petitioners*, where he did not mention his role in advising the association to take the risk. Later, in 1963, when others claimed that tremendous progress had been made in race relations with the *Brown* decision, an outraged Miller, fully aware that little had changed, not the transformation of the American psyche or its old-time Jim Crow policies, wrote that those claims "marks the supreme triumph of tokenism." He continued,

> To date not a single Negro child has been enrolled in a South Carolina "white" grade school or high school. The original plaintiffs have long since graduated from or dropped out of school. As one of the attorneys who participated in the case I can't even remember the names of the plaintiffs. All that has happened in South Carolina is that one Negro has been enrolled in Clemson University. He got there a few weeks ago to the accompaniment of loud cheers and hosannas from people who believe that one swallow makes a summer and one daisy makes a spring. South Carolina was even hailed as a great example of an honorable and law abiding state. . . . Acceptance of tokenism as the goal in the quest for racial equality has led to a letdown in the struggle for civil rights.[75]

Four decades later, Charles J. Ogletree Jr., professor at Harvard Law School, affirmed Miller's 1960s position: "If *Brown I* made integration a legal imperative, *Brown II*, with its decision to proceed with 'all deliberate speed,' ensured that the imperative was not implemented as a social imperative. . . . As an expression of moral rectitude, *Brown I* was the least the Court could have done but the timidity expressed in *Brown II* nullified its import."[76] Essentially, as long as the Supreme Court continues to abandon the legacy of *Brown* as demonstrated by the Rehnquist court and subsequent court decisions, black children will be stuck in poorly funded public schools.

For all of Miller's efforts to keep the *Eagle* above water, two years after he took it over, he confirmed the rumors reported by the *Chicago Defender* that the "oldest Negro weekly in the west has reached the end of the trail." Only "immediate financial aid" would save the newspaper.[77] According to Abie Robinson, the *Eagle*'s sports editor, crime reporter, and all around everything, the paper barely had enough to pay his salary, let alone that of additional staff. The newspaper's "inability to pay our bills" was "for the simple reason that Loren was tainted by the government. . . . You have to understand that. . . . The *California Eagle* in 1951 was taking on the housing authority, the realty association, and police brutality, three of the most influential agencies in this city that controls the minds of white people." On top of that, William H. Parker III, appointed chief of the Los Angeles Police Department in 1950, publicly called Miller a Communist. In addition to government agencies discrediting Miller, which in turn affected the newspaper's ability to attract advertisers, Robinson said, "J. Edgar Hoover and company bugged the office."[78] Distressed, Miller, scrounged up the money from two investors—and added their names to the ownership title—in order to make two two-thousand-dollar installments. By 1955, he averred the newspaper was free of debt.[79] Charlotta Bass took much umbrage to his claim. Faithful to her reputation as a formidable and relentless adversary, Bass, though now retired, claimed that Miller owed her a percentage of the profits. Miller responded to E. Leonard Richardson, Bass's attorney at the time, that the claim "is unjustified." He explained that after providing a twenty-thousand-dollar down payment toward the forty-thousand-dollar purchase price, he made annual installments of four thousand dollars between 1951 and 1955. A balance, according to the contract, would be "paid from the profits, at the rate of 10% of the net profits," if there were any profits; otherwise "nothing is due." The *Eagle*, Miller contended, instead of making a profit, lost money. Perhaps in an attempt at diplomacy, he added that once a complete accounting of the paper's finances was complete, "I am sure you will be satisfied that no profits have accrued."[80] Despite Miller's insistence that he owed Bass nothing, she remained unconvinced. The issue of the debt would follow Miller well into the next decade. By then, Bass replaced Richardson with attorney Ben Margolis, known for defending the blacklisted Hollywood Ten and for reversing the conviction of twenty-three Mexican Americans in the infamous Sleepy Lagoon murder case. The situation was awkward; Margolis, the "grand poobah" of Communist attorneys, and Miller were members of the National Lawyers Guild and, as such, worked cases together. Moreover, as members of the Hollywood Arts, Sciences and Professions Council of Progressive Citizens of America, the two served on the organizing committee for its 1947 Thought Control Conference.[81] Interestingly, around the time Miller was urging the Supreme Court to review the contempt of Congress convictions of Hollywood Ten defendants Dalton Trumbo and John Howard Lawson, Margolis said that Miller "stopped his associations with people like me."[82]

During the 1940s, Miller and Margolis worked "very closely" on the well-publicized restrictive covenant case of Anna and Henry Laws, a respectable Los Angeles African American family hauled off to jail for five days. Urged by Thurgood Marshall, Miller and Thomas Griffith, Jr., defended the Laws for two years. Subsequently, the case passed out of their hands and into the hands of Ben Margolis, Charles J. Katz, and John T. McTernan, three left-wing gunslingers who successfully represented the Laws family before the California State Supreme Court.[83] Margolis told an interviewer that after having read an article on what constitutes "Negro blood," he asked, "Loren, why don't we attack restrictive covenants on the ground that there is no legal way of telling whether a person is or is not black. And therefore there is no way of enforcing it? I thought that was a good, progressive position to take." Miller, who occasionally used that argument, replied angrily, "We're fighting for the right of black people to be black. Not on the right that you can't tell who's black and who's white."[84]

Apparently, Miller had a penchant for playing around the edges of conflict when he dodged Margolis's numerous attempts to reach him. He continued to ignore Margolis even after returning from attending Sargent Shriver's Peace Corps conference in Washington, D.C.[85] On January 24, 1962, Margolis tried again: "I need hardly tell you that I am most reluctant to file a lawsuit for the purpose of enforcing Mrs. Bass's rights under her contract, but if you will not even talk to me about the matter you will leave me no alternative."[86] Awkward though it may have been for the two attorneys, the situation apparently lay dormant until 1964, when Miller sold the newspaper to James L. Tolbert for twenty-five thousand dollars—"one-half in cash and one-half within five years with interest thereon at 6 percent."[87] Predictably, like an old penny, Bass turned up again, this time to dispute the sale price.

On the face of a *Los Angeles Times* report that mentioned that the *Eagle* was sold somewhere in the neighborhood of $60,000, Bass revived her original complaint. When Miller replied to Elaine B. Fischel, an associate with Margolis's law firm, he reiterated that the price was $25,000 not $60,000. Then he attached a copy of the sales contract for review.[88] Unconvinced, Fischel threatened that if he did not appear at the office of notary public Nathan Akin on West Sixth Street and "produce then and there at the taking of said all documents"[89] in his possession pertaining to the sale of the *California Eagle*, he would be "served without further notice."[90] Miller refused to comply, which subsequently led to the court issuing an official deposition notice. However, according to Miller's nephew, Halvor Miller, Jr.—by then an attorney assisting his uncle—"Nothing ever came of it."[91] Finally, it was over.

> December 6, 1961
> 5:30 A.M.
> Dear Loren:
>
> I want you to read this letter rather carefully and give it considerable thought as your decision will have a direct effect upon your, mine and the community's future. There are many compelling reasons why you shouldn't run for congress. Some of them are personal and you know them much better than I do. Most of them are real, and I think some of them are fancy.
>
> There are many compelling reasons why you SHOULD run for congress. . . . On balance, it is my firm conviction that . . . you just cannot afford to let this opportunity that time and circumstances have placed you in, go by. . . . I know you are a proud, sensitive shy person. I also recognize the almost overwhelming frustrations that engulf you because of the many missed opportunities you see for progress and achievement on a community and personal basis.[92]

When Wendell Green composed his urgent early morning plea for Miller's consideration—a run for the newly created Twenty-first Congressional District seat from south central Los Angeles—he admitted to a "continual envy" of his friend's

ability to say in a beautiful way that the average man wants to say, in language that
he can understand, is truly one of your greatest assets. . . . You are the only person in
the community who can beat Gus Hawkins. Not because you have a more outgoing
personality. . . . You represent the "man on horseback" type of leadership. Not based
on demagoguery, but enlightened understanding leadership. The man who can give
the white man spades and still beat him. This "hero" image is what is necessary to
project. The community needs a leadership symbol.[93]

Green, a former Tuskegee Airman, had harsh words for Leon Washington,
whom he called "petty, jealous and egocentric." According to Green, the behavior of Miller's cousin was like that way well before his 1948 stroke. The only reason Wash was flirting with Hawkins as a possible candidate "is his petty jeal-
ousy," he wrote. "You and I know he would still be selling suits in Kansas City if
it hadn't been for you. . . . With Wash solidly behind you, the task would have
been simple. Perhaps, too simple. . . . I will give my notice to Mrs. Washington
[who had taken over running the *Sentinel* since her husband's stroke] effective
January 5. I will then assume all the responsibilities for the campaign."[94] Then
he set out to form, along with fellow co-chairs Thomas Neusom, Nira Hardon,
and Raymond Johnson, the Temporary Organizing Committee to Draft Loren
Miller for Congress. They believed "by virtue of his training, experience, and
30 years of unswerving devotion to the cause of Negroes and civil rights in Los
Angeles," Miller "is the most qualified and uniquely fitted to become California's
first Negro congressman."[95]

According to an FBI informant, Miller's run for Congress was at the top of
the September 11, 1961, agenda of the Moranda Smith section of the Southern
California district Communist Party. The group's reasoning "for wanting LOREN
MILLER to run against GUS HAWKINS is because GUS HAWKINS has not helped to
organize the Negro community politically in all the years he has been in office
as a politician in Sacramento."[96] Still, the Smith committee felt that it would be a
"fatal mistake" if the two candidates ran against one another. The group was of
the opinion that it "not support either LOREN MILLER or GUS HAWKINS . . . but that
a candidate must be chosen on issues alone in the Negro community." Green's
campaign flier had all the right stuff: a photograph of Miller, a slogan, "Mr. Civil
Rights," and the where and when. "We need a fighter like Mr. Civil Rights to
represent us in our nation's capital. . . . We need you to form a committee to
draft Loren Miller for this vital position. Join Your Fellow Citizens."[97] Attorney
Thomas Neusom, gratified by the turnout, told the group, "You represent the
intelligence, energy and know-how that can beat the machine that would impose
its will on our community. I see nothing but success for the venture."[98] Throughout September, meetings were held, but in the end Miller endorsed Gus Hawkins, as did the American Federation of Labor and the Congress of Industrial
Organizations (AFL-CIO), the Council of Democratic Clubs, and others. With
84 percent of the votes, Hawkins won the Twenty-first District seat, an office he

held for the next twenty-eight years.[99] Might Miller have fared better if his cousin had backed him?

Ronald X. Stokes's death hit Malcolm X particularly hard. "He wept for the reliable and trustworthy Stokes, whom he had known well from his many trips to the West Coast,"[100] according to historian Manning Marable. Before Malcolm X left for Los Angeles to attend Stokes's well-attended funeral he turned to Brooklyn activist Jane Kerina for advice. Malcolm needed the name of Los Angeles's best and most trusted attorney. Jane directed him to her uncle, Loren Miller.[101]

It started after 11:00 P.M. on April 27, 1962, when two police officers of the Los Angeles Police Department spotted two members of Muhammad Temple 27 "taking some clothes from a parked car."[102] Soon after the officers finished questioning Monroe X. Jones and Fred X. Jingles, others from the LAPD entered the mosque at 56th and Broadway. When they finished, six unarmed Muslims had been shot down "in cold blood," including William X. Rogers, who was paralyzed for life; Korean War veteran Ronald X. Stokes, a newcomer to Los Angeles, lay dead.[103] One newspaper reported that the street battle or near riot where "one Negro was killed," involved about "50 policemen and 50 Black Muslims."[104]

Seven days later, Malcolm X held a press conference at L.A.'s Statler Hilton Hotel, at Figueroa Street and Wilshire Boulevard. He accused the LAPD of "Gestapo-type atrocities."[105] On May 13, at a major protest rally held at the Second Baptist Church, Malcolm said, "If we don't hate the white man, then you don't know what you are talking about."[106] By June, black ministers, representing five hundred black churches, essentially "the entire Negro-populated areas of Los Angeles"—who earlier had condemned the Muslims—now demanded the "cessation of brutality against Negro citizens at the hands of police officers."[107] They pressured Sam Yorty, Los Angeles's thirty-seventh mayor, to establish a police review board. Police Chief Parker, adamant that there would be no newly created separate review board, refused on the basis that there already existed a police commission.[108]

During the grand jury investigation, Officer Donald L. Weese admitted that he fatally shot Stokes. In the end, the county coroner's office ruled that "the police slaying of a member of the Negro extremist cult"[109] was justifiable homicide. By summer, the story garnered such national attention it made it onto the pages of *Newsweek* magazine.[110] When Miller and Malcolm X met, according to his nephew Halvor Miller, Jr., "Loren agreed to take the case on condition that the Muslims hire Earl Broady to help him."[111] In 1991, Broady told Taylor Branch, Martin Luther King, Jr.'s, biographer, that he put Malcolm off "about three times" before he agreed to meet: "The only thing I know is, they went to Loren Miller first, and he sent them to me. Of course, after they came to me and I finally agreed to represent them, then I associated with Loren Miller with me in their defense."[112]

However, before the final decision to hire the defense team, Miller and Broady traveled to Arizona to meet with Elijah Muhammad, the head of the Nation of Islam. Broady recounted, "He wanted to check us out. He wanted to defend 'my mens.'" Broady laughed as he retold historian Taylor Branch how Muhammad pluralized "men," an indication of the leader's lack of education: "He just wanted to talk about my *mens*. He told us stories . . . silly things. As a matter of fact, Loren Miller sat there and he looked at me like this from time to time," averting his eyes to keep from laughing during their meeting. Sympathetic toward the Muslims, as a former police officer with the LAPD, Broady knew their stance was one of defense, not aggression. He was astonished that Muhammad, who had such a large following, was so "uninformed and non-intelligent." According to Broady, Stanley Malone, Miller's law partner at the time, set the fee and handled the money. "Only decent fee I ever got. Altogether I think it was $120,000. . . . We split it. But they handled it."[113]

If we take the FBI at its word, Miller, during the trial, became an "informant" who "telephonically" agreed to make his Muslim defendants available for interview at the Oasis Restaurant at 5108 South Main Street: "MR. MILLER also advised that he would make a copy of the transcript of the grand jury available to the FBI when he received it."[114] It is unclear why Miller would do something as illegal as providing the transcript. Perhaps he knew that when his former New York colleague Ben Davis, Jr., the national secretary of the CPUSA, visited him in his office on February 25, 1963, the FBI followed him there.[115] Or when Miller called the FBI on May 31, perhaps it was an attempt at placating the agents in some way to avoid being interviewed as they had done years before. Or was it a quid pro quo offer, access to his clients in exchange for a parallel FBI investigation? Despite Malcolm X's "muzzling" orders from Elijah Muhammad, to stay put, take no revenge, and tone down the public rhetoric—contrary to the Nation of Islam's dogmatic absurdism—he continued to participate with civil rights organizations in Los Angeles, where he encouraged people to come together "against the common enemy. Remember . . . it's not a Muslim fight. It's a black man's fight."[116] Although Malcolm pursued "a strategy of limited political engagement," he felt persecuted nonetheless. Eventually, because of his active role in Los Angeles, followed by comments he made later about President John F. Kennedy's assassination in Dallas (and accusations that Muhammad had fathered children with several of his young secretaries), Malcolm X was censored, suspended, stripped of all of his authority, and drummed out of the religious cult he once loved.[117]

Before the Muslim trial began, Miller was appointed by the United States Commission on Civil Rights in Washington to the California Advisory Committee (CAC)—one of fifty-one advisory committees in every state and the District of Columbia. Bishop James A. Pike of the Episcopal Diocese of California, chair of the CAC, picked Miller as both its public face and its liaison between the police and the black community, where Miller immediately called for public hearings on policing.[118] Sgt. Norman Moore, of the Los Angeles Fire and Police Research Association, who wasted little time accusing Miller of "unsubstantiated accusations of police brutality,"[119] demanded Miller's ouster as the committee's vice chair. Miller assured the association, "I have consistently insisted that the hearing, which is in the nature of a fact find inquiry, must place major emphasis on the causes of tensions and upon proposals for solution." He added, "I would, of course, step aside and will not participate"[120] if the Muslim trial came up during hearings. Republicans such as Joseph C. Shell, member of the California State legislature, accused Miller "of violating a public law prohibiting formal hearings."[121]

On the upside, once the hearings were set for September 13 and 14, Miller was free to accept an invitation from President Kennedy. "It would be useful to me," wrote the president, "to have an exchange of views with you on state, regional and national problems."[122] On August 3, 1962, Miller joined the president and others for a White House luncheon meeting, where they dined on Salmon à la hollandaise, peas à la Française, and chokes Farcis and drank California Chablis. This was Miller's second invitation from President Kennedy. On January 20, 1961, Miller and Juanita danced at the President and Mrs. Kennedy's inaugural ball at the National Guard Armory.[123]

When Miller returned to Los Angeles, he resigned his position with the CAC, he said, in order to preserve the appearance of objectivity. However, before stepping down, Miller invited the mayor again, who earlier decided to boycott the meeting. Chief Parker, who did attend, denied allegations that his officers were "bigoted" or that his police force had a "bad image among the Negro community." It was not the black community who suffered, but rather "the police are the maligned minority,"[124] according to Parker.

On the home front, Belmont High School, concerned with the Miller's younger son's school performance, requested that they meet with Eddie's eleventh-grade counselor. Afterward, Miller informed the principal, Iona Lord, that they had met with the counselor, "who was very cooperative and informative in reference to our son's unsatisfactory performance in his academic courses." Using diplomacy, he assured the principal that he and his wife were taking steps to "secure tutorial service for him. . . . Meanwhile, we request that he be continued in an academic course. . . . If it becomes advisable, we may even seek private school training for him."[125] Four months later, Eddie was called into the office of Mr. Condit, the vice principal, for wearing his "shirt outside his trousers." Loren Miller replied that he had spoken with his son, who he assured the vice principal, "must abide by the regulations."[126] By today's dress code standards, the incident is laughable.

Five years later, Miller was writing Eddie, now in the Navy, a weekly letter—a promise he planned to keep. "Nothing of any moment has happened since you left," he reported, other than "Duke [the family dog] seems to have disappeared permanently. My opinion is that somebody has him tied up, or at least hemmed in so that he cannot get out. . . . Poor Barkey is lonely for you and Duke but she is too timid to go very far."[127] He mentioned some remaining champagne celebrating Eddie's entry into the Navy but no "appropriate occasion to drink it." He said he would call the registrar of voters on his son's behalf, adding that when Eddie got back, "you will be far and away the most widely traveled member of the Miller family." During the quagmire of the Vietnam War, Eddie, who was a member of the U.S. Navy river units, was exposed to Agent Orange/dioxin. On his return, after a period of training, Eddie found employment—ironically, on the other side of the bench—as a court reporter. Edward's first marriage ended in divorce; prior to the death of his second wife, Angela Miller, the mother of Noelle and Brandon, in 2002, the couple donated a small collection of Langston Hughes's papers to the Huntington Library.[128]

Influenced by the rising tide of 1960s black militancy, Miller began writing a series of well-defined articles that pronounced that the time had come for whites, from either the Left or the Right, cede control to emergent black leadership. The "new militants," wrote Miller, "don't want *progress*; they *demand* Freedom." It is only they, he agreed, who "can desegregate a café or a hotel or an airport by a sit-in." On October 20, 1962, the *Nation* magazine published "FAREWELL TO LIBERALS: A Negro View." "The conflict," wrote Miller,

> flares into the open when liberals exercise the prerogative, long held by them, of speaking *for* the Negro, and of espousing views which the Negro is abandoning. . . . Young Negro militants . . . influenced by the overthrow of white colonialism in Asia and Africa . . . not only want Freedom Now, but insist on substituting a grand strategy for the liberal tactics of fighting one civil-rights battle at a time. . . . Their message is plain: To liberals a fond farewell, with thanks for services rendered, until you are ready to re-enlist as foot soldiers and subordinates in a Negro-led, Negro-officered army under the banner of Freedom Now.[129]

Over the course of the next few years, the *Nation* carried more similar-themed articles by Miller.[130] Imbued with that awareness that the time had come to make equality a reality, he turned his attention to the Muslim trial.

On April 8, 1963, two days shy of the first anniversary of the killing of Ronald Stokes, the trial of the fourteen Black Muslims, now charged with forty-two felony counts of assault and resisting arrest, resumed. The *Chicago Defender* reported that the bailiff swore in an "all-Caucasian panel of 11 women and one man," despite defense team charges that African Americans were systematically excluded from jury service in a county where blacks at the time were 13 percent of the population.[131] According to the *Defender*, only five African Americans—between 1949 and 1959—had served on grand juries in Los Angeles County.[132] Once the trial began, it proceeded in an atmosphere of sarcasm and rudeness, similar to that experienced by the 1940s Sleepy Lagoon defendants, in which the judge consistently overruled objections by the defense. Frustrated, Broady "simply sat with his head in his hands for five minutes,"[133] to keep from losing his temper inside the courtroom. While the tense atmosphere inside the courtroom continued, Muslims were outside handing out leaflets. Broady, a seasoned criminal attorney, handled most cross-examinations. Later, he said the case was not particularly complex. "It was a brawl, a fight" between the Muslims and the police, he observed. "It wasn't anything you had to work up a scientific test or experts or anything of that kind. One side said one thing and one side said something different."[134]

It is difficult to gauge whether the contentiousness of the trial, the undercurrent of fear and hostility held by the community toward the police, or the commotion outside on the courthouse steps encouraged Miller to focus his attention more on housing issues. Undeniably, Broady was the better attorney in this instance. He had litigated countless criminal cases. Or was it simply that Miller tired easily since his heart attack on December 3, 1959? A trial of such magnitude was an obvious threat to the health of a man who presented closing arguments for two hours. Whatever the reason, as vice president of the National Committee Against Discrimination in Housing, Miller directed his focus in part on insuring the passage of the Rumford Fair Housing Act. The measure, which the California legislature passed later that year, prohibited "discrimination in the sale or rental of all private housing" and extended enforcement of the Fair Employment Practices Commission.[135]

Despite Miller's digressions, he, not Broady, delivered the closing arguments in the Muslim trial. Halvor Miller, Jr., profusely indebted to his uncle's influence and guidance through law school said, "Loren argued to the jury for more than two hours without a note. I was there it was spellbinding." In the largest superior court courtroom, he continued,

> There were probably 500 spectators, 75% of which were lawyers. Spectators occupied every seat and stood around the environs of the court. The general reaction was that nobody had ever seen a performance like that. Loren's health had been frail about this time. . . . He was exhausted. After his presentation, as reflected in the [newspaper] photographs, he sat for a long time before he was able to leave the court. Many of the lawyers waited and applauded when it became appropriate.[136]

For more than twenty-four days, from May 21 through June 14, the jury deliberated. They returned on June 10 with the first of four convictions. Four days later, they returned with the remaining verdicts. Of the fourteen on trial, two were found not guilty; one was freed because the jury failed to agree; and the remaining eleven were convicted of violating section 69, obstructing a police officer and knowingly resisting arrest.[137]

After the verdict, two women jurors, both white, told Broady how, during deliberations, the bailiff came into the jury room. "You've got the niggers on one side and whites on the other," the bailiff told them, recalled Broady. "What's the delay here? Are you going to believe these niggers or are you going to believe these officers"? Broady said it struck him as odd because he knew the bailiff. "I'd been around the courts a long time. I was just amazed that he would do that or say that. . . . That's very unusual for a bailiff to intrude himself up [into] the deliberations of a jury. . . . The weakness of the thing was, [the women] weren't willing to give us affidavits and they weren't willing to publicly state what they'd told us."[138]

Apparently, the passage of time did little to assuage well-known Los Angeles attorney Leo Branton's opinion of the Muslim trial, its results, or his personal animosity toward Miller. Branton believed that Miller, along with Dr. Claude Hudson and Franklin H. Williams, red-baited both he and Charlotta Bass. As for the Muslim defense team, he said it did a "terrible" and ineffectual job. Afterward, he found it rather strange that Earl Broady, Stanley Malone, and Loren Miller "all became judges."[139] The implication was that the three attorneys sold out their clients for seats on the bench.

By the early 1950's, Branton's relationship with Miller had soured around the time Branton defended Henry Steinberg and Ben Dobbs, two of the fifteen Communists indicted under the Smith Act. A member of Ben Margolis's law firm noted for defending Communists, Branton released a statement during the 1951 trial: "I understand that many prominent attorneys influenced by fear have declined to be associated with such cases."[140] Steinberg and Dobbs were found guilty the following year of conspiring to commit offenses against the U.S. government; they were sentenced to the maximum prison term of five years. Forty-five years later, Branton was more specific with Julieanna Richardson: "Nobody would join this case at the height of the anti-Communist era. Ben went to major black lawyers like Miller, [Earl] Broady and Crispus Wright. They turned him down saying it takes too long and cannot afford it."[141] Branton, lead attorney in Angela Davis's acquittal on murder charges, contends that Miller was "a stool pigeon," a friendly witness who testified privately, naming names during the House Un-American Activities Committee era of the 1950s. Otherwise, why would he testify in private? "Despicable," he said. Branton's wife, Geraldine, who, like Juanita Miller, belonged to the Wives of Bench and Bar, an auxiliary to the National Bar Association, refused to speak to Miller in public afterward. Branton said his wife told him, "Don't you ever forgive him. He's a stool pigeon."[142]

After four years with Margolis, Branton turned to entertainment law, where he became the attorney to such celebrities as Dorothy Dandridge, Nat King Cole, and Miles Davis, among others. In time, Branton said he became "somewhat of a libel expert." When one of his client's sued *Jet* magazine "for libeling her . . . they got Loren Miller, who was the dean of all the black lawyers here in town at the time to represent them in the trial. I won the trial, got a judgment against them and a judgment for punitive damages."[143]

On June 21, 1963, Miller was at the White House, along with 244 lawyers, for the purposes of discussing race relation issues with President Kennedy. "We were gratified and heartened by the favorable reaction to the President's suggestions about the special contribution which lawyers might be expected to make," wrote Robert F. Kennedy, attorney general of the United States. "We sincerely believe that great good can come from your taking affirmative action now along the lines the President indicated" by helping to "initiate, help organize, and participate in local bi-racial committees."[144]

By the time Miller returned to Los Angles, the CAC published its forty-page police minority report for the Civil Rights Commission. In it, the CAC acknowledged, "the committee did not attempt to determine the truth or falsity of [police brutality] allegations."[145] The most the committee could do—because the police opposed a separate review board—was to recommend and urge cooperation, mutual understanding, and good relations between various county agencies, minority communities, and the Los Angeles Police Commission. Though a warning, the report proved dramatically insufficient. Watts erupted on August 11–17, 1965 (over a six-day period), resulting in thirty-four deaths and more than one thousand injuries. Interestingly, in the Jewel Report of May 25, 1964, submitted to California attorney general Stanley Mosk, Miller is credited with having predicted, "Violence in Los Angeles is inevitable and nothing can or will be done about it until after the fact."[146]

When Miller testified on the Watts riots before Warren Christopher, chair of the McCone Commission, and the other commissioners, including Earl Broady, by then a Los Angeles County Superior Court judge, it was in the capacity of vice president of the National Committee Against Discriminatory Action in Housing. Miller blamed the city. He said that "ghettoes are the fruit of governmental policy" and that Watts, where his mother, sister, and nephews lived, was "ringed on every side by highly restricted [white] areas." He added that "the greatest problem faced by cities in the United States is racial residential segregation. It is in my view an open invitation to conflict. . . . It fosters racial distrust which breeds the ghetto. And the ghetto exaggerates racial divisions—makes strangers of people—makes them hostile and distrustful of one another."[147]

Miller cited the need for a presidential executive order "preventing banks . . . from lending funds for discriminatory housing . . . and prohibiting the Federal Housing Administration from guaranteeing loans for public housing where there is any racial discrimination." He offered a variety of other recommendations, suggesting, "Los Angeles should institute its own WPA-type . . . public works projects." But, he warned, "until Los Angeles tackles its own ghetto problem, it will always be ripe for an accident like the one that triggered the riots in Watts."[148] Though Miller, after giving his testimony, praised the McCone Commission, few of the panel's recommendations, such as community-based policing, were implemented. Interestingly, Miller's former law partner Stanley Malone defended Marquette Frye, who was arrested for starting the riot.[149]

Miller knew better than anyone what the risks were politically and personally when he decided in 1958 to represent alleged Communists Donald Wheedin and

Stella Choyke Biber in hearings before the House Un-American Activities Committee in Room 229 of the Spring Street Court House.[150] Was it simply loyalty to his old friend Wheedin, who, according to historian Josh Sides, "Remembered that Miller was so dynamic that other lawyers would actually postpone their own cases just to hear him," or to A. L. Wirin, co-counsel, which overrode any fear Miller might have of future political repercussions? Or was it his nature as a contrarian or that his attacks on Communists in the *Eagle* was some sort of sham to protect his social standing? Had he, like Langston Hughes, revived his radical engagement and had a political "reawakening"?[151] Certainly, it was less risky— now that the Red Scare was declining. Whatever his reasoning for supporting leftist clients, nonetheless, he held out hope for a future judicial appointment at the urging of his wife but mostly because "Miller was," according to publisher Almena Lomax, "the closest Negro figure in the entire state to Brown during the Governor's campaign."[152] Still, it is little wonder that Miller received a judicial appointment, considering that since the 1940s the FBI had monitored his activities, most likely beginning when he took a position against Japanese internment camps.

In the mid-1950s, Miller—propelled perhaps by some interior contrition— treaded carefully as he moved to the political center. When Lester Granger asked him to add his name to an Urban League proposal to the United Nations Educational, Scientific and Cultural Organization, Miller, though grateful for the offer, declined on the grounds that it might embarrass the league:

> As you know, I never have been a Communist but I do have a background of association with what we now call Red Front groups. All such activities on my part stopped in 1938 but the doctrine of permanent guilt still obtains. Any such proposal would only lead to dredging up the fact that I was with New Masses etc. . . . I have therefore formed a policy of not involving any organization with which I am connected in such a hassle. . . . I think the principle is particularly important in light of the fact that the Hate Groups are out after the League as they are at present time. It would be far better for the League to propose a safe person.

That said, Miller closed as he often did with an update on the family: Pete was enjoying himself as a student at the University of Oregon; Juanita was "inspecting nursery schools" for the California Department of Social Welfare; and "Eddie," he wrote, "is still on the loose."[153]

When Miller's appointment did come, it followed on the heels of two brothers, even though the governor had boasted publically of Miller's early confidence in him "before he was elected to his first public office."[154] In 1960, under patronage pressure from black Angelinos to "appoint a Negro," Governor Edmund Brown, Sr., made his first African American appointment to the bench when he appointed Bernard Jefferson to the Los Angeles Municipal Court. The next year, Governor Brown elevated Jefferson's brother, Judge Edwin Jefferson, the first black judge west of the Mississippi, from the Superior Court of California to California's Second District Court of Appeal. According to Lionel J. Wilson, former mayor of Oakland, California, it was common practice before 1965 to appoint African Americans to the municipal court from private practice, whereas white attorneys went from "private practice to courts of appeals."[155]

Vaino Hassan Spencer was the governor's next municipal court appointee. Spencer, a native black Angelino, whose Buddhist father had emigrated from Sri Lanka in 1910, founded the Democratic Minority Conference (of which Miller and Tom Bradley, Los Angeles's future mayor were members).[156] According to the *Los Angeles Sentinel*, Spencer, along with fellow Democratic Minority Conference founder and neighbor, Leo Branton, worked tirelessly to elect Brown to the state's highest office. Spencer's 1961 appointment "represents a tribute to the sagacity and tenacity of SENTINEL publisher Leon H. Washington," who for three years demanded "that the Governor appoint her." The article continued, "Mrs. Spencer, is a happy combination of charm, beauty, brains, ability and a purposefully organized personality. . . . As prime mover and financial angel behind the Democratic Minorities Conference, she brought into sharp focus the demands of California's large Negro and Mexican-American minorities for a voice and hand in government."[157] Hailed as the first black woman in the state appointed to the California court system (the third black woman in the nation), the former real estate broker and member of Los Angeles's Consolidated Realty Board was admitted to the State Bar of California in 1952 (twenty-four years after Miller passed the Kansas bar). Spencer retired as presiding judge of Division One California Court of Appeal, Second Appellate District in 2007.[158]

When Sherman W. Smith and Earl Gilliam were appointed in 1963 to the Los Angeles Municipal Court and to the San Diego Municipal Court, respectively, Miller felt demeaned and angered that lesser experienced attorneys preceded his appointment.[159] What was being said in legal circles is that Miller's "heart attack . . . was really a 'broken heart,'" the result of Brown's snub. However, according to Marion Maddox, the wife of Miller's law partner, Edward C. Maddox, "Loren blew an initial appointment as a judge before 1964 because he announced his appointment in the California Eagle when the powers that be wanted to make the announcement first."[160]

One wonders whether Miller ever would have been appointed had not Judge Ernestine Stahlhut died in 1964. In Brown's defense, the governor inquired about Miller's background with the FBI, taking umbrage when, without providing proof, they alleged that Miller was a Communist.[161]

On Tuesday, May 12, 1964, Governor Brown appointed Miller to the Los Angeles Municipal Court. To Miller's shower of accolades, Brown added that, more than an outstanding Los Angeles attorney, Miller was "one of the ablest attorneys I have known. I know he will distinguish himself on the bench as he has in private practice, and as a citizen."[162]

Less impressed was George Putnam. On May 25, from the broadcast studios of KTTV, Channel 11, Putnam, Los Angeles's most conservative news commentator, spewed vitriol and scorn. Quoting from the previous year's *Congressional Record*, Putnam informed his audience that Miller "defended Communists in court . . . worked as a reporter for THE DAILY WORKER . . . was named editor of NEW MASSES,"[163] a Communist periodical. Within a few days of that broadcast, the Los Angeles office of the FBI received Putnam's transcript as well as complaints and copies of letters sent to the editor of the *Los Angeles Times*, Nick B. Williams, Sr., protesting Miller's appointment.[164]

Before Miller walked through the portals of the Municipal Court Traffic Building 833, there were matters that needed his attention. First, he set about transferring ownership of the *Eagle* to James L. Tolbert, who planned to switch the newspaper to a tabloid format.[165] In the rush to wrap up his office and any remaining cases, Miller took the time to praise his nemesis, the *Los Angeles Times*, for supporting effective civil rights legislation. "It is my considered opinion that responsible conservatives, such as the *Times*, were the deciding factors in favor of cloture and final passage of the legislation. They tipped the almost evenly balanced scales,"[166] wrote Miller.

At the top of Miller's list of unresolved cases were the homes of Pasadena's Pepper neighborhood, which were in jeopardy. On June 4, at an all-day meeting of the Community Redevelopment Agency board members, held in the main library of Pasadena, Miller said that the $9.44 million Pepper Redevelopment Project— which he called a "gilded, golden ghetto"—would displace the residents, most of whom were black. He called the plan a "joke" if it involved the cooperation of the Pasadena Realty Board, a board with "a long history of supporting residential segregation."[167] Speaking to protestors assembled at Calvary Christian Methodist Episcopal Church on Pepper Street, Miller added, "The sad fact is that as these plans are applied predominately to Negro areas, the Negroes are 'developed out' of the community and are with no comparable place to go."[168]

Perhaps it could be called his last hurrah before walking away from forty years of journalism when Miller entered the brawl between a local Catholic priest, the archbishop of Los Angeles, and His Holiness in Rome. On Thursday, June 11, Reverend William H. Du Bay of Compton wrote to Pope Paul VI, demanding the ouster of the archbishop of Los Angeles, Cardinal James Francis McIntyre. The young priest charged the cardinal with inexcusable abuses: "He has failed to exercise moral leadership among the white Catholics of this diocese on racial discrimination," and he has "conducted a vicious program of intimidation and repression against priests, seminarians and laity."[169] In the support of the priest, the *California Eagle* carried an editorial defending Du Bay, as did the Jewish weekly *Heritage*, and the lay organization Catholics for Racial Equality. The chancery denied allegations that the cardinal failed to speak out on racial issues, that "priests of the archdiocese live under a reign of terror, muted and repressed," or even that "Catholics have been kept in the dark on the church's stand on principles of racial equality."[170] "The cardinal," asserted the *Eagle*, "is clearly out of step with the Catholic Church and has done his best to impose his out-of-date views on his own church and on the community."[171] In time, the priest dropped his campaign—under threat of excommunication. "Afterwards he would become a parish priest at some undisclosed location."[172] By year's end, according to the *Times*, Father Du Bay had been exiled to a "Negro parish in Chicago."[173]

The weather was a sunny eighty-three degrees, on Friday, August 21, the day Miller took the oath of office at the county's courthouse. A good omen for Miller.[174] His appointment brought applause from the black community and by year's end the local NAACP honored him with a banquet testimonial, where Dr. H. Claude Hudson declared, "Rarely can we point to an individual and truthfully say, 'There goes a man who has earned the right to be considered as something extra special. . . . He was my boyhood hero. He was and is a source of inspiration to many, and he has earned the respect of fair-minded citizens throughout this country. His name is LOREN MILLER.'"[175] Earlier that July, Women of Today, an African American women's political action club, honored him along with sixteen other "Negroes serving in elective public offices in California."[176]

From the outset Miller took a firm but fair judicial tone. When Roberto Martinez's wife and eleven children drove seventy miles from their Lancaster home to Los Angeles to plea for the release of the husband and father "25 days early on a 30-day sentence of drunk driving," Judge Miller held his ground. It was Martinez's fifth drunk-driving arrest in six years. His attorney, David Marcus (who argued *Mendez v. Westminster*), foolhardily claimed, "With 11 children, Martinez has a good reason for drinking." Judge Miller was firm: 'No,' he said."[177]

As for switchboard operator Virginia W. Evans, arrested at her home on Alexandria Street for ignoring fifty-nine parking tickets, Miller observed "a deliberate pattern of breaking the law, over a two-year period." Although she explained in traffic court that she "couldn't afford to park in the lot," Miller assessed the penalty: "Five days in jail (one suspended) on each two violations plus three months to pay $10 each (or serve two days in jail) on the 57 others." After phoning her boss, she decided to go on "vacation for the duration of her jail sentence."[178]

The kindest words came from former political reporter Chester G. Hanson, who wrote the *Los Angeles Times* that he was in the downtown traffic court at "the invitation of a motorcycle officer." After the case was concluded, he dropped into "a neighboring courtroom," where he was pleasantly surprised to see Judge Miller. Although as a young reporter some years earlier Hanson had said that Miller "was too rare for my conservative taste," he nonetheless wrote:

> It was a rewarding session. Judge Miller, handling scores of cases . . . passed out
> even handed justice regardless of race, color or creed. . . . He did it in a very human
> way—a chuckle over this one's improbable story, a sympathetic ear to another—and
> a stern lecture and 10 days in jail for a serious offense . . . unlike some judges who
> carry on a sort of tête-à-tête with defendants at the bench, Judge Miller used his

microphone. It let the many waiting their turn hear some of the troubles others got into and what happened to them. He gave a course in driving education. And there was not very many suspended sentences.[179]

On the bench, as in the course of his life, Miller proved that he was fair and just. He had come far—from a Kansas farm to the United States Supreme Court to dancing with his wife at two presidential inaugurals. Along the way, he compromised his radical principals once he "plunged into the law"[180] full-time those many years ago. Still, it was during Miller's service as a municipal judge that he found the time to complete his magnum opus, *The Petitioners: The Story of the Supreme Court of the United States and the Negro*, a book he had been working on for decades. In the preface, he wrote that it was a "grave risk . . . a calculated risk that must be run," in attempting such a specific history of the "Supreme Court's decisions" as it relates to "the Negro, as slave, freeman, and citizen."[181] He took the self-imposed challenge and wrote the first definitive study of African Americans and the Supreme Court; and we are the better for it. In it, he placed "[Charles] Houston's litigation at the center of a heroic narrative, and popularized that story just as the civil rights movement was searching for historical predecessors,"[182] writes Kenneth Mack. The very lawyer Miller challenged in his youth he came to admire in the end.

On Sunday, January 23, 1966, in the Beverly Hills home of Judge Earl Broady, "a highly selective audience assembled" for an autograph party sponsored by the League of Allied Arts on the publication of Miller's *The Petitioners*. As the smartly dressed crowd enjoyed champagne and hors d'oeuvres, league president Antoinette Atkinson, reported the *Los Angeles Sentinel*, introduced Judge Miller, who gave "a brief but hilarious account of his encounters while writing the book."[183]

Leon Washington waxed lyrically and loud when he endorsed his cousin's "commendable" publication. "We have already paid high tribute to Loren as a lawyer, but now it is a privilege to salute him as an author of high merit." The book, wrote Washington, "vividly portrays the Negro's background of toil, ambition and strife and dramatically traces his progress through the ponderous channels of legal procedure.[184] The *Chicago Defender* called it a provocative and lively account of the "changing relationship between law and society as seen in the history of the court . . . that will appeal to the general reader as well as the scholar."[185] Roy Wilkins joined the polyphony of voices praising the work: "For all its legal asides, the book is a thrilling adventure story, abounding in courage, sacrifice, and ingenuity, never before spread on a canvas of such overwhelming proportions."[186]

Eleanor Holmes Norton, future delegate from Washington, D.C., to the U.S. House of Representatives, at the time the assistant legal director of the ACLU, in her book review said, "Loren Miller looks back at the Court, records its often dreary performance toward the Negro, and ends in celebrations of its redemption." Norton called the book "a significant contribution to the literature of race and of the Court. . . . Nowhere else will the layman find a complete and readable account of the Court's long-time dealings with the Negro."[187] *The Journal of Negro Education* and *Pylon*, among other publications, weighed in too. Judge Richard F. C. Hayden of the Los Angeles Superior Court reviewing the book for the *Los Angeles Times*, writing, "This book is powerful advocacy because it does not appeal to easy emotions. It is based on hard logic and hard facts. . . . It is lucidly and compellingly written with a narrative that moves the reader as if in a novel."[188]

Loren Miller bought a newspaper to say what he wanted to say, though by then he had mellowed. It is hoped that after he set out to frame the law as he saw it, he realized in the end his role in making America, the America he so loved, a better America. As he entered the sunset of his life, he wrote with inimitable frankness that "no man can be sure his intentions came to good ends, I'll just have to let the whole thing go with the hope that I did more good than wrong. You can be the judge. . . . We cannot undo our yesterdays. . . . Let us as literal and free men work to overcome the restrictions our yesterdays impose."[189] Never one to forget those to whom he owed his success and his strength, he expressed that debt in the opening dedication of his magnum opus, *The Petitioners*:

> To my wife, Juanita, for her unflagging faith;
> To my father, John Bird Miller, born a slave,
> whose love of liberty inspired me to become a lawyer,
> and to my mother, Nora Herbaugh Miller, whose love of
> my father led her across the color line and to my birth,
> I dedicate this book.

Notes

Archival Sources and Abbreviations

ACLU   American Civil Liberties of Southern California. Charles E. Young Library. University of California, Los Angeles.

ALP   Alain Locke Papers, Moorland Spingarn Research Center. Howard University, Washington, D.C.

BMP   Ben Margolis Papers. Center for Oral History Research. University of California, Los Angeles.

CMP   Carey McWilliams Papers. Center for Oral History Research. University of California, Los Angeles.

LDG   Lawrence de Graaf. Center for Oral and Public History. California State University, Fullerton.

LGP   Lester B. Granger Papers. Beinecke Rare Book and Manuscript Library. Yale University.

LMP   Loren Miller Papers. Huntington Library. San Marino, California.

LHP   Langston Hughes Papers. Huntington Library. San Marino.

LHYP   Langston Hughes Papers. Beinecke Rare Book and Manuscript Library. Yale University.

LTP   Louise Thompson Patterson Papers. Emory University, Atlanta.

LOC   Library of Congress, Washington, D.C.

NAACP   Papers of the NAACP. Manuscript Division, Library of Congress. Washington, D.C.

NARA   National Archives Records Administration, Washington, D.C.

TBP   Taylor Branch Papers. University of North Carolina, Chapel Hill.

UCSB   Donald C. Davidson Library. Center for the Study of Democratic Institutions. University of California, Santa Barbara.

Introduction

1. Marshall, T. (May 1951), The Supreme Court as protector of civil rights: Equal protections of the laws, *Annals of the American Academy of Political and Social Sciences*, 275.

2. Miller, L. (1932, June 3), On second thought, *California Eagle*, 12.

3. Granger, L. (1962, March 22), Battleaxe and bread, *California Eagle*, 4.

4. Miller named judge by Brown (1964, May 14), *Los Angeles Sentinel*, A1.

5. Loren Miller, Transcript: KFOX radio broadcast (circa 1944), 7, LMP.

Chapter 1

1. Rites pending for municipal Judge Miller (1967, July 16), *Los Angeles Times*, G6; *Medical Alumni Magazine* (Fall 2006): 16.

2. Thousands pay homage (1967, July 27), *Los Angeles Sentinel*, D1; Church to fete birthday (1939, August 17), *Los Angeles Sentinel*, 1; Pye, B. (1967, July 20), I worked for Loren, *Los Angeles Sentinel*, D1; Gardner, D. (2010, May 11), Lena Horne, first black superstar who took on racists in showbiz, dies aged 92, *Daily Mail*, retrieved from http://www.dailymail.co.uk/tvshowbiz/article-1275946/Lena-Horne-iconic-jazz-singer-Broadway-star-dies-aged-92.html. Along with Loren Miller, Ms. Horne was a member of the International Film and Radio Guild. Show Time (1946, January 3), *Los Angeles Sentinel*, 18; International Film and Radio Guild Fetes Press (1946, February 28), *Los Angeles Sentinel*, 20; Leon L. Lewis to Loren Miller (1946, October 8), LMP.

3. Langston Hughes died in New York on May 22, 1967. Rampersad, A. (1986), *The Life of Langston Hughes*, vol. 1, *1902–1941, I, too, sing America* (New York: Oxford Press), 236.

4. First AME will close 75th celebration next Sunday night (1947, August 28), *Los Angeles Sentinel*, 6.

5. Farrell, R., & Mounts, B. (1967, July 20), Nation mourns Loren Miller, *Los Angeles Sentinel*, A1; Valenzuela, R. (2010, December 10), *Bridget "Biddy" Mason*, retrieved from http://www.socalhistory.org/biographies/bridget-biddy-mason.html.

6. Ibid.

7. Jeremiah 8:22.

8. Funeral services held Tuesday M. V. Ellsworth (1947, August 21), *Los Angeles Sentinel*, 6.

9. International Film and Radio Guild Fetes Press (1946, February 28).

10. Loren Miller's contributions (May–August 1967), *Crisis*, 336.

11. Ostrow, R. J. (1967, July 20), Marshall says he bears southerners no ill will, *Los Angeles Times*, 5.

12. A. L.Wirin on Loren Miller (n.d.), eulogy, LMP.

13. Pye (1967, July 20).

14. Judge Loren Miller, 64, dead; backed open housing on coast (1967, July 16), *New York Times*, 64; Farrell & Mounts (1967, July 20); Tribute to Nathaniel Colley Program Book, LMP.

15. Work begins on ultra-modern church (1967, July 20), *Los Angeles Sentinel*, D6. Following Miller's death the first AME church announced plans to build a new church to be designed by Paul R. Williams, with a seating capacity of 1,500. It would be located at Harvard Boulevard. Rampersad (1986), 241; Peoples funeral home to open doors Sunday (1938, August 11), *Los Angeles Sentinel*, 1A. Norman, Irma, and their daughter, Faye Hudson, were neighbors of the Millers in 1935, living at 207. E. 45th Street; Architect James Garrott designed the Miller home at 647 Micheltorena Street; Garrott designed the one next door at 653, where he lived with his mother, Fannie, his brother, Curtis, and his wife, Helen Duncan.

16. Photo standalone 1 (1967, July 27), *Los Angeles Sentinel*, A1.

17. Letter to the editor (1967, September 14), *Los Angeles Sentinel*, A6.

18. Robertson, S. (1979, August 9), L. A. Confidential, *Los Angeles Sentinel*, A6; H. Miller, Jr., personal communication (2010, October 5).

19. Farrell & Mounts (1967, July 20).

20. Negro wants rights now, Miller tells governor (1964, May 7), *Los Angeles Sentinel*, A1.

21. Pye (1967, July 20).

22. Loren Miller to be elevated to high court? (1948, March 4), *Los Angeles Sentinel*, 8.

23. Ben Margolis, interview by Michael Balter (1984, July 2), tape 4, side 2, 108, BMP.

24. Earl C. Broady, Sr., interview by Taylor Branch (1991, March 25), #05047, TBP.

25. Washington, L. (1967, July 20), Wash's Wash—A tribute to my cousin, *Los Angeles Sentinel*, A6.

26. Higginbotham quoted in Robertson (1979, August 9).

27. *Communist Party v. Peek*, 20 Cal.2d 536 [L.A. No. 18354. In Bank, July 11, 1942].

28. Loren Miller (hereafter LM) to Lester Granger (1955, November 30), LMP; Loren Miller, FBI File, No. 100–18291, 100–4621, U.S. Department of Justice.

29. Miller FBI file (1947, February 9), Judge Loren Miller in the *Congressional Record* by George Putnam. The FBI's first report on Loren Miller is dated July 15, 1943; the last report is dated November 11, 1967. Apparently, the Millers were burgled. Miller's FBI file contains a December 17, 1964, article from the *Los Angles Sentinel*: "Empty bottle may jail burglar."

30. LM to Edward Miller (1967, April 5), LMP.

31. Eagleton, T. (2011, April 15), In praise of Marx, *Chronicle Review*, B8.

32. Loren Miller, interview by Lawrence de Graaf (1967, March 3), transcript 174.1, 12, LDG.

33. Urquhart, B. (1993), *Ralph Bunche: An American life* (New York: Norton), 454.

34. E. Miller, personal communication (2007, December 6).

35. J. Miller Kerina, personal communication (2006, October 18).

36. Loren Miller, interview by Lawrence de Graaf (1967, March 3 and April 29); The legend of Loren Miller (1967, July 20), *Los Angeles Sentinel*, D.

37. J. Miller Kerina, personal communication (2006, October 18); Miller, Loren (1963, November 21), A Negro looks at the Fourteenth Amendment, two audio tapes, program 77, UCSB.

38. LM to Edward Miller (1967, April 5), LMP; L.A. Judge, noted rights fighter, dies at 64 (1967, August 3), *Jet*.

39. Moon, H. (1967, August–September), Loren Miller: Legal scholar, *Crisis*, 346–47.

40. Aldridge, C. W. (1967, May 6), P.S., *New York Amsterdam News*, 7.

41. Weds blonde Boston heiress (1950, July 22), *Chicago Defender*, A11; Van Alstine, B. (1967, May 24), Poet Hughes dies, *Chicago Defender*, 1.

42. Rousseau, J. (1923), *The social contract and discourses* (G. D. H. Cole, Trans.) (London: Dent, 1923).

43. Carey McWilliams, interview by Joel Gardner (1975, July 14), transcription of audio recording, tape 5, side 2, p. 19, CMP. McWilliams was a Los Angeles attorney, writer, and activist who addressed race and labor issues. He headed California's Division of Housing and Immigration and defended both the Sleepy Lagoon and Hollywood Ten defendants. From 1955 to 1975, he edited the *Nation*; McWilliams lived in the Echo Park area at 2041 N. Alvarado, less than three miles from Miller, who lived at 647 Micheltorena Street.

44. Menand, L. (2011, September 5), Browbeaten, *New Yorker*, 72.

45. Miller, L. (1931, March 13), On second thought, *California Eagle*, 8.

46. Ibid.

47. Granger, L. (1962, March 22), Battleaxe and bread, *California Eagle*, 4.

48. Transcript: KFOX radio broadcast (circa 1944), 7, LMP.

Chapter 2

1. Wabash strike averted (1903, April 5), *New York Times*, 1; Burning corn in Nebraska (1903, January 13), *New York Times*, 2; Works shut down in Iowa (1903, January 10), *New York Times*, 1; Coal shortage closes schools (1903, January 7), *New York Times*, 2; Guarding coal with rifles (1903, January 9), *New York Times*, 2; Grossman, J. (1902, October 3), The coal strike of 1902—Turning point in U.S. policy, retrieved from United States Department of Labor website, http://www.dol.gov/oasam/programs/history/coalstrike.htm.

2. According to the 1870 Census, John Miller was born in 1862; on the 1880 Census, his birth year is recorded as 1865; Loren Miller, who signed his father's death certificate, gave May 4, 1861, as his birth year. Nora Miller confirms that date in her autobiographical diary, hereafter referred to as NM diary, located in LMP. A genealogical family tree lists John's birth as 1858. Foner, E. (2010), *The fiery trial: Abraham Lincoln and American slavery* (New York: Norton).

3. Miller, L. (ca. 1933), Unto you (unpublished manuscript), 4, 5, 62, LMP (hereafter Miller [1933]). "Unto You" is Loren Miller's unpublished thinly veiled autobiography. It is used here as a primary source; too much of the manuscript replicates real people and real events to be easily dismissed. Storytelling and memories of childhood shape and strengthen our sense of who we are. It is what psychologists call "narrative identity." Perhaps Miller planned to change the names of the characters if "Unto You" was ever published. Nevertheless, the manuscript retains identical first names of people such as his father and mother, John and Nora; Hugh Eubanks, John's Kansas neighbor; Herschel Essex, Loren Miller's part American Indian playmate and Herschel's mother, Pearl Essex; as well as Jim Malloy, saloon proprietor and John Miller's part-time employer. Other names mentioned are found on the U.S. census: Lina Belle Ammons, classmate; Mar-

tha Hubbard, Miller's grandaunt; and Vogt's Saloon, run by the German William Vogt. However, Miller does alter some names. Instead of the surname "Miller," he substitutes "Merrill" in its place, and of his siblings, Cloyd becomes "Floyd." Loren is "Rollin." Helen is "Hilda." Roland is "Ronald." The village of Pender, Nebraska, is "Penwood." Highland, Kansas, is "High Point." Much of what Miller wrote in "Unto You" is corroborated by his brother Halvor Miller, Sr., in his lengthy "Note Book" (circa 1970) (private Miller family collection), hereafter referred to as NB, expressly written to preserve Miller family history as he remembered it. Further, though inconclusive, Loren Miller began writing "Unto You" sometime between 1932 and 1933, either during his trip to Moscow while he worked on a novel about the "petty middle class" or later in 1933 when he married. The address 207 East 45th Street, where the newly wedded Miller couple lived in 1933, is on the first manuscript page. That address is substantiated by the March 18, 1933, *Chicago Defender* article "Banquet Hall Decorated for Newlyweds."

Another document used here is the 85th Anniversary, 1882–1967 Souvenir Program, Saint Martha's AME Church (1967, October 29), Highland, Kansas, LHP. This particular document contains short biographies of Miller's grandaunt and granduncle Martha Hubbard and Joseph Miller, respectively, as well as stories, dates, and photographs of Loren Miller, his siblings, and his schoolmates who attended Saint Martha's church schoolhouse in Highland, Kansas, in 1915. Moreover, "Let Tomorrow Come" (n.d.), another of Miller's unpublished manuscripts located in the LMP, though brief, is another firsthand account of his life from his early childhood to his college years. Perhaps Miller's decision to write in the third person allowed him greater freedom to write what must have been painful memories of his early life.

4. Halvor Miller, Sr., NB #23, 62 (private Miller family collection). According to the 1900 U.S. Census, Washington D.C., Nancy Bruce had been married to Henry Clay Bruce for eleven years. In the 1910 U.S. Census, Nancy Bruce lived in Wyondotte, Kansas, with Loren Miller's cousin Leon Washington, Jr.

5. 1880 U.S. Census; NM diary, LMP. In the 1880 U.S. Census for Kansas, Anna Weaver Herbaugh's birthplace is listed as Indiana. In the 1900 U.S. Census for Nebraska, Henry lists his mother's birthplace as Kentucky; Henry's birthplace is listed in the 1880 Census and 1900 Census as Kentucky and Indiana, respectively. In 1970, Nora's surviving siblings were Flora Kelly, Sarah Richardson, Mary Jones, Dorothy Bahelder, and Everett Herbaugh. Mrs. Miller's rites held (1970, December 17), *Los Angeles Sentinel*, D3.

6. Halvor Miller, Sr., NB #1–3.

7. 1900 U.S. Census; 1885 U.S. Census; Nebraska Resident Military Roster, June 1, 1891; National Park Service, U.S. Civil War Soldiers, 1861–1865, database; backside of photograph of Anna Weaver Herbaugh provides family genealogy (private Miller family collection).

8. Ravenna, earlier known as the township of Garfield, Nebraska. Save America's Heritage (1993), *Nebraska historic buildings survey reconnaissance survey final report of Buffalo County, Nebraska*, prepared for Nebraska State Historical Society State Historic Preservation Office, retrieved from http://www.nebraskahistory.org/histpres/reports/buffalo _county.pdf.

9. Between 1886–1888, Nora, who held a teacher's certificate, taught school. Mrs. Baker (Pender, Nebraska schoolteacher) to Loren Miller (hereafter LM) (1924, July 24), LHP, mentions that Nora had problems with her eyes.

10. Miller (1933), 5, LMP; 1880 and 1900 U.S. Census.

11. Miller (1933), 5; John Miller and Nora Herbaugh Marriage Certificate, both in LMP.

12. Miller (1933), 5, LMP.

13. Cloyd was born on November 19, 1901, according to the Miller family genealogical tree, in possession of Halvor Miller, Jr. Cloyd is listed as eight years old on the 1910 Census for Thurston County, Pender Township, Nebraska.

14. 1920 U.S. Census. From the Miller family genealogy tree: Cloyd Blanchard Miller, 11/19/1901–3/10/1933; Loren Miller, 1/20/1903–7/14/1967; Cecil Everett Miller, 11/28/1904–5/30/1973; Ruby Lillie Miller, 1/16/1906–9/10/1929; Halvor Thomas Miller, 9/14/1907–3/19/1986; Helen Mae Miller, 7/5/1909–2/2006; Roland Jay Miller, 4/18/1911–3/12/1993. Virtual Nebraska (2005), *Nebraska . . . our towns: Pender—Thurston County*, retrieved May 4, 2011, from http://www.casde.unl.edu/history/counties/thurston/pender/. Halvor Miller, Sr., NB #92. In general, in the postbellum era of Reconstruction, lynching became a common method to control newly freed African Americans. In 1900, in two separate incidents in nearby Fort Scott, Kansas, George and Ed Silsbee were lynched; and in Saint Louis, Missouri, an unidentified black man was lynched; Allen, J., & Littlefield, J., *Without sanctuary: Photographs and postcards of lynching in America* (2005), retrieved from http://withoutsanctuary.org. From May to September 1919, there "were 25 race riots" across the nation. On September 28, 1919, a heinous lynching took place in Omaha; Nebraskastudies.org (1994), *Racial tensions in Nebraska after World War I: Racial tensions in Omaha—A horrible lynching*, retrieved from http://www.nebraskastudies.org/0700/stories/0701_0130.html. After WWI, between 1917 and 1921, there was a significant increase in racial violence across the United States with major riots in Omaha, Nebraska, and Tulsa, Oklahoma. Moreover, in 1921, the KKK founded its first "Klaven" in Omaha, Nebraska.

15. Miller (1933), 4–5, 62, LMP; Miller, *Let tomorrow come*, LMP; Halvor, NB; 85th Anniversary.

16. Ibid.; 1880 U.S. Census.

17. Chesapeake Bay Program (2012), *African-Americans in the Chesapeake Region*, retrieved from www.chesapeakebay.net/discover/bayhistory/africanamericans; National Park Service (December 10, 2014), *Park ethnography program*, retrieved from http://www.nps.gov/history/ethnography/aah/aaheritage/histcontextsd.htm.

18. Halvor Miller, Sr., NB #32–36; 1870, 1880 U.S. Census, Kansas. Kentucky Slave Schedule for Clay County (September 10, 1850), lists Leander Miller, owner of ten slaves. J. Miller Kerina, personal communication (2006, October 17).

19. Halvor Miller, Sr., NB #36.

20. Jane Gee Miller's siblings were Martha, Greenbury, Smith, Bird, Catherine, Nancy, Sally, and Fanny.

21. Miller (1933), 62, LMP; Halvor Miller, Sr., NB #35–36.

22. 85th Anniversary, LHP; Wyandotte Museums (2009), *A Brief History of the City of Wyandotte*, retrieved from http://www.wyandottemuseums.org/dotnetnuke/Research/LocalHistoryFacts/ABriefHistoryoftheCityofWyandotte/tabid/112/Default.

23. 85th Anniversary, LHP.

24. Halvor Miller, Sr., NB #88; 1870 and 1875 U.S. Census.

25. The First Regiment, Kansas Colored Volunteer Infantry was organized on December 13, 1864. They were the first black troops permitted to engage in combat, known

afterward as the Seventy-Ninth United States Colored Infantry (New). Many of those in the Seventy-Ninth would in turn become members of the famous buffalo soldiers of the Old West.

26. In the 1870 U.S. Census for Iowa Township, Doniphan County, Kansas, Thomas and Jane are the parents of Nancy, fifteen; Green, thirteen; Mahalia, nine; John, eight; Lucita, six; William, four; and Sarah, one. U.S. Census 1865, 1870, 1880, Kansas. In the various censuses, Bird and his siblings are listed as mulatto; on the March 1875 U.S. Census for Iowa Township, Kansas, Jane Miller is not listed; John is listed as living nearby with his aunt Martha Hubbard, Jane's sister. Thomas, also nearby, was living with his brother Joseph Miller.

27. Smith Gee, Claim No. 1208183, Department of the Interior, Bureau of Pensions, July 14, 1898; 1890 U.S. Veterans Schedule Record, Civil War Pension Index, NARA. On the 1870 U.S. Census for Doniphan County, Kansas, Bird Gee, at age of twenty-four, is living with his parents. 1900 U.S. Census; American Civil War Soldiers Record; Cornish, D. (1987). *The sable arm: Black troops in the Union Army, 1861–1865* (Lawrence: University Press of Kansas), 77–78.

28. Declaration of Widow's Army Pension (March 7, 1866), No. 109415, NARA. Included in Mary Catherine Gee's widows pension application, notarized on November 13, 1865, by Private Isaac White. In addition Thomas Miller, Greenbury's brother-in-law, and William Cunningham affirmed the October 25, 1863, marriage of Greenbury and Mary.

29. Cooke, Michael A. (1984), *The health of blacks during Reconstruction, 1862, 1870* (Dissertation), University of Maryland, College Park.

30. Downs, J. (2012), *Sick for freedom: African-American illness and suffering during the Civil War and Reconstruction* (NY: Oxford University Press), 22.

31. Bird's Declaration for Original Invalid Pension (May 6, 1896), Claim No. 117369, NARA; Smith's Declaration for Pension (June 29, 1898), No. 1208183, NARA; Surgeon's Certificate (1898, October 12); 1890 U.S. Veterans Schedule Record, Civil War Pension index, NARA 1; 1900 U.S. Census; American Civil War Soldiers Record; Skocpol, T. (1992), *Protecting soldiers and mothers: The political origins of social policy in the United States* (Cambridge, MA: Harvard University Press). The U.S. Dependent Pension Act of 1890 provided a small government pension to all soldiers who served the requisite ninety days or more in the military whether disabled or not.

32. Affidavit of an Officer or Comrade (1900, January 18), signed by Jackson Wright, NARA. Wright's statement implies that Bird Gee, who mustered out of service on May 15, 1865, served his entire service while hospitalized. At age sixty-three (1909) Bird applied for membership in the Grand Army of the Republic (GAR) in Oklahoma City, Oklahoma, stating that he enlisted on March 8, 1865, and mustered out on May 15, 1865, whereas other documents state he mustered in two days later on March 10. Rules and Regulation GAR.

33. Declaration (1896, May 6); C. B. Bradford, M.D. (1901, January 14), Physician's Affidavit, NARA 1; Surgeon's Certificate (1896, July 22); Affidavit of an Officer or Comrade, signed by William Montgomery (1908, August 31), NARA.

34. Received by Southern Division of the Medical Division, Bureau of Pensions (1909, March 13), NARA; Skocpol (1992). In 1865, of the surviving civil war veterans 62 percent received their invalid pension. Downs (2012), 155–57. In 1904, veterans had to be over sixty-two and have served ninety days to be eligible. Born in 1846, Bird was neither old enough nor had served long enough.

35. 1920 and 1930 U.S. Census; Order of Birth: Cloyd Blanchard—November 19, 1901–March 10, 1933; Lorin Raymond—January 20, 1903–July 14, 1967; Cecil Everett—November 28, 1904–May 30, 1973; Ruby Lillie—January 16, 1906–September 10, 1929; Halvor Thomas—September 14, 1907–March 19 (18?) 1986; Helen Mae—July 5, 1909–February 2006; Roland Jay—April 18, 1911–March 12, 1993, LMP.

36. NM diary, 1, LMP.

37 Halvor Miller, Sr., NB #14–16.

38. Miller (1933), 9, 13, LMP; Virtual Nebraska (2005), *Nebraska . . . our towns: Pender—Thurston County*, retrieved May 4, 2011, from http://www.casde.unl.edu/history/counties/thurston/pender/.

39. Miller (1933), 13, LMP; *The McGuffey Reader*, published from 1836 to 1922, was among the best-known schoolbooks of the era. Wikipedia (2014, Sept. 4), *McGuffey Readers*, retrieved from http://en.wikipedia.org/wiki/McGuffey_Readers.

40. Miller (1933), 13, LMP.

41. Ibid., 28; Virtual Nebraska (2005), *Nebraska . . . our towns: Pender—Thurston County*, retrieved May 4, 2011, from http://www.casde.unl.edu/history/counties/thurston/pender/.

42. NM diary, 23, LMP.

43. Miller (1933), 13–14, LMP; Halvor Miller, Sr., NB #19.

44. Miller (1933), 50, LMP. The Frank series of adventure books was written by Harry Castlemon.

45. Ibid., 49.

46. Halvor Miller, Sr., NB #19–20.

47. Ibid., #95.

48. Retrieved from Flickr (May 26, 2008), *Old Thurston County courthouse (Pender, Nebraska)*, http://www.flickr.com/photos/courthouselover/2680619643/; Halvor Miller, Sr., NB #93, 95; 1920 U.S. Census, Nebraska; World War I, Registration draft card (1918, September 12); Judge Frank Flynn to LM (1920, June), LMP; Rampersad (1986), 236.

49. Darrow, C. (1932), *The story of my life* (New York: Scribner's), 29; Darrow, C. (1936, May), How to pick a jury, *Esquire*.

50. Halvor Miller, Sr., NB #95.

51. Judge Flynn to LM (1920, June), LMP.

52. Godsil, R. D. (2006), Race nuisance: The politics of law in the Jim Crow era, *Michigan Law Review*, 105 (December): 549; 245 U.S. 60 (1917).

53. Miller, L. (1966), *The Petitioners: The story of the Supreme Court of the United States and the Negro* (Cleveland: Meridian Books), 1.

54. Ibid.

55. *Gray's Doniphan County History: A Record of the Happenings of Half a Hundred Years*, chap. 1, pp. 1, 32, retrieved from doniphan/history/1905/I-In.html (March 22, 2015); Kansas Historical Society (September 2012), *Doniphan County, Kansas*, retrieved from https://www.kshs.org/kansapedia/doniphan-county-kansas/15277.

56. Miller (1966), p.1.

57. 1895 Kansas Census for Brown County. Allen McCowan, a speculator, was born in Indiana in 1844.

58. Miller (1966), 1.

59. *Hiawatha World* (1883, October 25), 2; 1900 U.S. Census, Doniphan County, Kansas. Murray Stanley was born in Illinois in 1848.

60. KSGenWeb (2004, January 18), *Biographical sketch of Casper W. Shreve, Doniphan County, Kansas*, retrieved from http://www.ksgenweb.com/archives/doniphan/bios/cwshreve.htm.

61. Miller (1966), 1.

62. Ibid., 4; Biographical sketch, retrieved from http://www.justice.gov/usao-ks/history (March 22, 2015); Department of Justice (2014, December 16), *History of the United States Attorney District of Kansas*, retrieved from http://www.justice.gov/usao/ks/history.html.

63. *U.S. vs. Stanley*, held on April 10, 1876, in Circuit Court No. 1568, Case No. 1578 filed on May 8, 1876, in the District Court of the United States, District of Kansas, Topeka.

64. $500 Bond on capias (1876, June 12), Case No. 1578.

65. Defendant's demur (1876, April 27).

66. Weaver, V. W. (1969, October), The failure of Civil Rights 1875–1883 and its repercussions, *Journal of Negro History*, 54(4): 368–82.

67. Miller (1966), 4.

68. *Hiawatha World* (1883, October 25), 2.

69. *U.S. v. Stanley, Ryan, Nichols, Singleton and Robinson*, 109 U.S. 3, was submitted to the October 1882 term of the U.S. Supreme Court on November 7, 1882. The Robinson case was submitted to the court on March 29, 1883; it appears that Kansas went without a U.S. attorney from 1879 to 1897. Perhaps for that reason, Bird's case lacked representation before the U.S. Supreme Court in 1883. See Department of Justice (2014, December 16), *History of the United States Attorney District for Kansas*, http://www.justice.gov/usao/ks/history.html.

70. Miller (1966), 422.

71. Weaver, W. V. (1969, October).

72. In 1892, Homer Plessy was arrested for sitting in the white section of a Louisiana train station. His suit reached the U.S. Supreme Court in 1896, where the court granted sanction to the "separate but equal" doctrine of segregated facilities.

73. Miller (1966), 4.

74. Ibid.

75. Ibid.

76. Statement by Bird Gee (1900, April 11), Affidavit of Claimant, Pension No. 1177369, U.S. Pension Office, that after discharge from military service he lived in Highland, Kansas, from June 1865 to 1876; from August 1 to September 1, 1876, New York City; from September 1876 to August 1878, Philadelphia; from August 1878 to November 1880, Chester Town, Maryland; from 1881 to 1885 Leavenworth, Kansas; from December 1885 to October 1886, Highland, Kansas; from 1886 to 1889 Beeler, Kansas; from 1889 to 1900 (present), Edmond, Oklahoma; NARA.

77. Miller, *Let tomorrow come*, 1, LMP.

78. Miller (1933), 32, 45, LMP.

79. Ibid., 33.

80. Ibid., 25.

81. Ibid., 34.

82. Ibid., 16.

83. Ibid., 17.

84. Ibid., 20, 35, 38.

85. Rampersad (1986), 236.

86. Miller (1933), 21, LMP.

87. Ibid., 22.

88. Ibid., 23.

89. Ibid.

90. Miller, *Let tomorrow come*, LMP.

91. Miller (1933), 46, LMP.

92. Ibid., 49.

93. Ibid. According to the 1910 U.S. Census for Pender, Nebraska, Emma Bohling, nine, was born in Nebraska. Her father, William, was from Germany. Lina Belle Ammons, white, was born in Nebraska in 1904. Fred Ammons, Lina's father, owned a barber shop.

94. NM diary, 12, LMP.

95. Ibid., p.14.

96. Miller (1933), 40. *Grit*, a weekly newspaper targeted rural areas, was founded in 1882 in Williamsport, Pennsylvania.

97. LM to Dave Farrell (circa 1940s), *People's Daily World*, LMP.

98. Helen Miller, born July 5, 1909, in Pender. 1910 U. S. Census, Nebraska.

99. Halvor Miller, Sr., NB #26–27.

100. Ibid., #93. On the 1910 U.S. Census, Pearl Essex is categorized as part Omaha Indian; Fred, her husband, is listed as white. On the 1920 U.S. Census, Kansas, Pearl, her husband, and all of their children are listed as white.

101. 1910 U.S. Department of Labor and Commerce, Indian Population.

102. Miller (1933), 41, LMP; Halvor Miller, Sr., NB #27.

103. Miller (1933), 41, LMP.

104. Ibid., 42.

105. Ibid., 41. Dr. Gifford, a graduate of the University of Michican, Ann Arbor, in 1882, was a professor in 1903 at the Nebraska College of Medicine and Omaha Medical College. His Omaha, Iowa, ophthalmology practice was located at 1404 Farnam. Directory of Deceased American Physicians, 1804–1929.

106. Miller (1933), 43, LMP.

107. Halvor Miller, Sr., NB #13.

108. 1900 U.S. Census; NM diary, 9, 38, LMP.

109. Ibid., 9.

110. In 1910, African Americans were 0.6 percent of the population of Nebraska; of the 8,804 people who lived in Thurston County, 13 were African American. The total population for Pender was 804. However, there are no specific statistics for the number of African Americans living in Pender when Loren Miller and his family lived there; 1910 U.S. Census.

111. Halvor Miller, Sr., NB #92.

112. Miller (1933), 4, LMP. On several pages of "Unto You," Jim Malloy, the saloon proprietor, is mentioned specifically by name.

113. Marable, M. (2011), *Malcolm X: A life of reinvention* (New York: Viking), 15.

114. Miller (1933), 47, LMP.

115. Ibid., 2, 4.

116. Ibid., 50. Nora Miller makes no mention of her husband's drinking in her diary.

117. Halvor Miller, Sr., NB #44–45, italics added. According to the 1875 U.S. Census, Iowa Township, Donaphan County, Kansas, Hugh Eubanks and Thomas Miller were neighbors. In 1880, Kansas was the first state to enact Prohibition on intoxicating beverages. In 1919, the U.S. Congress, over the veto of President Woodrow Wilson, passed the Eighteenth Amendment to the Constitution, to prohibit beverages, and to regulate the manufacture, production, and sale of spirits for other than beverage purposes. The Anti-Saloon League, established in the late 1890s, lobbied at all levels of government on Prohibition legislation. It was considered one of the first pressure organizations focusing on one issue.

118. Miller (1933), 55–56, LMP. The Webster Street Station, a connector station for people traveling from Pender, Nebraska—located at Webster and North 15th Streets, Omaha, Nebraska—was built in 1887.

119. Ibid., 54; The parallel story of why the family moved to Kansas turns on the arrest of a Native American man, awaiting trial on charges of rape and the decision of Miller's father to let the man escape. "My father," recalled Halvor, "always seemed to be quite soft at heart." As Thurston County's part-time night jailer and janitor, John Miller held the keys to the jail cells. Talk of lynching the Indian, according to family lore, brought back memories of the lynching of John's friend, Loris Higgins, in Bancroft, the township over from Pender. On May 12, 1907, Higgins, a twenty-six-year-old farmhand working in Rosalie, Nebraska, charged with two murders, was on his way to court when he was taken off the train and hung from a tree; Higgins is lynched (1907, August 30), *Red Cloud Chief*, 7.

120. Miller, L. (1931, September 11), On second thought, *California Eagle*, 8.

121. Mary to Cloyd Miller, November 26, 1910, LMP.

122. Miller (1933), p.57, LMP.

123. Ibid., 54.

124. NM diary, 9, LMP.

125. Miller (1933), 58, LMP.

126. Ibid., 59.

127. Ibid., 60.

128. NM diary, 9, LMP.

129. Miller (1933), 61, LMP.

130. Ibid., 61–62.

131. Ibid., 63.

132. Ibid., 63–64; 85th Anniversary, 1915 class photograph, LHP.

133. NM diary, 10, LMP.

134. Miller, *Let Tomorrow Come*, 2, LMP.

135. Miller (1933), 64, LMP.

136. Ibid.; Halvor Miller, Sr., NB #112.

137. 85th Anniversary, 6, LHP; 1900 U.S. Census, Iowa, Kansas.

138. Miller (1933), 65, LMP.

139. NM diary, 11, LMP.

140. Miller (1933), 67, LMP.

141. Ibid.

142. William H. Starr, born on March 21, 1899, in Kansas, was the son of Charles Starr, Martha Hubbard's grandson and Loren Miller's second cousin, once removed. 1900 U.S. Census.

143. Miller (1933), 68, LMP.

144. Ibid.

145. Ibid., 69.

146. Ibid.

147. Ibid., 70.

148. Ibid., 69.

149. Kansas Collection Books (1999), *William G. Cutler's history of the state of Kansas: Doniphan County*, pt. 3, retrieved from http://www.kancoll.org/books/cutler/doniphan/doniphan-co-p3.html.

150. Miller (1933), 64, LMP.

151. NM diary, 12, LMP.

152. Ibid., 13–14.

153. Ibid., 14.

154. Miller (1933), 70, LMP.

155. 85th Anniversary, 10, LHP.

156. Miller (1933), 71, LMP.

157. Ibid., 72.

158. NM diary, 15, LMP.

159. Miller (1933), 73, LMP.

160. Ibid., 74.

161. Ibid., 74–75.

162. Ibid., 75.

163. Mrs. Baker to LM, July 24, 1914, LHP.

164. 85th Anniversary, LHP; Miller (1933), 74, LMP.

165. Miller (1933), 35, LMP.

166. Douglass, F. (2003), *The narrative of the life of Frederick Douglass, an American slave* (New York: Barnes and Noble Classics), 69.

167. Miller (1933), 69, 76, LMP; Loren Miller, Howard University transcript, Fall 1926.

168. Miller (1933), 76.

169. Ibid.

170. NM diary, 13, LMP.

171. Halvor Miller, Sr., NB #107. Carver, according to Halvor Miller, "remained in Highland for some time and worked in an orchard by day and stayed at the Old JP Johnson hotel and did janitorial work in the evenings"; Wikipedia (2014, 9 October), *Highland University*, retrieved from http://en.wikipedia.org/wiki/Highland_University.

172. Miller (1933), 80, LMP; Highland High School transcript.

173. Miller (1933), 81, LMP.

174. NM diary, 15, LMP.

175. Ibid., p.16.

176. Ibid., p.17.

177. Ibid., p.16; Eighth grade graduation diploma July 21, 1916; Highland High School diploma, May 14, 1920, LMP.

178. Judge Flynn to LM, June 1920, LMP.

179. NM diary, 16, LMP.

180. Ibid., 16–17.

181. Halvor Miller, Sr., NB #109, 111.

182. NM diary, 18, LMP.

183. Nebraskastudies.org (1994), *Racial tensions in Nebraska after World War I: Racial tensions in Omaha—A horrible lynching*, retrieved from http://www.nebraskastudies.org/0700/stories/0701_0130.html.

184. Ibid.

185. Lincoln, C. E. (1970), Black nationalism: The minor league, in R. K. Baker (Ed.), *The Afro-American* (New York: Van Nostrand Reinhold), 284.

186. Wikipedia (2015, 20 March), *1920 Duluth Lynchings*, retrieved from http://en.wikipedia.org/wiki/1920_Duluth_lynchings.

187. NM diary, 19, LMP; Miller's FBI file contained a 1941 vital statistic report from the Los Angeles Sheriff Department.

188. Miller FBI File, City of Los Angeles physical exam.

189. Death certificate signed by L. M., LMP.

190. Miller, L. (1927, January), College, *Crisis*, 138.

191. Wikipedia (2015, March 20), *Memorial Stadium (University of Kansas)*, retrieved from http://en.wikipedia.org/wiki/Memorial_Stadium_(University_of_Kansas). In 1920, construction began on Memorial Stadium; it opened on October 29, 1921.

192. Miller (1927).

193. Tulsa aflame: 85 dead in riot (1919, June 4), *Chicago Defender*, 1.

194. Ibid.; Sulzberger, A. G. (2011, June 19), As survivors dwindle, Tulsa confronts past, *New York Times*, A16.

195. NM diary, 32, LMP.

196. McCullough, D. (2001), *John Adams* (New York: Simon and Shuster), 19; Highland High School transcript.

197. University of Kansas archives; Miller (1933), 88, LMP; Miller, L. (undated, unpublished), Novelists and clowns, 6, LMP.

198. Miller, L. (1935, August 3), Hectic Harlem, *New York Amsterdam News*, 11.

199. Miller, *Let tomorrow come*, 2, LMP.

200. Loren Miller, interview by Lawrence de Graaf (1967, March 3 and April 29).

201. Ivan Johnson, Loren Miller associate in law practice (1936, September 3), *Los Angeles Sentinel*, 1. Johnson finished his legal training at Southwestern University in Los Angeles. Imparato, M. (Summer 2007), Washburn alumni were leaders in early California civil rights movement, *Washburn Alumni Magazine*, 14; Brown, J. M. (1980, October 23), Your social chronicler, *Los Angeles Sentinel*, C2; H. Miller, Jr., personal communication (2010, October 5); Washington, L. (1967, July 20), Tribute to my cousin, *Los Angeles Sentinel*.

202. Miller transcripts from Howard University, Washburn University, and the University of Kansas. At KU, he studied English, Spanish, Psychology, Logic, Ethics, Economics, Plane Trigonometry, History, and College Algebra.

203. Miller (1962, February 1); Howard University opens 59th term (1926, October 2), *New York Amsterdam News*, 4.

204. Howard student wins art, literature prizes (1926, November 28), *Washington Post*, M16; Miller (1927).

205. Miller, L. (1998), College, in S. K. Wilson (Ed.), *The Crisis reader: Stories, poetry, and essays from the NAACP's Crisis magazine* (New York: Modern Library).

206. Crisis magazine awards prizes (1926, October 27), *New York Amsterdam News*, 9.

207. Cullen takes second prize in the Crisis poetry award (1926, October 30), *Baltimore Afro-American*, 10; Crisis presents literary prizes (1926, October 30), *Chicago Defender*, 5.

208. Weeks, P. (1964, May 17), New judge reluctant member of profession, *Los Angeles Times*, E4.

209. Hilton, A. (2014, April 28), On the mountain, *New Yorker*, 14.

210. Smith, R. J. (2007), *The great black way: L.A. in the 1940s and the lost African-American renaissance* (New York: Public Affairs), 235.

211. Miller, L. (unpublished poem, 1926), Notes from a suicide—To my father, LMP.

212. Mills, C. W. (2002), *White collar: The American middle classes* (Oxford: Oxford University Press), 372.

213. Byrd, R. P., & Gates, H. L., Jr. (2011, February 11), Jean Toomer's conflicted racial identity, *Chronicle Review*, B6.

214. Miller (1962, February 1). Studying English, economics, and political science earned Miller seven credits.

215. Kerr, A. (2006–2007); The history of color prejudice at Howard University. *Journal of Blacks in Higher Education*, 54 (Winter): 85.

216. High school notes: Howard University (1927, April 16), *Chicago Defender*, A7.

217. Miller (1966), 186.

218. Du Bois, W. E. B. (1968), *The autobiography of W. E. B. Du Bois: A soliloquy on viewing my life from the last decade of its first century*, H. Aptheker (Ed.) (New York: International Publishers), 121.

219. H. Miller, Jr., personal communication (2006, April 22).

220. Hughes, L. (1999), Our wonderful society: Washington, in S. K. Wilson (Ed.), *The opportunity reader: Stories, poetry, and essays from the Urban League's Opportunity Magazine* (New York: Modern Library), 366, 367.

221. LM to Langston Hughes (1931, October 28), LMP.

222. Keith, V. M., & Herring, C. (1991, November), Skin tone and stratification in the Black community, *American Journal of Sociology*, 97(3): 775.

223. Cashmore, E., & Jennings, J. (Eds.), *Racism: Essential Readings* (London: Sage, 2001.

224. Keith & Herring (1991), 761.

225. Frazier, E. F. (1957), *The Black bourgeoisie* (New York: Free Press), 257.

226. U.S. Census 1920, Los Angeles, California.

227. Loren Miller, interview by Lawrence de Graaf (1967, March 3 and April 29).

228. Du Bois (1968), 108.

229. Miller, *Let tomorrow come*, LMP.

230. NM diary, 36; Washburn College Graduation Program, LMP.

Chapter 3

1. Loren Miller (hereafter LM) to Nora Miller, circa September 1929, LHP.

2. Halvor Miller, Sr., NB #109, 111.

3. Ibid., #112; NM Diary, 49, LMP, states that Nora's daughter Ruby died on a Tuesday at 2:00 A.M.; whereas in NB, #111, it is recorded that she died at 10:00 P.M.

4. Halvor Miller, Sr., NB #113.

5. NM diary, 49, LMP. On November 20, 1927, Nora Miller joined Aimee McPherson's Angelus Temple, the International Church of the Foursquare Gospel. After receiving the Holy Ghost, Nora said she left her work "and went into the bedroom to get ready for him. Something I had never done before. I put-on a clean dress, combed my hair, and looked at my shoes, when suddenly it came to me that 'You are married.' I said married, who to? When suddenly the answer came, 'married to Jesus.'" On May 1, 1928, Roland was "saved"; Ruby and Helen followed on June 25, 1928.

6. Ibid., 35, 37.

7. Ibid., 36.

8. LM to Nora Miller (n.d.), LHP.

9. Loren Miller, interview by Lawrence de Graaf (1967, March 3 and April 29).

10. NM diary, 33, LMP; Loren Miller, interview by Lawrence de Graaf (1967, March 3 and April 29).

11. NM diary, 34, LMP.

12. Ibid.

13. H. Miller, Jr., personal communication (2006, October 3). Bessie Seals (Elizabeth Miller), Evergreen Cemetery, buried on Nov. 4, 1924, Lot 3698 Section B; Death Record of Bessie Seals, Los Angeles Health Department, 1088-V01.224.

14. NM diary, 34–37, LMP. By spring 1926, Halvor Miller, Sr., was living in Los Angeles. On June 8, 1926, Nora left Kansas for Los Angeles; Helen left on September 3, 1927; Ruby and her children moved by November, 1927; Cloyd, along with his first family, left with Roland for California on January 18, 1928; Fred Holmes, Ruby's husband, arrived in winter 1927–1928. Before they moved to east 22nd street, the Millers shared four rooms.

15. The weather (1929, September 15), *Los Angeles Times*, 14; Rain (1929, September 18), *Los Angeles Times*, 1.

16. 1930, U.S. Census. The single-family, 1,200-square-foot home at 1446 E. 22nd Street was built in 1902.

17. Tone of the market shaky (1929, September 10), *Los Angeles Times*, 14.

18. Sudden avalanche wipes out $3,000,000,000 in paper values (1929, October 24), *Washington Post*, 1.

19. Schuyler, G. S. (1929, December 4), *New York Amsterdam News*, 20.

20. Langston Hughes, undated speech circa spring 1932, Los Angeles, LHP.

21. Loren Miller, interview by Lawrence de Graaf (1967, March 3 and April 29).

22. Ibid., 4.

23. Ibid.

24. Ibid., 5.

25. Miller, L. (1931, February 13), On second thought, *California Eagle*, 8.

26. Streitmatter, R. (1994), *Raising her voice: African-American women journalists who changed history* (Lexington: University of Kentucky Press), 97.

27. Freer, R. M. (2005), Charlotta Bass: A community activist for racial and economic justice, in R. Gottlieb, M. Vallianatos, R. M. Freer, & P. Dreier, *The next Los Angeles: The struggle for a livable city* (Berkeley: University of California Press), 51.

28. Ibid., 49.

29. Miller's "On Second Thought" ran from February 13, 1931, to July 30, 1933. In the masthead of the *California Eagle* edition of April 17, 1931, he is listed as city editor. 1930

U.S. Census, California; Washington, L. (1931, February 27), Dance dope, *California Eagle*, 8.

30. California Eagle (1933, June 30), *California Eagle*, 12.

31. Wilkerson, D. A. (1947, Autumn), The Negro press, *Journal of Negro Education*, 16(4): 512.

32. California Eagle (1931, January 21), *California Eagle*, 7.

33. Streitmatter (1994), 96–97.

34. Loren Miller, interview by Lawrence de Graaf (1967, March 3 and April 29), 5.

35. Ibid., 6; the *California Eagle* would change politically when Loren Miller bought it in May of 1951, from its "extreme left-wing" stance where it had lost ground to a more "liberal Fair Deal-New Deal policy," according to Miller (1952, July 29), To Whom it May Concern, LMP.

36. NAACP members defeat move to oust Griffith (1947, January 16), *California Eagle*; Agreement for Sale and Agreement Extending Time; William B. Easterman, esq. to LM (1955, July 6). Letter is receipt of $4,000 payment from Miller regarding fulfillment of 1954 "Agreement Extending Time" on the sale of the *Eagle* to Miller in 1951. Ben Margolis to Herbert Simmons, esq. (1960, November 14). Ben Margolis to LM (1961, December 4), LMP: "At that time you said that apparently Mrs. Bass did have some cause for complaint with respect to compliance with regard her contract for the sale of The Eagle."

37. Miller (1931, February 13), On second thought, *California Eagle*, 8; Betty Smith, executive secretary John Reed Club, Hollywood Chapter, to LM (1934, November 30), LMP; Dilling, E. (1934), *The Red Network: A "who's who" and handbook of radicalism for patriots* (published by author), 226.

38. LM to Langston Hughes (hereafter LH) and Louise Thompson (hereafter LT) (1932, March), LHP.

39. Ibid.

40. Betty Smith to Comrade Miller (1934, November 30), LMP.

41. Denning, M. (1996), *The cultural front: The laboring of American culture in the twentieth century* (New York: Verso), 66.

42. Ibid., 15; Gale Encyclopedia of U.S. history (2014, December 30), *International Labor Defense*, retrieved from http://www.answers.com/topic/international-labor-defense.

43. Miller, L. (1966), 266.

44. Miller (1931, May 15), On second thought, *California Eagle*, 8.

45. LM to LH (1931, October 28), LHP.

46. LM to LH (1931, May 15).

47. Miller (1931, March 4), On second thought, *California Eagle*, 8. In 1933, according to *The Red Network*, Miller was on the national executive committee of the National Scottsboro Committee of Action along with Roger Baldwin (ACLU); Harry Haywood, Communist Party of America; Cyril Briggs, editor of the *Liberator*; A. Clayton Powell of Abyssinian Baptist Church; and scores of others.

48. Miller (1932, May 15).

49. Miller (1931, March 6), On second thought, *California Eagle*, 8.

50. Complaints delayed in red rioting (1931, November 1), *Los Angeles Times*, A6

51. Rabid red captured (1931, November 14), *Chicago Defender*, 4.

52. Greek farce to continue (1932, January 9), *Los Angeles Times*, A1; Greek comedy players arrested in show raid (1932, January 8), *Los Angeles Times*, A1.

53. LM to LH and LT (1932, March), LHP; *Babbit*, written by Sinclair Lewis, was published in 1922.

54. Ibid.

Chapter 4

1. McWilliams, C. (2001), Water. Water. Water!, in C. McWilliams, *Fool's Paradise: A Carey McWilliams Reader* (Santa Clara, CA: Heyday Books), 147. Mutavilya, god of the Mojave Indians created the Colorado River. Langston Hughes to Matthew Crawford (1932, May 24), LHP; Harden, T. G. (1932, June 18), California News, *Chicago Defender*, 20 (Harden writes they left "Sunday afternoon"); Rampersad (1986), 241. Hughes to Miller written possibly on May 29, 1932, LHP: "That's why we gotta Leave Los Angeles as soon as we can—Sunday morning—to be sure to make it by Ford." Correspondence to and from Miller, Hughes, Matt Crawford, Louise Thompson Patterson, and Juanita Ellsworth Miller are primarily located in LMP and LHP; other correspondence concerning their Russian travels are in the Louise Thompson Patterson Papers (No. 869) Emory University (LTP); a few others are in the Langston Hughes Papers (LHYP) at the Beinecke Rare Book and Manuscript Library, Yale University.

2. Drizzling weather will end (1932, June 6), *Los Angeles Times*, A1; Rain fails (1932, June 5), *Los Angeles Times*; June rain (1932, June 5), *Los Angeles Times*.

3. Hughes, L. (1956), *I wonder as I wander* (New York: Hill and Wang), 80.

4. Miller (1932, June 3), On second thought. *California Eagle*, 12.

5. Hughes (1956), 65.

6. Miller (1932, June 3).

7. Patterson, L. (1995), With Langston Hughes in the USSR, in D. L. Lewis (Ed.), *The portable Harlem renaissance reader* (New York: Penguin), 183.

8. Rampersad (1986), 161–62.

9. Loren Miller to Nora Miller (hereafter LM to NM), (1932, September 16), LMP.

10. Come out for Foster and Ford (1932, June 20), *Daily Worker*, 2; Russia to produce film of race life in America soon (1932, March 19), *Chicago Defender*, 5.

11. Langston Hughes (hereafter LH) to LM (1930, August 21), LHP.

12. LM to LH (ca. 1930), LHP.

13. LH to LM (1930, August 21), LHP.

14. LM to LH (1931, October 26), LHP.

15. Miller (1931, March 18), On second thought, *California Eagle*, 8.

16. Miller (1931, May 20), On second thought, *California Eagle*, 8.

17. W. A. Domingo to Louise Thompson (hereafter LT). (1932, May 31), in Berry, F. (1992), *Before and beyond Harlem: Langston Hughes, a biography* (New York: Carol Publishing Group), 155n8.

18. Ibid., 156.

19. Sue E. Bailey (1901–1996) was a 1926 graduate of Oberlin College. As a member of the Pilgrimage of Friendship, she and her husband, Howard Thurman, traveled to India and to what was then called Burma and Ceylon. In 1944, along with her husband, she established America's first interracial, nondenominational church, the Church of the Fellowship of All Peoples in San Francisco, box 12, LTP; Rampersad (1986), 162, 235;

Baldwin, K. A. (2002), *Beyond the color line and the iron curtain: Reading encounters between Black and Red, 1922–1963* (Durham: Duke University Press), 96.

20. Patterson (1995).

21. LT to Henrietta (1932, May 18), LTP.

22. LM to LT and LH (circa March 1932), LHP.

23. On November 16, 1933, the United States recognized the Soviet Union. LH to Gilbert Porter, March 26, 1932; LT to Zell, May 18, 1932; LT's Cooperating Committee statement of money received and disbursed: "The two different rates of $95 and $110 are due to the rise in steamship fares that went into effect before all registrations were in," LTP.

24. Hauke, K. A. (1998), *Ted Poston: Pioneer American journalist* (Athens: University of Georgia Press), 236n38.

25. Hughes (1956), 70.

26. Hughes, L. (1973) Moscow and Me. In Berry, F. (Ed.), *Good morning, revolution: Uncollected social protest, writings by Langston Hughes* (New York: Lawrence Hill), 67.

27. Hughes (1956), 70.

28. LT to LH (1932, May 16), LHP.

29. LT to LH (1932, May 10); LH to LM (1932, May 29), LHYP.

30. LT to LH (1932, May 27); LT to LH (1932, May 16), LHYP.

31. LH to LM (1932, May 29), LHYP.

32. Press release to Henry Moon (1932, May 11), *New York Amsterdam News*; LT to LH (1932, May 27), LTP; Wilentz, S. (2012), *360 sound: The Columbia Records story* (San Francisco: Chronicle Books).

33. Quast, S. (2003), *How the fight to free Tom Mooney fueled the nation's first general strike*, Pacific Northwest Labor and Civil Rights Projects, retrieved from http://depts.washington.edu/labhist/strike/quast.shtml; Wilson, E. (1931, August 26), The freight-car case, *New Republic*.

34. McKay, C. (1923), Soviet Russia and the Negro, *Crisis*, 27, 61–65, 114–18.

35. Baldwin (2002), 5.

36. In 1932, U.S. Route 80 was the best westward route to Yuma, Arizona; from Sinclair, U. (2007), *Oil!* (New York: Penguin), 4, 6.

37. Workers of the Writers Programs of the Works Project Administration (Comp.) (1989), *WPA guide to Arizona* (Phoenix: University of Arizona Press), 274; Hughes, L. (1946, March 30), Here to Yonder, *Chicago Defender*, 14.

38. LM, no date, title, or known recipient, LHP.

39. Ibid.; Hughes (1946, March 30).

40. Ibid.

41. Miller, L., Look down, look down (unpublished essay), LMP.

42. LH to LT (1932, May 5), LHYP; Weather report (1932, June 6), *Los Angeles Times*, 12.

43. LM to NM (1932, June 9), LHP.

44. Miller, L., Look down.

45. Hughes (1946, March 30), LMP.

46. LM to NM (1932, June 9), LHP.

47. Ibid.

48. Rampersad (1986), 241; LM to NM (1932, June 9), LHP.

49. Ibid.

50. Miller, L., Look down.

51. Berry (1992), 152.

52. Hughes (1956), 75.

53. German Lloyd line marks a birthday (1932, February 12), *New York Times*, 43.

54. Rampersad (1986), 241.

55. Hughes (1956), 69.

56. Leave for U.S.S.R. to work on Soviet film (1932, June 16), *Daily Worker*, 2.

57. Garder, J. L. (1999), African Americans in the Soviet Union in the 1920s and 1930s: The development of transcontinental protest, *Western Journal of Black Studies*, 23(3): 193.

58. Miller, L. (1935, March 2), The way out, Crusader News Agency. Miller was assistant editor, along with editor Cyril Briggs and assistant editor Ben Davis, Jr. Haywood, H. (1978), *Black Bolshevik. Autobiography of an Afro-American Communist* (Chicago: Liberator Press), 253.

59. Whitney, B. (1932, June 11), Actors to sail for Russia on June 14, *Baltimore Afro-American*, 3; Cabaret party friday night (1932, June 3), *Daily Worker*, 2.

60. New York society (1932, June 18). *Baltimore Afro-American*, 3.

61. Hughes (1956), 69; Friends attend rites for Wallace Thurman (1934, December 29), *New York Amsterdam News*, front page.

62. Bourne, S. C., Louise Patterson on Langston Hughes, *Langston Hughes Review* 15(2) (Winter 1997), 42.

63. Box Lacrosse games off (1932, June 15), *New York Times*, 43; The weather (1932, June 15), *New York Times*, 41; Europa sails with 1,950 (1932, June 15), *New York Times*, 41; Shipping and mails (1932, June 14), *New York Times*, 43.

64. Hauke (1998), 45.

65. Rampersad (1986), 132, 172.

66. Ibid., 242; Hughes (1956), 69; Hauke (1998), 236n38.

67. Hughes (1956), 81.

68. Ibid., 70.

69. Rampersad (1986), 243.

70. Dorothy West, interview by Genii Guinier (1978, May 6), in Hauke (1998), 44.

71. Ibid., 45.

72. Ibid., 42.

73. Ibid., 38.

74. Ibid., 38–39, 57, 189.

75. Rampersad (1986), 243; He fought for equality (1996, September 5), *Sun Reporter*. Matt Crawford died at age ninety-three.

76. El-Hai, J. (1991, May/June), Black and white and red, *American Heritage Magazine*, 42(3): 89–92, retrieved from https://www.librarything.com/series/American+Heritage+Magazine.

77. Hughes (1956), 70.

78. LTP box 12:6, item no. 8; Rampersad (1986), 243; Announce players for Soviet picture (1932, June 8), *New York Amsterdam News*.

79. Rampersad (1986), 243.

80. Miller, L. (1932, October 11), Negro gets high post with red post offices, *Atlanta Daily World*, A2; Rampersad (1986), 243.

81. Boyle, S. T., & Bunie, A. (2001), *Paul Robeson: The years of promise and achievement* (Boston: University of Massachusetts Press); Matusevich, M. (2008), An exotic subversive: Africa, Africans and the Soviet everyday, *Race and Class*, 49(4), 80n13.

82. Press release to Henry Moon (1932, June 11), *New York Amsterdam News*: "The scenario avoids the sentimentality and buffoonery . . . of the Negro. It is written by a Russian, a German and Lovett Forte-Whiteman, an American Negro"; To aid Soviet Negro film (1932, June 14), *New York Times*, 26; Soviet seeks negroes to make film of conditions Here (1932, March 9), *New York Amsterdam News*, 7; Matusevich (2008), 63–64.

83. Moser, C. (1966, July), Mayakovsky and America, *Russian Review*, 25(3): 249.

84. LM to NM (1932, June 24); LM to Juanita Ellsworth (hereafter JE) (1932, June 25), LMP.

85. Hughes (1956), 70; Rampersad (1986), 246.

86. Captain of ship halts debate on Scottsboro case (1932, June 19), *Chicago Defender*, 13; Alain Locke to Charlotte Mason (hereafter AL and CM), (1932, June 16). Letters between Locke and Mason and Locke and Hughes are located in ALP.

87. LM to JE (ca. 1932, August), LHP; Dilling (1934), 226.

88. Berry (1992), 157.

89. Howard U profs sail for Europe (1932, June 25), *Chicago Defender*, 2; Lewis, D. L. (1981), *When Harlem was in vogue* (New York: Knopf), 117.

90. Rampersad (1986), 242.

91. Ibid.; Berry (1992), 154.

92. Rampersad (1986), 92.

93. LH to AL, written sometime in early 1926. "You are out on such a snowy night! Or do you think I'm a robber and wont let me in?"; postmark on back of envelope is dated February 22, 1926, 4:30 P.M. "Dear Locke, are you home? I'm on way back to school"; LH to AL (n.d.): "I want to stay with you. I need to know," ALP (164–68, folder 4).

94. Berry (1992), 154.

95. Shakespeare, W. (1916), *Twelfth Night*, in W. J. Craig (Ed.), *The complete works of William Shakespeare* (Oxford: Oxford University Press), 1.5.293

96. AL to CM (1932, June 16), ALP.

97. AL to CM (1932, July 7), ALP.

98. Ibid.

99. Miller, L. (1935, April 16), Mail-order dictatorship: The Rosenwalds and 12,000,000 Negroes, *New Masses*; Miller, L. (1935, February 19), Shadow of philanthropy (book review), *New Masses*, 23–24. Miller was not the first to accuse the Rosenwald Fund of racism. In 1931, a group of Harlem physicians rejected the foundation's hospital plan because "Rosenwald hospitals are Jim Crow in spirit and in fact." Harlem physicians reject Rosenwald's hospital plan (1931, February 7), *Chicago Defender*, 3.

100. Miller (1935, April 16), Mail-order.

101. Henry, C. P. (2005), *Ralph Bunche: model Negro or American other?* (New York: New York University Press), 66–68.

102. LM to Joseph North (1935, February 25), box 42, folder 5, LMP.

103. Juanita Miller 1955 resumé, LMP; Nobleprize.com: Official website of the Nobel Prize (2015, March 23), *Ralph Bunche—Biographical*, retrieved from http://www.nobel prize.org/nobel_prizes/peace/laureates/1950/bunche-bio.html. Photograph of Juanita and

Ralph, ca. 1940, in the Miller family album. Halvor Miller, Jr., Miller's nephew, said they were high school sweethearts.

104. A photograph of Miller and Bunche standing together appeared on the front page of the first edition following Miller's purchase of the *California Eagle* in May 1951.

105. Rampersad (1986), 243.

106. Hauke (1998), 212n12.

107. LM to JE (n.d.), LHP.

108. Thompson, L. (1934, November), Southern terror. *Crisis*, 327.

109. Miller (1952, July 29), To whom it may concern.

110. Patterson (1995), 183.

111. LM to JE (possibly 1932, June 23), LHP.

112. Miss Juanita Lewis back after visit to Russia (1933, April 29), *Chicago Defender*, 4.

113. LM to JE (possibly 1932, June 23), LHP.

114. Patterson (1995), 183.

115. Hughes (1956), 71.

116. Dorothy West to Rachel West (1932, June 29), in Hauke (1998).

117. LM to JE (1932, June 23), LHP; Hughes (1956), 71.

118. Statement of film's cancellation, LMP.

119. Hughes (1956), 70.

120. LM to JE (1932, June 23), LHP.

121. Ibid.; Patterson (1995), 184.

122. LM to JE (1932, June 23), LHP.

123. Hughes (1956), 72. In 1945, Stettin, Germany, now called Szczecin, is part of Poland.

124. LM to JE (1932, June 23), LHP. The *Ariadne*, built in 1914, and scrapped in 1969, was owned by the Finland Steamship Company; Finland Steamship Co. (2005), *Ariadne*, retrieved from http://www.simplonpc.co.uk/FinlandSSCo.html#anchor1407754.

125. Hughes (1956), 69, 72.

126. Patterson (1995), 184.

127. LM to JE (1932, June 25), LHP.

128. Hughes (1956), 73.

129. Ibid.

130. Ibid.

131. Robinson, R. (1988), *Black on red: My 44 years inside the Soviet Union* (Washington, D.C.: Acropolis Books), 37; Haywood (1978), 143.

132. Bread bringing high prices in Soviet Russia (1932, June 26), *Chicago Daily Tribune*, E3; Berry (1992), 67.

133. Film cancellation, LMP.

134. Hughes (1956), 83.

135. Hughes (1973), 68.

136. Hughes (1956), 83–86.

137. Ibid., 86.

138. LM to LH and LT (ca. 1932); LM to JE (1932, July 17), both in LHP.

139. Rampersad (1986), 215; Miller and Hughes always denied that they were ever card-carrying Communists.

140. Miller, L. (1932, June 20), Hughes says lot of Negro worker is growing worse. *Atlanta Daily World*, 2.

141. Patterson (1995), 185.

142. Hughes (1956), 76; Langston "and I are rooming together here in the Soviet Union. Matt Crawford also stays with us." LM to JE (1932, July 17), LHP.

143. LM to JE (1932, July 7), LHP.

144. Hughes (1956), 77.

145. Thompson, L. (1933), The Soviet Film, *Crisis*.

146. LM to JE (1932, July 7), LHP.

147. Harden, T. (1932, June 18), City News, *Chicago Defender*, 20.

148. Hughes (1956), 79.

149. Ibid., 77.

150. Ibid., 80; Hughes (1973), 67; To aid Soviet Negro film (1932, June 14), *New York Times*, 26.

151. Baldwin (2002), 14–15; To aid Soviet Negro film (1932, June 14), *New York Times*, 26; Robinson (1988), 361.

152. Smith, H. (1964), *Black man in red Russia: A memoir* (Chicago: Johnson), 26.

153. LM to JE (1932, July 7), LHP.

154. Haywood (1978), 146.

155. Robinson (1988), 361; National affairs: Black and Red (1925, November 9), *Time*; Klehr, H., Haynes, J. E., & Anderson, K. M. (1998), *The Soviet world of American communism* (New Haven: Yale University Press), 222–27.

156. LM to JE (1932, July 7), LHP.

157. Ibid.

158. Ibid.

159. Robinson (1988), 320; Hughes (1956), 87.

160. Miller, L. (1932, November 15), Inventor is honored by the Soviets, *Atlanta Daily World*, 1.

161. Keys, B. (2009), An African-American worker in Stalin's Soviet Union: Race and the Soviet experiment in international perspective, *Historian*, 71(1): 31–54.

162. Haywood (1978), 111–12.

163. LM to JE (1932, July 7), LHP.

164. Ibid.

165. Hauke (1998), 49.

166. LM to JE (1932, July 7), LHP.

167. Hughes (1956), 89.

168. LM to JE (1932, July 7), LHP.

169. Ibid.

170. Miller, L. (1931, August 14), On second thought, California *Eagle*.

171. LM to JE (1932, July 7), LHP.

172. Hughes (1956), 89.

173. Hauke (1998), 51.

174. Ibid., 212n11, telephone interview by Hauke and Thurston Lewis.

175. Ibid., 212n10; Dorothy West, interview by Genii Guinier, in Hauke (1998).

176. Smith (1964), 28.

177. Dorothy West, interview by Rachel West (1933, March 6), in Hauke (1998), 49. In 1938, Boris Pilnyak was executed for counterrevolutionary activities and spying.

178. Hughes (1956), 88.

179. Gilmore, G. (2008), *Defying Dixie: The radical roots of civil rights, 1919–1950* (New York: Norton), 143; Nelson, C. N. (2004), Black and white, in C. D. Wintz and P. Finkelman (Eds.), *Encyclopedia of the Harlem Renaissance*, vol. 1 (New York: Routlege), 123. Clare Nee Nelson, says it was "probably" Sylvia Garner who attempted suicide and it was "probably" Constance White who was Sylvia's lover. I agree with Gilmore that it was Sylvia who attempted suicide, though she does not mention who the other woman was. From the evidence of Miller's letter that White was a lesbian and that Dorothy acknowledged that she had a lesbian affair with "M" in her letter to Langston (i.e., Mildred), I take the position that White, as the third lesbian on the trip, was the woman who spurned Sylvia's affections.

180. Hughes (1956), 88, Langston did not name Sylvia as the woman who attempted suicide.

181. LM to JE (n.d.), North Caucasus, LHP.

182. LM to JE (1932, July 17), LHP.

183. Miss Ellsworth is named case work inspector (1936, April 16), *Los Angeles Sentinel*, 4.

184. LM to JE (1932, July 17), LHP.

185. Ibid.

186. LM to JE (1932, August 16), LHP.

187. Ibid.

188. Ibid.

189. LM to JE (n.d.), Moscow, USSR, LHP.

190. LM to JE (1932, July 17), LHP.

191. LM to JE (1932, August 16), LHP.

192. To publish works of Negro poets in Russia (1932, August 13), *Pittsburgh Courier*, A3.

193. Hughes (1956), 80.

194. Rampersad (1986), 248; Hughes (1956), 80.

195. Bourne (1997), 43.

196. Hughes (1956), 81.

197. Ibid., 82.

198. LM to JE (1932, July 17), LHP.

199. Ibid.; Berry (1992), 162; Hughes (1956), 91.

200. Berry (1992), 163; Hughes (1956), 94.

201. Hughes (1956), 92.

202. Ibid., 93.

203. Miller, L. (1932, October 12). Poe once tried to snub Pushkin, great Russian author, investigator reveals, *Atlanta Daily World*, 6A.

204. Miller, L. (1932, September 10), Negro film group tours U.S.S.R.; Race problem studied, *Pittsburg Courier*, 3.

205. LM to JE (1932, August), Odessa, LHP.

206. Miller, L. (1932, August 13), New Russia's liberality towards Negroes is graphically described, *Pittsburgh Courier*, A3.

207. Ibid.; LM to JE (1932, August 7), LHP.

208. LM to NM (1932, August 7),Odessa, LHP; Hughes (1956), 94.

209. Miller, L. (1932, October 12), Poe once tried to snub Pushkin, great Russian author, investigator reveals, *Atlanta Daily World*, 6A.

210. LM to NM (1932, August), Odessa, LHP.

211. Miller, Poe, *Atlanta Daily World*.

212. Ibid.; Hughes (1956); LM to JE (1932, August), Odessa, LHP.

213. LM to JE (1932, August 16), LHP. The term "dicty" supposedly is taken from a 1927 black silent film meaning a con man. However, as Miller uses it, the term implies a snobbish intellectual. In general, "dicty" is a term for acting white.

214. LM to NM (1932, August), Odessa, LHP.

215. Ibid.

216. Ibid.

217. To publish works of Negro poets in Russia (1932, August 13), *Pittsburgh Courier*, A3. It is likely that Miller wrote this article.

218. Berry (1992), 163.

219. Smith (1964), 28.

220. Rampersad (1986), 249

221. Ibid.

222. Hauke (1998), 50.

223. Ibid.

224. Hughes (1956), 94.

225. LM to JE (1932, August), Odessa, LHP.

226. LM to JE (n.d.), North Caucasus, LHP.

227. A.N.P. correspondent writes for Soviet books (1932, December 3), *Pittsburgh Courier*, A10.

228. Berry (1992), 162.

229. LM to JE (1932, August) Odessa, LHP.

230. LM to JE (1932, August 8 and 11), LHP; LM to JE (1932, August), Odessa, LHP; Rampersad (1986), 249.

231. LM to JE (1932, August 16), Odessa, LHP.

232. Sleeping car officials pay visit to west (1932, August 27), *Baltimore Afro-American*, 18; Ross, A. (1932, July 30), San Diego, Calif., *Chicago Defender*, 11.

233. LM to JE (1932, August 16), Odessa, LHP.

234. Henry Moon, interview by Hauke (1982, July 15), in Hauke (1998), 217n62. In the interview, Moon discussed how he revised his original version announcing the film's cancellation.

235. *Paris Herald-Tribune* (1932, August 12).

236. Hughes (1956), 95.

237. Ibid.

238. Rampersad (1986), 249.

239. Film cancellation, LMP.

240. Hughes (1956), 96.

241. Ibid.

242. Berry (1992), 157.

243. Page, M. (1932, September 8), Langston Hughes spikes lies on Negro film, *Daily Worker*, 3.

244. Unsigned film statement, LMP; Rampersad (1986), 424n.

245. Rampersad (1986), 249.

246. Film statement signed by Moon, Poston, Lewis, Alberga, LMP.

247. Patterson (1995).

248. Film cancellation, LMP.

249. Hughes (1956), 98; quote from Rampersad (1986), 250; Hauke (1998), 54.

250. Negroes rebuke Soviet for order to drop film plan (1932, August), *Paris Herald-Tribune*; Poston, T., & Moon, H. (1932, October 5), Amsterdam news reporters tell why Soviet Russia dropped film, *New York Amsterdam News*, 1.

251. The fifteen signers were Louise Thompson, Matt Crawford, Mildred Jones, Dorothy West, Constance White, Sylvia Garner, Lloyd Patterson, Frank Montero, Langston Hughes, Juanita Lewis, Loren Miller, Alan McKenzie, Homer Smith, Wayland Rudd, and Mollie Lewis, LMP.

252. Poston & Moon (1932, October 5).

253. Thompson (1933).

254. Hughes (1956), 98.

255. Unsigned film statement, LMP.

256. Ibid.

257. Fifteen signers, LMP.

258. LM to JE (n.d.), North Caucasus, LHP.

259. "Negroes adrift in 'Uncle Tom's' Russian Cabin" (1932, August 12), *New York Herald-Tribune*.

260. LM to NM (1932, September 16), LHP.

261. Miller, L. (1932, September 22), Moving picture group in Russia is laughing at fears of U.S. Friends, *Atlanta Daily World*, 6.

262. Calvin, F. (1932, October 8), Claims Soviet betrayed race for "big money," *Pittsburgh Courier*, 4; Miller, L. (1932, October 8), On Calvin, *Pittsburgh Courier*, A2.

263. LM to JE (n.d.), from Moscow, LHP.

264. Apropos Soviet Negro film (1932, November), *New Masses*, 28.

265. Poston, T., & Moon, H. (1932, October 5), Russian Negro film is finally banned, *Atlanta Daily World*, A1; Newspaper men expose tactics of Soviet in making film (1932, October 15), *Baltimore Afro-American*; Soviets consider plan to harness Dnieper (1926, October 29), *New York Times*, 21.

266. Smith (1964), 29.

267. Carew, J. G. (2008). *Blacks, Reds, and Russians: Sojourners in search of the Soviet promise* (New Brunswick, NJ: Rutgers University Press), 84.

268. McClellan, W. (1993), Africans and black Americans in the comintern schools, 1925–1934, *International Journal of African Historical Studies*, 26(3): 383n49.

269. Russia completes big power project (1932, August 21), *New York Times*, F1; Soviets consider plan to harness Dnieper (1926, October 29), *New York Times*, 21.

270. Russia completes big power project (1932, August 21); Giant power plant is opened in Russia (1932, October 11), *Washington Post*, 8.

271. H. L. Cooper wants Russia recognized (1926, November 6), *New York Times*, 11.

272. Ibid.; Colonel H. L. Cooper hopeful of Russia (1926, October 2), *New York Times*, 30; Address by Litvinoff at farewell dinner here (1933, November 25), *New York Times*, 3. In 1933, in honor of renewed diplomatic relations between the United States and the

U.S.S.R., and to honor Maxim M. Litvinov, the Soviet commissar for foreign affairs, who negotiated the terms, Colonel Cooper, as president of the Russian-American Chamber of Commerce, hosted a dinner—attended by 1,500 dignitaries—at the Waldorf Astoria in Litvinov's honor.

273. Declassified file 861.5017 (No. 928), NARA (College Park, MD), RG 59, Central Decimal File, 1930–39.

274. Gilmore (2008), 146.

275. Hughes (1956), 98.

276. El-Hai (1991).

277. Rampersad (1986), 251.

278. Poston & Moon (1932, October 5).

279. LH to Van Vechten, November 15, 1932, LHYP; LM to JE (1932, September 4), LHP; LM to JE (1932, n.d.), North Caucasus; Hughes (1956), 104. Miller lists twelve traveling to central Asia: himself, Hughes, Thompson, Crawford, McKenzie, Jones, White, Mollie Lewis, West, Jenkins, Sample, and Juanita Lewis.

280. LH to JE (1932, September 21), LHP.

281. Page, M. (1932, October 15), Negro film group visits Tashkent region USSR; to study free life of people, *Daily Worker*, 3; Members of the group who would remain when the others returned to the states were Langston Hughes, Homer Smith, Wayland Rudd, Mildred Jones, Dorothy West, Lloyd Patterson, and Alan McKenzie.

282. Hall, C. (1932, October 5), U.S. actors in Russia "throw up sponge"; return to America, *Chicago Defender*, 2; Returns scoring Soviet attitude (1932, October 5), *New York Amsterdam News*, 3; What happened during the year 1932? (1932, December 28), *New York Amsterdam News*, 7.

283. Make new plans for Soviet film (1932, October 19), *New York Amsterdam News*.

284. Ibid.; Records of the Immigration and Naturalization Passenger and Crew Lists, NARA.

285. Hughes (1956), 103.

286. LM to JE (n.d.), Somewhere-in-Asia, LHP; LH to Evelyn (Nebby) Crawford (1932, September 23), LTP.

287. Hughes (1956), 105.

288. Ibid., 255–56.

289. Miller, L. (1932, November 8), Negro experts describe Reds' experiments with cotton, *Atlanta Daily World*, 2A.

290. LM to JE (1932, October 6), LHP.

291. Hughes (1956), p.106.

292. LM to JE (1932, August), Odessa; LM to JE (1932, October 6), both in LHP.

293. Hughes (1956), 105; Rampersad (1986), 257.

294. Hughes (1956), 106.

295. Rampersad (1986), 258.

296. Hughes (1956), 107.

297. Ibid., 230.

298. Miller, L. (1932, November 9), Negro heads fire dep't in Russia, *Atlanta Daily World*, 1A.

299. LM to JE (n.d.), North Caucasus, LHP; Norman Macleod to LM (1933, January 1), LMP; LH to LM (1933, March 2), LMP.

300. LM to JE (n.d.), North Caucasus, LHP.

301. Ibid.

302. Ibid.

303. Ibid.

304. West, D. (1995), An adventure in Moscow, in D. West (Ed.), *The richer, the poorer: Stories, sketches, and reminiscences* (New York: Anchor Books), 206.

305. Christopher, M. (1934, March), Room in Red square, *Challenge*, 1(1): 15

306. Support new magazine (1937, July 5), *Atlanta Daily World*, 1.

307. LM to JE (n.d.), North Caucasus, LHP.

308. Miller, L. (1931, August 21), On second thought. *California Eagle*, 8.

309. LM to JE (n.d.), North Caucasus, LHP.

310. Cooke, M. (1938, August 27), Exotic Mollie Lewis weds Henry Moon, *New York Amsterdam News*, 9.

311. LM to Henry Moon (1944, December 27), LMP.

312. Hauke (1998), 218n66.

313. Williams, J. A., & Williams, L. (Eds.) (2008), *Dear Chester, Dear John: Letters between Chester Himes and John Williams* (Detroit: Wayne State University Press), 21, 204.

314. Bearden, B. (1942, March 21), New York Society: Art center's annual beaux arts ball, *Chicago Defender*, 17.

315. Himes, C. (1965), *Pinktoes* (New York: Putnam, 1965), 26.

316. LM to JE (n.d.), North Caucasus, LHP.

317. Rampersad (1986), 286. The League of Struggle for Negro Rights was organized in 1930 by the Communist Party.

318. LM to NM (1932, September 9), LHP.

319. LM to NM (1932, August), Odessa, LHP.

320. Smith, V. (1935, January 1), I am at home, *Daily Worker*.

321. LM to NM (1932, August), Odessa, LHP.

Chapter 5

1. Loren Miller (hereafter LM) to Langston Hughes (hereafter LH) (n.d., ca. fall 1932), after Baku, LHP.

2. Ibid.

3. LM to Juanita Ellsworth (hereafter JE) (n.d.), North Caucasus, LHP.

4. The Soviet Revolution, also known interchangeably as the October or Bolshevik Revolution, took place in the Julian calendar on October 25, 1917 (November 7, 1917, in the Gregorian calendar). 1,000,000 in parade in Soviet Capital (1932, November 8), *New York Times*, 25.

5. LM to Nora Miller (hereafter NM) (1932, November 18), LHP.

6. LM to NM (1932, September 16); LM to NM (1932, November 11), both in LHP.

7. LM to JE (n.d.), North Caucasus, LHP.

8. Miller, L. (1932, December 10), Negro is editor of fine German labor magazine, *Pittsburgh Courier*, 5.

9. Padmore hits Soviet again (1934, September 15), *New York Amsterdam News*, 1.

10. LM to Leon Washington (1932, November 22), LHP.

11. LM to Mrs. Ellsworth (1932, November 18), LHP; New York Passenger list.

12. LH to LM (1932, May 27 and 29), LHYP.

13. LM to LH (n.d.), from Asia, LHP.

14. LM to JE (n.d.), North Caucasus, LHP.

15. Norman Macleod to LM (1933, January 19), LMP. See also Rampersad (1986), 237–38.

16. LM to Macleod (1933, March 3), LMP.

17. Ibid.

18. Hughes, L. (1990), Cora Unashamed, in L. Hughes, *The Ways of White Folks: Stories of Langston Hughes* (New York: Vintage Classics).

19. Redding, J. (1956, December 23), *New York Herald Tribune*; LH to LM (1956, October 20), LMP.

20. Hughes (1956). Hughes mentions that Lloyd Patterson, Wayland Rudd, and Homer Smith remained in Russia when the others returned to the United States (101). Sylvia Garner is the only other member of the film group he mentions by name (70). In "Moscow and Me" (1933), Hughes lists the names of those who remained in Russia.

21. Ibid., 214.

22. U.S. Congress, *Hearings before the House Committee on Un-American Activities, Investigation of Communist activity in the San Francisco area*, December 1, 1953 (Washington: U.S. Government Printing Office), Testimony of Louis Rosser, Rosser Exhibit No. 4, *New York Herald Tribune*, June 14, 1932, retrieved from http://www.archive.org/stream/investigationofcsf195401unit/investigationofcsf195401unit_djvu.tx.

23. Ross, A. (1932, December 31), California News, *Chicago Defender*; Harden, T. G. (1932, December 24), California News, *Chicago Defender*, 18.

24. Harden, T. G. (1933, January 7), Los Angeles, *Chicago Defender*, 12.

25. Miller, L. (1933, March, unpublished), The Ellsworth-Miller Weakly Blather 1(1), LMP.

26. Rout, M. (1930, March 22), *Chicago Defender*, 19.

27. Schalk, T. (1945, September 8), Toki types, *Pittsburgh Courier*, 8; Census (1980, March 27), *Jet*.

28. Juanita Miller's 1956 resumé (Training and Experience of Juanita E. Miller), LMP. Helen Clum, District Case Supervisor California State Relief Administration to Raymond E. Nelson, Housing Manager, Los Angeles County (1940, August 8), LMP.

29. H. Miller, Jr., personal communication (2010, October 5); Juanita Miller's 1956 resumé.

30. Juanita Miller's 1956 resumé.

31. Banquet hall decorated for newlyweds (1933, March 18), *Chicago Defender*, 6.

32. Ibid.; Hardon, T. G. (1933, March 25), Los Angeles, *Chicago Defender*, 24.

33. LH to LM (1933, March 21), LHP.

34. Miller, L. (1933, March 10), To my brother dying in a hospital, unpublished, LMP.

35. Hardon (1933, March 25).

36. LH to LM (1933, March 21), LHP.

37. Strand, C. (1997), *Seismic monitoring and actuation*, retrieved from http://www.strandearthquake.com/sma.html; Ransome, S. (1933, March 13), Experts fixes quake source, *Los Angeles Times*, 4; Southern California Earthquake Data Center (2013, Janu-

ary 31), *Long Beach earthquake*, retrieved from http://scedc.caltech.edu/significant/longbeach1933.html; Aid sum backed by Roosevelt (1933, March 16), *Los Angeles Times*, 6; Quake inquest to open today (1933, March 21), *Los Angeles Times*, A1.

38. Last schools to reopen (1933, April 4), *Los Angeles Times*, A5; Jefferson High School Commencement Program (1926, January 27).

39. Public Broadcasting System (1999), *The black press: Soldiers without swords*, transcript of interview with Libby Clark, retrieved from www.pbs.org/blackpress/film/transcripts/clarke.html. Clark said the throwaway paper was called the *Central Avenue Shopper*; Loren Miller said in an interview with Lawrence de Graaf that its name was *Town Talk*. Beneath the *Sentinel*'s June 24, 1948, masthead, it states: "It was founded by Leon H. Washington Jr. as the Eastside News Shopper and developed into its present form and size"; Trailblazers of Los Angeles (2006), Los Angeles Branch of the Association for the Study of African American Life, Inc., City of Los Angeles Department of Cultural Affairs, 21.

40. Loren Miller, interview by Lawrence de Graaf (1967, March 3), 8.

41. Miller (1952, July 29), To whom it may concern, LMP; Leon Washington said to be getting better (1948, November 27), *New York Amsterdam News*, 21; LM to Thurgood Marshall (1949, February 6), LMP; Green, W. (1953, May 14), Sounding Off, *California Eagle*.

42. H. Miller, Jr., personal communication (2015, March 3).

43. Broadcast script: KFOX (1945, August 11, 10:00 A.M.), LMP.

44. LM to Thurgood Marshall (1949, February 6), LMP.

45. Washington, L. (1967, July 20), Wash's Wash—A tribute to my cousin, *Los Angeles Sentinel*, A6.

46. H. Miller, Jr., personal communication (2007, May 22); Negro publisher placed on board (1940, November 3), *Los Angeles Times*, A12; LaMar, L. F. (1941, November 9), Publisher named to housing post. *Chicago Defender*, 6.

47. Miller (1952, July 29), LMP.

48. Sentinel is antiunion, labor leaders charge (1953, June 14), *California Eagle*, 1, 3.

49. Green, W. (1953, May 14), Sounding off, *California Eagle*. Sentinel publisher, wife honored with soiree (1966, July 14), *Los Angeles Sentinel*, D3.

50. Miller in group admitted to bar (1934, June 14), *Los Angeles Sentinel*, 5.

51. Pupil sues skate rink (1934, July 19), *Los Angeles Sentinel*, 1; Paul R. Williams Project (2010), *Second Baptist Church, Los Angeles*, retrieved from http://www.paulrwilliamsproject.org/gallery/1920s-churches/.

52. Pupil sues skate rink (1934, July 19), *Los Angeles Sentinel*, 1.

53. Mack, K. (2012), *Representing the race: The creation of the civil rights lawyer* (Cambridge, MA: Harvard University Press), 196.

54. Pair seeks damages for discrimination (1936, January 30), *Los Angeles Sentinel*, p.1; Wind damages against coast eating place (1937, March 20), *Chicago Defender*, 1; Prepare evidence in Hampton case (1936, August 13), *Los Angeles Sentinel*, 1; Mystery "other woman" promises spicy developments in coast divorce case (1937, March 13), *Pittsburgh Courier*, 21.

55. Drug store loses $200 suit for bias (1935, March 14), *Los Angeles Sentinel*, 1.

56. Card of thanks (1937, February 11), *Los Angeles Sentinel*, 2.

57. Refuse collectors to fight one man trucks (1939, July 27), *Los Angeles Sentinel*, 1; George Farley receives manslaughter (1938, May 26), *Los Angeles Sentinel*, 1A.

58. Vera H. Forte delightfully entertained (1932, July 16), *Chicago Defender*, 7; Hardon, T. (1933, May 27), Los Angeles, *Chicago Defender*, 22; Greenaway-Clark, G. (1938, January 29), Los Angeles Society, *Chicago Defender*, 11.

59. Patton, B. (1935, March 2), Swanky dancing party for smart coast visitors, *Pittsburgh Courier*, 8.

60. Deltas cover angel city's social service field (1935, February 2), *Pittsburgh Courier*, 9; Los Angeles society (1927, June 11), *Pittsburgh Courier*, 6; De Amicus Puellas (1933, May 20), *Chicago Defender*, 7; Lovely Mrs. Loren Miller fetes her bridge club (1933, October 28), *Chicago Defender*, 6; Greenaway-Clark, G. (1938, December 31), Los Angeles Society, *Chicago Defender*, 13; Brown, J. M. (1980), Your social chronicler, *Los Angeles Sentinel*, C2; League of Allied Arts Program brochure: A Langston Hughes Salon (2007, April 22); Ivan Johnson, Loren Miller associate in law practice (1936, September 3), *Los Angeles Sentinel*, 1; Club Corner (February 20, 1947), *Los Angeles Sentinel*, 17.

61. Greenaway-Clark (1938, December 31).

62. Kurashige, S. (2008), *The shifting grounds of race: Black and Japanese Americans in the making of multiethnic Los Angeles* (New Jersey: Princeton University Press), 77.

63. Miller, L. (circa 1933), "Unto You," unpublished manuscript, 33, LMP.

64. Juanita Miller's 1956 resumé.

65. Greenaway-Clark, G. (1938, May 7), *Chicago Defender*, 15.

66. Delta Sigma Theta tells plans for education week (1945, May 19), *Pittsburgh Courier*, 11.

67. Ben Davis to LM (1934, January 3), LMP. In June 1934, the *Harlem Liberator* changed its name to the *Negro Liberator*.

68. Ben Davis to LM (1934, October 8), LMP.

69. Ben Davis to LM (1934, November 4); Maude White to LM (1933, December 22). See also Elizabeth Lawson to LM (1934, December 22); Ben Davis to LM (1934, October 8), all in LMP. Both Ben Davis and Elizabeth Lawson would repeatedly ask Miller to stay within the five-hundred-word guidelines.

70. Elizabeth Lawson to LM (1934, November 27), LMP.

71. Elizabeth Lawson to LM (1934, December 8), LMP.

72. Ibid.

73. Ben Davis to LM (1935, January 21), LMP.

74. Ben Davis to LM (1935, February 1), LMP.

75. LM to Ben Davis (n.d.), LMP.

76. Hawkins defeats Roberts by 1,500 (1934, November 8), *Los Angeles Sentinel*, 1.

77. Law maker (1934, December 1), *Chicago Defender*, 2; Kurashige (2008), 93; Liberian future to be discussed (June 21, 1934), *Los Angeles Sentinel*, 1.

78. Miller, L. (1934, October 22), Sinclair is big puzzle of today, *Atlantic Daily World*, 1.

79. Miller, L. (1934, December 15), Preacher sues Upton Sinclair, *Pittsburgh Courier*, 4.

80. Sinclair retracts statement about Negro ministers in letter sent to Nation (1935, January 26), *Atlanta Daily World*, 1.

81. Juanita Miller's 1956 resumé. Juanita Miller new welfare administrator (n.d., publication unknown), LMP.

82. Heads news agency (1936, February 15), *New York Amsterdam News*, 17.

83. Davenport, T. (Ed.) (2007), Cyril Briggs to Theodore Draper (1958, March 17), retrieved from http://www.marxisthistory.org/history/usa/groups/abb/1958/0317-briggs -todraper.pdf.

84. Horne, G. (1994), *Black liberation/red scare: Ben Davis and the Communist Party* (Newark: University of Delaware Press), 45.

85. LM to Juanita Miller (hereafter JM) (1935, May 27), LMP.

86. LM to JM (1935, June 15), LMP.

87. Jackson, M. (1935, May 11), Topical types in filmland, *Baltimore Afro-American*, 8; Cairns, K. (2007), *Fay Jackson (1902–1988)*, retrieved from http://www.blackpast.org/aaw/jackson-fay-1902-1988.

88. Hughes-Watkins, L. (2008), *Fay M. Jackson: The Sociopolitical narrative of a pioneering African American female journalist* (Unpublished masters thesis, Youngstown State University), 12. Jackson's newsweekly, Flash, lasted two years, from 1928 to 1930.

89. Moore, L. (2010, November), Show time, *Smithsonian Magazine*, 72.

90. Burroughs, N. H. (1935, April 13), Declaration of 1776 is cause of Harlem riot: Nannie Burroughs compares smashing and pillaging of New York stores to Boston tea party, *Baltimore Afro-American*, 12.

91. Miller, L. (1935, August), Harlem without make-up, *New Masses*.

92. Ibid.

93. Naison, M. (1983), *Communists in Harlem during the Depression* (New York: Grove), 147; Toney's removal from commission sought in Harlem (1935, July 6), *Baltimore Afro-American*, 16.

94. LM to JM (1935, June 15), LMP.

95. Miller (1935, August), Harlem without make-up.

96. LM to JM (1935, June 15), LMP.

97. Editorial (1935, December 19), *Los Angeles Sentinel*, 1; Naison (1983), 78; Dr. Vincent exposes Harlem Hospital conditions; Resigns: Reveals Jim Crow policy of its heads, *Chicago Defender*, 1; Doctors launch attack on Harlem Hospital (1932, December 31), *Chicago Defender*, 1.

98. To study Soviet Russia (1935, April 27), *Chicago Defender*, 3; January 1934, letterhead League of Struggle for Negro Rights.

99. Miller, L. (1935, April 16), Mail-Order; Eugene Gordon to LM (1935, February 4).

100. Miller, L. (1935, August 24), The crisis in the socialist party, *New Masses*; Miller, L. (1935, July 16), The screen: No "escape" for Negro artists, *New Masses*, 29–30.

101. Miller, L. (1935, September 9), Last in peace, last in war, *New Masses*, 16–18.

102. LM to JM (1935, July 1), LMP.

103. LM to JM (1935, June 15); LM to JM (1935, June 8), LMP.

104. LM to JM (1935, October 17), LMP.

105. Miller is listed on the Crusader News Agency masthead as assistant editor from March 1935 to February 1938. Benjamin Davis, Jr., to LM (1935, July 3), LMP; Charles Angoff, editor of the *American Spectator*, to LM (1935, September 19), LMP.

106. New magazine will be published in N.Y. (1935, October 26), *Baltimore Afro-American*, 12.

107. Miller, L. (1935, October 5), Was F. D. talking through his hat when he lamented Long's death?, *Baltimore Afro-American*, 10.

108. Miller, L. (1935, August 3), Hectic Harlem, *New York Amsterdam News*, 11.

109. Miller (1935, August), Harlem without make-up; Miller (1935, August 3), Hectic Harlem.

110. Ben Davis to LM (1935, July 3), LMP.

111. Miller, L. (1935, July 27), Wilkins is all wet on his inferiority theory, *Baltimore Afro-American*, 12.

112. Ibid.

113. Miller, L. (1935, July 16), How "Left" is the NAACP?, *New Masses*, 12–13.

114. Ibid.

115. "Two-Girl war" on NAACP may cause swing to left (1935, June 29), *Baltimore Afro-American*, 2. Incidentally, this author's granduncle, Jesse Ball (Moore), was one of the thirteen soldiers court-martialed and hung.

116. McNeil, G. R. (1983), *Groundwork: Charles Hamilton Houston and the struggle for civil rights* (Philadelphia: University of Pennsylvania Press), 102.

117. Ibid.

118. LM to JM (1935, July 1), LMP.

119. LM to JM (1935, June 15), LMP.

120. LM to JM (1935, September 8), LMP.

121. LM to JM (1935, October 17), LMP.

122. LM to JM (1935, October 6), LMP.

123. Social workers' conference to open Thursday: Weaver will address body (1935, June 8), *New York Amsterdam News*, 2.

124. Granger, L. (1953, May 16), Manhattan and beyond, *New York Amsterdam News*, 16.

125. LM to JM (1935, June 10), LMP.

126. Ibid.

127. Cooke, M. (1935, June 8), Rockland is packed but show's just so, *New York Amsterdam News*, 6.

128. LM to JM (1935, October 8), LMP. The Girl Friends, an African American elite social club, was established in 1927 in New York.

129. LM to JM (1935, October 17), LMP.

130. LM to JM (1935, September 8), LMP.

131. LM to JM (1935, October 6), LM.

132. LM to JM (1935, October 30), LMP.

133. LM to JM (1935, November 4), LMP.

134. LM to JM (1935, October 30), LMP.

135. LM to JM (1935, October 17), LMP.

136. LM to JM (1935, October 30), LMP.

137. LM to JM (1935, October 8), LMP.

138. N.Y. newspaper discharges all of its writers (1935, October 19), *Chicago Defender*, 5.

139. Sympathizers support ousted newspaper men (1935, November 16), *Chicago Defender*, 5.

140. LM to JM (1935, October 30), LMP.

141. Ibid.

142. LM to JM (1935, October 17), LMP.

143. Ibid.

144. LM to JM (1935, October 30), LMP.

145. Amsterdam News is sold; strikers back (1936, January 4), *Chicago Defender*, 4.

146. LM to JM (1935, October 6), LMP.

147. Miller, L. (1935, November 5), The theater, *New Masses*, 29–30.

148. Menand, L. (2011, September 5), Browbeaten, *New Yorker*, 72.

149. Loren Miller, interview by Lawrence de Graaf (1967, March 3), 10.

150. LM to LH (n.d.), LMP.

151. LM to JM (1935, October 6), LMP.

152. Burgchardt, C. R. (1980, December). Two faces of American Communism: Pamphlet rhetoric of the third period and the popular front, *Quarterly Journal of Speech*, 66(4): 375–91.

153. LM to JM (1935, October 6), LMP.

154. LM to JM (1935, October 10), LMP.

155. LM to JM (1935, October 17), LMP.

156. LM to JM (1935, November 4), LMP.

157. Ibid.

158. LM to JM (1935, October 17), LMP.

159. LM to JM (1935, November 4), LMP.

160. LM to LH (1935, November 20), LMP.

161. J. Miller Kerina, personal communication (2006, October 18).

162. E. Miller, personal communication (2007, December 6).

163. J. Miller Kerina, personal communication (2006, October 18); H. Miller, Jr., personal communication (2010, October 6).

164. Pair seek damages for discrimination (1936, January 30), *Los Angeles Sentinel*, 1.

165. Prepare evidence in Hampton case (1936, August 13), *Los Angeles Sentinel*, 1.

166. Benny Goodman to be at dance (1936, October 10), *New York Amsterdam News*, 11.

167. IRA (1936, October 9), Pot-pie, *California Eagle*, 14.

168. In 1930, Miller was a registered Republican. Between 1932 and 1954, he registered as a Democrat; however, he is not on the Index to Register of Voters for 1936, 1938, 1940, and 1950.

169. Miller, L. (1934, July), One way out—Communism, *Opportunity*, 12 (July): 215.

170. Ibid.

171. Miller FBI File.

172. J. Miller Kerina, personal communication (2006, October 18).

173. Son born Sunday to Loren Millers (1937, March 8), *Los Angeles Sentinel*, 1.

174. Ibid.

175. Men's day at Scott Methodist (1958, October 23), *Los Angeles Sentinel*, A13; Covenant suit arguments on August 22 (1947, July 31), *Los Angeles Sentinel*, 3; Resume of annual convention of the political study club (1948, November 11), *Los Angeles Sentinel*, 9; Links demonstrate community interest with special conference meeting (1951, February 22), *Los Angeles Sentinel*, C1; NAACP plans mass meeting in Arkansas (1952, November 15), *Chicago Defender*, 6.

176. Reward for Fitts assassins planned today in hunt for gang (1937, March 9), *Los Angeles Times*, 1; Prosecutor in fighting pose (1937, March 8), *Los Angeles Times*, 1.

177. Los Angeles Almanac (1998–2014), *Frank Shaw—First U.S. mayor successfully recalled from office*, retrieved from http://www.Laalmanac.com/history/hio6f.htm.

178. Clinton bomb case studied (1937, October 30), *Los Angeles Times*, A1; Clinton bombers elude police net (1937, October 31), *Los Angeles Times*, 3.

179. Frank L. Shaw served as mayor of Los Angeles from July 1, 1933, to September 26, 1938. He was replaced by Fletcher Bowron, who served from September 26, 1938, to July 1, 1953.

180. Wins damages against coast eating place (1937, March 20), *Chicago Defender*, 1.

181. Loren Miller to speak (1937, March 25), *Los Angeles Sentinel*, 9; Clubs invited to opening of new center (1939, August 3), *Los Angeles Sentinel*, 6; Thru Hollywood (1937, April 3), *Chicago Defender*, 20.

182. Loren Miller, interview by Lawrence de Graaf (1967, March 3), pt. 1, 10.

183. LM to Lester Granger (1955, November 30), LMP and LGP.

184. Singh, N. P. (2005), *Black is a country: Race and the unfinished struggle for democracy* (Cambridge, MA: Harvard University Press), 11.

185. *Communist Party v. Peek*, 20 Cal.2d 536, 127 P.2d 889 (1942).

186. Mack (2012), 199.

187. Smith (2007), 235.

188. Evangelist Aimee ruins Langston Hughes' lunch (1940, November 30), *Chicago Defender*, 2.

189. Ibid.

190. Langston Hughes, FBI File, No. 108–1960, U.S. Department of Justice; Report of February 5, 1941, includes flier "Attention Christians!!"

191. Fingerprinting of aliens termed unconstitutional: Civil liberties union spokesman protests (1940, June 12), *Los Angeles Times*, 7.

192. Alien registration (1940, June 6), *Los Angeles Times*, A4.

193. Alien registry foes scored (1940, June 7), *Los Angeles Times*, 7.

194. Ibid.

195. Alien registration (1940, June 6), *Los Angeles Times*, A4.

196. Kurashige (2008), 97.

197. Editorial, Democracy in peril (1940, August 15), *Los Angeles Sentinel*, 1.

198. Councilmen rant against Japanese home buyers (1940, August 15), *Los Angeles Sentinel*, 1.

199. Editorial (1940, August 15), *Los Angeles Sentinel*, 1.

200. Tajiri, L. (1944, winter). Farewell to little Tokyo, *Pacific Citizen*.

201. Kurashige (2008), 91.

202. Democracy in peril (1940, August 15), *Los Angeles Sentinel*, 1.

203. Kurashige (2008), 98.

204. Harrison, S. (2012, February 14), *Framework: Alien registration act of 1940*, retrieved from http://framework.latimes.com/2012/02/14/alien-registration-act-of-1940/.

205. Kurashige (2008), 99.

206. Constable, P. (2012, March 14), For Japanese Americans WWII leaves a mixed legacy, *Washington Post*, H15.

207. E. Miller, personal communication (2007, December 6).

208. Irons, P. (1983), *Justice at war. The story of the Japanese American internment cases* (Berkeley: University of California Press), ix.

209. Ibid., 130.

210. Ibid., ix.

211. Brilliant, M. (2010), *The color of America has changed* (New York: Oxford University Press), 31.

212. Kurashige (2008), 127.

213. A. L. Wirin on Loren Miller (n.d.), eulogy, LMP.

214. Hurewitz, D. (2007), *Bohemian Los Angeles and the making of modern politics* (Berkeley: University of California Press), 24.

215. E. Miller, personal communication (2007, December 6).

216. Index to Register of Voters, Los Angeles City, 1928, 1942–1954. It is unclear why James and Helen Garrott used 1808 W. 36th for their voting address unless they preferred voting in a different precinct from that of James Garrott's mother and brother, who lived at 653 Micheltorena. E. Miller, personal communication (2007, December 6).

217. Committee to Save Silver Lake's Reservoir (2000, October 22); Banquet hall decorated for newlyweds (1933, March 18), *Chicago Defender*, 6; 200 petition school board on behalf of our teachers (1934, September 13), *Los Angeles Sentinel*, 1; Henderson, W. H. (2004), James Homer Garrott, in D. S. Wilson (Ed.), *African American architects: A biographical dictionary, 1865–1945* (New York: Routledge), 165–66; *Negro who's who in California* (1948) (California Eagle Publishing Company), 84; Negro architect to build Calif sheriff station (1953, November 12), *Jet*, 49. Miller was occasional legal counsel for Golden State Mutual Insurance Company, according to Halvor Miller, Jr.

218. Nichols, C. H. (1990), *Arna Bontemps—Langston Hughes Letters, 1925–1967* (New York: Paragon House).

219. Ibid., 91.

220. LH to Maurice Murphy (1941, October 11), LMP.

221. LH to LM (1941, October 11), LMP.

222. Rampersad (1986), 385.

Chapter 6

1. Man will bite dog if former is famous (1943, May 1), *Chicago Defender*, 19; Sugar Hill residents battle to keep homes (1943, March 24), *California Eagle*, front page; Coast whites move to oust movie stars (1943, March 27), *Baltimore Afro-American*, 24.

2. On May 24, 1945, Miller and Jones responded to *Anderson v. Auseth et al.* (No. 484808); Attorneys for the defense were Miller, Jones, Willis Tyler, George Cryer, Hugh MacBeth, Clore Warne, and Louis M. Brown of Pacht, Pelton, Warne, Ross and Bernhard, who represented Hattie McDaniel Crawford and her husband, James Lloyd Crawford. In time, Miller would become lead attorney in *Anderson v. Auseth et al.*, representing all the defendants, including Earl and Helen Auseth, Hattie McDaniel, Ethel Burke Waters, Juan Tizol, Hallie D. Johnson, Arthur Twyne, Russell T. Smith, Omelia Crawford, Truman R. Lott, Sidney Dones, Sydnetta Dones Smith, and others. Attorneys for the plaintiffs were represented by Joseph Guerin, Kenneth Kearney, and Alfred MacDonald; According to Gunnar Myrdal's 1944 *An American Dilemma: The Negro Problem and Modern Democracy*, neighborhood associations served as "organized extra-legal agencies to keep Negro and white residences separated" (624).

3. Weaver, R. (1945), *Hemmed in: The ABC's of race restrictive housing covenants* (Chicago: American Council on Race Relations).

4. Lamar, L. (1944, October 7), Film stars face eviction from West Coast homes, *Chicago Defender*, 1; Watts, J. (2005), *Hattie McDaniel: Black ambition, white Hollywood* (New York: Amistad).

5. Bogle, D. (2005), *Bright boulevards, bold dreams: The story of black Hollywood* (New York: One World Ballantine Books), 259.

6. Kurashige (2008), 61.

7. Watts (2005), 238.

8. Walter White to Thurgood Marshall (hereafter TM) (1944, October 5), NAACP Papers, pt. 17, National Staff Files, 1940–1955, LOC.

9. *Anderson v. Auseth.*

10. Race zoning case in supreme court (1946, March 10), *Los Angeles Times*, A3.

11. Victory on Sugar Hill (1945, December 17), *Time.*

12. Hughes, L. (1946, January 26), Here to yonder, *Chicago Defender*, 14.

13. Harold Lloyd heads anti-Negro drive (1945, July 28), *Chicago Defender*, 1; according to Gunnar Myrdal's 1944 *An American Dilemma*, there are three main factors determining residential concentration: poverty, ethnic attachment, and "segregation enforced by white people," 619; Bengston, J. (2012, February 29), *How Harold Lloyd filmed the* Safety Last! *finale (at three places)*, retrieved from http://silentlocations.wordpress.com/2012/02/29/how-harold-lloyd-filmed-safety-last.

14. To air ouster move in court (1941, May 31), *New York Amsterdam News*, 21.

15. Whites protest brother of Hattie McDaniel as neighbor (1941, May 31), *Chicago Defender*, 20.

16. Ibid.

17. Ibid.; Watts (2005), 237; Postpone restrictive covenant court case (1941, June 14), *Chicago Defender*, 3.

18. To air ouster move in court (1941, May 31), 21.

19. Whites protest (1941, May 31), 20.

20. Restrictive covenant thrown out of California court by judge (1943, September 11), *Chicago Defender*, 2.

21. Arellano, G. (2010, May 6), Mi casa es mi casa, retrieved from http://www.ocweekly.com/2010-05-06/news/alex-bernal-housing-discrimination/.

22. Restrictive covenant thrown out (1943, September 11), 2. *Doss v. Bernal* was not the first case where a school district was sued for racial discrimination. In 1934, attorney, Thomas Griffith, Jr., president of the Los Angeles chapter of the NAACP, sued the Monrovia school district, claiming that it had "no right to subdivide it into subdistricts and then penalize those who refuse to send their children to one of the so-called subdistricts." Miller, L. (1934, December 18), Coast Negroes battle segregation in school, *New York Amsterdam News*, 2.

23. Dismiss charges against 2 in Maywood bias case (1942, May 14), *California Eagle*, 3B.

24. Murray, P. (1987), *Song in a weary throat: An American pilgrimage* (New York: Harper and Row), 253.

25. Mack (2012), 205; Murray (1987), 253.

26. Murray (1987), 253.

27. Ibid., 181.

28. Documenting the American South (2004), P. Murray, interview by G. R. McNeil (1976, February 13), interview G-0044, retrieved from Southern Oral History Program Collection (#4007), http://docsouth.unc.edu/sohp/G-0044/G-0044.html.

29. Murray, P. (1944, September 2), Pauli Murray will not move, *Baltimore Afro-American*, 13.

30. Miller urges Kenny support for state senator (1950, May 18), *Los Angeles Sentinel*, B4.

31. Abdullah, M., & Freer, R. (2010), Bass to Bass: Relative freedom and womanist leadership in Black Los Angeles, in D. Hunt & A. Ramón (Eds.), *Black Los Angeles: American dreams and racial realities* (New York: New York University Press), 328.

32. Myrdal, G. (1944) 1996, *An American dilemma: The Negro problem and modern democracy* (New York: Harper), 618.

33. Ibid., 619; see also Sugrue, T. J. (2008), *Sweet land of liberty: The forgotten struggle for civil rights in the north* (New York: Random House), 201–202.

34. Miller, L. (1966), *The Petitioners: The story of the Supreme Court of the United States and the Negro* (New York: Meridian Books), 321.

35. McWilliams, C. (1999), *California: The great exception* (Berkeley: University of California Press), 8.

36. Miller, L. (1946, May), Covenants in the bear flag state, *Crisis*, 140.

37. Miller, L., & Sheil, B. (1946), *Racial restrictive covenants* (Chicago: Chicago Council Against Racial and Religious Discrimination), 5.

38. Ibid., 6.

39. Miller (1966), 246; see also Streator, G. (1947, June 26), Housing problem called "explosive," *New York Times*, 18.

40. McWilliams, C. (2001), The long-suffering Chinese, in *Fool's Paradise: A Carey McWilliams reader* (Santa Clara, CA: Heyday Books), 91.

41. Modern American Poetry (1997), *About Angel Island*, retrieved from http://www .english.illinois.edu/maps/poets/a_f/angel/about.htm (March 24, 2015); Gold, S. (2006), *Korematsu v. United States: Japanese-American internment* (New York: Marshall Cavendish Benchmark); Maryland State Archives (2005), *The Chinese Exclusion Act*, retrieved from http://teaching.msa.maryland.gov/000001/000000/000136/html/t136.html (March 24, 2015).

42. McWilliams (1943).

43. McWilliams (1999), 141.

44. Opinion of U.S. Supreme Court on California Alien Land Law (1948, January 24), *Los Angeles Daily Journal*.

45. de Graaf, L. (2007), Changing face and place: Race in Los Angeles City government, in H. L. Rudd. (Ed.), *The development of Los Angeles city government: An institutional history, 1850–2000* (Los Angeles: Los Angeles City Historical Society), 745.

46. Modern American Poety (1997), *About Angel Island*, retrieved from http://www .english.illinois.edu/maps/poets/a_f/angel/about.htm (March 24, 2015).

47. Miller (1966), 246.

48. *In re Lee Sing*, 43 Fed. 259; McWilliams (1943), 87.

49. Miller (1966), 246.

50. Miller (1946, May), Covenants in the bear flag state, 138.

51. *Gandolfo v. Hartman* (1892), 16 LRA 277, 49 Fed. 181.

52. Miller (1946, May), Covenants in the bear flag state; Miller (1947, October), Covenants for Exclusion, *Survey Graphic*; *Gandolfo v. Hartman* (1892).

53. Miller (1946, May), Covenants for exclusion, 541; *Gandolfo v. Hartman* (1892).

54. Miller & Sheil (1946), 6.

55. Miller (1946, May), Covenants in the bear flag state, 140.

56. Miller (1946, May), Covenants for exclusion, 542.

57. Miller & Sheil (1946), 6. The treaty guaranteed those living in the newly annexed territory the right of citizenship, which brought along with it the privileges of whiteness. Soon after, those guarantees were racialized. Over the years, the court—e.g. *In re Rodriquez*, 1897—debated whether Mexicans are white. While many Mexicans are considered white, most are considered Indian; according to Mike Davis (2006) in *City of Quartz* (New York: Verso), when a single black Los Angeles family moved in east of Budlong Avenue in 1922, whites immediately formed the Anti-African Housing Association and campaigned "for a restrictive agreement to exclude non-whites (Japanese as well as Blacks) from the neighborhood," 162.

58. Miller, L. (1948, September), Supreme Court: Covenant decision—An analysis, *Crisis*, 266.

59. Miller (1944) 1996, 246. According to Gunnar Myrdal, *American dilemma*, the earliest legal enforcement of covenants occurred in 1910, in Baltimore, Maryland, following the moving in of a black family (623–24).

60. Miller (1966), 248.

61. Ibid.

62. von Hoffman, A. (1998, August), *Like fleas on a Tiger? A brief history of the Open Housing Movement* (Cambridge, MA: Joint Center for Housing Studies of Harvard University), 6.

63. *Buchanan v. Warley*, 245 U.S. 60 (1917).

64. Miller (1966), 250–51.

65. von Hoffman (1998, August), 6.

66. Miller (1966), 252.

67. Vose, C. (1959), *Caucasians only: The Supreme Court, the NAACP, and the restrictive covenant cases* (Berkeley: University of California Press), 52.

68. *Corrigan v. Buckley*, 271 U.S. 323 (1926), decided May 24, 1926; Vose (1959), 17–18.

69. Miller (1966), 253, 254.

70. Miller (1946, May), Covenants for exclusion, 542.

71. Miller (1966), 244.

72. Ibid., 323.

73. Vose (1959), 53.

74. Miller (1966), 322.

75. Meier, A., & Rudwick, E. (1976, March), Attorneys black and white: A case study of race relations within the NAACP, *Journal of American History*, 62(4): 930.

76. Wynn, J. A., & Mazur, E. P. (2004), "Grounds to stand on: Charles Hamilton Houston's legal foundation for Dr. King," *North Carolina State Bar Journal* (Spring): 8, retrieved from http://www.ncbar.com/journal/archive/journal_9,1.pdf.

77. McWilliams, C. (1949, March), The evolution of Sugar Hill, *Script*, 24; U.N. cited by negroes in appeal for homes (1964, October 3), *New York Times*, 38.

78. Electric Railway Historical Association of Southern California, *Henry E. Huntington*, retrieved from http://www.erha.org/henrhunt.htm.

79. McWilliams, C. (1979), *The education of Carey McWilliams* (New York: Simon and Schuster), 323; McWilliams (1949, March), 24.

80. McWilliams (1949, March), 25.

81. Moss, R. (Fall 1996), Not quite paradise: The development of the African American community in Los Angeles through 1950, *California History*, 234.

82. McWilliams (1949, March), 26.

83. Sugar Hill defendants' generosity to GIs told (1945, December 10), *Los Angeles Tribune*, front page.

84. Hopper, H. (1947, December 14), Screen and stage, *Los Angeles Times*, H3.

85. Sides, J. (2004), *L.A. city limits: African American Los Angeles from the Great Depression to the present* (Berkeley: University of California Press), 98.

86. *Anderson v. Auseth*; according to the 1941 city directory of Los Angeles, Hattie McDaniel lived at 2177 W. 31st Street and Louise Beavers lived at 2130 W. 29th Street before the two moved to the West Adams district.

87. *Anderson v. Auseth*; Graham, L. O. (2000), *Our kind of people: Inside America's Black upper class* (New York: Harper Perennial), 363.

88. Graham (2000), 363.

89. Stars aid IFRG in fight for international unity in films (1945, April 21), *Chicago Defender*, 17.

90. McWilliams (1949, March), 28.

91. Ibid., 29.

92. Ibid.

93. *Anderson v. Auseth*; Miller (1966), 323.

94. *Anderson v. Auseth*. Hattie McDaniel Crawford was originally represented by Louis M. Brown and Clore Warne of Pacht, Pelton, Warne, Ross and Bernhard (May, 1945, 500–057). The following cases—500–054; 500–055; 500–056; 500–057; 500–058; 503–450; and 503–976—were consolidated into *L.A. Sup Ct case 484–808* with Miller as lead defense counsel of fifty-one defendants. One Korean family is among the defendants. See Court battle looms (1945, December 1), *Pittsburgh Courier*, 4. On May 1, 1943, the case began; the preliminary trial was held on December 5, 1945, with Judge Thurmond Clarke presiding; the plaintiffs appealed to the Supreme Court of California in 1946; however, the decision was set aside along with many other covenant cases in anticipation of the decision by the U.S. Supreme Court in *Shelley v. Kraemer*.

95. Watts (2005), 236.

96. Hattie to sing "ice cold Katie" (1943, March 22), *Baltimore Afro-American*, 2; Sam McDaniel, retrieved from http://www.movie2.nytimes.com; Red Hot Jazz Archive, *Hattie McDaniel*, retrieved from http://www.redhotjazz.com/hattiemcd.html.

97. *New York Times Online*, Movies & TV, "Sam McDaniel," retrieved from http://www.nytimes.com/movies/person/47223/Sam-McDaniel (March 24, 2015).

98. Rasmussen, C. (2000, December 3), L.A. then and now; a life that defied racial stereotypes, *Los Angeles Times*, B3.

99. Dove, R. (2004), *American Smooth* (New York: Norton), 92–94.

100. Ibid.

101. Rasmussen (2000, December 3).

102. Schallert, E. (1940, May 1), Cocoanut Grove throngs give stars gay ovation, *Los Angeles Times*, A.

103. Hedda Hopper's Hollywood (1940, March 4), *Los Angeles Times*, 22.

104. Thomas, T. L. (1945, February 24), Assails Uncle Tom in movies, *Chicago Defender*, 10.

105. Hughes, L. (1943, March 13), Here to yonder, *Chicago Defender*, 14. In his *I Wonder as I Wander*, Hughes states that by 1932 he had "never been offered" a job in Hollywood

(65). However, according to Loren Miller's letter of October 6, 1935, to his wife Juanita, Hollywood had offered Hughes a job, but, Miller explained, "he doesn't know exactly what there is to it."

106. Rampersad (1986), 368.

107. Miller, L. (1934, November), Uncle Tom in Hollywood, *Crisis*, 329, 336.

108. Jones, R. (1947, August), How Hollywood feels about Negroes, *Negro Digest*.

109. Miller (1934, November), 448, 450.

110. Ibid.

111. Miller, L. (1938, February), The Negro market, *Opportunity*, 38.

112. Hughes, L. (1943, May 27), Here to yonder, *Chicago Defender*, 14.

113. Smith, W. T. (n.d.), The Negro in Hollywood (unpublished essay), folder 32, box 1, Los Angeles Urban League Records (Collection 203), Department of Special Collections, Charles E. Young Library. University of California, Los Angeles.

114. Hughes (1943, May 27); Stine, W., & Davis, B. (1974), *Mother Goddam: The story of the career of Bette Davis* (New York: Hawthorne Books).

115. McWilliams (1949, March), 30; Court battle looms (1945, December 1), *Pittsburgh Courier*, 4; Snelson, F. G. (1944, October 7), This is Hollywood, *Chicago Defender*, 16.

116. Vose (1959), 59.

117. Loren Miller (hereafter LM) to Rachel B. Noel (1945, June 2), Fisk University, Social Science Institute, LMP. In 1965, Noel became the first African American woman elected to public office in Colorado.

118. McWilliams, C. (1945, November), Critical summary, *Journal of Educational Sociology*, 19(3): 196.

119. Predicts covenant breakdown in Los Angeles (1946, February 23), *Chicago Defender*, 13

120. Celebrities in spotlight as "Sugar Hill" trial begins (1945, December 5), *California Eagle*, 4.

121. Negro owners win contest on occupancy (1945, December 7), *Los Angeles Times*, A1.

122. LM to Louise Cooper (1945, December 12), LMP.

123. McWilliams (1949, March), 30.

124. Sugar Hill victory sets U.S. precedent (1945, December 10), *Los Angeles Tribune*, front page.

125. McWilliams (1949, March), 30; Sugar Hill victory sets U.S. precedent (1945, December 10).

126. Negro owners win contest on occupancy (1945, December 7), *Los Angeles Times*, A1.

127. Sugar Hill victory sets U.S. precedent (1945, December 10).

128. Good neighbors, California judge knocks out race restrictive covenants as unconstitutional (1946, January), *Architectural Forum*.

129. Jackson, C. (1990), *Hattie: The life of Hattie McDaniel* (Lanham, MD: Madison Books), 91.

130. Negro owners win contest on occupancy (1945, December 7); Sugar Hill victory sets U.S. precedent (1945, December 10).

131. LM to TM (1945, December 6), LMP.

132. TM to LM (1945, December 11), LMP.

133. LM to TM (1946, February 16), LMP.

134. TM to LM (1946, March 13), LMP.

135. California Birth Index, 1905–1995, retrieved from http://search.ancestry.com; 1920 U.S. Census.

136. Hughes arrives here for Sunday lecture at L.A. City College (1946, January 3), *Los Angeles Sentinel*, 9.

137. Snelson, F. G. (1946, January 19), This is Hollywood, *Chicago Defender*, 17.

138. Hughes (1946).

139. Mack (2012).

140. A. L. Wirin to LM (1945, December 10), LMP.

141. Scovel Richardson to LM (1945, December 18), LMP. In 1935, Charles W. Anderson became the first African American elected to the Kentucky State Legislature. Jesse S. Heslip to LM (1945, December 13), LMP. Heslip graduated from Harvard Law School in 1922. He "petitioned Congress to establish an officer training camp for African American college students during World War I. After its establishment, Heslip attended the camp before serving in the U.S. Army overseas." Heslip served on national legal committee of the NAACP. Heslip-Ruffin Family Papers, Amistad Research Center, Tulane University, New Orleans.

142. Walter White to LM (1945, December 19), LMP.

143. White, W. (1946, February 9), People, Politics and Places: Emancipation from the slums, *Chicago Defender*, 15.

144. Moreno, P. (2007, September 1), The strange career of affirmation action, *Wall Street Journal*, 7.

145. LM to Lester Granger (1945, December 18), LMP. The *New York Times* (1945, December 1) reported that after attending the annual National Bar Association conference in Cleveland, where he was elected vice president, Miller stopped in New York to discuss restrictive agreements with the Urban League.

146. Hollywood executives to support better jobs policy (1942, August 29), *Chicago Defender*, 23.

147. Vaughn, S. (1992), Ronald Reagan and the struggle for black dignity in cinema, 1937–1953, *Journal of Negro History*, 77(1): 6. In spring 1942, according to Vaughn, the famous actor Franchot Tone chaired the newly formed SAG committee, which met with black members "upset by White's stand."

148. Another group speaks on the question Negroes in pictures (1942, September 19), *Chicago Defender*, 20.

149. Film stars answer charges by public protesting "Uncle Tom" roles (1942, August 29), *Chicago Defender*, 7.

150. Watkins, M. (2005), *Stepin Fetchit: The life and times of Lincoln Perry* (New York: Pantheon), 231.

151. Hollywood and Walter White (1946, February 23), *Chicago Defender*, 14.

152. Muse, C. (1940, January 27), What's going on in Hollywood, *Chicago Defender*, 21.

153. Covington, F. (1929), The Negro invades Hollywood, *Opportunity*, 7; Washburn alumni were leaders in early California civil rights movement (2007, Summer), *Washburn Alumni Magazine*, 14.

154. Hill, H. (1946, February 2), Hollywood stars rap interference, *Pittsburg Courier*, 24.

155. Celebrities flay, laud move for NAACP in Hollywood (1946, January 31), *Los Angeles Sentinel*, 5.

156. Hollywood and Walter White (1946, February 23), *Chicago Defender*, 14.

157. Muse quoted in ibid.

158. Carter quoted in Celebrities flay (1946, January 31).

159. Beaver quoted in H. Hill (1946, February 2).

160. Beaver quoted in Walter White tells plans for Hollywood bureau (1946, January 24), *Los Angeles Sentinel*, 16.

161. That Hollywood bureau (1946, January 1), *Los Angeles Sentinel*, 7.

162. Vaughn (1992), 6.

163. Hardwick, L. (1946, September 19), Special committee to meet producers, directors and writers for changed policy, *Los Angeles Sentinel*, 18.

164. Jones (1947, August), 8.

165. Riley, R. (1947, May 3), This is Hollywood, *Chicago Defender*, 18.

166. Watts (2005), 238.

167. Miller, L. (1952, November 13), *California Eagle*.

168. Undated *Los Angeles Sentinel* KFOX radio script, LMP.

169. Russell, B. (1922), *Free thought and official propaganda* (London: Watts).

170. McWilliams, C., April 3, 1944, endorsement of Loren Miller for Los Angeles's Fourteenth Congressional District, LMP.

171. "Times" recommends candidates for house (1944, May 14), *Los Angeles Times*, A2.

172. LM to Helen Gahagan Douglas (1946, October 15), LMP; Notables at Coast cocktail party (1948, October 23), *Chicago Defender*, 8.

173. LM to Henry Lee Moon (1946, October 11), LMP.

174. Attorney Miller and other prominent Democrats join Staten's swelling tide (1948, April 8), *Los Angeles Sentinel*, 11; Atty. Loren Miller supports Moody Staten for Congress (1948, May 20), *Los Angeles Sentinel*, 16.

175. Vose (1959), 58.

176. TM to LM (1945, June 26), LMP.

177. LM to TM (1945, July 2), LMP.

178. TM to LM (1945, June 26), LMP.

179. LM to Mrs. Wilkie C. Mahoney (1945, July 2), LMP. Mr. Mahoney had written film scripts for Brewster's Millions (1945) and Ziegfeld Follies (1945) and many other films between 1939 and 1961.

180. Pritchett, W. (2008), *Robert Clifton Weaver and the American city: The life and times of an urban reformer* (Chicago: University of Chicago Press), 128.

181. Tushnet, M. V. (1994), *Making civil rights law: Thurgood Marshall and the Supreme Court, 1936–1961* (Oxford: Oxford University Press), 88.

182. Vose (1959), 58.

183. Ibid., 59.

184. Tushnet (1994), 88.

185. Vose (1959), 56.

186. Vose (1959), 64.

187. Tushnet (1994), 89.

188. TM to LM (1945, July 30), LMP.

189. Sources Select Resources, Japanese American Internment, retrieved from http://www.sources.com/SSR/Docs/SSRW-Japanese_American_Internment.htm (March 24, 2015); *Ex parte Mitsuye Endo* 323 U.S. 283 (1944); Japanese American National Museum, *Korematsu v. U.S.*323 U.S. 214 (1944); retrieved from http://caselaw.lp.findlaw.com/scripts/getcase.pl?court=US&vol=323&invol=283 (March 24, 2015).

190. Seattle Civil Rights and History Project, *After Internment* retrieved from http://depts.washington.edu/civilr/after_internment.htm (March 24, 2015).

191. Kurashige (2008), 166.

192. Hansen, A. (2011), *Resettlement: A neglected link in Japanese America's narrative chain*, retrieved from http://content.cdlib.org/view?docId=ft358003z1&doc.view=frames&chunk.id=d0e566&toc.depth=1&toc.id=&brand=calisphere&query=redress; H. Miller, Jr., personal communication (2006, April 22). However, there is only anecdotal evidence to substantiate whether Loren Miller held deeds for his Japanese neighbors.

193. Iwamura, A. (1946, October 14), Ex-Sgt. Akira Iwamura is puzzled, *Los Angeles Times*, A4.

194. Kurashige (2008), 166, 191; McBroome, D. N. (2001), Harvest of gold: African American boosterism, agriculture, and investment in Allensworth and Little Liberia, in L. B. de Graaf, K. Mulroy & Q. Taylor (Eds.), *Seeking El Dorado: African Americans in California* (Los Angeles: Autry Museum of Western Heritage), 166.

195. *Oyama v. California*, 332 U.S. 633 (1948); Robinson, G., & Robinson, T. (2005), Korematsu and beyond: Japanese Americans and the origins of strict scrutiny, *Law and Contemporary Problems*, 68(2): 29–56, retrieved from http://scholarship.law.duke.edu/lcp/vol68/iss2/5/.

196. A. L. Wirin to LM, Morris Cohn, Hugh MacBeth, Jr., and Daniel G. Marshall (1945, October 24), LMP.

197. A. L. Wirin to LM (1945, October 30), LMP.

198. Vinson quoted in Robinson & Robinson (2005).

199. Other attorneys for the respondents in *Masaoka v. People*, 39 Cal. 2d 883 [L.A. No. 21479. In Bank. July 9, 1952] were James C. Purcell, Willaim E. Ferreter, and Guy C. Calden.

200. Ibid. Another important case was *Takahashi v. California Fish and Game Commission*, 334 U.S. 410 (1948), which barred Japan-born aliens from owning a fishing license. It too was overturned.

Chapter 7

1. Miller leaves for battle on covenant (1947, September 4), *Los Angeles Sentinel*, 1; City broils in heat, smog (1947, September 3), *Los Angeles Times*, 1.

2. In late 1940, the Millers moved into their newly built home on Micheltorena Street. The street is named for Manuel Micheltorena, commandant-general and governor of California, who, in 1845, led a team of mixed Mestizo and Amerindians against Juan Bautista Alvarado and lost; unlike most elite educated black Angelenos, the Miller family remained in bohemian Silver Lake, rather than move in the 1960s to the upscale black neighborhoods of View Park, Ladera Heights, and Baldwin Hills.

3. Watts (2005), 245; King Cole can occupy home—temporarily (1946, June 6), *Los Angeles Sentinel*, 1.

4. Parker, G. (2013, April 29), Don't look down, *New Yorker*, 72; Loren Miller (hereafter LM) to Lester Granger (1955, November 30), LMP.

5. Party hosts (1947, June 19), *Los Angeles Sentinel*, 17. In 1924, Juanita Miller, while a student at USC cofounded the Upsilon chapter of Delta Sigma Theta.

6. Theodore Spaulding to Loren Miller (hereafter LM) (1947, March 3), LMP.

7. Lawyers: corp of 1,300 attorneys (1947 April), *Ebony*.

8. Kluger, R. (2004), *Simple Justice: The history of* Brown v. Board of Education *and black America's struggle for equality* (New York: Knopf), 252.

9. Thurgood Marshall (hereafter TM) to C. L. Dellums (1944, July 31), LMP; William Hastie to LM (1945, January 10), LMP.

10. TM to Dorothy L. Height (1945, November 14), LMP.

11. Christine Sterling is credited with restoring Olvera Street, beginning in 1926. When the project faltered, she turned to Harry Chandler, who provided "publicity and support for the development plan in the the *Times*." Wikipedia (2014, December 2), *Olvera Street*, retrieved from http://en.wikipedia.org/wiki/Olvera_Street.

12. Study of restrictive covenants aid Negro (1946, January 1), *Atlanta Daily World*, 1.

13. Plan national attack on housing barriers (1947, September 13), *Chicago Defender*, 1.

14. Miller (1966), 258–59; *Buchanan v. Warley*, 245 U.S. 60 (1917). Although in 1940, in *Hansberry v. Lee*, 311 U.S. 32, the Supreme Court decided that restrictive covenants could be contested, nothing really had been decided "because 95 per cent of the white property owners" had not signed the covenant, which "called for 95 per cent of the signers."

15. White, W. (1947, September 20), Walter White: People, politics and places, *Chicago Defender*, 18. On September 17, 1947, Miller submitted a $312.02 reimbursement statement to the NAACP for railroad and Pullman fare. On October 16, Anne M. Brown, Marian Perry's secretary, sent Miller a $400 check for round-trip travel expenditures from Los Angeles; business memos/invoices in LMP.

16. Simon, J. (1947, September 27), West Coast Atty: To argue covenants in top U.S. Court, *Chicago Defender*, 7. From 1929 to 1935 Charles H. Hamilton was vice dean at Howard University School of Law. He was legal counsel for the NAACP from 1935 to 1938. Thurgood Marshall replaced Houston in 1938 as legal counsel, one year prior to the incorporation of the NAACP Legal Defense and Educational Fund; in 1947, Houston chaired the Legal Committee of the Legal Defense Fund, of which Loren Miller was one of its thirty-seven members; Ruth Weyland to TM, July 26, 1947; TM to John Doebele, July 25, 1947, both in NAACP Papers, box 2-B-131. The date of the "Methods of Attacking Restrictive Covenants" had been changed from August 30 to September 6, because most of the attorneys were unable to meet on the earlier date; Marian Perry to George M. Johnson, August 22, 1947, NAACP Papers, box 2-B-133. Johnson (dean of Howard University's School of Law) believed that the conference would not last beyond Saturday, although he admitted, "There is a possibility that we may want to do some work on Sunday." Forty-three were in attendance of the September 6 meeting, according to the Minutes of Meeting NAACP, Lawyers and Consultants on Methods of Attacking Restrictive Covenants (1947, September 6), NAACP Papers, group 2, box 133, Library of Congress; JRank.org (2015), *Constance B. Motley biography*, retrieved from http://biography.jrank

.org/pages/2924/Motley-Constance-Baker.html; Constance Baker Motley 1921–2005 (2005, September 30), *Washington Post*.

17. *Mendez v. Westminster*, 64 F. Supp.544 (1946); Court brands segregated schools as illegal, vicious (1947, April 17), *Los Angeles Sentinel*, 1; A. L. Wirin on Loren Miller's death (n.d.), LMP: "In 1947, [Miller] appeared as a friend of the court in the ACLU case challenging racial segregation of students of Mexican descent in Orange County." According to Wirin, he and Miller in 1955 together secured a federal court ruling barring African and Mexican American children in public schools in Imperial County.

18. Carter, R. (2005), *A matter of law: A memoir of struggle in the cause of equal rights* (New York: New Press), 66. "The brief was really my baby," wrote Carter. "Loren Miller . . . was the only person with a real opportunity to modify what I had written, but he liked what was presented to him. I made certain that Thurgood had the opportunity to study the brief and suggest changes before it was filed, but he let it go as written." Miller was on the National Lawyers Guild (NLG) Los Angeles branch lower court amicus brief along with Charles F. Christopher and Ben Margolis. By the time the case reached the appellate court, Christopher is singularly on the NLG appellate brief as amicus counsel.

19. Robinson, T., & Robinson, G. (2003, May), Mendez v. Westminster: Asian-Latino coalition triumphant?, *Asian Law Journal*, 10(2): 170nn103–104; earlier in the lower court, Wirin submitted a brief on behalf of the ACLU; *Mendez v. Westminster* 64 F.Supp. 544 (S.D Cal 1946); *Westminster v. Mendez* 161 F.2d 744,1947, US App; Atty. Miller scouts fears of bigots (1946, April 18), *Los Angeles Sentinel*, 11; Simon (1947, September 27); Weeks, P. (1964, May 17), New judge reluctant member of profession, *Los Angeles Times*, B4; Streator, G. (1947, April 26), Negro home needs rise as coast issue, *New York Times*. The petitioning attorney in *Mendez* was David C. Marcus. However, prior to the Mendez case, Milton Smith, a floor finisher, was arrested under the state truancy laws for refusing to send his children to a "school called a 'fire hazard' and 'unsafe' by a state architect." Smith had earlier attempted to gain admittance for his children in two other Monrovia schools. However, they were refused and sent back to the segregated unsafe Huntington Drive School. Attorney Thomas Griffith, Jr., president of the Los Angeles NAACP, sued the city on the grounds that it "has no right to subdivide it into subdistricts and then penalize those who refuse to send their children to one of the so-called subdistricts" Miller, L. (1934, December 8), Coast Negroes battle segregation in School, *New York Amsterdam News*, 2.

20. Blanco, M. (2010, March), Before *Brown*, there was *Mendez*: The lasting impact of *Mendez v. Westminster* in the struggle for desegregation, Immigration Policy Center *Perspectives*, retrieved from http://lawprofessors.typepad.com/files/mendez_v._westminster_0324101.pdf.

21. Moton, T. (1947, August 4), *Los Angeles Sentinel*, 24.

22. Funeral services held Tuesday for M. V. Ellsworth (1947, August 21), *Los Angeles Sentinel*, 6. Milton V. Ellsworth had been born in New Mexico and moved from Albuquerque to Los Angeles in 1915.

23. LM telegram to Marian Wynn Perry (NAACP) (1947, September 9), LMP: "Please secure me reservations on Broadway Limited or Century directly to Los Angeles via Santa Fe Chief." LM handwritten note (n.d.): "Broadway Ltd all filled. Try for bedroom or compartment"; LM letter to Marian Wynn Perry and $312 expense statement (1947,

September 17); he was reimbursed $400, all in LMP; Miller leaves (1947, September 4), *Los Angeles Sentinel*.

24. Miller, Look down, 5, LMP. On July 30, 1945, Earl B. Dickerson wrote to thank Miller for his promise to "aid in securing transportation for my return to California. . . . I wonder to what extent I may be certain of obtaining first class return transportation on the Super Chief."

25. Miller, Look down, 5.

26. Ibid., 1–2.

27. Ibid., 2.

28. Miller (1966), 367.

29. Wendell Green to LM (1961, December 6, 5:30 A.M.), LMP; Pleasant, B. (1987, December 24), Former Sentinel editor dies. *Los Angeles Sentinel*, A1.

30. F. Hopkins Duffy, personal communication (2007, April 18). Faye is the daughter of Norman Hopkins, owner of the People's Funeral Home and his social worker wife, Irma Hopkins, Juanita's Delta sister.

31. Aurelius, M. (2006), *Meditations* (M. Hammond, Trans.), (London: Penguin Classics).

32. H. Miller, Jr., personal communication (2007, May 22).

33. Granger, L. (1962, March 22), Battleaxe and bread, *California Eagle*, 4.

34. "Justice is a certain rectitude of mind whereby a man does what he ought to do in the circumstances confronting him." Aquinas, T. (1981), *Summa Theologica* (Fathers of the English Dominican Province, Trans.) (London: Christian Classics).

35. NAACP chief lauds Loren Miller (1967, August 3), *Los Angeles Sentinel*, A5.

36. McWilliams, transcription of audio recording, tape 5, side 2, p. 19. McWilliams, like Miller, was a Los Angeles attorney, writer, and activist spoke against the internment of Japanese-American citizens and other race and labor issues. California historian Kevin Starr is said to have called him the finest nonfiction writer on California. McWilliams headed California's Division of Immigration and Housing; defended both the Sleepy Lagoon and Hollywood Ten defendants, along with Robert Kenny and other progressive attorneys. From 1955 to 1975, he was editor of the *Nation* magazine; McWilliams lived in the Echo Park area at 2041 N. Alvarado, less than three miles from Miller's 647 Micheltorena Street Silver Lake address.

37. Du Bois, W. E. B. (1994), *The Souls of Black Folk* (New York: Gramercy Books); Myrdal (1944) 1996, 1385.

38. Graham (2000), 94.

39. Ibid., 362.

40. Miller (1966), 261.

41. Though Miller was from a rural township such as Highland, Kansas, one hundred miles or so from major cities such as Topeka and Lawrence, in itself it did not hinder him from attaining rousing personal accomplishments.

42. Pritchett (2008), 16–17.

43. Ibid., 17.

44. Graham (2000), 61.

45. Linder, D. O. (2015), *Before* Brown: *Charles H. Houston and the* Gaines *case*, retrieved from http://law2.umkc.edu/faculty/projects/ftrials/trialheroes/charleshouston essayF.html.

46. U.S. 1870, 1880 Census, Kansas; Nancy Gee, Loren Miller's paternal grandaunt, a schoolteacher, married Henry Bruce, brother of U.S. senator (1875–1881) Blanche Kelso Bruce from Mississippi, the first black American to serve a full term in the U.S. Senate.

47. Pritchett (2008), 8; Phillips-Fein, K. (2008, December 22), Living for the city: Robert Clifton Weaver's liberalism, *Nation*, retrieved from http://www.thenation.com/article/living-city-robert-clifton-weavers-liberalism; Steffen, H. (2010, December 3), Intellectual proletarians, *Chronicle Review*, B10.

48. Pritchett (2008), 24.

49. Ibid., 6.

50. Ibid., 75

51. LM to Lester Granger (1945, December 18).

52. LM to Leon L. Lewis, attorney (1945, October 8), LMP: "I shall be very glad to serve on the Advisory Council for the ILGWU radio station."

53. Miller, L. (1947, January), The power of restrictive covenants, *Survey Graphic*; Miller, L. (1947, May–June), Race restrictions on ownership or occupancy of land, *Lawyers Guild Review*; Miller (1947, October), Covenants for exclusion.

54. Miller, L. (1935, July 21), Anti-Negro campaign launched, *Atlanta Daily World*, 1.

55. Miller (1966), 322.

56. Roy Wilkins to Robert Carter (1947, August 13), memo, LMP.

57. Vose (1959), 71.

58. LM to Roy Wilkins (1947, July 8), LMP. A petition for writ of certiorari is a document that the losing party files with the Supreme Court asking the court to review a lower court's decision.

59. Roy Wilkins to Robert Carter (1947, August 13), LMP.

60. NAACP Restrictive Covenant Chicago Conference (1945, July 9–10), LMP. Also in NAACP Papers box 2-B-131.

61. Vose (1959), p.161

62. LM to Robert Weaver (1946, January 1), LMP.

63. Vose (1959), 275n45.

64. Minutes on Conference on Restrictive Covenants held at Howard University, Sunday 1/26/1947 11:30 A.M. to 2 P.M., (1947, February 4), NAACP Papers, box 2-B-131.

65. Vose (1959), 128.

66. Miller (1966), 323; Farley, R. (May 2013), *The Orsel and Minnie McGhee home*, retrieved from http://www.detroit1701.org/McGheeHome.html#.VY1VnEaavnG.

67. Sugrue (2008), p.208.

68. Perry, M. W. (1947, January 27), memo, LMP.

69. Irons, P. (1988), *The courage of their convictions: Sixteen Americans who fought their way to the Supreme Court* (New York: Penguin), 70.

70. Restrictive Covenants at Howard University (1947, February 4), NAACP Papers, box 2-B-133.

71. Perry, M. W. (1947, January 27), memo, LMP.

72. Tushnet (1994), 90.

73. Rubenstein, W. B. (1997, April), Divided we litigate: Addressing disputes among group members and lawyers in civil rights campaigns, *Yale Law Journal*, 106(6): 1623, 1630.

74. Vose (1959), 157. On June 23, 1947, the U.S. Supreme Court granted certiorari in *Shelley v. Kraemer* and *McGhee v. Sipes*.

75. Kluger (2004), interview with Franklin Williams, 248.

76. Irons (1988), 65–66, 74.

77. Vaughn, G. L. (1949, October), *Journal of Negro History*, 34(4): 490; Miller (1966), 323. The Kraemers lived at 3542 Labadie Avenue. Vose (1959), 112; Irons (1988), 65–66.

78. Tushnet (1994), 90.

79. Irons (1988), 68.

80. Vose (1959), 114; Miller (1966), 323; Judge rules out covenant suit (1945, December 1), *Chicago Defender*, 9A; George L. Vaughn to TM (1947, January 30), LMP; Tushnet (1994), 92–93.

81. TM to LM and Charles H. Houston (1947, January 10), LMP.

82. LM to TM (1947, July 18), LMP.

83. LM to TM (1947, April 3), LMP.

84. Plan national attack on housing barriers (1947, September 3), *Chicago Defender*, 1.

85. Meeting NAACP (1947, September 7), NAACP Papers, box 2-B-133. The pending cases were *McGhee v. Sipes, Shelley v. Kraemer, Trustees of Monroe Avenue Church vs. Fred C. Perkins, Hurd v. Hodge*, and *Urciola v. Hodge*. Eventually, the Supreme Court decided not to hear *Trustees of Monroe Avenue Church vs. Fred C. Perkins*. According to Clement Vose (1959), that case raised "peripheral issues of church-state relations," 158.

86. Meeting NAACP (1947, September 7), afternoon session. State action doctrine is a legal principle maintaining that the Fourteenth Amendment applies only to state and local governments, not to private entities.

87. Minutes of Meeting NAACP (1947, September 6), NAACP Papers, box 2-B-134; *Fairchild v. Raines*, 2 Cal.2d 818 [L.A. No. 18735. In Bank. Aug. 31, 1944.] Though Judge Traynor of the California Supreme Court concluded in *Fairchild v. Raines* that "there was a public interest in the fact that residential districts for Negroes in Los Angeles were crowded," covenants, he declared, "must yield to the public interest in the sound development of the whole community," according to Vose (1959), 24.

88. Minutes of Meeting NAACP. September 6, 1947.

89. Tushnet (1994), 91. By the time the four cases were argued before the U.S. Supreme Court, twenty-one organizations filed briefs in support of *Shelley v. Kraemer*, according to Miller (1966), 324. Surprisingly, the opposing side, too, filed a large number of amici curiae briefs; see Vose (1959), 276n49.

90. Levy quoted in White (1947, September 20), Walter White: People, politics and places, *Chicago Defender*, 18.

91. Smallwood, B. (1947, September 25), Delightful side, *Los Angeles Sentinel*, 19.

92. TM to LM (1947, October 27), LMP.

93. LM to TM (1947, October 28), LMP. *McGhee v. Sipes* 334 U.S. 1 (1948) was bundled into *Shelley v. Kraemer*, the first of the combined cases; *Hurd v. Hodge* and *Urciolo v. Hodge* [334 U.S. 24 (1948)], companion cases to *Shelley* and *McGhee*, were treated differently because, according to Miller "the 14th District of Columbia and relief had to be sought in the due process of law clause of the Fifth Amendment." Miller (1966), 324.

94. LM to TM (1947, October 28).

95. Marshall, T. (2001), Tribute to Charles H. Houston (Amherst Magazine), in T. Marshall, *Thurgood Marshall: His speeches, writings, arguments, opinions, and reminiscences* Mark V. Tushnet (Ed.) (Chicago: Lawrence Hill Books), 272.

96. Miller (1966), 260. In 1930, New York attorney Nathan Margold produced a legal plan for a campaign against segregation for the NAACP. See Vose (1959), 43.

97. *Hurd v. Hodge, Urciolo v. Hodge*, 162 Fed.2d 233 (D.C.Cir.,1947); the U. S. Supreme Court granted certiorari, 332 U.S. 789 (1947).

98. TM to LM (1947, October 27), LMP.

99. LM to TM (1947, October 28), LMP.

100. Miller (1966), 261; Kluger (2004), 252.

101. Kluger (2004), 252.

102. TM to John Doebele (1947, January 25), LMP.

103. Marshall (2001), 1.

104. In *Brown v. Board of Education of Topeka*, 347 U.S.483 (1954), Miller wrote appellant briefs Nos. 2 and 4; in the case commonly referred to as "all deliberate speed," 349 U.S. 294 (1955), he wrote appellant briefs Nos. 1, 2, and 3 and respondent brief No. 5.

105. Miller (1966), 322.

106. Ibid., 260.

107. Ibid., 261.

108. McNeil, G. R. (1993), 180. Louis Brandeis served as associate justice of the U.S. Supreme Court from 1916 to 1939.

109. Strum, P. (1984), *Louis D. Brandeis: Justice for the people* (New York: Schocken Books), 332; *Encyclopaedia Britannica*, "Louise Brandeis," retrieved from http://www .britannica.com/EBchecked/topic/77644/Louis-Brandeis (March 24, 2015).

110. Photo Standalone 5—no title (1947, November 6), *Los Angeles Sentinel*, 17; Loren Miller to argue race ban case in supreme court (1947, September 18), *Los Angeles Sentinel*, 1; (1947, September 27), Attys. Miller, Houston to eye bias writ cases: Supreme court hears important suit Nov. 10–17, *Atlanta Daily World*, 1.

111. Miller (1966), 265.

112. Covenants get final supreme court test Monday (1947, December 4), *Los Angeles Sentinel*, 1; Detroit will take restrictive covenants to U.S. high court (1947, March 8), *Chicago Defender*, 7. In Detroit, Rev. Horace A. White helped to coordinate the campaign to raise funds to cover the NAACP's legal costs. Contributions from churches and business associations, including Jewish merchants, figured largely. Supreme court to hear 4 covenant cases in December (1947, November 1), *Chicago Defender*, 1; LM to TM (1947, October 28), LMP.

113. L.A. County brands all Negroes degenerates; "Ungodly" to fight ghetto says white pastor (1947, October 9), *Los Angeles Sentinel*, 1.

114. Ibid.; Jurist refuses to uphold covenant (1947, November 1), *Baltimore Afro-American*, 1.

115. California judge outlaws covenant (1947, November 1), *Chicago Defender*, 1.

116. Ibid. By November 1947, Judge Mosk had made five "decisions that race covenants are unconstitutional," Covenanters work feverishly to blanket Echo Park area (1947, November 13), *Los Angeles Sentinel*, 1.

117. Rasmussen (2007, November 11), L.A. then and now: Dream home came with racial restrictions, *Los Angeles Times*, B2; A. Drye and F. Drye, personal communication (2007, December 11).

118. Ministers told to be tolerant (1947, November 5), *Los Angeles Times*, A18; Rasmussen (2007, November 11).

119. High court test of covenants delayed month (1947, December 11), *Los Angeles Sentinel*, 1.

120. TM to LM (1947, December 29), LMP.

121. TM to Charles Hotel (1947, December 29), LMP.

122. LM to Santa Fe Railway (1947, December 29), LMP.

123. Marian W. Perry to Statler Hotel (1947, December 30), LMP.

124. Covenanters seek to oust Jew: Suit to test legality (1947, September 25), *Los Angeles Sentinel*, 1. See also Vose (1959), 276n66.

125. Kluger (2004), 251.

126. Government aid against housing bias writs urged (1947, September 20), *Atlanta Daily World*, 1. The American Jewish Committee, B'Nai B'rith, Jewish War Veterans of U.S.A. and Jewish Labor Committee filed its consolidated brief in support of *Shelley v. Kraemer, et al.*

127. Vose (1959), 277n84 (Perlman to I. Miller, October 30, 1947). On December 5, 1946, the President's Committee on Civil Rights was established by Executive Order 9808; its findings were published as the 178-page *To Secure These Rights*. Perlman served as solicitor general from 1947 to 1952 under President Truman.

128. Elman, P. (1987), The Solicitor General's Office, Justice Frankfurter, and civil rights litigation, 1946–1960: An oral history, *Harvard Law Review*, 100(4): 818.

129. Ibid.

130. Ibid., 819.

131. Lautier, L. (1947, December 6), *New York Amsterdam News*, 10.

132. Clark to demand strong rights law (1947, December 6), *Baltimore Afro-American*, 1. The NBA acknowledged Miller's contributions by reelecting him first vice president; Thurman L. Dodson of Washington, D.C., replaced Earl B. Dickerson as president.

133. Race prejudice blasted at Nat'l Bar convention (1947, December 6), *Pittsburgh Courier Press Service*, 4.

134. Mate barred, but white wife can live in house (1946, November 23), *Baltimore Afro-American*, 6. At the 1946 annual NBA conference, the entire slate of association officers was reelected, with Miller elected second vice president. The conference was presided over by Earl B. Dickerson of Chicago, president of the association (1945–1947).

135. National Bar Ass'n to meet in Detroit, site of covenant fight (1946, November 28), *Los Angeles Sentinel*, 1. Dickerson also served as president of the National Lawyers Guild (1951–1954).

136. Lawyers map bias fight in Detroit meet (1946, December 7), *Chicago Defender*, 1. See also Jesse S. Heslip to Loren Miller (1945, December 13), LMP.

137. Tushnet (1994), 93, 168; see also Vose (1959), 200.

138. Ibid., 3.

139. Graves, L. (1948, January 24), Secret Ballot, *Pittsburgh Courier*, 1.

140. Murphy, C. (1948, January 24), Truman plea for Fifth freedom in high court, *Baltimore Afro-American*.

141. Ibid.; Vose (1959), 178.

142. Racism must go, high court told by Houston (1948, January 24), *Baltimore Afro-American*, 1.

143. Clark condemns race property bias (1947, December 6), *New York Times*, 10.

144. Elman (1987, February), 819.

145. Miller (1966), 324.

146. Vose (1959), 201.

147. Graves (1948, January 24), 1.

148. Elman (1987, February), 820.

149. Irons (1988), 78.

150. J. Williams (1998), 150–51. Though Thurgood Marshall's description of George Vaughn is attributed by Juan Williams (nn 13–15) to the *Pittsburgh Courier* and the *Baltimore Afro-American* (1948, January 24), this author found no such references.

151. Graves (1948, January 24).

152. Racism must go (1948, January 24), 1.

153. Graves (1948, January 24).

154. Ware, L. (1989), Invisible walls: An examination of the legal strategy of the restrictive covenant cases, *Washington University Law Quarterly*, 67 (Fall): 766.

155. Racism must go (1948, January 24), 1. The U.S. Supreme Court advised Miller in his application to argue before the court to provide proof of bar membership in Kansas. On September 22, 1947, Miller wrote the Kansas Supreme Court for a certificate showing the date he was admitted to the bar and proof that there were no disciplinary actions against him.

156. Graves (1948, January 24); see also Vose (1959), 202.

157. Allen, F. (1989), Remembering Shelley v. Kraemer: Of public and private worlds, *Washington University Law Quarterly*, 67 (Fall): 719–20.

158. Brief for Petitioners, *McGhee v. Sipes* [334 U.S.1 (1941)].

159. Ware (1989); subordinate to the legal claims, the "sociological points . . . were drawn almost wholly from the trial record." See also Vose (1959), 186.

160. Ware (1989), 766n148.

161. Graves (1948, January 24).

162. NAACP Restrictive Covenant Howard University (1947, September 6), NAACP Papers, box 2-B-134; see also Vose, 277nn81.

163. Racism must go (1948, January 24), 1.

164. Graves (1948, January 24).

165. Racism must go (1948, January 24), 1.

166. Stokes, D. (1948, January 17), Covenant case arguments end; Decision unlikely for months, *Washington Post*, 1.

167. Graves (1948, January 24).

168. Racism must go (1948, January 24), 1.

169. Ibid.

170. Strum (1984), 332.

171. Allen (Fall 1989), 720.

172. Tushnet (1994), 94.

173. Graves (1948, January 24).

174. Before returning to business as usual, on January 20, three days after he returned to Los Angeles, Miller submitted an invoice of $381.44 to the NAACP for travel expenses to Washington: roundtrip rail fare from L.A. to D.C. $293.73; hotel, $32.96; meals $52.50; taxi fare $2.25.

175. Jewish Congress to hear speakers of various races (1948, January 29), *Los Angeles Sentinel*, 11.

176. Dinner highlights brotherhood week (1948, February 26), *Los Angeles Sentinel*, 11; N. Peter Rathvon of RKO Radio Pictures to LM (1948, January 6), LMP.

177. City welcomes delegates to NAACP regional confab (1948, March 4), *Los Angeles Sentinel*, 1; Political action NAACP meet topic (1948, January 25), *Atlanta Daily World*, 2; Six justices to decide L.A. Negro home rights (1948, Janaury 22), *Los Angeles Sentinel*, 1.

178. Protest stymie attempt to block job fight at Sears (1948, March 25), *Los Angeles Sentinel*, 2.

179. NAACP leader denies U.S. disloyalty (1948, June 16), *Los Angeles Sentinel*, 1.

180. Ibid.

181, LeMar, L. (1948, December 25), Postal worker wins case in "Red" firing, *New York Amsterdam News*, 3. Members of the postal board were: E. B. Jackson, Hugh E. Alford, and Roy Frank, attorney for the Post Office Loyalty Board.

182. Santa Monica seeks emergency law to block job fight at Sears (1948, March 18), *Los Angeles Sentinel*, 1.

183. LeMar (1948, December 25).

184. Community leaders pledge support to Moody Staten (1948, April 22), *Los Angeles Sentinel*, 4; Atty. Loren Miller supports Moody Staten for Congress (1948, May 20), *Los Angeles Sentinel*, 16.

185. Garlington, S. W. (1948, May 1), Randolph, Reynolds upheld in fight on Army bias as leaders close ranks, *New York Amsterdam News*, 1. In 1946, Granger played a significant role in the setting aside the conviction of the fifty sailors in the Port Chicago incident. Sailors freed of mutiny (1946, January 10), *Los Angeles Sentinel*, 1, 4.

186. Miller tells leaders' plan to boycott Jim crow Army (1948, May 13), *Los Angeles Sentinel*, 11.

187. Lester Granger to LM (1948, September 29), LMP.

188. Clearing forecast today (1948, May 3), *Washington Post*, B2; National weather summary (1948, May 3), *Washington Post*, B10; Little Harp wins opener at Pimlico (1948, May 4), *Washington Post*, 18.

189. Vose (1959), 205.

190. Text of AP story on Supreme Court decision (1948, May 3), LMP.

191. Races: A house with a yard (1948, May 17), *Time*.

192. Proposed act asks ban of all restrictive pacts (1948, May 15), *Baltimore Afro-American*, 1.

193. Text of AP story (1948, May 3), LMP.

194. Vose (1959), 207.

195. Miller (1946, May), Covenants in the bear flag state, 140; McGovney, D. (1945, March), Racial residential segregation by state court enforcement of restrictive agreements, covenants or conditions in deeds is unconstitutional, *California Law Review*, 33(1); Robert W. Kenny, *My First Forty Years in California Politics, 1922–1962*, Robert W. Kenny Papers, Department of Special Collections, Charles E. Young Library, University of California, Los Angeles (My first forty years in politics), 278–88.

196. Tushnet (1994), 97

197. Miller, L. (1948, May 6), No loophole in court ruling, *Los Angeles Sentinel*, 1.

198. Ibid.

199. *News from NAACP* (newsletter) (1948, May 6), LMP.

200. Marshall, T. (1951, May), The Supreme Court as protector of civil rights: Equal protections of the laws, *Annals of the American Academy of Political and Social Sciences*, 275.

201. *Washington Star*, quoted in ibid., 200.

202. TM to George A. Beavers, Jr. (1948, May 13), LMP.

203. Triumph for democracy (1948, May 6), *Los Angeles Sentinel*, 1.

204. *News from NAACP* (1948, May 6).

205. Quantity discount held illegal where effect is lessened competition (1948, May 4), *Wall Street Journal*, 5; Supreme Court upholds government's major anti-trust charges against film distributors (1948, May 4), *Wall Street Journal*, 3; What's news (1948, May 4), *Wall Street Journal*, 1.

206. L.A. citizens happy over court ruling (1948, May 6), *Los Angeles Sentinel*, 9.

207. Testimonial dinner honoring Loren Miller (1948, May 20), *Los Angeles Sentinel*, 3; Brown, V. (1948, May 20), Social sidelights, *Los Angeles Sentinel*, 19; Watts group to honor Loren Miller (1948, May 20), *Los Angeles Sentinel*, 2; Lake Elsinore Community Center opens Sunday eve (1948, May 27), *Los Angeles Sentinel*, 10.

208. Citizenship group plans benefit cocktail party (1948, October 14), *Los Angeles Sentinel*, 6.

209. Coast rights honors 2 attorneys (1948, December 18), *Chicago Defender*, 5.

Chapter 8

1. Loren Miller (hereafter LM) to Gloster Current, Director of NAACP Branches (1948, October 16), LMP.

2. NAACP members defeat move to oust Griffith (1947, January 16), *California Eagle*, front page.

3. Let the ladies do it (1948, December 11), *Los Angeles Tribune*, 20.

4. Mary Cutler to Roy Wilkins (1948, December 11), LMP; Communist threat to "take over" local NAACP fought: Griffith accused of bargaining with "Reds" (1948, December 18), *Los Angeles Tribune*, 1; It's time for a change (1948, December 23), *Los Angeles Sentinel*, 25; NAACP at crossroads (1949, January 31), *Los Angeles Sentinel*, 23. In March 1942, according to Rodger Streitmatter, FBI "agents arrived unannounced at the *Eagle* office" and interrogated Griffith's supporter, Charlotta Bass, "suggesting that her newspaper was financed by Germany and Japan"; Streitmatter (1994), 102.

5. LM to Gloster Current (1948, October 16), LMP. Dr. Thomas L. Griffith, Sr., a supporter of black-owned businesses, served from 1921 to 1940, as the pastor of the Second Baptist Church, Los Angeles's first African American Baptist church.

6. Gloster Current to Mary Cutler (1948, October 19), LMP.

7. Gloster Current to LM (1948, October 20), LMP.

8. Miller, L. (1948, October), "For my wife at noontime," unpublished, box 33(02)DSC 6046–6048, LMP.

9. Let the ladies do it (1948, December 11), *Los Angeles Tribune*, 20.

10. Atty. Loren Miller declines presidency of Los Angeles Branch NAACP (1948, December 16), *California Eagle*, 7.

11. Gloster Current to Noah Griffin (1948, December 30), LMP.

12. LM to Thurgood Marshall (hereafter TM) (1949, February 6), LMP.

13. Leonard, K. (2005), "I am sure you can read between the lines": Cold war anti-Communism and the NAACP in Los Angeles, *Journal of the West*, 44(2): 22.

14. Will not run for re-election (1949, November 3), *Los Angeles Sentinel*, A7.

15. Attorneys over-look wealthy financier's "meeting" behavior (1950, February 2), *Los Angeles Sentinel*, A1.

16. Find Howard guilty on two charges (1950, November 18), *Chicago Defender*, 1; B'way savings must hold new election Feb. 24 (1950, February 9), *Los Angeles Sentinel*, A2.

17. Headless chicken creating quite a stir in southeast Los Angeles (1949, April 7), *Los Angeles Sentinel*, A1.

18. L.A. attorney made judge (1953, March 7), *Chicago Defender*, 1; Pioneering Black lawyer, judge dies (1986), *Los Angeles Times*.

19. W. Gordon, personal communication (2007, August 14); *O'Rourke v. Teeters*, 63 Cal. App.2d 349 (1944).

20. Pupil sues skate rink (1934, July 19), *Los Angeles Sentinel*, 1.

21. LM to Juanita Miller (1935, September 8), LMP. Walter Gordon said Lloyd Griffith, though polished and a good orator, failed the state bar exam six times before he passed. In 1945 and 1953, Miller, first with Thomas Griffith and later with Harold Sinclair, represented Lloyd Griffith before the state bar. In 1945, the bar suspended Lloyd for misconduct for three years; in 1953, he was suspended for two years (26 Cal.2d 273, *Griffith v. State Bar* April 20, 1945, L.A. No. 19285; *Griffith v. State Bar*, March 13, 1953, L.A. No. 22506. 52 Cal.2d 762).

22. Fair practices act assailed as menace (1946, October 27), *Los Angeles Times*, A2; Little FEP law proposed in California (1943, January 16), *Chicago Defender*, 9. Miller worked for the Eastside Chamber of Commerce, where he and Clarence A. Jones drafted an employment discrimination amendment for the California State Constitution.

23. Letterhead of the California Committee for Fair Employment (1955, August 30); Miller is a sponsor; Co-Chairs Loren Miller, Gilbert C. Anaya and Max Mont to sponsors of the Committee for Equal Employment Opportunity (1957, February 25); Loren Miller et al., Committee for Equal Employment Opportunity to Supervisor Warren M. Dorn (1957, February 18); Miller, L. (1958, February 17), Statement on Proposal to Establish Department of Human Relations in State Government, submitted to Assembly Committee Hearing, all in LMP.

24. Loren Miller, interview by Lawrence de Graaf (1967, March 3), 6. Miller was a registered Republican according to the 1930 Index to Register of Voters Los Angeles City, Precinct no. 636. He did not switch to the Democratic Party until 1932.

25. Smith (2007), 24.

26. Ibid., 208–209.

27. Freer (2005), 52–55.

28. Ibid.

29. IRA (1936, October 9), Pot-Pie, *California Eagle*, 14.

30. Kurashige (2008), 147.

31. Mack (2012), 184.

32. Ibid., 199.

33. Approval (1951, May 3), *California Eagle*, p.1.

34. Green, W. (1951, May 3), Policy shift in new Eagle is announced, *California Eagle*, 1.

35. Dunnigan, A. (1951, May 31), *Los Angeles Sentinel*, A1.

36. Miller, L. (1953, November 12), A new beginning, *California Eagle*.

37. Forest Lawn went to court to prevent burial of Negro (1951, November 22), *California Eagle*, 2.

38. Here's where we stand (1951, May 3), *California Eagle*, 1.

39. Editor returns home (1953, March 28), *Chicago Defender*, 6.

40. Miller, L. (1952, July 29), To Whom It May Concern; Agreement for Sale between C. Bass and Clyde B. Denslow; Reconveyance and Quitclaim (1954), LMP.

41. California paper "not to be sold" (1938, September 3), *Chicago Defender*, 5.

42. Miller (1952, July 29).

43. Sides, J. (1998) "You understand my condition": the Civil Rights Congress in the Los Angeles African American Community, 1946–1952, *Pacific Historical Review*, 67 (May): 256; Kurashige (2008), 214.

44. Miller, L. (1951), Prelude for suicide (unpublished poem), LMP.

45. Phoenix NAACP sues school on issue (1951, October 12), *Atlanta Daily World*, 1.

46. Loren Miller, Jr., Virgil Junior High School report cards (1949–1951), LMP. Virgil Junior High School (now Virgil Middle School) is located in Los Angeles, on Vermont Avenue.

47. LM to Henry Lee Moon (1962, October 26), LMP.

48. Franklin H. Williams to LM (1962, July 3), LMP.

49. Gilbert, A. (2012, June 4), *Judge Loren Miller, Jr.*, retrieved from http://gilbertsubmits .blogspot.com/2012/06/judge-loren-miler-jr.html.

50. Passings: Loren Miller Jr. (2011, December 15), *Los Angeles Times*; FEPC wins Long Beach home fight (1967, November 9), *Los Angeles Sentinel*, A3; Wikipedia (2013, 7 February), *Loren Miller*, retrieved from https://en.wikipedia.org/wiki/Loren_Miller _(judge).

51. Respondent's Brief on Certiorari to U.S. Supreme Court, October Term, 1952 (*Barrows v. Jackson*, 346 U.S. 249 [1953]).

52. Short shift (1953, March 28), *Chicago Defender*, 2; Supreme Court will review covenant case (1953, May 11), *Atlanta Daily World*, 1; Off the memo pad (1953, May), *Chicago Defender*, 2.

53. Granger, L. (1953, May 16), Manhattan and beyond, *New York Amsterdam News*, 16.

54. Supreme Court of the United States (2015, March 23), *Supreme Court Building*, retrieved from http://www.supremecourt.gov/about/courtbuilding.aspx.

55. Smart party welcome the Loren Millers (1953, March 14), *New York Amsterdam News*, 9.

56. LM to Franklin H. Williams (1953, March 21), LMP.

57. Covenants back in Supreme Court (1953, May 9), *Chicago Defender*, 3.

58. *Barrows v. Jackson*, 346 U.S. 249 (1953).

59. Granger, L. (1953, May 16), Manhattan and beyond, *New York Amsterdam News*, 16.

60. A shabby performance (1953, December 17), *California Eagle*, 4; The path to solution (1953, May 14), *California Eagle*, 4; Broadway Dept. Store (1954, January 7), *California Eagle*, front page.

61. Memo to the mayor (1953, December 31), *California Eagle*, 3.

62. Negroes threaten new fire department move (1953, October 9), *Los Angeles Times*, 21; Hearings airs fire dep't segregation (1954, March11), *Los Angeles Sentinel*, A1.

63. A lawsuit? Maybe! (1955, July 28), *Los Angeles Sentinel*, editorial page.

64. NAACP draws up petition (1955, July 28), *Los Angeles Sentinel*, 1.

65. Ibid.

66. Dear chief: bye bye! (1955, November 3), *Los Angeles Sentinel*.

67. *Brown v. Board of Education of Topeka*, 347 U.S. 483 (1954). In *Brown I*, Miller wrote brief No. 2 (*Briggs v. Elliot*) and brief No. 4 (*Davis v. County School Board of Prince Edward County, Virginia*). Later, Miller wrote briefs Nos. 1, 2, and 3 for appellants and No. 5 for respondents in what is known as the "all deliberate speed" appeal. *Brown v. Board of Education of Topeka*, 349 U.S. 294 (1955); Carter (2005), 96, 122.

68. Botsch, R. E., and Botsch, C. B. (2010, December), *Briggs v. Elliot (1954)*, retrieved from http://www.usca.edu/aasc/briggsvelliott.htm.

69. Charles V. Bush, 72: First black page at U.S. Supreme Court (2012, December 2), *Washington Post*, C8.

70. Carter (2005), 148.

71. Ibid., 150.

72. Ibid., 151.

73. Ibid., 152.

74. Miller (1966), 377.

75. Miller, L. (1963, April 4), Loren Miller says, *California Eagle*, 4.

76. Ogletree, Charles J., Jr. (2004), *All deliberate speed: Reflections on the first half century of* Brown v. Board of Education (New York: Norton), 306–307.

77. Concedes end of the California Eagle (1953, November 7), *Chicago Defender*, 2.

78. Public Broadcasting System (1999), *The black press: Soldiers without swords*, transcript of interview with Abie Robinson, http://www.pbs.org/blackpress/film/transcripts/robinson.html.

79. LM to E. Leonard Richardson (1957, September 2), LMP; *Herbert W. Simmons, Jr., v. Loren Miller, Clyde Denslow, Vi Brown and Wendell Green*: Complaint for Claim and Delivery (1954), LMP.

80. LM to E. Leonard Richardson (1957, September 2), LMP.

81. Charlotta Bass to Ben Margolis (n.d.); Ben Margolis to Loren Miller (1961, December 4), both in LMP; 15 top Cal leaders face court (1952, February 1), *Los Angeles Times*, 1; Fourth Report of the Senate Fact-Finding Committee on Un-American Activities, 1948—Communist Front organizations, 148.

82. Ben Margolis, interview by Michael S. Balter (1984, July 2), tape 4, side 2, BMP; Group urges rehearing for film writers (1950, May 2), *Los Angeles Times*, 8. On the brief for the appellants in *Lawson v. U.S.* 176 F.2d 49 (1949) and *Trumbo v. U.S. Nos. 9872, 9873* were Ben Margolis, Charles J. Katz, and Robert W. Kenny (pro hac vice) and Charles H. Houston and Martin Popper. Following the U.S. Supreme Court's refusal to review that case, Trumbo and Lawson, on June 9, 1950, began their prison term.

83. Cal.App.2d 230 *Burkhardt v. Lofton* (1944, March 8), Civ. No. 14117; Notice of Appeal to the Supreme Court, No. 474 800, to the clerk of the Superior Court of the State of California in and for the County of Los Angeles, from Loren Miller and Thomas Griffith (1942, December 1), LMP; Ordered colored families to move in Lofton Case (1942,

September 1), *Atlanta Daily World*, 1; Secret meeting plans to uphold restrictions (1946, March 21), *Los Angeles Sentinel*, 5; On local scene (1947, January 2), *Los Angeles Sentinel*, 1; Clerk of Supreme Court of California to TM (1946, May 27), NAACP Papers, box 2-B-131:9; Martin, D. (2005, April 16), McTernan Obituary, *New York Times*; Tarrow, B. (1999, May), *In memoriam—Ben Margolis*, National Association of Criminal Defense Lawyers, retrieved from www.nacdl.org.

84. Margolis, interview by Balter (1984, July 2), BMP.

85. Vivian C. Mason with the Peace Corps to Loren Miller (1962, January 12), LMP.

86. Ben Margolis to LM (1962, January 24), LMP.

87. LM to James L. Tolbert (1964, June 1), LMP.

88. Loren Miller, now a judge, sells paper (1964, June 24), *Los Angeles Times*, 20; Elaine B. Fischel for Margolis and McTernan to Loren Miller (1964, October 7), LMP. The last issue of the *California Eagle* was published on June 25, 1964. Possession of the *Eagle* took place on July 1, 1964. LM to James Tolbert (1964, June 1). Miller rejected the $20,000 offer and instead stated that he would accept $25,000; Miller's co-owners of the *Eagle* were Clyde B. Denslow and Wendell Green; sales contract, LMP.

89. *Charlotta A. Bass v. Loren Miller, et al.*, No. 789 286, Notice of Taking of Deposition (1964, November 25), LMP; *Charlotta A. Bass v. Loren Miller, et al.* No. 789 286, Declaration of Elaine B. Fischel in Support of Taking of Deposition (1964, November 25), LMP (and Charlotta Bass Papers, Southern California Library for Social Studies and Research).

90. Elaine B. Fischel to LM (1964, November 16), LMP.

91. H. Miller, Jr., personal communication (2014, June 30).

92. Wendell Green to LM (1961, December 6), LMP.

93. Ibid.; Former *Sentinel* editor dies (1987, December 24), *Los Angeles Sentinel*, A1.

94. Wendell Green to LM (1961, December 6), LMP; Leon Washington said to be getting better (1948, November 27), *New York Amsterdam News*, 2

95. Draft Loren Miller committee formed (1961, August 24), *Los Angeles Sentinel*, A4.

96. Miller FBI File (subject Moranda Smith Section [100–55455], October 17, 1961).

97. Join the Committee to Draft Loren Miller for Congress, FOIA/PA No. 1064028-000; Miller FBI File (subject Moranda Smith Section).

98. Draft Loren Miller committee formed (1961, August 24).

99. The Twenty-first Congressional District was changed in 1975 to the Twenty-ninth District.

100. Marable, M. (2011), *A life of reinvention: Malcolm X* (New York: Viking), 207.

101. Handwritten note by Halvor Miller, Jr., on back of article (author's possession): 4 Black Muslims convicted by jury (1963, June 11), *Los Angeles Herald Examiner*, A3.

102. Perry, B. (1991), *Malcolm: The life of a man who changed black America* (Barrytown, NY: Station Hill), 191–92.

103. Marable (2011), 207; Carson, C. (1991), *Malcolm X: The FBI File* (New York: Carroll and Graf); Malcolm X Little, FBI Field Office File, No. 105–8999; Bureau File, No. 100–399321, U.S. Department of Justice.

104. L.A. cop says Muslims ko'd him in riot (1962, November 29), *Chicago Defender*, 9.

105. Conduct rites for Calif. black Muslim riot victim (1962, May 7), *Chicago Defender*, 3; Marable (2011), 208.

106. Protest rally (1962, May 14), *Los Angeles Herald Examiner*.

107. Mayor hears pastors charges on police (1962, June 14), *Los Angeles Sentinel*, A4; 90 Negro Clergymen denounce Muslim Cult (1962, May 23), *Los Angeles Times*, 25.

108. Weeks, P. (1965, April 22), Causes of riots assessed by city, *Los Angeles Times*, 1; Weeks, P. (1963, June 25), Law enforcement hit by Negroes, *Los Angeles Times*, 2.

109. Calif. jury opens probe (1962, May 17), *Chicago Defender*, 10.

110. The Muslim message: All white men devils, all Negroes devine (1962, August 27), *Newsweek*, 26–27, retrieved from http://www.columbia.edu/cu/ccbh/mxp/images/source book_img_47.jpg.

111. Halvor Miller, Jr., handwritten notes, in author's possession.

112. Earl Broady, interview by Taylor Branch (1991, March 25), #05047, TBP.

113. Ibid.

114. Miller FBI File (1962, June 4).

115. Ibid., [LA 100–5589] (1963, February 25).

116. Marable (2011), 207.

117. Ibid., 207–209, 211, 272, 278, 282; Knight, F. (1994), Justifiable homicide, police brutality, or governmental repression? The 1962 Los Angeles police shooting of seven members of the Nation of Islam, *Journal of Negro History*, 79(2): 182–96.

118. NAACP to sift charges of brutality (1934, July 5), *Los Angeles Sentinel*; Miller, L. (1964), Negroes and the police in Los Angeles, in A. F. Westin (Ed.), *Freedom Now: The civil rights struggle in America* (New York: Basic Books), 224–28; Begin jury selection in L.A. Muslim trial (1963, April 10), *Chicago Defender*, 2.

119. California Advisory Committee to the U.S. Commission on Civil Rights (1963, August), *Report on California: Police—Minority group relations*, 3, LMP; Miller, L., Letter to the editor of *Los Angeles Times* (1962, July 13), LMP (letter includes crime statistics). Fire and police group demand lawyer ouster (1963, August 13), *Los Angeles Times*, A1; LM to Bishop James A. Pike (1962, August 7), LMP.

120. Statement of Loren Miller in response to protests against participation on hearings on relations between police and minority communities (n.d.), 30, LMP.

121. Civil rights hearing illegal, says Shell (ca. August 1962), unidentified newspaper, LMP.

122. President Kennedy to LM (1962, July 26), telegram, LMP.

123. Inaugural Committee 1961 to Mr. and Mrs. Loren Miller (1961, January 9), LMP. In addition to JFK's inaugural ball of January 20, the Millers attended the Governors' Reception at the Sheraton Park Hotel on January 19, 1961. Later, in 1965, the Millers would attend the inaugural ball of President Johnson.

124. Parker quoted in California Advisory Committee report (1963, August).

125. LM to Iona Lord (1962, January 25), LMP.

126. LM to Mr. Condit (1962, May 3), LMP.

127. LM to Edward Miller (1967, April 5), LMP.

128. Edward Miller married Linda Ann Smith on September 12, 1970; he and his second wife, Angela (mother of Brandon and Noelle), who later died, donated Langston Hughes's papers to the Huntington Library.

129. Miller, L. (1962, October 20), Farewell to liberals: A Negro view, *Nation*, 235–38.

130. Miller, L. (1963, June 29), Freedom now—but what then?, *Nation*; Miller, L. (1963, September 21), Prosperity through equality, *Nation*.

131. Row flares over jurors in Muslim riot trial (1963, April 25), *Los Angeles Times*, A1; Legal battle brews over riot indictments of 9 Muslim followers (1962, September 4), *Chicago Defender*, 5; Los Angeles trial of 14 black Muslims opens (1963, April 9), *Chicago Defender*, 2; U.S. Bureau of the Census (1995, March 27), *Population of Counties by Decennial Census: 1900 to 1990*, retrieved from http://www.census.gov/population/cencounts/ca190090.txt.

132. Legal battle brews over riot indictments of 9 Muslim followers (1962, September 4), 5.

133. Marable (2011), 239.

134. Earl Broady, interview by Taylor Branch (1991, March 25), #05047, TBP.

135. Top fair housing law backer heads anti-bias meet speakers (1963, April 24), *Chicago Defender*, 9; Levette, H. (1959, December 27), Atty. Loren Miller suffers heart attack, *Atlanta Daily World*, 7; Schiesl, M. (2003), "Pat" Brown, the making of a reformer, in M. Schiesl (Ed.), *Responsible liberalism: Edmund G. "Pat" Brown and reform government, 1958–1967* (Los Angeles: Edmund G. "Pat" Brown Institute of Public Affairs, 2003), 1–21; photo standalone 1—no title (1963, June 11), *Chicago Defender*, 1 (photo of Black Muslim defendants and Miller seated in wheelchair); Lomax, A. (1959, December 11), Miller heart attack laid to judicial disappointment, *Los Angeles Tribune*, 1, 2. The California Real Estate Association immediately began an acrimonious constitutional campaigning to amend the Rumford Act, which went before the voters as Proposition 14. In November 1964, by a wide margin, the voters approved it. Eventually, Prop 14 was overturned in court as unconstitutional.

136. Halvor Miller, Jr., handwritten notes.

137. *People v. Buice*, 230 Cal. App.2d 324 (1964); Legal battle brews over riot indictments of 9 Muslim followers (1962, September 4), 5.

138. Earl Broady, interview by Taylor Branch (1991, March 25), #05047, TBP.

139. Earl Broady was appointed to the Los Angeles Superior Court on June 7, 1965; Stanley Malone was appointed to the Los Angeles Superior Court in 1975.

140. Atty. Branton defends 2 of communist 15 (1951, November 12), *California Eagle*, 2.

141. *U.S. v. Schneiderman et al.* U.S. District Court, S.D. California, Central Division. August 18, 1952; Hill, G. (1952, August 18), 14 Reds on coast get maximum of 5 years, *New York Times*, 1; Leo Branton, Jr., interview by Julieanna Richardson (2001, July 27), retrieved from www.thehistorymakers.com/biography/leo-branton-40.

142. L. Branton, Jr., personal communication (2006, December 9 and 28). Branton did not clarify if he referred to the September 2–3, 1958, Southern California District of the Communist Party, House Un-American Activities Committee Hearings (54), where Miller, on behalf of his subpoenaed client, Don Wheedin, attempted to read his client's statement. Fred Okrand, interview by Michael Balter (1982, July 24), Forty years defending the Constitution, oral history transcript, vol. 2, 332–33, Department of Special Collections, Charles E. Young Library, University of California, Los Angeles.

143. Leo Branton, Jr., interview by Julieanna Richardson (2001, July 27).

144. Robert F. Kennedy to LM (1963, June 28), LMP.

145. California Advisory Committee report to the U.S. Commission on Civil Rights, Statement of Loren Miller, 39; Miller's twenty-five-page statement was presented on January 24–28, 1960. As vice chair of the fact-finding California Advisory Committee to the

U.S. Commission on Civil Rights, Miller warned the commission during hearings in San Francisco on residential segregation that "the widespread character and degree of residential segregation is such that the problems it breeds will plague us for a long time to come. We are at a crisis. What the federal government does in the immediate future will either point the way towards a solution of the problem or intensify it." See also Cornelius P. Cotter, Commission on Civil Rights to LM (1962, April 20), LMP.

146. Roberts, C. (1965, September 3), Los Angeles riot was prophesied in report to officials last year, *Washington Post*, A1; Horne, G. (1995), *Fire this time: The Watts uprising and the 1960s* (Charlottesville: University Press of Virginia), 45; [McCone] Testimony before the Governor's Commission on the Los Angeles riots, Testimony of Loren Miller (1965, October 7), LMP.

147. Miller (1965, October 7), McCone Testimony; Judge blames city for riot (1965, October 8), *Los Angeles Times*, A1.

148. Judge blames city for riot (1965, October 8).

149. Oliver, M. (2000, December 19), Stanley R. Malone, Jr., Leading L.A. civil rights lawyer, judge, *Los Angeles Times*.

150. U.S. Congress, *Hearings before the House Committee on Un-American Activities*, Southern California District of the Communist Party, September 2 and 3, 1958 (Washington: U.S. Government Printing Office), 54, 98. In 1958, Miller was equally busy representing Oliver Ming (*Ming v. Horgan*, 3 Race Rel, L.Ref. 693 [Cal. Super.Ct. 1958]) (FHA and VA insured subdivision). This landmark case involved California's largest builders, who received financing from the FHA and the VA, but refused to sell to minorities. Judge James H. Oakley found that Ming had been discriminated against.

151. Sides (2004), 99; Singh (2005), 118–19, 131.

152. Lomax (1959, December 11); H. Miller, Jr., personal communication (2010, October 5); Miller (1962, November 4), KRCA radio speech, LMP.

153. LM to Lester Granger (1955, November 30).

154. Lomax (1959, December 11).

155. Jefferson Gets Municipal Judgeship (1960, January 7), *Los Angeles Sentinel*, A1; Wash's Wash (1961, October 5), *Los Angeles Sentinel*, A6; Oliver, M. (1989, August 22), Pioneer black Judge Edwin Jefferson dies, *Los Angeles Times*; Lionel Wilson, interview by Gabrielle Morris, *University of California Black Alumni series (1985)*, Bancroft Library, University of California, Berkeley. In 1953, Thomas L. Griffith Jr., was appointed to L.A.'s municipal court, followed in 1956 by the appointment of David W. Williams, a Republican, and, later, the first African American federal judge in the West.

156. Disclosure: Vaino Hassan Spencer's brother, Alfred Hassan, is the author's engineer father.

157. Judge Spencer (1961, October 12), *Los Angeles Sentinel*, A6.

158. African American women appeal court justices (2012, March 29), *Los Angeles Sentinel*; Board installs officer for '53 (1953, April 8), *Los Angeles Sentinel*, E8; Vaino Hassan Spencer, owner of Hassan Realty Company, located at 4525 South Main Street, graduated from Southwestern Law School; Hassan Spencer worked as a Hollywood bit player in the 1930s, along with her father, Abdul Hassan (also known as Alfred de Livera), who immigrated from Sri Lanka (at fifteen Hassan Spencer was the lead Southeast Asian dancer in Laurel and Hardy's 1935 *Bonnie Scotland* and other films that starred Errol Flynn).

159. Weeks, P. (1964, May 17), New judge reluctant member of profession, *Los Angeles Times*, E4; California publisher named interim judge (1964, May 23), *Atlanta Daily World*, 1; Sherman Smith's appointment hailed (1963, February 14), *Los Angeles Sentinel*, A.1; Wikipedia (2013, 18 January), *Earl Ben Gilliam*, retrieved from http://en.wikipedia.org/wiki/Earl_Ben_Gilliam; L.A. attorney Loren Miller named judge (1964, May 13), *Los Angeles Times*, 22. Sherman W. Smith passed the California bar in 1949 and Earl Gilliam passed it in 1957.

160. Lomax (1959, December 11); Marion Maddox, personal communication (2008, July 1).

161. Miller FBI File (1963, December).

162. Miller named Judge by Brown (1964, May 14), *Los Angeles Sentinel*, A1; NAACP membership fete will honor Judge Loren Miller (1964, September 3), *Los Angeles Sentinel*, D4.

163. Putnam, G. Judge Loren Miller in the Congressional Record (1964, May 24), Los Angeles, KTTV.

164. Miller FBI File.

165. Tried, but failed (1966, April 20), *Los Angeles Times*, B2; Los Angeles weekly changes ownership (1964, July 18), *Baltimore Afro-American*, 16.

166. Miller, L. (1964, June 29), Rights stand, *Los Angeles Times*, A4.

167. Birkinshaw, J. (1964, June 5), Pepper renewal plan lauded, hit at hearing, *Los Angeles Times*, G8.

168. Weeks, P. (1963, September 4), CORE to propose strike at Jordan High School, *Los Angeles Times*, A2.

169. Priest urges removal of Cardinal McIntyre (1964, June 12), *Los Angeles Times*, A1.

170. Thrapp, D. (1964, June 19), End of priest's dispute with cardinal expected, *Los Angeles Times*, A1.

171. *Eagle*, quoted in ibid.

172. Ibid.

173. Priest "exile" to serve Negro parish in Chicago (1964, December 29), *Los Angeles Times*, A1.

174. Brown appoints Clinco to superior judgeship (1964, August 22), *Los Angeles Times*, B7; 121 Soldier Girl in easy Crosby win (1964, August 23), *Los Angeles Times*, D10.

175. Tolbert, J. (1964, October 15), Honor Loren Miller at NAACP dinner Friday night, Oct. 16, *Los Angeles Sentinel*; NAACP life membership banquet set for Statler (1964, September 17), *Los Angeles Sentinel*, C5.

176. Women honor 17 elective Negro officials (1964, July 26), *Los Angeles Times*, F3.

177. Tried, but failed (1966, April 20).

178. 59 tickets prove wrong number: Phone girl vacations in jail (1967, February 24), *Los Angeles Times*, A1.

179. Hanson, C. (1966, January 29), Praise given traffic judge, *Los Angeles Times*, B4.

180. Miller (1998), 237–41.

181. Miller (1966), preface.

182. Mack (2012), 182.

183. Judge Miller's book "sell out" at League's autograph party (1966, January 27), *Los Angeles Sentinel*, C2.

184. Washington, L. (1966, January 22), Wash's Wash: A new book and honors for Judge Miller, *Los Angeles Sentinel*, A6.

185. Judge writes book on Supreme Court, Negro (1966, January 15), *Chicago Defender*, 4.

186. Wilkins, R. (1966), Book Department, *Annals of the American Academy of Political and Social Science*, 367(1): 205.

187. Norton, E. H. (1966, May 2), The end of a period, *Nation*, 529.

188. Hayden, R. (1966, January 30), Supreme Court and the Negro, *Los Angeles Times*, 26.

189. Farrell & Mounts (1967, July 20).

References

Books

Abdullah, M., & Freer, R. (2010). Bass to Bass: Relative freedom and womanist leadership in Black Los Angeles. In D. Hunt & A. Ramón (Eds.), *Black Los Angeles: American dreams and racial realities*. New York: New York University Press.

Aquinas, T. (1981). *Summa Theologica*. (Fathers of the English Dominican Province, Trans). London: Christian Classics.

Aurelius, M. (2006). *Meditations*. (M. Hammond, Trans). London: Penguin.

Baker, R. K. (1970) (Ed.). *The Afro-American*. New York: Van Nostrand Reinhold.

Baldwin, K. A. (2002). *Beyond the color line and the iron curtain: Reading encounters between black and red, 1922–1963*. Durham, NC: Duke University Press.

Berry, F. (1992). *Before and beyond Harlem: Langston Hughes, a biography*. New York: Carol Publishing Group.

Bogle, D. (2005). *Bright boulevards, bold dreams: The story of black Hollywood*. New York: One World Ballantine Books.

Boyle, S. T., & Bunie, A. (2001). *Paul Robeson: The years of promise and achievement*. Boston: University of Massachusetts Press.

Brilliant, M. (2010). *The color of America has changed*. New York: Oxford University Press.

Burgchardt, C. R. (1980). Two faces of American Communism: Pamphlet rhetoric of the third period and the popular front. *Quarterly Journal of Speech* 66, no. 4 (December): 375–91.

Carew, J. G. (2008). *Blacks, Reds, and Russians: Sojourners in search of the Soviet promise*. New Brunswick, NJ: Rutgers University Press.

Carson, C. (1991). *Malcolm X: The FBI file*. New York: Carroll and Graf.

Carter, R. (2005). *A matter of law: A memoir of struggle in the cause of equal rights*. New York: New Press.

Cooke, Michael A. (1984). *The health of blacks during Reconstruction, 1862, 1870*. PhD diss., University of Maryland, College Park.

Cornish, D. (1987). *The sable arm: Black troops in the Union Army, 1861–1865*. Lawrence: University Press of Kansas.

Cox, T. C. (1982). *Blacks in Topeka, Kansas, 1865–1915: A social history*. Baton Rouge: Louisiana State University Press.

Darrow, C. (1932). *The story of my life*. New York: Scribner's.

Davis, M. (2006). City of Quartz: Excavating the Future in Los Angeles. New York: Verso.

de Graaf, L. (2007). Changing face and place: Race in Los Angeles City government. In H. L. Rudd (Ed.), *The development of Los Angeles city government: An institutional history, 1850–2000*. Los Angeles: Los Angeles Historical Society.

de Graaf, L., Mulroy, K., & Taylor, Q. (2001). *Seeking El Dorado: African Americans in California*. Los Angeles: Autry Museum of Western Heritage.

Denning, M. (1996). *The cultural front: The laboring of American culture in the Twentieth Century*. New York: Verso.

Dilling, E. (1935). *The red network: A "who's who" and handbook of radicalism for patriots*. Published by the author.

Douglass, F. (2003). *The narrative of the life of Frederick Douglass, an American slave*. New York: Barnes and Noble Classics.

Dove, R. (2004). *American Smooth*. New York: Norton.

Downs, J. (2012). *Sick for freedom: African-American illness and suffering during the Civil War and Reconstruction*. New York: Oxford University Press.

Du Bois, W. E. B. (1968). *The autobiography of W. E. B. Du Bois: A soliloquy on viewing my life from the last decade of its first century*. H. Aptheker (Ed.). New York: International Publishers.

——— (1994). *The Souls of Black Folk*. New York: Gramercy Books.

Flamming, D. (2005). *Bound for freedom: Black Los Angeles in Jim Crow America*. Berkeley: University of California Press.

Foner, E. (2010). *The fiery trial: Abraham Lincoln and American slavery*. New York: Norton.

Frank, W. (1932). *Dawn and Russia: The record of a journey*. New York: Scribner's.

Frazier, E. F. (1957). *The Black bourgeoisie*. New York: Free Press.

Freer, R. M. (2005). Charlotta Bass: A community activist for racial and economic justice. In R. Gottlieb, M. Vallianatos, R. M. Freer, & P. Dreier, *The next Los Angeles: The struggle for a livable city*, 49–66. Berkeley: University of California Press.

Gilmore, G. (2008). *Defying Dixie. The radical roots of civil rights, 1919–1950*. New York: Norton.

Gold, S. (2006). Korematsu v. United States: *Japanese-American internment*. New York: Marshall Cavendish Benchmark.

Gore, D., Teoharis, J., & Woodard, K. (Eds.) (2009). *Want to start a revolution: Radical women in the black freedom struggle*. New York: New York University Press.

Graham, L. O. (2000). *Our kind of people: Inside America's Black upper class*. New York: Harper Perennial.

Hauke, K. A. (1998). *Ted Poston: Pioneer American journalist*. Athens: University of Georgia Press.

Haywood, H. (1978). *Black Bolshevik. Autobiography of an Afro-American Communist*. Chicago: Liberator Press.

Henderson, W. H. (2004). James Homer Garrott. In D. S. Wilson (Ed.), *African American architects: A biographical dictionary 1865–1945*. New York: Routledge.

Henry, C. P. (2005). *Ralph Bunche: model Negro or American other?* New York: New York University Press.

Himes, C. (1966). *Pinktoes*. New York: Dell Putnam.

—— (1971). *The quality of hurt.* London: Michael Joseph.

Horne, G. (1994). *Black liberation/red scare: Ben Davis and the Communist Party.* Newark: University of Delaware Press.

—— (1995). *Fire this time: The Watts uprising and the 1960s.* Charlottesville: University Press of Virginia.

Hughes, L. (1940). *The big sea: An autobiography.* New York: Knopf.

—— (1973). Moscow and me. In Faith Berry (Ed.), *Good morning revolution: Uncollected social protest writings of Langston Hughes,* 67–75. New York: Lawrence Hill.

—— (1990). Cora Unashamed. In L. Hughes, *The Ways of White Folks: Stories of Langston Hughes,* 3–18. New York: Vintage Classics.

—— (1999). *I wonder as I wander: An autobiographical journey.* 2nd ed. New York: Hill and Wang.

—— (1999). Our wonderful society: Washington. In S. K. Wilson (Ed.), *The opportunity reader: Stories, poetry, and essays from the Urban League's Opportunity Magazine,* 364–67. New York: Modern Library.

Hughes-Watkins, L. (2008). *Fay M. Jackson: The Sociopolitical narrative of a pioneering African American female journalist.* Master's thesis, Youngstown State University.

Hurewitz, D. (2008). *Bohemian Los Angeles and the making of modern politics.* Berkeley: University of California Press.

Irons, P. (1983). *Justice at war. The story of the Japanese American internment cases.* Berkeley: University of California Press.

—— (1988). *The courage of their convictions: Sixteen Americans who fought their way to the Supreme Court.* New York: Penguin.

Jackson, C. (1990). *Hattie: The life of Hattie McDaniel.* Lanham, MD: Madison Books.

Kelley, R. D. G. (1990). *Hammer and Hoe: Alabama Communists: During the Great Depression.* Chapel Hill: University of North Carolina Press.

Klehr, H., Haynes, J. E., & Anderson, K. M. (1998). *The Soviet world of American communism.* New Haven: Yale University Press.

Kluger, R. (2004). *Simple Justice: The history of* Brown v. Board of Education *and black America's struggle for equality.* New York: Knopf.

Koestler, A. (1954). *The invisible writing: An autobiography.* Boston: Beacon Press.

Kurashige, S. (2008). *The shifting grounds of race: Black and Japanese Americans in the making of multiethnic Los Angeles.* New Jersey: Princeton University Press.

Leonard, K. A. (2006). *The battle for Los Angeles: Racial ideology and World War II.* Albuquerque:University of New Mexico Press.

Lewis, D. L. (1981). *When Harlem was in vogue.* New York: Knopf.

Lincoln, C. E. (1970). Black nationalism: The minor leagues. In R. K. Baker (Ed.), *The Afro-American.* New York: Van Nostrand Reinhold.

Mack, K. (2012). *Representing the race: The creation of the civil rights lawyer.* Cambridge, MA: Harvard University Press.

Marable, M. (2011). *Malcolm X: A life of reinvention.* New York: Viking.

Margolies, E., & Fabre, M. (1997). *The several lives of Chester Himes.* Jackson: University of Mississippi Press.

Marshall, T. (2001). *Thurgood Marshall: His speeches, writings, arguments, opinions, and reminiscences.* Mark V. Tushnet (Ed.) Chicago: Lawrence Hill Books.

McBroome, D. N. (2001). Harvest of gold: African American boosterism, agriculture, and investment in Allensworth and Little Liberia. In L. B. de Graaf, K. Mulroy, & Q. Taylor (Eds.), *Seeking El Dorado: African Americans in California.* Los Angeles: Autry Museum of Western Heritage.

McCullough, D. (2001). *John Adams.* New York: Simon and Shuster.

McNeil, G. R. (1983). *Groundwork: Charles Hamilton Houston and the struggle for civil rights.* Philadelphia: University of Pennsylvania Press.

McWilliams, C. (1979). *The education of Carey McWilliams.* New York: Simon and Shuster.

——— (1999). *California: The great exception.* Berkeley: University of California Press.

——— (2001). The long-suffering Chinese. In C. McWilliams, *Fool's paradise: A Carey McWilliams reader.* D. Stewart & J. Gendar (Eds.) Santa Clara, CA: Heyday Books.

——— (2001). Water. water. water! In C. McWilliams, *Fool's paradise: A Carey McWilliams reader.* D. Stewart & J. Gendar (Eds.) Santa Clara, CA: Heyday Books.

Miller, L. (1966). *The Petitioners: The story of the Supreme Court of the United States and the Negro.* Cleveland: Meridian Books.

——— (1998). College. In S. K. Wilson (Ed.), *The* Crisis *reader: Stories, poetry, and essays from the N.A.A.C.P.'s* Crisis *magazine,* 237–41. New York: Modern Library.

Miller, L., & Sheil, B. (1946). *Racial restrictive covenants.* Chicago: Chicago Council Against Racial and Religious Discrimination.

Mills, C. W. (2002). *White collar: the American middle classes.* Oxford: Oxford University Press.

Murray, P. (1987). *Song in a weary throat: An American pilgrimage.* New York: Harper and Row.

Myrdal, Gunnar (1944) 1996. *An American dilemma: The negro problem and modern democracy.* New Jersey: Transaction Publishers.

Naison, M. (1983). *Communists in Harlem during the Depression.* New York: Grove.

Negro who's who in California (1948). Los Angeles: California Eagle Publishing Company.

Nichols, C. H. (Ed.) (1990). *Arna Bontemps—Langston Hughes Letters, 1925–1967.* New York: Paragon House.

Nelson, C. N. (2004). Black and white. In C. D. Wintz & P. Finkelman (Eds.), *Encyclopedia of the Harlem Renaissance,* vol. 1, 122–24. New York: Routlege.

Ogletree, C., Jr. (2004). *All deliberate speed: Reflections on the first half century of* Brown v. Board of Education. New York: Norton.

Patterson, L. (1995). With Langston Hughes in the USSR. In D. L. Lewis (Ed.), *The portable Harlem renaissance reader,* 182–89. New York: Penguin.

Perry, B. (1991). *Malcolm: The life of a man who changed black America.* Barrytown, NY: Station Hill.

Pritchett, W. (2008). *Robert Clifton Weaver and the American city: The life and times of an urban reformer*. Chicago: University of Chicago Press.

Rampersad, A. (1986). *The life of Langston Hughes*. Vol. 1, *1902–1941. I, too, sing America*. New York: Oxford Press.

Robinson, R. (1988). *Black on red: My 44 years inside the Soviet Union*. Washington, D.C.: Acropolis Books.

Russell, B. (1922). *Free thought and official propaganda*. London: Watts.

Schiesl, M. (2003). Pat Brown, the making of a reformer. In M. Schiesl (Ed.), *Responsible liberalism: Edmund G. "Pat" Brown and reform government of California, 1958–1967*. Los Angeles: Edmund G. "Pat" Brown Institute of Public Affairs.

Schiesl, M., & Dodge, M. M. (Eds.) (2006). *City of promise: Race and historical change in Los Angeles*. Claremont, CA: Regina Books.

Sides, J. (2004). *L.A. city limits: African American Los Angeles from the Great Depression to the Present*. Berkeley: University of California Press.

Sinclair, U. (2007). *Oil!* New York: Penguin.

Singh, N. P. (2005). *Black is a country: Race and the unfinished struggle for democracy*. Cambridge, MA: Harvard University Press.

Skocpol, T. (1992). *Protecting soldiers and mothers: The political origins of social policy in the United States*. Cambridge, MA: Harvard University Press.

Smith, H. (1964). *Black man in red Russia: A memoir*. Chicago: Johnson.

Smith, R. J. (2007). *The great black way: L.A. in the 1940s and the last African American renaissance*. New York: Public Affairs.

Stine, W., & Davis, B. (1974). *Mother Goddam: The story of the career of Bette Davis*. New York: Hawthorne Books.

Streitmatter, R. (1994). *Raising her voice: African-American women journalists who changed history*. Lexington: University of Kentucky Press.

Strum, P. (1984). *Louis D. Brandeis: Justice for the people*. New York: Schocken Books.

Sugrue, T. J. (2008). *Sweet land of liberty: The forgotten struggle for civil rights in the north*. New York: Random House.

Tushnet, M. V. (1994). *Making civil rights law: Thurgood Marshall and the Supreme Court, 1936–1961*. Oxford: Oxford University Press.

Urquhart, B. (1993). *Ralph Bunche: An American life*. New York: Norton.

von Hoffman, A. (1998). *Like fleas on a Tiger? A brief history of the Open Housing Movement*. Cambridge, MA: Joint Center for Housing Studies of Harvard University.

Vose, C. (1959). *Caucasians only: The Supreme Court, the NAACP, and the restrictive covenant cases*. Berkeley: University of California Press.

Watkins, M. (2005). *Stepin Fetchit: The Life and Times of Lincoln Perry*. New York: Pantheon.

Watts, J. (2005). *Hattie McDaniel: Black ambition, white Hollywood*. New York: Amistad.

Weaver, R. (1945). *Hemmed in: The ABC's of race restrictive housing covenants*. Chicago: American Council on Race Relations.

West, D. (1995). The richer, the poorer: Stories, sketches and reminisces. New York: Anchor Books.

Wilentz, S. (2012). *360 sound: The Columbia Records story.* San Francisco: Chronicle Books.

Williams, J. (1998). *Thurgood Marshall: American Revolutionary.* New York: Random House.

Williams, J. A., & Williams, L. (Eds.) (2008). *Dear Chester, dear John: Letters between Chester Himes and John Williams.* Detroit: Wayne State University Press.

Newspapers

Annals of the American Academy of Political and Social Science
Architectural Forum
Atlanta Daily World
Baltimore Afro-American
California Eagle
Chicago Defender
Crusader News
Esquire Magazine
Jet Magazine
Journal of American History
Journal of Educational Sociology
Journal of the West
Liberator
Los Angeles Sentinel
Los Angeles Times
Nation
Negro Digest
New Masses
New York Amsterdam News
New York Daily Worker
New Yorker
New York Times
Opportunity: Journal of Negro Life
Pacific Citizen
Pacific Historical Review
San Francisco Chronicle
San Francisco Examiner
Smithsonian Magazine
Survey Graphic
Washington Post

Index

Page numbers in italics indicate illustrations.